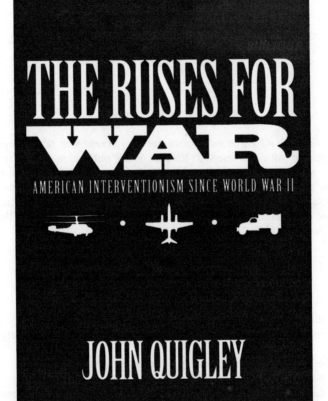

THE RUSES FOR
WAR

AMERICAN INTERVENTIONISM SINCE WORLD WAR II

JOHN QUIGLEY

PROMETHEUS BOOKS · BUFFALO, NEW YORK

To Shirley Adele Shank
who didn't have to save me in Cambodia

Published 1992 by Prometheus Books

The Ruses for War: American Interventionism since World War II. Copyright © 1992 by John Quigley. All rights reserved. No part of this publication may be reproduced, stored in a retrieval system, or transmitted in any form or by any means, electronic, mechanical, photocopying, recording, or otherwise, without prior written permission of the publisher, except in the case of brief quotations embodied in critical articles and reviews. Inquiries should be addressed to Prometheus Books, 59 John Glenn Drive, Buffalo, New York 14228, 716-837-2475. FAX: 716-835-6901.

96 95 94 93 92   5 4 3 2 1

Library of Congress Cataloging-in-Publication Data

Quigley, John B.
    The ruses for war : American interventionism since World War II / by John Quigley.
        p.   cm.
    Includes bibliographical references (p.   ) and index.
    ISBN 0-87975-767-1 (cloth : acid free)
    1. United States—Foreign relations—1945–1989. 2. United States—Foreign relations—1989-   3. United States—Foreign relations—1945–1989—Citizen participation. 4. United States—Foreign relations—1989-   —Citizen participation. 5. United States—Military policy. 6. United States—Military policy—Citizen participation. I. Title.
E744.Q54   1992
973.92—dc20   92-19288
                                                                              CIP

Printed in the United States of America on acid-free paper.

Acknowledgments

I am grateful to colleagues in the international law field with whom I have maintained a dialogue in my earlier work on military intervention that has led to the writing of this book. I am also indebted to the College of Law, Ohio State University, which provided research support, and whose library staff made heroic efforts to trace out-of-the-way source material.

Contents

7

List of Abbreviations

Abbreviations are used in the notes for a few frequently cited sources. They are:

DSB   United States, Department of State Bulletin
FRUS   Foreign Relations of the United States
GAOR   United Nations, General Assembly Official Records
SCOR   United Nations, Security Council Official Records

Full data on the major works cited in the notes will be given in the bibliography.

Preface

The cold war is no more, but hot war has hardly gone out of style. Our daily news remains full of war and rumors of war. Despite some downscaling, the United States retains a far-flung network of air, naval, and land forces prepared for combat on short notice. How and when those forces are used depends in large part on how the public perceives the need for their use. As the Vietnam war showed, a president cannot use U.S. forces, at least for very long, if the public is hostile to his action.

In a developing crisis situation, the public gets its information from the media. In the initial stages of a military conflict, the media get most of their information from the White House, the Defense Department, and the State Department. If troops are sent into combat, the president appears on television. "My fellow Americans," he says solemnly, "it is my duty to inform you that at dawn this morning our forces landed in far-off Ruritania."

Then the president explains that civil order in Ruritania has broken down, or that the tyrant who runs Ruritania has threatened something unspeakable. If there are Americans living in Ruritania, he may say that their lives are at stake. At this early stage in a crisis, the media and the public may have little independent factual basis on which to

13

assess the president's statement. Thus, the public perception of a crisis comes largely from its reaction to what he says.

Still another military scenario is an overthrow of a foreign government, and here, too, the president may explain. "Last night the tyrannical president of Ruritania was replaced by the prime minister of Ruritania. We have recognized the new government and wish it well." A reporter asks, "Did we have anything to do with this?" The president replies, "This was a purely Ruritanian matter. Despite our long-standing concern for Ruritania's welfare, the United States was not involved in the change of Ruritania's government."

Whatever the scenario, can the public rely on this kind of information from the president? Do presidents explain the true reasons for the military action they take, or do they shade the truth to get public support? The evidence on which this book draws is that presidents do not always divulge the truth, at least not the whole truth. In the interest of gaining public backing, they omit inconvenient details and exaggerate hazards, like potential risk to U.S. nationals, or the actions of our potential adversary. They may act in the utmost good faith, confident that they are serving the best interests of the country, yet they feel the need to modify the truth in order to put their action in the most favorable light.

If presidents do shade the truth when they send troops into combat, the implications for our system of governance are serious. After all, one of the premises of democracy is that the public keeps tabs on the government. Congress and the media call the president to account, informing the public of wrongdoing. If we don't like the administration, we throw the rascals out at the next election. But, particularly with events that occur in far-off places like Ruritania, Congress and the media may not get the full picture, and the public may not know what the administration has done, or, more importantly, why it has done it.

In this book we explore U.S. military actions abroad over the past half-century. There have been many such involvements, and we examine the most significant of them. We look in each instance at what the president and his administration said about an action, and what reasons they gave. Then we examine the situation in light of what is known today to determine whether the administration was truthful, or whether it gave a distorted picture.

My own life has spanned the years covered by this book and has been affected by them directly and indirectly. I served in the United States Marine Corps Reserve during the early 1960s and faced the possibility of being dispatched to participate in the interventions of that period, although I was never asked to do so. Later in the decade I did research at Moscow State University as part of a student exchange program, an experience that forced me to rethink the cold war, which was a central factor in American military policy. The threat of nuclear conflict that hung over the planet began to shape my activity.

Since the time of the American military involvement in southeast Asia in the 1960s, I have had an active interest in military intervention. I have visited many of the countries where interventions occurred and have written on interventions, to analyze them from the legal standpoint.

As I discussed these interventions, I saw that the stated explanations did not conform to the facts. In instance after instance, the American public gave tacit consent to military action, the reasons for which it did not understand because it accepted the White House's skewed presentation of the facts.

The subject matter of this book is of extreme interest as a matter of public policy, namely, how a government convinces the public to go to war. In a more immediate sense, however, the topic poses a serious dilemma for every citizen. Does anyone have an obligation to take the trouble to find out whether the government is telling the truth when it initiates military action? For a citizen who answers that question in the affirmative, is it possible to find out the truth in time to take effective action to stop a military action that is being presented on false premises? Do the media have a responsibility to help concerned citizens uncover the facts, and do they fulfill that responsibility? Do elected representatives in Congress have such a responsibility, and do they fulfill it?

Ultimately the issue comes down to one of citizen responsibility, because in the final analysis it is the individual, acting as part of the collective citizenry, who consents to military action, by paying taxes to maintain the military establishment, or by actually participating in the fighting. Thus the issue explored in this book goes to the heart of a system of governance. In my view, that nation is stronger whose citizens feel a sense of responsibility for how their government impacts on the rest of the world.

1

Do We Get the Truth?

Supreme Court Justice Hugo Black said it well when he wrote, "Paramount among the responsibilities of a free press is the duty to prevent any part of the government from deceiving the people and sending them off to distant lands to die of foreign fevers and foreign shot and shell."[1] Nothing could be worse, Black thought, than for an administration to deceive the public about the need to get into a war. The administration's true reasons might be valid or invalid, but those actually fighting the war haven't been consulted, and might go to their graves for a cause they did not know.

The issue of foreign military involvement and unclear facts took center stage after Iraq invaded Kuwait in 1990. Explaining that Iraq was about to do the same to Saudi Arabia, President George Bush sent 200,000 American troops to the deserts of Saudi Arabia. Although Bush did not have hard evidence that Iraq would invade Saudi Arabia, he said it was a fair supposition that it would, since Iraq had just invaded Kuwait, and since it had put into Kuwait large numbers of troops that could be used against Saudi Arabia. To show Iraq's bad intent, Bush reminded the American public that in 1980 Iraq had invaded Iran. Iraq, he said, was therefore on a path of conquest.

President Bush's assertion that Iraq was about to invade Saudi Arabia was hardly airtight, however, because Iraq's invasion of Kuwait had grown out of a specific dispute between the two countries. Iraq harbored a series of grievances against Kuwait, one being that Kuwait had been taking oil from a pool lying under a piece of land on the two countries' common border. Iraq claimed that Kuwait was siphoning its oil.

Beyond that, Iraq objected that Kuwait was keeping world oil prices low, which was making it difficult for Iraq to survive economically. Finally, Kuwait held two islands in the Persian Gulf that Iraq claimed, and which it wanted in order to have better access to the waters of the Persian Gulf. Iraq and Kuwait were in closed talks on all these issues during July, but no resolution emerged.

In addition to these specific grievances, Iraq had a long-standing territorial claim to all of Kuwait. Early in the century, Great Britain had controlled the area, and the Iraqi view was that it unfairly carved Kuwait out of Iraqi territory as the old Ottoman Empire fell apart. When Britain granted Kuwait its independence in 1962, Iraq made a claim to Kuwait, and both Britain and the Arab League put troops in Kuwait to prevent an Iraqi takeover.

While Iraq had all these disputes with Kuwait, it had no similar grievances against Saudi Arabia, except perhaps on oil prices. As a result, Saudi officials, while concerned that Iraq might attack them some time in the future, did not, according to press reports, expect an imminent invasion.[2] Immediately after Iraq invaded Kuwait, President Bush sent Secretary of Defense Richard Cheney to Riyadh, where he spent several days convincing Saudi leaders they were about to be attacked by Iraq, and that they should invite the United States to send in troops.[3]

Iraq meanwhile denied any intent to invade Saudi Arabia,[4] and administration officials who spoke "on background" thought that Iraq was not likely to move against Saudi Arabia. Although they acknowledged there was some Iraqi deployment near the Kuwait-Saudi border, they said that it did not mean that Iraq was about to invade; it might be installing those troops there simply to consolidate its hold on Kuwait against a possible counteroffensive staged from Saudi Arabia. Or this troop buildup in Kuwait, the officials reasoned, might be aimed at creating fear of an invasion of Saudi Arabia, so that the West and the Arab states would accept Iraq's occupation of Kuwait. But they did not think Iraq so foolhardy as to go after Saudi Arabia, a much more difficult military target than tiny Kuwait.[5]

One piece of supposed U.S. intelligence information that surfaced in the press was an account of Iraqi troops entering the Saudi portion of a neutral zone between Kuwait and Saudi Arabia. According to this story, Iraqi troops had entered the neutral zone in force.[6] If true, this might portend an Iraqi invasion of Saudi Arabia. But this report, whose origin was unclear, turned out to be false, as no substantial Iraqi force could be found in the neutral zone.[7]

There had been a report, apparently accurate, that a small number of Iraqi troops entered the zone on the night of August 3, but they left when confronted by Saudi border forces.[8] *Newsday* quoted a "senior State Department official" that while Iraqi troops had entered the neutral zone, they "have made no threatening movements toward the south," no "massing of troops . . . as they did before the invasion of Kuwait."[9] Although the reports of an Iraqi buildup in the neutral zone were false, they added to the impression that Iraq might be planning to move against Saudi Arabia.

Whether an imminent Iraqi invasion of Saudi Arabia was, or was not, in the works turned into a sticky issue for President Bush. To convince the public, Bush had to make a persuasive argument that Iraq was about to invade Saudi Arabia. If Bush did send troops, then Congress had a right to make its own judgment about the Iraqi threat to Saudi Arabia. By law, the president must notify Congress if he sends troops into "imminent involvement in hostilities," and Congress may then force the president to withdraw the forces within sixty days.[10]

When President Bush announced on August 7 that he was sending troops to Saudi Arabia, State Department spokesperson Marlin Fitzwater, citing unspecified intelligence information (probably the erroneous report about the neutral zone), said in a press conference briefing that there was "an imminent threat to Saudi Arabia" from the way that the Iraqi forces were "positioned and located in Kuwait."[11]

President Bush, however, in a less publicized communication, said just the opposite. On August 9, Bush sent a letter to Congress, informing it, as the law required, that he had sent troops to Saudi Arabia. As for what they might face there, Bush wrote, "I do not believe involvement in hostilities is imminent; to the contrary, it is my belief that this deployment will facilitate a peaceful resolution of the crisis."[12] Elaborating for the press, Bush said, "There is no evidence right now that Saddam Hussein would be foolish enough to cross that border [into Saudi Arabia]."[13]

Thus, the administration's apparent position was that on August 7 there was an imminent threat of an Iraqi attack on Saudi Arabia, but by August 9 there was no such threat. For both propositions to be true, Iraq would have had to be planning an invasion on August 7, which it aborted once it had heard Bush's announcement. Although this scenario was questionable, the press did not force the administration to explain. For the selling of the deployment to the public, an imminent Iraqi threat was an advantage, but with Congress it was a liability.

Beyond the question of whether Iraq was about to invade Saudi Arabia lay that of why the United States should care, and in particular why it should send troops to defend Saudi Arabia. On this point, President Bush explained that if Iraq took the Saudi oil fields, and perhaps those of the nearby Gulf emirates, it would control over half the world's known oil reserves. Then, Bush said, Iraq might drive up the price or withhold the oil, causing devastation for oil-dependent economies around the world, particularly the United States.

This rationale was not self-evident, however, because the United States was not heavily dependent on Persian Gulf oil. Besides, even if Iraq did control a great deal of the world's oil, it would still need to sell the oil abroad, and if it drove up the price too high, other countries could pump more oil. If oil got too expensive, other energy sources would become more competitive on the world market.

These flaws in logic apparently came across to the public, because it reacted negatively to Bush's call to arms to fight for oil. At public speeches Bush was dogged by placard slogans like "No blood for oil." A president can sell a war as a fight to protect freedom, but not to get a natural resource that we have no inalienable right to in the first place. Promptly reacting to the criticism, Bush changed the emphasis in his public statements from oil to the defense of Kuwait: "naked aggression" became his rallying cry. We must stand up against aggression, he said, because if it can happen in one place it can happen anywhere.

The "naked aggression" rationale, while potentially a better selling point for Bush, had some practical drawbacks. Specifically, in late July our ambassador in Baghdad, April Glaspie, had asked Iraqi President Saddam Hussein what he would do if his negotiations with Kuwait failed. When Hussein hinted that Iraq might invade Kuwait, Glaspie replied that the United States had no opinion on Iraq's territorial dispute with Kuwait and did not want to be involved. Hussein, thought many analysts, may well have concluded from Glaspie's reply that Bush would see in an Iraqi invasion of Kuwait not "naked aggression" but at most a minor peccadillo.[14]

Like the oil rationale, the aggression rationale did not sit well with the public, the major problem being a lack of evenhandedness. Other recent aggressive activity by Iraq had not drawn a lift of the presidential eyebrow. In fact, when Iraq invaded Iran in 1980, we supplied it with weapons. In that war, disdain for Iran apparently took precedence over concern about aggression. Skeptics suspected that Bush's actual motive in sending troops to Saudi Arabia was to show a need for a large military establishment. The Soviet Union had just bowed out of the arms race, leaving the West with little reason for major weapons systems. Perhaps Bush's interest was to make it appear that sophisticated weaponry was still needed.

The Persian Gulf plot thickened in November 1990, when Bush doubled our force in Saudi Arabia to give it, as he said, an offensive capability to attack Iraq and to drive it out of Kuwait. To justify this new and larger deployment, President Bush floated a third rationale for our involvement. Iraq, he said, was developing nuclear weapons, and in the hands of a country bent on aggression, this was a danger to world peace. While this new rationale held some appeal, it, too, had its flaws. Although the full scope of Iraq's nuclear capability remained unclear, Iraq evidently was still some years away from being ready to deliver a nuclear weapon against an enemy. Moreover, Iraq's adversary, Israel, had nuclear weapons ready to deliver.

Bush's nuclear rationale gained some public following, but each change of focus cast doubt on the sincerity of his previous arguments for a military buildup. To skeptics Bush looked like a child caught in a lie, who made up a new story each time his previous story was exposed.

Later in November, Bush followed up on the Saudi troop deployment by getting United Nations backing for an invasion of Iraq. The UN Security Council adopted a resolution authorizing any UN member country to use "all necessary means" to get Iraq out of Kuwait if it didn't leave by January 15, 1991. Council members, however, said that military force was to be only a last resort, and that their hope was that the threat of force would convince Iraq to withdraw peacefully.

Even as they voted on the resolution, Council members emphasized that intensive diplomacy should precede any shots.[15]

President Bush, however, his offensive formation now in place, did not negotiate with Iraq. After the Security Council vote, his administration held only one meeting with Iraq, a session in Geneva during which Secretary of State James Baker simply told Iraq to leave Kuwait. Baker, by his own account, did not explore ways of resolving Iraq's differences with Kuwait.[16] Iraq floated peace feelers, but the administration ignored them.

Instead, on January 16, 1991, the administration launched a blistering aerial attack on Iraq. In his address to the nation, President Bush defended his position by saying that he had acted "in accord with United Nations resolutions," and that the attack followed "months of constant and virtually endless diplomatic activity."[17] But if there had been "endless diplomatic activity," Bush had not involved Iraq in it.

On February 23, 1991, after a month of air strikes, President Bush launched a ground assault on Iraqi forces, explaining that his objective was "to eject the Iraqi Army from Kuwait."[18] The previous day, however, the administration had demanded that Iraq evacuate Kuwait over a one-week period, after the Soviet Union, having engaged in intense talks with Iraq, had convinced it to leave Kuwait over a three-week period. But Bush said he could not wait three weeks, because Iraq was following a "scorched-earth" policy in Kuwait.

Bush's rejection of a three-week withdrawal period created doubt that he was being truthful when he said that an Iraqi withdrawal from Kuwait was his only objective. Even if Iraq were causing extensive damage in Kuwait, a ground offensive would only result in further destruction. When National Security Adviser Brent Scowcroft was asked about our aims, he acknowledged a purpose that Bush had not mentioned, namely, that the administration hoped to leave Iraq with "no offensive capability."[19] This aim was confirmed by General Thomas Kelly, director of operations for the Joint Chiefs of Staff (JCS), who said that Bush had asked the JCS both to get the Iraqis out of Kuwait and to "destroy their ability to conduct offensive operations" outside Iraq in the future.[20] If Scowcroft and Kelly were accurate—and there is no reason to doubt them—the rationale Bush had given the public for the ground offensive was only part of the truth.

Secretary of State Baker hinted at an additional reason for the ground offensive when he suggested that removing Iraqi President Saddam Hussein from power might be authorized by the Security Council resolutions.[21] In any event, the administration's aims went beyond what it had disclosed to the public.

Shortly after the commencement of the ground offensive, Iraq ordered its forces to withdraw from Kuwait immediately, which they began to do. The Bush administration, however, refused to stop its offensive, arguing that Iraq must comply not only with the Security Council resolution calling on it to leave Kuwait, but with other resolutions the Council had passed concerning the situation.[22] The other resolutions, however, related to Iraq's occupation of Kuwait and to sanctions aimed at getting it to leave. One resolution demanded that Iraq allow foreign nationals to leave Iraq, but Iraq had already done that. One other held Iraq responsible for financial loss resulting from the invasion, but that was hardly an issue that could be resolved quickly. The administration's reference to the other resolutions was merely a smokescreen thrown up to allow it more time to destroy Iraq's military infrastructure.

As the Iraq war showed, a president who sends troops abroad is automatically confronted with a public relations problem. Our soldiers must be willing to go, and Congress must be willing to provide the funds. In general, presidents have been successful in convincing both Congress and the public to go along with their interventions. This success is perhaps to be deemed remarkable, since the purported reasons for many of the interventions were vague at the time; but with historical hindsight it has become clear that much of what the presidents have told the public was untrue. We proceed now to examine how successive presidents have dealt with the public as they entered into military conflict.

Notes

1. *New York Times* v. *U.S., U.S. Reports,* vol. 403, p. 717 (1971).

2. Youssef M. Ibrahim, "Bush Sends U.S. Force to Saudi Arabia as Kingdom Agrees to Confront Iraq," *New York Times,* August 8, 1990, p. A1, col. 3.

3. Andrew Rosenthal, "Bush Sends U.S. Force to Saudi Arabia as Kingdom Agrees to Confront Iraq," *New York Times,* August 8, 1990, p. A1, col. 6. Bob Woodward, *The Commanders* (1991), pp. 263–77.

4. Ibrahim, "Bush Sends U.S. Force to Saudi Arabia as Kingdom Agrees to Confront Iraq."

5. Thomas Friedman, "Bush, Hinting Force, Declares Iraqi Assault 'Will Not Stand'; Proxy in Kuwait Issues Threat," *New York Times,* August 7, 1990, p. A1, col. 6.

6. John Kifner, "Arabs' Summit Meeting Off; Iraqi Units in Kuwait Dig in; Europe Bars Baghdad's Oil," *New York Times,* August 5, 1990, p. A1, col. 1.

7. "Chronology of the Crisis," *Middle East International,* August 31, 1990, p. 24.

8. "British Troops Feared Held by Saddam's Men," *Daily Telegraph,* August 5, 1990, p. 1.

9. Fred Bruning, "Enter 'Neutral Zone'; Won't Attack Saudi Land, Top Arabs Say," *Newsday,* August 5, 1990, p. 3.

10. U.S. Code, vol. 50, §§1543–44.

11. Rosenthal, "Bush Sends U.S. Force to Saudi Arabia as Kingdom Agrees to Confront Iraq."

12. Letter to the Speaker of the House and the President Pro Tempore of the Senate on the Deployment of United States Armed Forces to Saudi Arabia and the Middle East, August 9, 1990, *Weekly Compilation of Presidential Documents,* August 13, 1990, p. 1225; R. W. Apple, Jr., "U.S. Says Its Troops in the Gulf Could Reach 100,000 in Months," *New York Times,* August 11, 1990, p. A1, col. 4.

13. Dan Balz, "Bush Warns Iraq Against Sending Out Oil Tankers," *Washington Post,* August 11, 1990, p. A23, col. 4.

14. Elaine Sciolino, "U.S. Gave Iraq Little Reason Not to Mount Kuwait Assault," *New York Times,* September 23, 1990, p. A1, col. 3.

15. UN Security Council, *Provisional Verbatim Record,* 2963d meeting, UN Doc. S/PV.2963 (1990).

16. "Excerpts from Bush's Remarks on Baker's Mission and Diplomacy's Fate," *New York Times,* January 10, 1991, p. A16, col. 1.

17. "Transcript of the Comments by Bush on the Air Strikes Against the Iraqis," *New York Times,* January 17, 1991, p. A6, col. 1.

18. "Announcement by Bush on Start of Ground War," *New York Times,* February 25, 1991, p. A13, col. 5.

19. "Meet the Press," interview on NBC, February 24, 1991.

20. "Sunday Today," interview on NBC, March 31, 1991.

21. "This Week," interview on ABC, February 24, 1991.

22. Patrick E. Tyler, "Baghdad Cites Soviets' Plan; Administration Wants More," *New York Times,* February 26, 1991, p. A1, col. 5; Martin Yant, *Desert Mirage: The True Story of the Gulf War* (1991), pp. 135–50.

2

How It Began

The United States is unique in maintaining abroad a large establishment of battleships and military bases. Even at the height of the cold war, the Soviet Union did not maintain military forces abroad on anything like the scale of ours. No other country has so frequently sent troops to fight in distant locations.

The United States has fashioned a set of interests for itself around the globe, largely stemming from commercial activity. Our companies are everywhere, buying and selling, making investments, digging mines, cultivating cash crops, and setting up assembly lines that employ cheap labor. By the early part of this century we needed raw materials unavailable at home to fuel the mass-assembly production system we had mastered. Our industry, which rapidly became the most robust in the world, needed markets for its expanding products.

We spread first through regions close to home, as our companies set up shop in Latin America. Our banana plantations were the most visible form of this activity. With the decline, in the nineteenth century, of Spanish and Portuguese colonial activity in Latin America, the United States declared, through the Monroe Doctrine, that Europe was not to recolonize in our hemisphere. Our business activity in Latin America grew, with our government intervening militarily to protect our companies. By 1895, Secretary of State Richard Olney could assert that the United States was "practically sovereign" in the western hemisphere, because "its infinite resources combined with its isolated position render it master of the situation."[1] Many Latins doubtless agreed with Olney's assessment, although they may not have viewed the U.S. role so benignly.

Exercising our role of "master of the situation," President Theodore Roosevelt claimed a right to intervene in any Latin country that defaulted on its public debt. To put a country's finances in order, we would operate its customs houses and put its finances back on a proper footing. Roosevelt first used this rationale, which became known as the Roosevelt corollary to the Monroe Doctrine,[2] to intervene in the Dominican Republic in 1905.

When Colombia balked at giving us Panama to build a canal, we fomented a rebellion in Panama and sent ships to stop Colombia from putting it down. In the early decades of the twentieth century, we intervened over and over again in Latin America, anxious to see at the helm governments that let our companies operate without major restrictions. In U.S. strategic thinking, security and economic considerations became so intertwined as to be inseparable.[3]

In 1916, President Woodrow Wilson sent the Marines to occupy the Dominican Republic, arguing that Germany, which was conducting naval operations in the Atlantic Ocean, might take it over if we stayed out. There was little evidence of any such possibility, and it seems that our real aim was greater control over the Dominican Republic. The Marines remained for eight years, leaving only in 1924. By then, our military administration had let U.S. sugar companies gain title to much of the sugar-growing land in the Dominican Republic, driving off Dominican peasants and burning their villages in the process.[4]

Intervention in Latin America subsided in the 1930s, when President Franklin Roosevelt declared a "good neighbor" policy in the hemisphere. But after World War II, we resumed interventionism there, as a number of the chapters that follow will demonstrate.

At the same time, we began to spread our influence to the rest of the world. As Europe's colonial empires declined in Asia, Africa, and the Middle East, our companies became the main outside financial force in these regions. Since the economies of these areas were weak, outside capital could play a vital role. As with Latin America, we wanted friendly governments in power, to let us extract their minerals, employ their labor force, and sell our products.

Once more, as in Latin America, we sent our military forces out to make sure the right kinds of governments were in power. We thus set up a worldwide military apparatus, sending naval fleets to all the world's oceans and stationing ground troops in far-flung sites. We tried to preserve friendly governments and displace the unfriendly, giving the Monroe Doctrine and its Roosevelt corollary a global reach.[5]

In Third World areas once dominated by Europe, we came into a power broker role, taking Indochina from France and the Middle East from Great Britain. Our companies saw nothing wrong in what they were doing, and in some ways they benefited the countries where they operated. The companies were simply doing good business, looking for the cheapest raw materials and labor as well as new markets.

Our rising preeminence in the financial life of weaker countries was accompanied by a similarly influential role in their politics. Our companies, whose assets often exceeded those of the countries where they operated, could control events. Politicians, in return for payoffs, disguised or open, let the companies operate as they liked. In reaction to this practice, opposition to our role developed in Asia and Africa, as it already had in Latin America. Often this opposition was led by leftist parties on close terms with the Soviet Union or China.

When they sent troops overseas, U.S. administrations were not models of candor. It would hardly sound good to say to the people at home that we wanted to force Ruritania to switch to a government that would allow more profits to be returned to the United States. When the Senate was debating whether to enter World War I, Senator Hiram Johnson of Texas warned, "The first casualty when war comes is truth," but long before then American administrations had begun bending the truth to gain public support for interventions abroad.

The United States' westward and southern expansion provided the context for our first major foreign intervention. In 1846, President James Polk asked Congress to declare war on Mexico, telling it that Mexico had invaded U.S. territory and "shed American blood on the American soil."[6] Polk's claim of a Mexican invasion was based on a skirmish between U.S. and Mexican forces in the area between the Nueces River and the Rio Grande.[7] The Nueces, which parallels the Rio Grande 150 miles northeast of it, had long been the recognized border between Texas and Mexico, and at the time was governed by the latter.[8]

But Congress accepted Polk's argument, reciting in its war declaration that "by the act of the Republic of Mexico, a state of war exists between that Government and the United States."[9] This "act" by Mexico was the skirmish between the Rio Grande and the Nueces. Ulysses Grant, who as an army officer fought in the Mexican war, was on target when he wrote that the United States had initiated the war with Mexico "to acquire additional territory." Grant called the Mexican war "one of the most unjust ever waged by a stronger against a weaker nation."[10]

In 1898, we went to war with Spain under the slogan "Remember the *Maine*." Early that year, the USS *Maine* had exploded and sunk in the harbor at Havana, in Spain's colony of Cuba, with a loss of two hundred sixty-six crew members. President William McKinley ordered the Navy to conduct an inquiry, and the naval panel focused its attention on a section of the *Maine*'s hull, which was dented inward after the explosion. The panel decided that this indentation was caused by an external explosion, so it concluded that the *Maine* had been destroyed by an underwater mine. Although the panel could not determine who might have laid such a mine, the surmise was that it was Spanish, either private individuals or the government, who were afraid that the United States might encourage Cuba to revolt against Spain.[11]

The Spanish government, seeing that political hay was being made of the incident, conducted its own inquiry, and found no evidence of an external explosion. Of the many eyewitnesses to the event, no one noticed any disturbance of the water, which would have been visible if a mine exploded in the water. Havana harbor was home to abundant fish life, but no dead fish were reported, as one might expect from a mine exploding there.[12] The Spanish inquiry board concluded, therefore, that the explosion must have resulted from the spontaneous combustion of materials on the ship itself. It argued that the hull collapsed inward from the action of the water following the explosion.

Understanding that the United States was not likely to accept this conclusion, Spain proposed that the two countries hold a joint investigation, and also offered to submit the question of its liability to binding arbitration by an impartial international panel.

President William McKinley told Congress of Spain's proposal but informed it that he did not plan to reply. Instead he asked Congress to declare war on Spain, explaining that "the destruction of the *Maine,* by whatever exterior cause, is a patent and impressive proof of a state of things in Cuba that is intolerable." Spain, he said, was unable to "assure safety and security to a vessel of the American Navy."[13] Congress consequently authorized McKinley to go to war to drive Spain out of Cuba, giving as one reason "the destruction of a United States battle ship, with two hundred and sixty-six of its officers and crew, while on a friendly visit in the harbor of Havana."[14] We won the war with Spain, forcing it to set Cuba free, and in the process we also took from Spain its colonies of the Philippines and Puerto Rico. In all three territories we established our own control to a greater or lesser degree.

The cause of the *Maine* explosion was never authoritatively established. However, the U.S. Navy preserved the documentary evidence, and in a 1976 reexamination, Admiral Hyman Rickover arrived at the same conclusion that had been reached by the Spanish inquiry panel. Rickover found no evidence of an external explosion. Like the Spanish panel, Rickover concluded that the explosion was internal, and that the hull then collapsed inward from the action of the water.[15]

Another major U.S. intervention occurred in the wake of World War I, far from Latin America, and again the White House was reticent about publicly stating the real reasons. In Russia, the Bolshevik party had come to power, and Western governments worried that the Soviet ideas of collectivization and state property would limit foreign entrepreneurs. They also feared that the Soviet system would spread and that other countries would renounce capitalism.[16]

The military attachés of Italy, France, England, and the United States met in Moscow on May 27, 1918, and decided to propose military intervention to their respective governments.[17]

United States ambassador David Francis issued statements calling on the Russian people to overthrow the Bolsheviks.[18] In the northern port of Archangelsk (Anglicized as Archangel), British agents, working with anti-Bolshevik (White Russian) elements, organized an armed uprising against the local Soviet administration. On August 2, 1918, British and French warships occupied Archangelsk, and anti-Bolshevik Russian political parties overthrew the Soviet administration, setting up a government under British and French tutelage. British, French, and U.S. troops thus occupied Archangelsk and became the effective controllers of the area.[19]

As the allied force landed at Archangelsk, the Soviet troops retreated south with their supplies.[20] U.S. and other allied forces, along with White Russian troops, pursued the retreating Soviet forces.[21] The U.S. forces were put under British command, so that the British determined events on the ground.[22] The allied forces took up positions in towns to the south of Archangelsk and from there fought Soviet troops. George Chicherin, the Soviet commissar for foreign affairs, sent President Wilson a note offering an armistice and a withdrawal of U.S. forces, but Wilson did not reply.[23] The All-Russian Congress of Soviets then issued a public proposal to the allies to enter peace negotiations, but again got no response.[24]

For the United States, the avowed purpose of the continuation of hostilities was to prevent allied supplies from being given to the Germans, with whom we were still at war.[25] The *Chicago Tribune,* however, labeled this assertion "propaganda,"[26] and in later years a leading Western historian called it a pretext.[27]

The Wilson administration, in post-war meetings with other allied governments at Versailles, spoke for nonintervention in Russia, but on the ground, U.S. troops under British command continued fighting the Bolsheviks. In a proclamation to the troops, the British commander in north Russia stated, "We are up against Bolshevism," and that "the power is in the hands of a few men, mostly Jews, who have succeeded in bringing the country to such a state that order is nonexistent. Bolshevism has grown upon the uneducated masses to such an extent that Russia is disintegrated and helpless, and therefore we have come to help her get rid of the disease that is eating her up." The proclamation declared that the aim was "the restoration of Russia," by which was meant a non-Soviet Russia.[28]

In November 1918, when the armistice ending the war was signed with Germany, the allied troops in Russia thought they would be able to go home.[29] But Wilson left them there to fight the Soviet troops. This continuation of the battle even after the armistice had been signed showed that defeating Germany was not the true purpose of the allied military presence in Russia.[30] A British commander explained to the troops following the armistice that "there will be no faltering in our purpose to remove the stain of Bolshevism."[31] Even though the formerly stated purpose of intercepting supplies bound for Germany no longer applied, the Wilson administration still refused to divulge to the troops or the public the reason for the continued hostilities. Disaffection began to surface among the allied troops, who did not understand why they were still fighting.[32] Hunger and disease were widespread because of the privations brought about by the northern winter, and some mutinies occurred.[33]

Secretary of State Robert Lansing reported that troop morale was "not good and further weakened by considerable friction with [the] British."[34] According to Wilson's special envoy to Moscow, William C. Bullitt, the "American, British, and French troops at Archangelsk are no longer serving any useful purpose. Only 3,000 Russians have rallied around this force."[35]

By early 1919, we had 5,000 troops in the northern Russian theater.[36] A U.S. sergeant wrote a letter home that "we are absolutely ignorant of any cause for being here, and we appeal to the folks at home to enlighten us. If we are here to improve conditions of the Russians and to destroy bolshevism, which we must admit is a dangerous institution, does it not seem right the [R]ussians should assist us? But they refuse to go to the front and fight with us."[37]

Only in January 1919, six months after the intervention began, did Wilson publicly acknowledge that the U.S. troops were in Russia to stop the Bolsheviks. The allies were repelled by Bolshevism, he told the Paris Peace Conference, and for that reason had put troops into Russia.[38] Still, Wilson explained little of his reasoning behind the move, and he conceded to the allies at Paris that our intervention might actually strengthen the Bolsheviks by rallying support against the outside intervention.

In Washington, the administration's anti-Bolshevik intervention drew fire from Congress on the grounds that Wilson had not publicly explained his purpose. Senator Hiram Johnson said that U.S. soldiers "without warrant of law and in violation of the Constitution of the United States are killing and being killed in Russia today."[39] Johnson complained that "there is not a representative of the Government of the United States of America, there is not anybody in power or in position who has said to the American people or said to the American Congress what is the policy of this Government toward Russia or defined it in any degree or in any aspect."[40]

Johnson continued; the administration, he said, had insisted that "we entered Russia not to take any territory" or to interfere in local government, but these statements "were false in fact and were given to lull not only the Russian people into a false security but to lull the American people as well."[41] Johnson then quoted from the *Chicago Tribune,* which ran a story claiming that the aim of the military expedition was apparently to help Europe collect Russia's debt.[42] French and British citizens had loaned large sums to the czarist government, and the Bolsheviks had repudiated the debt.

The U.S. Senate accordingly passed a resolution in June 1919, asking Wilson to explain "the reasons for sending United States soldiers to Siberia."[43] U.S. Senator William Borah said that "while Congress has not declared war, we are carrying on war with the Russian people. We have an army in Russia; we are furnishing munitions and supplies." In Borah's estimation, the United States was engaged in a "military intervention to put down a certain force in Russia and establish a government satisfactory to the allied powers." He said that "every boy who dies in Russia is a sacrifice to the unlawful and intolerable scheme." While expressing no sympathy to Bolshevism, Borah continued, "if they see fit to have a soviet government, it is their business." Borah frequently demanded the withdrawal of the U.S. troops from Russia,[44] and in June 1919, President Wilson withdrew them.[45]

As these late-nineteenth- and early-twentieth-century examples show, prevarication to justify military intervention is not a new phenomenon for the United States, and hardly a product of the cold war. Nor is it the exclusive domain of a particular political party.

Such interventionism became particularly frequent after World War II, because of the political and economic preeminence the United States began to enjoy in the world as the French and British empires went into decline—a preeminence that this country has been resolutely prepared to maintain and to propagate as the stakes have grown steadily higher. We turn now to the post-war interventions, the first of which took place in an unlikely setting.

Notes

1. "Mr. Olney to Mr. Bayard," July 20, 1985, FRUS 1895, p. 558.
2. "Message from the President of the United States, Transmitting a Protocol of an Agreement between the United States and the Dominican Republic, Providing for the Collection and Disbursement by the United States of the Customs Revenues

of the Dominican Republic, Signed on February 7, 1905," February 15, 1905, FRUS 1905, pp. 334–42.

3. Piero Gleijeses, *The Dominican Crisis: The 1965 Constitutionalist Revolt and American Intervention* (1978), p. 15.

4. Ibid., pp. 17–18.

5. Thomas J. McCormick, *America's Half-Century: United States Foreign Policy in the Cold War* (1989), p. 75.

6. John H. Schroeder, *Mr. Polk's War: American Opposition and Dissent, 1846–1848* (1973), pp. 3, 11; Alfred Hoyt Bill, *Rehearsal for Conflict: The War with Mexico 1846-1848* (1947), p. 102.

7. David Wise, *The Politics of Lying: Government Deception, Secrecy, and Power* (1973), p. 25; Bill, *Rehearsal for Conflict,* p. 92.

8. Schroeder, *Mr. Polk's War,* pp. 8–11.

9. An Act Providing for the Prosecution of the Existing War between the United States and the Republic of Mexico, May 13, 1846, U.S. Congress, *Statutes at Large,* vol. 9, p. 9 (1846).

10. *Personal Memoirs of U. S. Grant* (1894), p. 37.

11. G. J. A. O'Toole, *The Spanish War: An American Epic—1898* (1984), pp. 138, 150.

12. John Edward Weems, *The Fate of the Maine* (1958), pp. 126–27.

13. William McKinley, "Message to the Congress of the United States," April 11, 1898, in *Papers Relating to the Foreign Relations of the United States, 1898* (1901), p. 758.

14. Joint Resolution: For the recognition of the independence of the people of Cuba, demanding that the government of Spain relinquish its authority and government in the Island of Cuba, and to withdraw its land and naval forces from Cuba and Cuban waters, and directing the President of the United States to use the land and naval forces of the United States to carry these resolutions into effect. U.S. Congress, *Statutes at Large,* vol. 30, p. 738 (1898).

15. H. G. Rickover, *How the Battleship Maine was Destroyed* (1976), p. 91.

16. Robert Murray, *Red Scare: A Study of National Hysteria, 1919–1920* (1964), p. 15.

17. John Cudahy, *Archangel: The American War with Russia* (1924), p. 27.

18. Michael Sayers and Albert E. Kahn, *The Great Conspiracy Against Russia* (1946), p. 11.

19. Cudahy, *Archangel: The American War with Russia,* pp. 47, 72.

20. *Foreign Relations of the United States: The Paris Peace Conference 1919,* vol. 3, p. 625 (1943) (statement of M. Noulens, former French ambassador to Russia); Cudahy, *Archangel: The American War with Russia,* pp. 47–48, 131.

21. Sayers and Kahn, *The Great Conspiracy Against Russia,* p. 28.

22. Cudahy, *Archangel: The American War with Russia,* p. 75.

23. Ibid., p. 30; E. H. Carr, *The Bolshevik Revolution 1917–1923* (1966), 3: 117.

24. Carr, *The Bolshevik Revolution 1917–1923,* 3: 117.

25. Adam Ulam, *A History of Soviet Russia* (1976), pp. 34–36; Georg von Rauch, *A History of Soviet Russia* (1959), p. 92; George Kennan, *The Decision to Intervene* (1967), p. 21; Cudahy, *Archangel: The American War with Russia,* p. 28.

26. *Congressional Record,* vol. 57, pt. 4, p. 3261 (February 13, 1919).

27. Carr, *The Bolshevik Revolution 1917–1923,* 3: 117.

28. Cudahy, *Archangel: The American War with Russia,* pp. 31–32.

29. *Congressional Record,* vol. 57, pt. 4, p. 3261 (February 13, 1919).

30. Ralph Albertson, *Fighting without a War: An Account of Military Intervention in North Russia* (1920), pp. 112–20.

31. Cudahy, *Archangel: The American War with Russia,* p. 37.

32. Albertson, *Fighting without a War,* pp. 74–75; Cudahy, *Archangel: The American War with Russia,* pp. 2–4, 71, 99–100, 159.

33. Cudahy, *Archangel: The American War with Russia,* pp. 161–62.

34. The Secretary of State to Colonel E. M. House, December 2, 1918, *Foreign Relations of the United States: The Paris Peace Conference 1919,* vol. 2, p. 465 (1943).

35. Memorandum for Colonel House, Withdrawal of American Troops from Archangel, January 30, 1919, Cudahy, *Archangel: The American War with Russia,* p. 120.

36. Albertson, *Fighting without a War,* p. 57; Sayers and Kahn, *The Great Conspiracy Against Russia,* p. 28; Cudahy, *Archangel: The American War with Russia,* p. 49.

37. *Congressional Record,* vol. 57, pt. 4, p. 3261 (February 13, 1919).

38. *Foreign Relations of the United States: the Paris Peace Conference 1919* (1943), 3: 648–49.

39. *Congressional Record,* vol. 57, pt. 4, p. 3259 (February 13, 1919).

40. Ibid., p. 3260.

41. Ibid., p. 3261.

42. Ibid., p. 3260.

43. Ibid., vol. 58, pt. 2, p. 1864 (June 27, 1919).

44. Ibid., pt. 5, p. 4897 (September 5, 1919).

45. Albertson, *Fighting without a War,* p. 57; Cudahy, *Archangel: The American War with Russia,* p. 169, 210–11.

3

Korea: Whose War?

Korea after World War II was divided north and south at the 38th parallel. The southern administration, with its capital at Seoul, had skirmished frequently across the parallel with the northern administration, based at Pyongyang. On June 25, 1950, the south reported an attack by the north and said fighting continued all across Korea along the parallel.[1] The north, on the other hand, claimed just the opposite, Pyongyang Radio announcing that the south "started a surprise invasion of the north along the whole front of the 38th parallel line at dawn on the 25th."[2] First reports from U.S. military intelligence in Korea were also that the south attacked first.[3] Our Korean Military Assistance Group (KMAG), which advised the southern army, had no reports on June 25 of northern troop movements or concentration of supplies near the 38th parallel.[4]

As was reported in the U.S. ambassador's first cable to Washington, the initial fighting was not taking place all along the 38th parallel, but only at its western end, on Korea's west coast, an area called the Ongjin peninsula.[5] Despite their public initial claims, both north and south, in their statements, agreed with the ambassador that the fighting had begun in the west. However, if the north was indeed assaulting the south, this was a strange location to choose. Moving south across the

35

38th parallel on the Ongjin peninsula, one goes only a few miles before dead-ending at the sea, with no access by land to Seoul or to the rest of Korea south of the 38th parallel. If, however, the south were assaulting the north, the Ongjin peninsula was a logical starting point, because Pyongyang, lying on the west coast, would be a prime objective for the south.[6]

One piece of evidence that suggested that the south made the first move is that, as announced June 25 by both the northern and southern administrations, the southern army had captured the northern city of Haeju, five miles above the 38th parallel on the Ongjin peninsula.[7] The south set the first fighting at 4:00 A.M., while Pyongyang Radio broadcast at 11:00 A.M. that the south attacked in the Haeju area "at dawn."[8] American military advisors who worked with the southern army confirmed this;[9] U.S. military intelligence also confirmed the south's capture of Haeju, identifying the southern army unit responsible as its 17th regiment, a crack unit.[10]

The south's assault on Haeju, it appears, started well before dawn of June 25. The northern army reported that the south had moved against Haeju on the night of June 23, a report that was later confirmed by Young Woon Lee, an admiral in the south's navy. The admiral recounted that on June 23, he led an assault by sea on Haeju, which is only one mile from the ocean; on that day the south's chief of staff issued a combat order directing commanders to "go into action at 5, June 25." The admiral said that to divert attention from the planned "full-force invasion of the North," the southern army started partial attacks beginning at 10 P.M. on June 23.[11] An early cable from the U.S. ambassador confirmed a southern advance, as he reported on June 26 that "North Korean armor and artillery are withdrawing all along the line," meaning the 38th parallel.[12] By then the fighting had spread eastward.

Although the facts behind the Korean fighting were unclear, and even despite the indication that an invasion had been initiated by the south, official Washington immediately concluded that the north was responsible. Two hours after receiving the first cable about the Korean fighting, the State Department approached the United Nations and arranged to have an emergency meeting scheduled in the Security Council. Wasting no time, the Department hastily drew up a resolution to submit to the Council, declaring that the north had committed an "act of aggression." Just before the Council met, Charles Noyes, the U.S. delegate, showed the draft resolution to the Security Council representatives of Great Britain, France, India, Egypt, and Norway. All five indicated "considerable hesitancy to take a position on which party was responsible for the invasion," Noyes reported. Egypt and Norway said there was not enough information to condemn the north, and in any event the fighting was between Koreans, and therefore a civil war. Moreover, they objected to the term "aggression" because it implied an invasion of one country by another.[13]

Worried that the resolution might fail, Noyes changed "act of aggression" to read "armed invasion."[14] Although this revised phraseology still implied an attack by one country against another, Noyes hoped the change might get the doubters to go along. Indonesia's delegate, however, was not satisfied. He told Noyes privately that the Security Council did not have enough information to confirm which side started the fighting.[15]

The Security Council did have some information, but it was far from conclusive. The Council had in hand a cable from the UN mission in Korea, which reported,

> South Korean troops apparently withdrawing to prearranged main line of resistance which runs along Imjin River 27 miles northwest of Seoul where crossing by northern forces has been reported at one point. Attack completely unexpected to both Korean Army and KMAG. Early fragmentary reports indicating complete surprise and withdrawals everywhere now being replaced by more confident statements. Situation reported being stabilized along main line of resistance.[16]

The mission's cable was apparently considered too sensitive to be published in UN documents, but it was read orally to Security Council members.[17] The cable suggested that the north attacked first, although it reported the north crossing the 38th parallel at only one point.

The mission, curiously, did not mention the south's capture of Haeju, although the world press had widely reported it. The omission was probably a result of the fact that the UN mission had no observers in the field and thus had received no firsthand information on the fighting. Moreover, the mission had not had an easy time in Korea, getting no cooperation from the north, which viewed the UN as partial to the south. Because the north did not cooperate, the mission did little by way of field operations, relying instead for its information on the southern army. Thus, its report to the Security Council was based largely on official southern sources.[18]

When the Security Council convened, the doubts had not been quelled. Yugoslavia announced, "we do not feel that the picture we have been able to obtain so far from the various dispatches that have come in, some of which are contradictory, and from the statements we have heard here, is sufficiently complete and balanced, nor one which would enable us to pass judgment on the merits of the case or assess the final and definite responsibility and guilt of either of the parties involved." Before adopting any resolution, the Council should "acquire all the factual knowledge which would make that final judgment and the action taken in pursuance of it incontrovertible," and, in particular, invite the north to tell the Council its side of the story. "We have heard the representative of South Korea," said Yugoslavia's delegate; "we should grant an opportunity for a representative of the Government of North Korea, which has now been accused of aggression, to receive a hearing."[19]

By this point, however, the U.S. delegation had managed to mollify most of the other Council members, and so the Council did not take up Yugoslavia's suggestion to hear the north's view. The U.S. delegation softened the wording of the resolution once more, from "armed invasion" to "armed attack." But the resolution still called the attack a "breach of the peace," which implied the international peace. Nevertheless, with the exception of Yugoslavia, those Council members who had insisted that whatever fighting was occurring was internal to Korea began to give ground.

During an adjournment in the Council's proceedings, a curious new piece of information surfaced. The UN Secretariat told Council members confidentially that tanks just captured by the southern army were manned by Russians. This information had not been included in any official record, but Australia's delegate mentioned it in a cable to the Australian government, adding that France and Egypt changed their view and voted for the U.S. resolution because of it.[20] The information, however, was quite erroneous, as no Russians could be confirmed to be involved in the fighting. Whether the information was deliberately planted or an honest error would never be determined.

The Soviet Union could not refute the information, because it was boycotting Council meetings over the Council's refusal to give mainland

China the Chinese seat on the Council. If it had participated, it would certainly have vetoed the U.S. resolution. But with the Soviet delegate absent, the U.S. resolution was put to a vote and, despite the initial doubts, it carried easily, with no negative votes and only Yugoslavia abstaining.[21]

Great Britain made a curious statement explaining its vote; it essentially cautioned the Council against any "action which might go beyond the bounds of the evidence which has been placed at its disposal by its own Commission in Korea." Britain said that the resolution "goes as far as the Security Council properly can go at this stage."[22] Thus Britain was apparently not fully convinced who had initiated the fighting but voted for the U.S. resolution anyway. Despite the softening of its language, the resolution charged the northern administration with international aggression,[23] as it had been initially construed by the U.S. delegation.[24]

This Security Council resolution, as well as another passed a few days later, provided the basis for the Truman administration to send troops to Korea. Although the administration consulted the Security Council, it did not ask Congress for a formal declaration of war. Secretary of State Dean Acheson explained later that Congress "might have completely muddied up the situation which seemed to be very clear."[25] While in Congress there was not substantial dissent, Senator Robert Taft of Ohio objected that there was "no legal authority" for Truman's action, and that Truman had made "no pretense of consulting the Congress." Taft called Truman's decision to send troops to Korea "a complete usurpation by the President of authority to use the Armed Forces of this country."[26]

One factor clouding the issue of responsibility for initiating the Korean conflict was that the June 25 fighting was not the first in Korea. Intermittent hostilities, in fact, had raged across the 38th parallel during the previous year.[27] The summer of 1949 had seen major fighting, most of it started by the south.[28] In April 1950, Philip Jessup, a U.S. ambassador at large, reported from Korea that the 38th parallel was "a real front line," and that there was "constant fighting," with "very real battles, involving perhaps one or two thousand men."[29] In May and June cross-parallel incidents picked up.[30] Our ambassador characterized this fighting as continuous probing along the parallel by both sides, which he said made it difficult to determine what was happening on that crucial morning of June 25.[31]

Despite the cross-parallel fighting, U.S. military intelligence did not anticipate a northern invasion in the summer of 1950.[32] One reason was that the northern army had a mobilization plan for an invasion of the south that called for fifteen divisions, but by June 1950 it had only six.[33] This left the north with fewer troops for engagement in the field than the south had at its disposal.[34]

Another reason for doubting a northern invasion was that the north was pressing its demand for reunification and had some prospects of achieving it without a war, because of the political vulnerability of the southern administration.[35] In elections held on May 30, 1950, the southern administration of President Syngman Rhee was dealt a severe blow when voters chose a parliament with a large anti-Rhee majority.[36] This defeat sapped Rhee's continued ability to convince the south to remain separate from the north and thus increased the prospects that unification could be achieved by political means.[37] For these reasons, both British intelligence and the CIA thought that the north had such a good chance of undermining Rhee from within that it would not need to invade.[38]

Rhee, on the other hand, had ample motive to provoke hostilities. The loss of support in parliament following the May 30 election threatened his hold on power, and his economy was collapsing. Beyond that, a serious guerrilla war in the south led by leftist elements and aimed at unification with the north was causing Rhee trouble.[39] A war against the north, then, while risky, might rally his opponents and bring military support from outside, particularly from the United States.[40] This explains why Rhee conducted raids across the 38th parallel in the summer of 1949, namely, to try to keep the United States in the picture. In the spring of 1950, in fact, Rhee announced his intention to invade the north and made actual war preparations, moving most of his troops and equipment up to the 38th parallel.[41] To General Douglas MacArthur, who would lead U.S. troops in Korea, that deployment suggested an offensive posture.[42] In the north, by contrast, only one-third of the available troops were close to the 38th parallel.[43]

Another factor suggesting that Rhee may have started the hostilities is that he thought he could draw the United States in on his side. On June 18, John Foster Dulles, a consultant to the State Department, addressed Korea's National Assembly and said that if the north attacked, we would respond. Rhee, who could barely contain his delight with the speech, pressed Dulles for details on our commitment. Although

Dulles did not say exactly what we would do, the speech may have convinced Rhee that the best way to save his faltering government was to provoke an attack by the north.[44] As the first reports of fighting began to filter into Seoul, our ambassador, who was with Rhee, reported that Rhee seemed unconcerned about the fighting. According to Rhee, doing battle "presented the best opportunity for settling the Korean problem once and for all"—an odd reaction for someone putatively caught off guard and fearful that he would be overrun.[45]

Some evidence for the proposition that the north began the fighting came years later when Soviet leader Nikita Khrushchev reported in his memoirs on a visit made to Moscow in December 1949 by Kim Il-sung, North Korea's leader. "The North Koreans," Khrushchev said, "wanted to give a helping hand to their brethren who were under the heel of Syngman Rhee."[46] Kim anticipated that if he launched an attack, the southerners would rise up against the unpopular Rhee.[47] If Khrushchev's account is accurate, it might mean that the northern army was planning to attack, or else that this was only a contingency plan. By June 1950, as we have seen, the political situation turned against the southern administration, so that if in the winter Kim Il-sung had been contemplating an attack, he might have changed his mind by mid-1950.

As soon as the Korean hostilities started, President Truman dispatched our Eighth Army to fight for the southern administration and sent the State Department rushing back to the Security Council to obtain an authorization for military action on a multilateral basis.[48] On June 27, the Council obliged by asking member states to assist South Korea "to repel the armed attack."[49] As before, the Council avoided the question of who started the hostilities. By this time the UN mission in Korea had given it no new information, other than a report based on the situation at the 38th parallel two days before the hostilities started.[50]

In the initial fighting, as it spread east across the 38th parallel, neither side got the better of it. For three days the two armies fought to a standstill, at which time the southern army withdrew southward. Its 17th regiment withdrew south from Haeju, even though it was not being pressed.[51] The northern army made its first major advance in the central area, where it took the southern town of Uijongbu, opening the road to Seoul, which it then took quickly. The north's speedy advance to Seoul is offered by some historians as proof that the northern army started the war. But one historian states that the southern army put up "suspiciously token resistance" at Uijongbu.[52] The south abandoned Seoul even before the northern army could catch up.

The southern army's rapid retreat is puzzling, because its forces outnumbered the north's, and there is no clear explanation why it could not have held its ground. The retreat, in fact, surprised the northern army, which anticipated heavier fighting. U.S. military actions as well are difficult to read. When our Eighth Army, commanded by General Douglas MacArthur, came in on the southern side, it did not attack the northern army but joined the southern retreat. One possible explanation is that Rhee and MacArthur wanted to make their situation appear desperate, so that President Truman would commit enough troops not only to halt the northern advance (Truman's stated objective) but also to bring down the northern administration.[53] In a memorandum to MacArthur in August, Rhee said, "we have been withdrawing from city to city in the hope that American reinforcements would arrive soon enough to launch an offensive."[54] Even though the U.S. and southern forces outnumbered those of the north, MacArthur continued the retreat, telling Truman that we were outnumbered by the north two or three to one.[55]

The retreat, on the other hand, may have been part of the Eighth Army's purpose all along. A contingency plan drafted by Colonel Donald McB. Curtis a few days before the hostilities anticipated not only our intervention but also a strategy to retreat south to a defensive perimeter around Pusan, to be followed by an amphibious landing at Inchon, a port city near Seoul. As the war began, MacArthur urgently requested fifty copies of the plan, and during the summer and fall of 1950 he appeared to follow it to the letter.[56]

The northern army, unprepared for an extended campaign in the south, needed a full week to regroup after taking Seoul, before it continued southward.[57] If the north had planned the attack for June 25, it had apparently not intended to go very far.[58] As the northern army moved south, it took 50,000 casualties and ran short on supplies.[59] When in September, the Eighth Army and the southern forces counterattacked, the northern army disintegrated and fled.[60] This lack of preparation for a sustained offensive casts doubt on whether the northern army had initiated the fighting, although if Khrushchev is to be believed, it could be that the north had launched a deliberate offensive with the expectation of an imminent southern collapse.

In 1951, the Truman administration released captured northern documents that, it said, proved that the north had launched an unprovoked attack on June 25, 1950. But the documents did not stand the test of scrutiny.[61] Wrote one historian, "what actually happened in those early hours of the war was never properly established."[62] Bruce Cumings, the leading historian of the Korean war, agrees that even with the evidence made available long after the events, it is hazardous to pin blame on either side.[63] Even with historical hindsight, we have little substantiation for the Truman administration's position of a premeditated general attack by the northern army all along the 38th parallel, with no provocation by the southern army.

Beyond the question of who started the hostilities was that of whether they were international, so that other countries might legitimately get involved. As we saw, the Truman administration got the Security Council to agree that the hostilities were international, despite the misgivings of some Council delegates.[64] But Korea had long been a single country, and at the time of World War II, it was held by Japan, which had invaded Korea early in this century. As we fought Japan, one of our war aims, as stated in the 1943 Allied Cairo Declaration, was to set Korea free, as a single country.[65]

When World War II was nearing an end, we encouraged the Soviet Union to undertake the task of seizing Korea from Japan.[66] But as Soviet troops entered Korea, we became skittish about a Soviet occupation and offered to take the southern part ourselves, proposing the 38th parallel as a dividing line.[67] The Soviet government agreed, although we had no troops in Korea and the Soviet army could easily have taken the opportunity to occupy the entire country. The fact that it did not suggests that the Soviet Union had no plans to control Korea.[68]

Soon separate administrations were established above and below the 38th parallel, each viewing Korea as a single country that would eventually be reunited and disregarding the 38th parallel as an international border.[69] In the late 1940s, the UN tried, unsuccessfully, to reunify Korea but confronted a difference in political persuasion between the southern and northern administrations. Korean leftists had been prominent in the anti-Japan resistance movement, and as a result were the most powerful political force in Korea as the war ended.[70] They had local administrations, called people's committees, throughout the country and began to assume control from the Japanese administration.[71]

After the Soviet Union took control above the 38th parallel, the people's committees there formed an administration for that territory, which became the Kim Il-sung government.[72] South of the 38th parallel, too, the people's committees tried to form an administration, but U.S. occupation authorities did not want a left-leaning government. General John R. Hodge, who ran our military government in Korea, said the country was headed for "a political-economic abyss" and that we had to "stop this drift."[73] Hodge's main aim in governing the southern half of Korea—an aim he did not conceal—was to keep the people's committees from consolidating power.[74] Hodge said he wanted to "break down" what he called "this Communist government" in the south of Korea.[75]

In the south as in the north, the people's committees called their overall administration the Korean People's Republic. When the Korean People's Republic called a convention in Seoul, Hodge made, as he termed it, a "declaration of war" against the People's Republic, even though, he admitted, this strong response "may result in temporary disorders" and "bring charges of political discrimination" from what he called the Korean "pinko press."[76]

To suppress the Korean People's Republic, Hodge formally outlawed it,[77] rounding up leftists and putting them behind bars.[78] He also suppressed the people's committees in the various localities,[79] jailing their members and replacing them with conservatives drawn from the business community.[80] To protest Hodge's suppression, southern workers went on strike in 1946, calling for a restoration of the people's committees. To put down the strike as well as the committees, Hodge arrested over a thousand workers,[81] banned leftist political parties, and formed a consultative council composed of conservatives. He excluded from official positions many Koreans who had been active in the anti-Japan resistance, out of concern that they were leftists.[82] The Korean police force that Hodge had set up was unable to put down the people's committees, however, so he created an army of Koreans, well before a Korean army was established under the Soviet occupation in the north.[83] To suppress the guerrillas who supported the people's committees, our KMAG helped the new southern army plan anti-guerrilla strategy.[84]

As a military occupier, the United States should have remained neutral in Korea's internal politics. But Hodge's suppression of the leftists and his promotion of the conservatives made the leftists, on both sides of the 38th parallel, feel that the United States had cheated them of a political victory that was rightfully theirs. Acknowledging this perception, Hodge said that the general view in the south was to blame the United States for the partition of Korea.[85] To make matters worse, many of the conservatives Hodge promoted had been collaborators of the Japanese colonial administration and thus were viewed with particular disdain by other Koreans.[86] In short, General Hodge sowed the seeds of a conflict that pitted an upper class that had collaborated with Japan against a lower class that resisted it, and thereby was he in large part responsible for the outbreak of war in Korea in 1950.

General Hodge particularly promoted Syngman Rhee, an expatriate Korean who had long lived in the United States and who had little following in Korea.[87] The administration he came to head acquired a reputation for brutality and corruption, starting with the run-up to the 1948 parliamentary elections, when Rhee used "goon squads" to terrorize his opponents. Leftists boycotted the elections, thus allowing the conservatives to win a majority.[88]

The U.S. military government, by promoting the conservatives, interfered with Korea's political process and kept it from being unified under a single administration. The hostilities that began in 1950, irrespective of who started them, were internal and aimed at reuniting Korea. They were no more international than the shooting that began at Fort Sumter in 1861.[89]

The Truman administration characterized the conflict as international to give itself a reason to intervene, but that still leaves the question of why Truman was so anxious to fight in Korea. To answer that question, we must look to the cold war, which formed the backdrop for the Korean hostilities.

Notes

1. "Telegram: The Ambassador in Korea (Muccio) to the Secretary of State," June 25, 1950, 10 A.M., FRUS 1950, vol. 7, p. 125.

2. Ibid., p. 132.

3. John Gunther, *The Riddle of MacArthur* (1950), p. 165.

4. "War Is Declared by North Koreans; Fighting on Border," *New York Times,* June 25, 1950, p. A1, col. 1.

5. "Telegram: The Ambassador in Korea (Muccio) to the Secretary of State," p. 125.

6. Bruce Cumings, *The Roaring of the Cataract, 1945-1950*, vol. 2 of *The Origins of the Korean War* (1990), pp. 568-72, 584-85.

7. "North Korean Communiques," *New York Times*, June 26, 1950, p. A3, col. 3; "U.N. Calls for Ceasefire in Korea," *New York Times*, June 26, 1950, p. A1, col. 4 (South Korean announcement).

8. "Telegram: The Ambassador in Korea (Muccio) to the Secretary of State," p. 132.

9. "Threefold Advance towards Seoul," *Guardian* (Manchester), June 26, 1950, p. 7, col. 1; "Defenders Launch Counterattack, Regain 5 Miles North of Capital," *Chicago Tribune*, June 26, 1950, p. A1, col. 8; Glenn D. Paige, *The Korean Decision June 24-30, 1950* (1968), p. 130.

10. Cumings, *The Origins of the Korean War*, 2: 572-73, 578-79.

11. Committee for a New Direction for U.S. Korea Policy, *Conference for a New Direction in U.S. Korea Policy* (1977), p. 100.

12. "Telegram: The Ambassador in Korea (Muccio) to the Secretary of State," p. 165.

13. "Memorandum of Conversations, by Mr. Charles P. Noyes, Adviser on Security Council Affairs, United States Mission at the United Nations," June 25, 1950, FRUS 1950, vol. 7, pp. 144-45.

14. SCOR, 5th yr., 473rd mtg., p. 7, UN Doc. S/PV.473 (1950).

15. "Memorandum of Conversations, by Mr. Charles P. Noyes, Adviser on Security Council Affairs, United States Mission at the United Nations," June 25, 1950, FRUS 1950, vol. 7, pp. 144, 145.

16. "The United States Representative at the United Nations (Austin) to the Secretary of State," June 26, 1950, FRUS 1950, vol. 7, p. 172.

17. "Cablegram dated 25 June 1950 from the United Nations Commission on Korea addressed to the Secretary General concerning aggression upon the Republic of Korea," UN Doc. S/1496, text in SCOR, 5th yr., 473rd mtg., p. 2 n. 2, UN Doc. S/PV.473 (1950).

18. Cumings, *The Origins of the Korean War*, 2: 548, 635.

19. SCOR, 5th yr., 473rd mtg., pp. 14-15, UN Doc. S/PV.473 (1950).

20. Gavan McCormack, *Cold War Hot War: An Australian Perspective on the Korean War* (1983), p. 75.

21. SCOR, 5th yr., 473rd mtg., p. 16, UN Doc. S/PV.473 (1950).

22. SCOR, 5th yr., 473rd mtg., p. 9, UN Doc. S/PV.473 (1950).

23. Res. 82, June 25, 1950, SCOR, 5th yr., *Resolutions and Decisions*, p. 4, UN Doc. S/INF/5/Rev.1 (1950).

24. SCOR, 5th yr., 474th mtg., p. 3, UN Doc. S/PV.474 (1950).

25. Cumings, *The Origins of the Korean War*, 2: 629.

26. *Congressional Record*, vol. 96, pp. 9320, 9323, June 28, 1950.

27. "Threefold Advance towards Seoul," *Guardian* (Manchester), June 26, 1950, p. 7, col. 1.

28. Cumings, *The Origins of the Korean War*, 2: 383, 388-90, 570-71.

29. Philip Jessup, "Report to the American People on the Far East," April 13, 1950, DSB, vol. 22, p. 627 (1950).

30. Cumings, *The Origins of the Korean War*, 2: 448-49, 575-76.

31. Ibid., p. 580.

32. Max Hastings, *The Korean War* (1987), p. 52.

33. Walter Sullivan, "Red Mobilization Termed 'Feverish'," *New York Times*, July 31, 1950, p. A1, col. 7; Cumings, *The Origins of the Korean War*, 2: 452, 584, 597.

34. Joyce and Gabriel Kolko, *The Limits of Power: The World and United States Foreign Policy, 1945-1954* (1972), pp. 573-74; Cumings, *The Origins of the Korean War,* 2: 452-53.

35. "Cablegram dated 26 June 1950 to the Secretary General from the United Nations Commission on Korea, transmitting a summary report on background events preceding the outbreak of hostilities on 25 June 1950," UN Doc. S/1505/Rev.1, SCOR, 5th yr., Supplement for June, July and August 1950, p. 24; I. F. Stone, *The Hidden History of the Korean War* (1952), p. 18; Kolko, *The Limits of Power,* p. 575.

36. Burton Crane, "Rhee's Slate's Rout Indicated in Korea," *New York Times,* May 31, 1950, p. A8, col. 3; Hastings, *The Korean War,* p. 43.

37. Hastings, *The Korean War,* p. 57; Stone, *The Hidden History of the Korean War,* p. 65.

38. Cumings, *The Origins of the Korean War,* 2: 450.

39. Ibid., p. 441.

40. McCormack, *Cold War Hot War,* pp. 90-91.

41. Kolko, *The Limits of Power,* pp. 567-75; Cumings, *The Origins of the Korean War,* 2: 437.

42. *Military Situation in the Far East,* Hearings before the Armed Services and the Committee on Foreign Relations, U.S. Senate, 82d Cong., 1st sess., Part I, p. 231 (1951) (statement of Gen. Douglas MacArthur); Cumings, *The Origins of the Korean War,* 2: 452, 476-77, 581.

43. Cumings, *The Origins of the Korean War,* 2: 452.

44. Kolko, *The Limits of Power,* p. 577; Cumings, *The Origins of the Korean War,* 2: 503, 505.

45. Cumings, *The Origins of the Korean War,* 2: 585.

46. *Khrushchev Remembers,* Strobe Talbott, ed. (1970), p. 368.

47. Ibid., p. 369.

48. SCOR, 5th yr., 474th mtg., p. 4, UN Doc. S/PV.474 (1950).

49. Res. 83, June 27, 1950, SCOR, 5th yr., *Resolutions and Decisions,* p. 5, UN Doc. S/INF/5/Rev.1 (1950).

50. SCOR, 5th yr., 474th mtg., p. 2, UN Doc. S/PV.474 (1950).

51. Cumings, *The Origins of the Korean War,* 2: 579.

52. Ibid., pp. 584-85.

53. McCormack, *Cold War Hot War,* p. 94.

54. Kolko, *The Limits of Power,* p. 591.

55. Cumings, *The Origins of the Korean War,* 2: 659.

56. Col. Donald McB. Curtis, "Inchon Insight," *Army: The Magazine of Landpower* (Ass'n. of the U.S. Army), July 1985, p. 5.

57. Hastings, *The Korean War,* p. 76.

58. Cumings, *The Origins of the Korean War,* 2: 617.

59. Hastings, *The Korean War,* pp. 82, 85. Roy E. Appleman, *United States Army in the Korean War: South to the Naktong, North to the Yalu (June-November 1950)* (Office of the Chief of Military History, Department of the Army, 1961), p. 263.

60. Hastings, *The Korean War,* p. 112.

61. Cumings, *The Origins of the Korean War,* 2: 588-93.

62. Phillip Knightley, *The First Casualty: From the Crimea to Vietnam: The War Correspondent as Hero, Propagandist, and Myth Maker* (1975), p. 336.

63. Cumings, *The Origins of the Korean War,* 2: 619.

64. Res. 82, June 25, 1950, SCOR, 5th yr., *Resolutions and Decisions,* p. 4, UN Doc. S/INF/5/Rev.1 (1950).

65. "Report by the State-War-Navy Coordinating Subcommittee for the Far East," Appendix B, FRUS 1945, vol. 6, p. 1098.

66. Bruce Cumings, *Liberation and the Emergence of Separate Regimes, 1945-1947*, vol. 1 of *The Origins of the Korean War* (1981), p. 118.

67. "Draft Memorandum to the Joint Chiefs of Staff," FRUS 1945, vol. 6, p. 1039.

68. Cumings, *The Origins of the Korean War*, 1: 121, 125.

69. Ibid., 2: 458, 619.

70. Ibid., 1: 32-33, 80, 100.

71. Ibid., pp. 193, 267-68.

72. Ibid., p. 196.

73. "General of the Army Douglas MacArthur to the Joint Chiefs of Staff," FRUS 1945, vol. 6, p. 1147 (quoting Gen. Hodge).

74. Cumings, *The Origins of the Korean War*, 1: 135.

75. Ibid., p. 194.

76. "Lt. Gen. John R. Hodge to General of the Army Douglas MacArthur, at Tokyo," FRUS 1945, vol. 6, p. 1134.

77. Cumings, *The Origins of the Korean War*, 1: 197.

78. Ibid., pp. 249, 252.

79. Ibid., p. 287.

80. Kolko, *The Limits of Power*, p. 285; Cumings, *The Origins of the Korean War*, 1: 148, 164, 263.

81. Kolko, *The Limits of Power*, p. 291; Cumings, *The Origins of the Korean War*, 1: 354-55.

82. Cumings, *The Origins of the Korean War*, 1: 127-30.

83. Ibid., pp. 169-72.

84. Ibid., 2: 399, 404-405.

85. "General of the Army Douglas MacArthur to the Joint Chiefs of Staff," FRUS 1945, vol. 6, p. 1145 (quoting Gen. Hodge).

86. Hastings, *The Korean War*, pp. 34-38; Cumings, *The Origins of the Korean War*, 1: 149-59, 263.

87. Cumings, *The Origins of the Korean War*, 1: 179-92.

88. Hastings, *The Korean War*, pp. 40-42.

89. Kolko, *The Limits of Power*, pp. 578-85; Cumings, *The Origins of the Korean War*, 2: 598.

4

Korea: The Russians Are Coming

As viewed from Washington, the attack in Korea was initiated only nominally by the northern army, because behind the northern administration stood the Soviet Union. According to the State Department's intelligence office, "the North Korean Government is completely under Kremlin control and there is no possibility that the North Koreans acted without prior instruction from Moscow. The move against South Korea must therefore be considered a Soviet move."[1] Dean Rusk, an up-and-coming diplomat who was assistant secretary of state for the Far East, declared that the "cold, cynical, flagrant aggression" had been "unleashed by the international Communist conspiracy."[2] According to President Truman, the attack showed "that the international Communist movement is prepared to use armed invasion to conquer independent nations."[3]

Not only was the Kremlin behind the Korea attack, but it made the move in Korea as part of a global plan to bring the capitalist world to its knees by force of arms. John Foster Dulles, just back from Korea, said, "Presumably the Soviet policy represented by the attack has its origin in planning of a global nature."[4] The invasion of the south, Dulles continued, showed that "international communism is prepared to use, in open warfare, the armed forces of puppet and satellite Communist states which are equipped with armament of Russian manufacture."

49

Dulles reasoned that "Stalin long ago calculated that the best way to conquer the West was to involve it in fighting the anticolonial aspirations of Asia and the Pacific. . . . No doubt the Korean venture is designed in part to draw the Western world back into that trap."[5]

Warren Austin, our UN representative asked, "Can there be any doubt that the armed attack upon the Republic of Korea is part of a Soviet Communist plan of world domination?" The "significance of the aggression upon the Republic of Korea," he said," lies in the fact that the Communist masters of the North Korean puppets revealed by the attack their willingness to resort to armed force . . . to achieve imperialistic aims of world domination."[6]

The Central Intelligence Agency stated that the north attacked "at Soviet direction" and that "the Soviet objective is the elimination of the last remaining anti-Communist bridgehead on the mainland of northern Asia, thereby undermining the position of the United States and the Western Powers throughout the Far East."[7] So the scenario developed: the attack in Korea was a move on a global chessboard, and Washington awaited the next move.

President Truman even thought that the Korea attack was the first of a planned series of Soviet-backed invasions in Asia.[8] To stem the tide, Truman rushed to plug other potential holes in the dike of anti-Communism. Earlier he had said we would not defend Taiwan (Formosa) if China attacked it, but Korea made him revise his thinking. "The attack upon Korea," Truman declared, "makes it plain beyond all doubt that communism has passed beyond the use of subversion to conquer independent nations and will now use armed invasion and war. . . . In these circumstances, the occupation of Formosa by Communist forces would be a direct threat to the security of the Pacific area and to United States forces performing their lawful and necessary functions in that area. Accordingly, I have ordered the Seventh Fleet to prevent any attack on Formosa."[9]

At the same time, Truman moved to shore up the French colonialists in Indochina, where they were under pressure from a nationalist insurgency in Vietnam. In May 1950, he had begun sending financial aid to France for Indochina,[10] and when hostilities began in Korea, he ordered an "acceleration in the furnishing of military assistance to the forces of France and the Associated States in Indo-China and the dispatch of a military mission to provide close working relations with those forces."[11]

Despite these statements of foreboding from the Truman administration, there was no evidence that the Soviet government had instigated a hostile advance by the northern army, or that the Korean hostilities were part of a Communist master plan.[12] From what can be determined of Soviet intentions, the Kremlin did not want a confrontation with us in Korea.[13] In 1945, as we saw, it had agreed to let the United States occupy Korea south of the 38th parallel, even though it could easily have taken the whole peninsula before we got there.[14] In 1948, the Soviet Union withdrew its occupation forces from Korea, well before we withdrew ours.[15] After withdrawing, the Soviets gave the northern administration arms and airplanes, but not the latest models (the planes it sent were props, not jets), and they charged the Koreans for every item.[16]

As for military advisors, the Soviet Union had only a handful in Korea, many fewer than we retained in the south.[17] Whereas our military advisors controlled the main airport in the south, the Soviet Union turned the northern airports over to the Koreans.[18] Khrushchev, although he may not be an unbiased source, said on the basis of Kim Il-sung's meeting with Stalin the previous winter, "the war wasn't Stalin's idea."[19] In fact, there is no historical evidence to show that the Soviet government knew that hostilities would commence when they did in Korea.[20] The CIA had nothing to show that the Soviet Union was giving the north equipment for a major assault on the south in early 1950.[21] Three days into the fighting, CIA Director Roscoe Hillenkoetter admitted to the National Security Council that he had no evidence that the Soviet Union would support the north's war effort. Beyond Korea, he said there was little Soviet military activity anywhere in the far east.[22] In private comments, the Truman administration was less sure of the Soviet role than in its bombastic public declarations.[23]

From all that can be determined, then, the Soviets did not help the northern administration plan military tactics as the fighting unfolded.[24] To make matters worse, the Soviet government even took tentative steps to assume the role of peacemaker in the Korean fighting. On July 6, Deputy Foreign Minister Andrei Gromyko informed the British ambassador in Moscow that his government wanted a peaceful settlement in Korea.[25] Our ambassador in Moscow thought the Soviet effort was "genuine," telling Secretary Acheson in a top-secret cable that the Soviet Union was "not disposed to enlarge the conflict into a general Asian or world conflagration."[26] Thus the ambassador's analysis directly contradicted the already shaky thesis that the Korean attack was part of a Soviet plan to take over the world.

One other inconvenient fact cast doubt on Washington's analysis. If the Soviet Union was responsible, it was strange that it absented itself from the UN Security Council, where the war would surely be discussed. But, as we saw, in June 1950, the Soviet Union was boycotting Security Council meetings because the Council had refused to give China's seat to the mainland China government.[27] Under Security Council procedures, the Soviet Union enjoyed veto power over Council decisions. Its absence allowed the Council to condemn the north and to set up a UN command to fight for the south. Had the Soviet Union orchestrated the Korean attack, staying away from the Council would have made no sense.[28]

Yet, despite this lack of evidence of a direct Soviet hand in Korea, Truman had little difficulty, given the cold war atmosphere of the time, convincing the public that the Kremlin was indeed behind the Korean fighting. Polls conducted in August 1950 showed a 75 percent approval rating for Truman's decision to send troops to Korea, and of this 75 percent, more than half said their reason was to stop the Soviet Union.[29]

To the extent our policy makers actually thought that the Soviet Union was pulling the strings in Korea—and some doubtless did—that belief was based on assumptions about Soviet ideology, not on hard facts. In the cold war thinking of the time, the West needed to confront communism sooner or later, and better sooner than later. Knowing little about Korea, administration officials interpreted the Korean hostilities on what they knew about Europe, where we were busily engaged in a push-pull with the Soviet Union for control of the continent. The same must be happening, they thought, in Korea.[30]

The key to Truman's strong reaction to the ambiguous hostilities in Korea may be found in the plans he had already inaugurated for dealing with the Soviet Union. Through the early months of 1950, administration staffers prepared a policy paper titled "United States Objectives and Programs for National Security." Designated by the National Security Council as NSC 68, and dated April 7, 1950, the paper called for permanent militarization to confront communism. In a major shift away from the massive U.S. demilitarization that followed World War II, NSC 68 affirmed that we should "develop a level of military readiness which can be maintained as long as necessary as a deterrent to Soviet aggression."[31] The outbreak of war in Korea gave Truman just the opportunity he needed to begin permanent militarization.[32]

While Truman embraced the NSC 68 philosophy, his primary concern was Europe, not Asia. He wanted Congress to build up our forces in Europe to oppose the Soviet Union, but he was having trouble convincing Congress of the need. From Truman's perspective, a conflict in Korea might help pry open the federal coffers for a European buildup.[33]

In addition to Truman, there was one other major player in U.S. policy on Korea. General Douglas MacArthur took Truman's confrontation with communism even more seriously than Truman himself. In MacArthur's thinking, the United States had to face down China, and soon, before it became too strong.[34]

Notes

1. "Intelligence Estimate Prepared by the Estimates Group, Office of Intelligence Research, Department of State: Korea," June 25, 1950, FRUS 1950, vol. 7, p. 149.

2. Dean Rusk, "Fundamentals of Far Eastern Foreign Policy," September 9, 1950, DSB, vol. 23, p. 466 (1950).

3. Harry S. Truman, "The Korean Situation: Its Significance to the People of the United States," July 19, 1950, DSB, vol. 23, p. 165 (1950).

4. "Memorandum by Mr. John Foster Dulles, Consultant to the Secretary of State," June 29, 1950, FRUS 1950, vol. 7, p. 238.

5. John Foster Dulles, "U.S. Military Actions in Korea," July 7, 1950, DSB, vol. 23, pp. 89–90 (1950).

6. John C. Ross, U.S. Deputy Representative in the Security Council, "The Threat of Communist Imperialism," August 23, 1950, DSB, vol. 23, p. 380 (1950).

7. Truman Papers, President's Secretary Files, June 28, 1950, in Rosemary Foot, *The Wrong War: American Policy and the Dimensions of the Korean Conflict, 1950–1953* (1985), p. 59.

8. Max Hastings, *The Korean War* (1987), p. 59.

9. "Statement by President Truman," June 27, 1950, DSB, vol. 23, p. 5 (1950).

10. Robert J. Donovan, *Tumultuous Years: The Presidency of Harry S. Truman 1949–1953* (1982), p. 146.

11. "Statement Issued by the President," June 27, 1950, FRUS 1950, vol. 7, p. 203.

12. Hastings, *The Korean War*, p. 51; Bruce Cumings, *The Roaring of the Cataract 1945-1950*, vol. 2 of *The Origins of the Korean War* (1990), p. 453.

13. I. F. Stone, *The Hidden History of the Korean War* (1952), p. 63.

14. Cumings, *The Origins of the Korean War*, 2: 631–32.

15. Harry S. Truman, "The Korean Situation: Its Significance to the People of the United States," July 19, 1950, DSB, vol. 23, p. 163 (1950); Hastings, *The Korean War*, p. 42.

16. Cumings, *The Origins of the Korean War*, 2: 446, 616.

17. *Khrushchev Remembers*, Strobe Talbott, ed. (1970), pp. 369–71; Cumings, *The Origins of the Korean War*, 2: 444.

18. Cumings, *The Origins of the Korean War,* 2: 444.

19. *Khrushchev Remembers,* p. 368.

20. Wilbur Hitchcock, "North Korea Jumps the Gun," *Current History,* March 1951, pp. 142–43.

21. Cumings, *The Origins of the Korean War,* 2: 447.

22. "Memorandum of National Security Council Consultants' Meeting," June 29, 1950, FRUS 1950, vol. 1, p. 329.

23. Joyce and Gabriel Kolko, *The Limits of Power: The World and United States Foreign Policy, 1945–1954* (1972), p. 586.

24. Hastings, *The Korean War,* pp. 116, 121.

25. "The Ambassador in the Soviet Union (Kirk) to the Secretary of State," July 6, 1950, 8:00 P.M., FRUS 1950, vol. 7, p. 312.

26. "The Ambassador in the Soviet Union (Kirk) to the Secretary of State," July 6, 1950, 9:00 P.M., FRUS 1950, vol. 7, pp. 315–16.

27. SCOR, 5th yr., 473rd mtg., pp. 1, 16–18, UN Doc. S/PV.473 (1950).

28. Stone, *The Hidden History of the Korean War,* p. 66; Cumings, *The Origins of the Korean War,* 2: 637.

29. John E. Mueller, *War, Presidents and Public Opinion* (1973), p. 48.

30. Bruce Cumings, *Liberation and the Emergence of Separate Regimes, 1945–1947,* vol. 1 of *The Origins of the Korean War* (1981), pp. 226–27.

31. "A Report to the President Pursuant to the President's Directive of January 31, 1950," April 7, 1950, FRUS 1950, vol. 1, p. 289.

32. Donovan, *Tumultuous Years,* pp. 241–47; Cumings, *The Origins of the Korean War,* 2: 627–28.

33. Kolko, *The Limits of Power,* p. 598.

34. Ibid., pp. 592–93.

5

Korea: The Chinese Hordes

The Truman administration did not blame China for the outbreak of hostilities in Korea, and no evidence ever surfaced to suggest it played any role.[1] In the early phases of the war, China did not engage in any strategies with the northern leadership, although China was wary of our intentions toward it, mainly because of President Truman's statement that we would defend Taiwan. Considering Taiwan to be a part of China, the Chinese leadership called Truman's declaration about defending Taiwan "criminal aggression against the territory of China."[2]

By August 1950, MacArthur's Eighth Army held only a small area around Pusan, but the northern army, try though it did, was unable to dislodge MacArthur from Korea. At that point a helping hand from China might have let the northern army succeed, but China stayed out. Had China been planning to enter the Korean war to help the north, that would have been the time; China's noninvolvement at this juncture suggests that it was planning to sit the war out.[3]

In September, deciding he had withdrawn far enough to the south, MacArthur staged an amphibious landing at Inchon, just west of Seoul, where he met little resistance because the northern forces were thin there. Simultaneously, from the area around Pusan MacArthur pushed northward, driving the northern army back up to the 38th parallel. By that time MacArthur's forces outnumbered the northern army ten to one, and the northern army could do little but retreat.[4]

When MacArthur reached the 38th parallel, he did not conceal his aim to go north, to reunite Korea under the southern administration. While others in the administration were of the same mind, they nonetheless asked themselves whether we would be invading another country if we pushed north. Secretary of State Acheson put the concern to rest, calling the 38th parallel only "a surveyor's line," meaning that Korea was a single country.[5] Warren Austin, our UN delegate, called the 38th parallel an "artificial barrier" that "has no basis for existence either in law or in reason," and one that was recognized by neither side. "An ancient people," Austin said, "has waited long and suffered much for freedom, independence, and unity."[6]

In taking this position, Acheson and Austin seemed untroubled by the UN's rationale for action; namely, that *North* Korea had committed aggression against *South* Korea. Once the administration decided it had a chance to take Communist territory, what in June had been an international border quickly became only an imaginary line.[7]

On October 7, MacArthur sent his troops north across the 38th parallel, which brought a reaction from China and a threat to enter the war. With the Truman administration viewing the Korean hostilities as a deliberate attack by world communism, China could not be sure that MacArthur would stop at the Korea-China border. Truman's announcement in June that we would defend Taiwan suggested to China that we were assuming a major military role in Asia, and that we might invade China itself.[8]

Although the administration had not in fact laid plans to invade China, the concern of the Chinese leadership was far from irrational. MacArthur, in fact, was hoping for a chance to invade China. In his memoirs on the Korean war, General Matthew Ridgway, the army's deputy chief of staff, reported that in August 1950, he discussed with MacArthur the possibility that China might intervene in Korea or in Taiwan. MacArthur responded to Ridgway, "I pray nightly that they will."[9] China's fears of a U.S. invasion were shared by Great Britain, whose prime minister, Ernest Bevin, cautioned the administration against military action in Chinese territory, asking Truman to tell MacArthur not to "take reprisals" inside China.[10]

Chinese fears were enhanced when MacArthur quickly pushed north against the collapsing northern army, occupying Pyongyang and moving up to the Yalu River, which separates Korea from China's province of Manchuria. On October 29, Peking radio called MacArthur's rapid advance a threat to China.[11] The Chinese government was concerned not only about an invasion of its own territory, but also about generating stations in Korea, just south of the Yalu River, that supplied electrical power to China. That concern brought China's first military involvement in Korea, when in late October, it sent troops across the Yalu to the area of the power installations.[12]

Analyzing China's move, the CIA said that its "main motivation" was "to establish a 'cordon sanitaire' south of the Yalu River" to "guarantee security of the Manchurian border from UN forces" and to "insure continued flow of electric power from the vital Suiho hydroelectric system to the industries of Manchuria." The CIA noted that "the UN has made no statement regarding the distribution of Suiho power after UN forces take possession, and Chinese Communist apprehension may have been increased by the recent statement of a South Korean general that all power to Manchuria would be cut off."[13] Thus, the insertion of Chinese troops into the area south of the Yalu River was the result of concern about protecting China and its power supply; it did not presage any general Chinese involvement in the Korean war.[14]

MacArthur's push to the Yalu was the more threatening to China because of his close relation with General Chiang Kai-shek, the ruler of Taiwan, who harbored aspirations to retake the Chinese mainland, from which he had been driven in 1949. According to an October 25 report from Canada's consul in Nanking, MacArthur's connection with Chiang was a major source of China's apprehension about U.S. intentions.[15]

Despite the CIA assessment of China's motives, MacArthur denounced China's troop entry into Korea as an act of deliberate aggression, calling it "one of the most offensive acts of international lawlessness of historic record."[16] But our allies were concerned more about MacArthur than about China. Typical was the reaction of Hume Wrong, Canada's ambassador to the United States, who told Washington he worried that MacArthur "might go ahead too rapidly in its reaction to Chinese intervention."[17] Although MacArthur was claiming a massive Chinese intervention, few Chinese soldiers were to be found in Korea.[18]

To make matters worse, MacArthur ordered attacks in Korea that seemed directed against China. On November 3, the Marines' Tenth Corps attacked the Changjin reservoir, site of a major hydroelectric complex near the Yalu River that produced power for China. One journalist called the attack "a deliberate invitation to a fight" with China, because holding the border area was unnecessary for effective control of the northern half of Korea.[19]

MacArthur's recklessness caused alarm even within the administration, when a report reached Washington that the U.S. Air Force planned to bomb a Yalu River bridge at Sinuiju, an important Korean border city. Secretary of State Acheson, Deputy Under Secretary of Defense Robert Lovett, and Assistant Secretary Rusk recommended against the bombing, because the Chinese might see it as a preface to a full-scale invasion of their country.[20] Reacting to the same report, the Joint Chiefs of Staff instructed MacArthur not to attack any target within five miles of the Yalu River.[21] But almost immediately, for reasons that remain unclear, the Joint Chiefs relented and told MacArthur he could bomb the "Korean end" of the Yalu River bridge at Sinuiju.[22]

MacArthur, quick to seize the opportunity, bombed Sinuiju on November 7, destroying 90 percent of the city.[23] From there he proceeded on to bomb Uiju, another major Yalu River city,[24] as well as a number of other Yalu River bridges.[25] This bombing brought a reaction from Great Britain, which pushed the administration to set up a demilitarized buffer zone south of the Yalu for the purpose of keeping MacArthur off China's doorstep.[26] MacArthur, however, rejected the idea, and the administration did not press him on the point.[27]

At the UN, delegates were frantic that MacArthur might provoke China into sending more troops into Korea, thereby escalating the war. France, Yugoslavia, and Australia all told our delegate that if MacArthur insisted on taking all Korea up to the Yalu River, the administration should at least assure China that its electric power would not be cut off and promise that the hydroelectric facilities would not be damaged.[28] However, for reasons that again are unclear, the administration refused to give China any such assurances.[29]

MacArthur was anxious to carry the war into China, and China got the message. Our consul general in Hong Kong reported in a cable that "non-Communist Chinese" told him that the "Chinese Communists actually fear U.S. intends [to] invade Manchuria and that this is [an] important reason for their intervention in Korea."[30] According to the

State Department's top China expert, Chinese government publications showed "that the Chinese Communist leaders view those UN actions as reflecting aggressive American intentions against China."[31] Our ambassador in the Netherlands passed along a cable from the Dutch chargé in Peking, expressing the chargé's view that the Chinese intervention in Korea was "primarily influenced by fear [of] U.S. aggression, particularly U.S. aims re Manchuria." The chargé said that China's expressed fear of our aggression against Manchuria was "real."[32]

MacArthur was not alone among the military in sounding belligerent, because other U.S. commanders were quoted in the press issuing similar verbal threats to invade China. These comments worried a top State Department official, who complained of "irresponsible and provocative statements attributed to high American officers. Undoubtedly they have served to arouse further the suspicions of the Chinese as to our intentions."[33]

As MacArthur bombed along the Yalu River, he claimed that his purpose was to stop a Chinese invasion; however, according to a U.S. military communique, the Chinese forces were by then retreating.[34] On November 9, our chargé d'affaires in Korea reported, in truncated cable language, "considerable decrease late yesterday and last night in number vehicles moving southward across Yalu; Chinese forces have withdrawn northward; Chinese intervention thus far cannot be regarded as of direct, open nature."[35] Despite MacArthur's claim that there were 60,000 Chinese troops in Korea,[36] the CIA on November 1 had estimated only 15,000 to 20,000,[37] and by November 8, 30,000 to 40,000.[38] On November 17, MacArthur reduced his own estimate to 25,000 to 30,000.[39]

MacArthur's apparently exaggerated and fluctuating estimates of Chinese troop strength were a further source of concern to U.S. allies.[40] Sir William Slim, chief of Britain's general staff, accused MacArthur of "colouring both intelligence and operational reports" during this period "to suit his own ends," which, Slim said, were to promote his aim of invading China.[41]

If Chinese troops were in Korea in large numbers, they were not doing much. Belying MacArthur's claims of massive Chinese action, our chargé d'affaires reported on November 14 that "no enemy aircraft were observed over northwestern Korea yesterday";[42] on November 18, "Contact with Chinese Communist forces in Eighth Army and Tenth Corps [in] areas [of] North Korea continued negligible yesterday";[43] and on November 19, "There continued yesterday to be virtually no contact between UN and CCF [Chinese Communist forces] forces in North Korea."[44] On November 23, our ambassador reported, "contact with Chinese both on ground and in air has been virtually negligible last three days."[45]

Far from starting an all-out assault on U.S. forces, the Chinese appeared content to protect the few positions they held just south of the Yalu River. The chargé reported, "Chinese Communist forces continue [to] remain strictly on defensive giving ground invariably in face [of] U.S. units moving northward; supplies and equipment are not coming from Manchuria in any substantial quantities." He concluded that Chinese forces were "not committed to all-out intervention."[46] While concerned about its own electricity supply as well as its own territory, China was apparently not anxious to engage MacArthur any more than necessary.[47]

As MacArthur continued to engage the vanishing Chinese, our allies continued to worry that he was provoking a general war with China. Acheson and Rusk reported "anxiety" among "friendly members of the UN" about "our becoming more deeply involved perhaps finally in war with Communist China."[48] Still, the administration said nothing to allay China's concern.

And instead of backing off, MacArthur planned a new offensive to take all the hydroelectric installations and to seize the small area south of the Yalu River that remained in Korean hands.[49] He launched his attack on November 24, but could not find Chinese forces to engage.[50] Our ambassador informed Washington, "Few if any Chinese troops were encountered," and that MacArthur met "little enemy resistance."[51]

On November 28, however, the Chinese and the northern army began a counteroffensive, in an apparent effort to push MacArthur away from the border area. Our ambassador reported a "general offensive" against our Eighth Army on the western side of the Korean peninsula by an estimated 48,000 Koreans and 101,000 Chinese.[52] His next report stated, "Enemy forces, composed mainly of Chinese, continued [to] exert heavy pressure yesterday in 8th Army sector. . . . There was no reported enemy air activity yesterday."[53] Thus, the Chinese were attacking on the ground, but without air support, as they were no match for U.S. forces in air power. MacArthur greeted the Chinese action as a full-scale offensive, telling the Joint Chiefs of Staff, "The Chinese military forces are committed in North Korea in great and ever increasing strength. No pretext of minor support under the guise of volunteerism or other subterfuge now has the slightest validity. We face an entirely new war."[54]

President Truman, too, said that China was launching an all-out invasion. So seriously did Truman view it that he indicated we might have to use the atomic bomb against China, a statement that prompted an international furor.[55] The allies, worried that a new world war might develop, demanded clarification. Our embassy in London reported "anxiety" in British public opinion over the "possibility that [the] atom bomb might be used in Korea thus setting off general atomic war."[56] Truman, however, refused to retract his nuclear threat, and the army drew up contingency plans to use atomic weapons in Korea.[57]

Shortly before Christmas 1950, Truman appealed to the Congress, arguing that because of the Chinese invasion, he needed an extra $16.8 billion for the military budget.[58] That represented more than a doubling of the budget, which at the time stood at $13 billion a year. Immediately after returning from Christmas recess, Congress, convinced by Truman that we were being attacked by world communism, approved the funds.[59] Thus, Truman was well on his way to carrying out the NSC 68 policy of putting the U.S. military on a permanent war footing.

Our policy makers, in a fit of cold war hyperbole, read the Chinese counteroffensive as part of a combined Sino-Soviet plan to attack the Western powers.[60] The CIA, despite the fact that there was no hint of a Soviet role, nevertheless saw the Soviet Union behind the Chinese counteroffensive: "The Soviet rulers have resolved to pursue aggressively their world-wide attack on the power position of the United States and its allies."[61] Secretary Acheson concurred in this doomsday analysis, saying, "the central enemy is not the Chinese but the Soviet Union."[62] Acheson cabled our ambassador in India to warn him that India might be next on China's hit list: "invasion Korea by Chi Commies is part of plan to over-run all countries of E. and S. Asia."[63] Even the State Department's China expert, who should have known better, declared that "the free world is now in the preliminary stage of World War III."[64]

In response to the Chinese counteroffensive, MacArthur ordered a retreat southward. On the eastern side of the peninsula, "The X [Tenth] Corps is being withdrawn into the Hamhung area as rapidly as possible," MacArthur notified the Joint Chiefs of Staff.[65] As for the western side, our ambassador reported, "UN forces in Eighth Army sector continued withdrawal and regrouping actions yesterday and day before. CCF forces moved southward, but there only light contact and that mainly in eastern sector of front."[66]

As the ambassador's cable suggested, the retreat was not required by any hostile action on the part of the Chinese forces. MacArthur said as much, stating that he retreated because of the overwhelming numbers of the Chinese forces, which he put at 200,000.[67] The Chinese and north Korean forces followed our retreat but did not attack.[68] The *London Times* reported that the Chinese had "made not the slightest attempt" to approach the rear of the Eighth Army, and that there was "no clear evidence that they strove to bar its road."[69] As the Eighth Army and Tenth Corps withdrew, the Chinese forces made some attempt to harass them,[70] but they did not seriously engage them.[71]

Reports from the field confirmed the lack of military action. General Omar Bradley, chairman of the Joint Chiefs of Staff, said on December 4 that "there had not been very much pressure on the western front during the last 24 hours; [t]he Tenth Corps is being concentrated in the Hamhung-Hungnam beachhead. . . . The Seventh Division was proceeding with its withdrawal without too much opposition," Bradley stated. "There has been very little enemy air lately."[72]

Similarly, our ambassador reported, "Contact between CCF [Chinese Communist Forces] and UN forces in Eighth Army sector remained light yesterday as latter forces continued withdrawal."[73] And two days later: "Contact between UN and CCF forces in Eighth Army sector remained virtually nil yesterday."[74] On December 12, the American ambassador said that during the previous three days there had been almost no hostile contact in the Eighth Army sector.[75]

MacArthur continued to withdraw, but still the Chinese, who were supposed to be starting World War III, did not attack. On December 15, the ambassador reported, "Past 3 days have seen no contact between 8th Army units and CCF. In X [Tenth] Corps area UN units continue withdrawal without any noteworthy CCF pressure."[76] And on December 18, "Eighth Army . . . remain[s] out of contact with Chinese Communist forces. Tenth corps continues withdrawal from Hungnam with increasing CCF pressure reported."[77] Finally, on December 21, "During past 3 days UN forces in Eighth Army sector continued out of contact with CCF. Light contact was maintained, however, with North Korean forces in 38th parallel area."[78]

The speed of our retreat and the low level of hostile contact suggested that MacArthur was doing the same thing he had done in July—withdraw to make the enemy look stronger and to gain political support for an all-out attack, this time on China.[79] The specter of a Chinese menace might move Truman to order an attack on that country. India's ambassador in Peking said that China's intervention in Korea "is what the Americans . . . want" for "a showdown with China. In any case MacArthur's dream has come true."[80]

MacArthur apparently saw in China's entry, which he had provoked, an opportunity to fight the inevitable war against communism.[81] As he withdrew southward, MacArthur called for air raids into China, telling the Joint Chiefs of Staff that our air power could destroy "China's industrial capacity to wage war."[82] MacArthur asked the Joint Chiefs of Staff for permission to make "naval and air attacks on objectives in Communist China," but the Joint Chiefs turned him down.[83]

By the end of 1950, Chinese forces had come as far south as the 38th parallel, and on New Years Day 1951, MacArthur announced that they had commenced a new offensive to go even farther.[84] MacArthur continued his retreat, evacuating Seoul and pulling his troops farther to the south.[85]

Again, however, the Chinese failed to appear for the attack MacArthur announced they had made, following at a respectful distance but not engaging MacArthur's troops. It was MacArthur, in fact, who initiated the first significant contact, when in mid-January 1951 he stopped and attacked, and the Chinese forces fell back without serious resistance.[86] By March of that year, MacArthur stood once again on the 38th parallel.

As for the Soviet Union, it did little to justify the CIA charge that it was behind China's move into Korea and eager to begin World War III. After Chinese troops entered Korea, the Soviet Union remained firmly on the sidelines. Taking no direct military role, it provided China with arms but demanded cash payment for them.[87]

Despite his best efforts, however, MacArthur did not get his wish of invading China. In April 1951, even Truman became frightened at MacArthur's aspirations and fired him. After that the Korean war continued for two more costly years, with desultory fighting around the 38th parallel, and as the stalemate dragged on, both Congress and the public lost their enthusiasm for the war. By the time the Korean war ended, however, we had lost 34,000 of our soldiers, while Korea had sustained over two million civilian dead.[88]

But the war cost Korea more than lives; it left the country in ruins; "in the capital at Seoul, hollow buildings stood like skeletons alongside streets paved with weird mixtures of concrete and shrapnel." In the north, "Pyongyang and other cities were heaps of bricks and ashes, factories stood empty, massive dams no longer held their water." As the war ended, "people emerged from a mole-like existence in caves and tunnels to find a nightmare in the bright of day."[89]

President Truman had convinced the public to support his intervention in Korea by painting a picture of the conflict that bore little relation to reality. He portrayed a civil war as international. The public, unaware of General Hodge's harsh occupation policy, and receptive to cold war claims, found no reason to object to Truman's analysis. Congress and the public thought we were responding to a major global challenge, when in fact it was we who turned a civil war in a small country into a global confrontation.

Notes

1. Max Hastings, *The Korean War* (1987), p. 133.
2. Rosemary Foot, *The Wrong War: American Policy and the Dimensions of the Korean Conflict, 1950-1953* (1985), p. 65.
3. Wilbur Hitchcock, "North Korea Jumps the Gun," *Current History*, March 1951, p. 139.
4. Joyce and Gabriel Kolko, *The Limits of Power: The World and United States Foreign Policy, 1945-1954* (1972), p. 595.
5. Hastings, *The Korean War*, p. 116.
6. "Statement by Austin to U.N. Committee on the Future of Korea," *New York Times*, October 1, 1950, p. A3, col. 1.
7. Bruce Cumings, *The Roaring of the Cataract, 1945-1950*, vol. 2 of *The Origins of the Korean War* (1990), pp. 710-11.
8. Hastings, *The Korean War*, p. 133.
9. Matthew Ridgway, *The Korean War* (1967), pp. 37-38.
10. "Memorandum of Conversation, by the Ambassador at Large (Jessup)," October 12, 1950, p. 932.
11. I. F. Stone, *The Hidden History of the Korean War* (1952), p. 161.
12. "Memorandum by the Director of the Central Intelligence Agency (Smith) to the President," November 1, 1950, FRUS 1950, vol. 7, p. 1025.
13. Ibid., pp. 1025-26.
14. Hastings, *The Korean War*, p. 341.
15. "Memorandum of Conversation, by the Deputy Director of the Office of Chinese Affairs (Perkins)," November 3, 1950, FRUS 1950, vol. 7, p. 1032.

16. "Text of MacArthur Statement," *New York Times,* November 6, 1950, p. A5, col. 1.

17. "Memorandum of Conversation, by the Acting Officer in Charge of Korean Affairs (Emmons)," November 6, 1950, FRUS 1950, vol. 7, p. 1065.

18. Walter Sullivan, "U.S. Bids U.N. Act on Chinese in Korea After M'Arthur Identifies Red Units; Foe Withdraws in Surprise Maneuver," *New York Times,* November 7, 1950, p. A1, col. 8.

19. Stone, *The Hidden History of the Korean War,* pp. 164–65.

20. "Memorandum of Conference Between Secretary Acheson, [Deputy] Under Secretary of Defense Lovett, and Mr. Dean Rusk," November 6, 1950, FRUS 1950, vol. 7, p. 1055.

21. "The Joint Chiefs of Staff to the Commander in Chief, Far East (MacArthur)," November 6, 1950, 11:47 A.M., FRUS 1950, vol. 7, p. 1057.

22. "The Joint Chiefs of Staff to the Commander in Chief, Far East (MacArthur)," November 6, 1950, 11:57 P.M., FRUS 1950, vol. 7, p. 1076.

23. Lindesay Parrott, "379 Planes Rip Foe's New Capital Below Manchuria," *New York Times,* November 9, 1950, p. A1, col. 1.

24. Lindesay Parrott, "Chinese Continue March into Korea Despite Air Blows," *New York Times,* November 11, 1950, p. A1, col. 8.

25. Lindesay Parrott, "60,000 Chinese Reds in War, More Ready, M'Arthur Says; West Asks U.N. Debate Now," *New York Times,* November 10, 1950, p. A1, col. 8; "The Chargé in Korea (Drumright) to the Secretary of State," November 12, 1950, FRUS 1950, vol. 7, p. 1135; "The Chargé in Korea (Drumright) to the Secretary of State," November 14, 1950, FRUS 1950, vol. 7, p. 1147.

26. Foot, *The Wrong War,* p. 92.

27. "The Commander in Chief, Far East (MacArthur) to the Joint Chiefs of Staff," November 9, 1950, FRUS 1950, vol. 7, pp. 1108–09.

28. "The United States Representative at the United Nations (Austin) to the Secretary of State," November 6, 1950, FRUS 1950, vol. 7, p. 1074.

29. Foot, *The Wrong War,* p. 95.

30. "The Consul General at Hong Kong (Wilkinson) to the Secretary of State," November 9, 1950, FRUS 1950, vol. 7, p. 1123.

31. "Memorandum by the Director of the Office of Chinese Affairs (Clubb) to the Assistant Secretary of State for Far Eastern Affairs (Rusk)," November 10, 1950, FRUS 1950, vol. 7, p. 1124.

32. "The Ambassador in the Netherlands (Chapin) to the Secretary of State," November 14, 1950, FRUS 1950, vol. 7, p. 1152.

33. "Memorandum by the Deputy Assistant Secretary of State for Far Eastern Affairs (Merchant) to the Assistant Secretary of State for Far Eastern Affairs (Rusk)," November 16, 1950, FRUS 1950, vol. 7, p. 1164.

34. Parrott, "379 U.S. Planes Rip Foe's New Capital Below Manchuria."

35. "The Chargé in Korea (Drumright) to the Secretary of State," November 9, 1950, FRUS 1950, vol. 7, p. 1116.

36. Parrott, "60,000 Chinese Reds in War, More Ready, M'Arthur Says; West Asks U.N. Debate Now."

37. "Memorandum by the Director of the Central Intelligence Agency (Smith) to the President," November 1, 1950.

38. "Memorandum by the Central Intelligence Agency: Chinese Communist Intervention in Korea," November 8, 1950, FRUS 1950, vol. 7, p. 1101.

39. "Memorandum of Conversation, by the Ambassador in Korea (Muccio)," November 17, 1950, FRUS 1950, vol. 7, p. 1175.

40. Hastings, *The Korean War*, p. 192.

41. Ibid., p. 200.

42. "The Chargé in Korea (Drumright) to the Secretary of State," November 14, 1950, FRUS 1950, vol. 7, p. 1147.

43. "The Chargé in Korea (Drumright) to the Secretary of State," November 18, 1950, FRUS 1950, vol. 7, p. 1184.

44. "The Chargé in Korea (Drumright) to the Secretary of State," November 19, 1950, FRUS 1950, vol. 7, p. 1190.

45. "The Ambassador in Korea (Muccio) to the Secretary of State," November 23, 1950, FRUS 1950, vol. 7, p. 1216.

46. "The Chargé in Korea (Drumright) to the Secretary of State," November 18, 1950.

47. Hastings, *The Korean War*, p. 132.

48. "Memorandum of Conversation, by the Ambassador at Large (Jessup)," November 21, 1950, FRUS 1950, vol. 7, p. 1205.

49. "Memorandum of Conversation, by the Political Adviser in Japan (Sebald)," November 14, 1950, FRUS 1950, vol. 7, pp. 1148–49.

50. Lindesay Parrott, "Allies Sweep Ahead on Korean Front," *New York Times*, November 25, 1950, p. A1, col. 8.

51. "The Ambassador in Korea (Muccio) to the Secretary of State," November 25, 1950, FRUS 1950, vol. 7, p. 1233.

52. "The Ambassador in Korea (Muccio) to the Secretary of State," November 28, 1950, FRUS 1950, vol. 7, p. 1238.

53. "The Ambassador in Korea (Muccio) to the Secretary of State," November 29, 1950, FRUS 1950, vol. 7, p. 1251.

54. "The Commander in Chief, Far East (MacArthur) to the Joint Chiefs of Staff," November 28, 1950, FRUS 1950, vol. 7, p. 1237.

55. "Statement by the President," November 30, 1950, and "President Clarifies Position on Use of Atom Bomb in Warfare," November 30, 1950, DSB, vol. 23, p. 925 (1950).

56. "The Chargé in the United Kingdom (Holmes) to the Secretary of State," December 1, 1950, FRUS 1950, vol. 7, p. 1296.

57. Hastings, *The Korean War*, p. 183.

58. "Special Message to the Congress Requesting Additional Appropriations for Defense," December 1, 1950, *Public Papers of the Presidents of the United States: Harry S. Truman, 1950* (1965), pp. 728–31.

59. Second Supplemental Appropriations Act, January 6, 1951, U.S. Congress, *Statutes at Large*, vol. 64, p. 1223 (1951).

60. Hastings, *The Korean War*, p. 177; Foot, *The Wrong War*, pp. 101–5.

61. "Memorandum by the Central Intelligence Agency," December 2, 1950, FRUS 1950, vol. 7, pp. 1309–10.

62. "United States Delegation Minutes of the First Meeting of President Truman and Prime Minister Attlee," FRUS 1950, vol. 7, p. 1366.

63. "The Secretary of State to the Embassy in India," December 4, 1950, FRUS 1950, vol. 7, p. 1377.

64. "Memorandum by the Director of the Office of Chinese Affairs (Clubb) to the Assistant Secretary of State for Far Eastern Affairs (Rusk)," December 7, 1950, FRUS 1950, vol. 7, p. 1444.

65. "The Commander in Chief, United Nations Command (MacArthur) to the Joint Chiefs of Staff," December 3, 1950, FRUS 1950, vol. 7, p. 1320.

66. "The Ambassador in Korea (Muccio) to the Secretary of State," December 4, 1950, FRUS 1950, vol. 7, p. 1346.

67. "The Commander in Chief, Far East (MacArthur) to the Joint Chiefs of Staff," November 28, 1950.

68. Hastings, *The Korean War,* pp. 187, 341.

69. "The Retreat in Korea," *Times* (London), December 18, 1950, p. 6, col. 3.

70. Hastings, *The Korean War,* pp. 157-59.

71. Ibid., pp. 137-38, 167.

72. "United States Delegation Minutes of the First Meeting of President Truman and Prime Minister Attlee," December 4, 1950, FRUS 1950, vol. 7, p. 1362.

73. "The Ambassador in Korea (Muccio) to the Secretary of State," December 5, 1950, FRUS 1950, vol. 7, p. 1381.

74. "The Ambassador in Korea (Muccio) to the Secretary of State," December 7, 1950, FRUS 1950, vol. 7, p. 1435.

75. "The Ambassador in Korea (Muccio) to the Secretary of State," December 15, 1950, FRUS 1950, vol. 7, p. 1548.

76. "The Ambassador in Korea (Muccio) to the Secretary of State," December 15, 1950, FRUS 1950, vol. 7, p. 1548.

77. "The Ambassador in Korea (Muccio) to the Secretary of State," December 18, 1950, FRUS 1950, vol. 7, p. 1565.

78. "The Ambassador in Korea (Muccio) to the Secretary of State," December 21, 1950, FRUS 1950, vol. 7, p. 1585.

79. Kolko, *The Limits of Power,* p. 605.

80. K. M. Panikkar, *In Two Chinas: Memoirs of a Diplomat* (1955), p. 111.

81. Hastings, *The Korean War,* p. 64.

82. "The Commander in Chief, Far East (MacArthur) to the Department of the Army," December 30, 1950, FRUS 1950, vol. 7, p. 1631; Hastings, *The Korean War,* p. 193.

83. "The Joint Chiefs of Staff to the Commander in Chief, Far East (MacArthur)," January 9, 1951, FRUS 1951, vol. 7, p. 42.

84. Lindesay Parrott, "Allies Fall Back to Fixed Line," *New York Times,* January 2, 1951, p. A1, col. 8.

85. "The Ambassador in Korea (Muccio) to the Secretary of State," January 6, 1951, FRUS 1951, vol. 7, p. 30; Lindesay Parrott, "Seoul Abandoned to Red Army, *New York Times,* January 4, 1951, p. A1, col. 8.

86. Hastings, *The Korean War,* pp. 195-98.

87. Ibid., pp. 230, 340.

88. Kolko, *The Limits of Power,* p. 615.

89. Bruce Cumings, *Liberation and the Emergence of Separate Regimes, 1945-1947,* vol. 1 of *The Origins of the Korean War* (1981), p. xix.

6

Guatemala: Deception and Timing

When I visited Guatemala City in 1963, soldiers patrolled the streets in pairs, with machine guns at the ready. Guatemala was in a state of seemingly permanent tension following a 1954 coup that overthrew its elected president. When that coup occurred, the administration of President Dwight Eisenhower portrayed it as one more incident in the long history of political instability south of the border, and that is how the press reported it. The reality, however, was somewhat different.

Guatemala's president in 1954, Jacobo Arbenz, had come to office in 1950 by a free election and was peacefully in control of the country. With thousands of peasants unable to make a living because they owned no land, Arbenz nationalized uncultivated fields belonging to the U.S.-owned United Fruit Company, a major landowner and banana producer in Guatemala. Although the nationalization did not affect United Fruit's current operations, it did take two-thirds of the land it owned in Guatemala. Arbenz offered compensation at the value United Fruit had declared its land worth for tax purposes, but the Eisenhower administration, which quickly rose to take up United Fruit's cause, demanded twenty-five times that amount.

Beyond making a financial claim on United Fruit's behalf, the Eisenhower administration denounced Arbenz as a Communist and a danger to Guatemala and the hemisphere. The United States Information Service (USIS), working with the CIA, placed unattributed articles in Latin American newspapers "labelling certain Guatemalan officials as Communists, and also labelling certain actions of the Guatemalan government as Communist-inspired."[1] These articles were reportedly "well received by both metropolitan and provincial papers as timely and effective and were widely printed, frequently without attribution to USIS."[2] The press followed the administration's lead, depicting Arbenz as a Communist threat.[3]

If the Arbenz government was in the Soviet camp, it did not act the part. It had no diplomatic relations with the Soviet Union, and at the United Nations it generally supported our view, not the Soviets'. Arbenz, while he himself had no affiliation with Guatemala's Communist party, had appointed Communists to posts in his bureaucracy, especially in his land reform agency. But of the fifty-two members of the Guatemalan congress, only four were Communists, and none served in Arbenz's cabinet.

When Arbenz refused to change his stand on the United Fruit land, President Eisenhower took the campaign against him one step farther by secretly instructing the CIA to overthrow him.[4] The CIA plotted psychological warfare and organized a military force, recruiting Guatemalans living abroad and putting at their head a former colonel in the Guatemalan army, Carlos Castillo Armas.[5] The CIA trained this paramilitary force at a secret location near Miami, set it up at secret bases in Honduras and Nicaragua, and gave it weapons and bomber aircraft.[6]

In January 1954, a hitch developed in the coup plotting, when one plot supporter betrayed it to Arbenz; he gave Arbenz incriminating letters between two conspirators, the CIA-recruited Castillo Armas and Miguel Ydígoras Fuentes, a military officer and politician who had lost the 1950 presidential election to Arbenz, but who now saw a chance to gain by coup what he had lost at the polls. Arbenz publicized the letters and charged publicly that the United States was colluding with the plotters.[7]

The State Department, however, denied any role, calling Arbenz's charge "ridiculous and untrue," and affirming, "It is the policy of the United States not to intervene in the internal affairs of other nations."[8] This false denial notwithstanding, our plotting continued and intensified.

The CIA set up a secret radio station to influence public opinion against Arbenz, and to cow the military into submission.[9] By June 1954, the groundwork had been laid, and the CIA set the coup in motion. Castillo Armas's force, which numbered only 150, entered Guatemala from Honduras on June 18 to take up positions just inside the border. The CIA radio station, inflating the number of troops to 5,000, "reported" a nonexistent battle with government troops.[10] At the same time, CIA airplanes, some piloted by Guatemalans, some by CIA mercenaries, bombed Guatemala City.[11]

Following the Republican presidential victory in 1952, top posts in Washington had been reshuffled, and John Foster Dulles, whom we saw as a consultant in the State Department under Truman, became secretary of state. President Eisenhower appointed Dulles's brother Allen to head the CIA; it was Allen Dulles, then, who ran the Guatemala coup operation. In a secret communication to Eisenhower, Dulles explained the CIA strategy: "The use of a small number of airplanes and the massive use of radio broadcasting are designed to build up and give main support to the impression of Castillo Armas' strength as well as to spread the impression of the regime's weakness. . . . From the foregoing description of the effort," Dulles continued, "it will be seen how important are the aspects of deception and timing."[12]

As soon as President Arbenz saw what was happening, he complained to the United Nations Security Council. Arbenz claimed that outside forces were responsible, although at that stage he was yet unsure about our exact role. Arbenz's main charge was not against the United States, but Honduras and Nicaragua, where the rebel forces had massed. But Soviet delegate Semyon Tsarapkin fingered the Americans as the perpetrators. "The United States," he said, "has prepared an armed intervention against this minute Central American country of 3,000,000 inhabitants"; Tsarapkin charged that Guatemala "has been subjected to an armed attack provoked, organized, and carried out by the United States of America."[13]

Publicly we denied any role. Our UN delegate, Henry Cabot Lodge, replied to Tsarapkin, "the situation does not involve aggression but is a revolt of Guatemalans against Guatemalans." Furthermore, Lodge protested that Tsarapkin's charge was "flatly untrue; I challenge him to prove it. He cannot do so."[14] Tsarapkin, to be sure, had no "smoking gun" and got little support at the UN for his charge.

In Washington, the State Department kept up the pretense of non-involvement, issuing a statement that it had "no evidence that indicates that this is anything other than a revolt of Guatemalans against the Government."[15] After Castillo Armas entered Guatemala, U.S. Ambassador John Peurifoy negotiated with top-level Guatemalan military officers to urge them to move against President Arbenz. President Eisenhower had hand-picked Peurifoy for this role, firing our previous ambassador, whom he found too soft on communism. Peurifoy, on the other hand, brought strong anti-Communist credentials to the job and enthusiastically approached his coup-instigation role.

The officers whom Peurifoy approached quickly understood that we controlled the insurgency. To gain their participation, Peurifoy told the officers that if the Communist party were suppressed, and Arbenz removed as president, the United States would "recommend" that the invading force call off its efforts. By giving that promise, Peurifoy got Colonel Carlos Díaz to pressure Arbenz to resign. "Throughout discussion [with Díaz]," Peurifoy reported to Washington, "I emphasized [the] necessity of acting quickly to round up leading Communists before they could mobilize forces."[16] As the air raids and radio broadcasts made Guatemalan military officials think they would be overwhelmed, President Arbenz resigned, viewing his situation as hopeless, and so Díaz assumed power.

That was not the end of the machinations, however, because Peurifoy was not satisfied with Díaz, either. As part of the takeover, Díaz let Arbenz make a resignation speech on radio, in which he laid out the U.S. role in ousting him, at least as much of it as he knew. Arbenz said on the broadcast that we had supplied pilots for the air raids over Guatemala City—which was true—and charged that we had used communism merely as a pretext to commit aggression against Guatemala.

Upset with the speech, Peurifoy told Díaz to bring another officer, Colonel Elfego Monzón, into the ruling group,[17] and he urged both Díaz and Monzón to negotiate with Castillo Armas.[18] Monzón, who replaced Díaz as president,[19] agreed to negotiate with Castillo Armas.[20] With the power change moving in a favorable direction, Peurifoy called the State Department to point out that the bombing of Guatemala City was still going on and to ask "if there wasn't some way to get word to Armas to stop it."[21] We had won, so it was time to call the CIA's army off.

Then Peurifoy convinced Monzón to take Castillo Armas into the new ruling junta and to elect him its president, and the junta complied.[22] Next the junta, canceling the Arbenz nationalization decrees, returned United Fruit's land; at the White House, President Eisenhower and his vice-president, Richard Nixon, held a secret celebration-cum-debriefing on the operation with the CIA operatives.[23]

For public consumption, Secretary of State Dulles gave a version of the coup that showed us squarely on the sidelines. "Led by Castillo Armas," he said, "patriots arose in Guatemala to challenge the Communist leadership—and to change it. Thus, the situation is being cured by the Guatemalans themselves."[24] For John Foster Dulles, Guatemala and its banana plantations were not unfamiliar territory. In 1936, as United Fruit's attorney, Dulles had drafted the concession agreements for the land Arbenz nationalized in the 1950s. The consummate lawyer, Dulles now engineered the observance of these 1936 agreements.

Peurifoy, too, alleged that we were not involved. Concealing his own role, Peurifoy declared in a speech, "The Guatemalan people themselves rose up and gave their support to a courageous leader, Col. Carlos Castillo Armas, in a brief encounter which pushed Arbenz' Communist clique from the seats of power." According to Peurifoy, "The task of liberation of Guatemala from communism was carried out by the Guatemalan people themselves."[25] When he received Guatemala's new post-coup ambassador in Washington, President Eisenhower also covered up our role, saying that "the people of Guatemala, in a magnificent effort, have liberated themselves from the shackles of international Communist direction."[26]

The pretense was successfully maintained, and little information surfaced on the CIA role in the Guatemala coup. A magazine article later in 1954 indicated that the CIA had sent guns and ammunition to Castillo Armas in Honduras, but this information was apparently "leaked" by the CIA itself, torn between keeping the operation secret and taking credit for it.[27] In his memoirs President Eisenhower acknowledged that he had authorized the CIA to fly bombing missions over Guatemala City while the coup was in progress, at a time when success was in doubt, but that made it look only as if we were helping at the last moment, when the coup makers ran into trouble.[28] Eisenhower never acknowledged that he authorized the entire operation.

Several of those involved, however, later wrote memoirs detailing the CIA role. David Atlee Phillips, a CIA principal in the affair, gave an extensive account.[29] John Moors Cabot, who, as assistant secretary of state for American republic affairs, had been marginally involved, described how the CIA "staged" the coup.[30] Cabot, having appointed a subordinate to coordinate planning for the coup between the State Department and CIA, wrote that his "principal concern" was "to keep secret any United States involvement in the projected coup."[31] Some years later, the Senate select committee on intelligence called the anti-Arbenz coup one of "the Agency's boldest, most spectacular covert operations."[32] A major policy initiative, it had lasting consequences for our Latin America policy. To this day, it is cited by Latin nationalists as evidence that the "Colossus of the North" cannot be trusted.

Although evidence did not emerge at the time to implicate the United States, the CIA's role was widely suspected, as reflected in Tsarapkin's charges, to the point that Cabot was upset that American prestige abroad had been hurt by the episode.[33] But in the United States the matter was quickly forgotten by both the press and the public. The Eisenhower administration for its part considered the Guatemala operation as a resounding success, for it had overthrown a government that dared to conflict with the interests of a major American company, and no one was the wiser. This success led us to try the same tactic again elsewhere.

Notes

1. "Report Prepared in the United States Information Agency," July 27, 1954, FRUS 1952–1954, vol. 4, pp. 1212–13.
2. Ibid., p. 1216.
3. Richard H. Immerman, *The CIA in Guatemala: The Foreign Policy of Intervention* (1982), pp. 112–14; Jim Handy, *Gift of the Devil: A History of Guatemala* (1984), pp. 140–41.
4. John Moors Cabot, *First Line of Defense* (1979), p. 90.
5. William Colby, *Honorable Men: My Life in the CIA* (1978), p. 181; Edwin C. Hoyt, *Law and Force in American Foreign Policy* (1985), p. 104; David Wise and Thomas B. Ross, *The Invisible Government* (1964), p. 166.
6. Andrew Tully, *CIA: The Inside Story* (1962), p. 66.
7. "Guatemala Says Neighbors and U.S. Plot an Invasion," *New York Times,* January 30, 1954, p. A1, col. 4.
8. "Charges of Intervention in Guatemala Denied," DSB, vol. 30, p. 251 (1954).
9. David Atlee Phillips, *Night Watch* (1977), pp. 38–48.
10. Ibid., p. 46.
11. Hoyt, *Law and Force in American Foreign Policy*, p. 104.

12. "Memorandum by the Director of Central Intelligence (Dulles) to the President," June 20, 1954, FRUS 1952–1954, vol. 4, p. 1176.

13. SCOR, 9th yr., 675th mtg., pp. 23, 33, UN Doc. S/PV.675 (1954).

14. SCOR, 9th yr., 675th mtg., pp. 29, 31, UN Doc. S/PV.675 (1954).

15. "Guatemalan Situation: Department Statement, June 19," DSB, vol. 30, p. 982 (1954).

16. "The Ambassador in Guatemala (Peurifoy) to the Department of State," June 27, 1954, 11 P.M., FRUS 1952–1954, vol. 4, pp. 1189–91.

17. "The Ambassador in Guatemala (Peurifoy) to the Department of State," June 28, 1954, 12 noon, FRUS 1952–1954, vol. 4, p. 1192.

18. "The Ambassador in Guatemala (Peurifoy) to the Department of State," June 28, 1954, 5 P.M., FRUS 1952–1954, vol. 4, p. 1193.

19. Immerman, *The CIA in Guatemala*, p. 175.

20. "The Ambassador in Guatemala (Peurifoy) to the Department of State," June 28, 1954, 8 P.M., FRUS 1952–1954, vol. 4, p. 1194.

21. "Memorandum of Telephone Conversation, by the Assistant Secretary of State for Inter-American Affairs (Holland)," June 29, 1954, FRUS 1952–1954, vol. 4, p. 1195.

22. "The Ambassador in Guatemala (Peurifoy) to the Department of State," July 7, 1954, FRUS 1952–1954, vol. 4, p. 1205; Immerman, *The CIA in Guatemala*, p. 177.

23. Phillips, *Night Watch*, pp. 49–51.

24. John Foster Dulles, "International Communism in Guatemala," June 30, 1954, DSB, vol. 31, p. 44 (1954).

25. "Meeting the Communist Challenge in the Western Hemisphere," August 28, 1954, DSB, vol. 31, pp. 335–36 (1954).

26. Immerman, *The CIA in Guatemala*, p. 178.

27. Richard and Gladys Harkness, "The Mysterious Doings of CIA," *Saturday Evening Post*, October 30, 1954, p. 20.

28. Dwight D. Eisenhower, *Mandate for Change 1953–1956* (1963), pp. 425–26.

29. Phillips, *Night Watch*, pp. 30–54.

30. Cabot, *First Line of Defense*, p. 94.

31. Ibid., pp. 90–91.

32. U.S. Senate, Select Committee to Study Governmental Operations with Respect to Intelligence Activities, *Final Report: Foreign and Military Intelligence*, Book I, 94th Cong., 2d sess., April 26, 1976, p. 111.

33. Cabot, *First Line of Defense*, p. 94.

7

Indonesia: Caught in a Coconut Tree

The next opportunity came on the other side of the globe. Ahmed
Sukarno, who headed Indonesia's government in the 1950s, had helped
free Indonesia from Dutch colonial rule in the 1940s, and he was a
popular leader. A neutralist, Sukarno befriended both the Soviet Union
and China and made overtures to the Eisenhower administration; but
Eisenhower kept Sukarno at arm's length. Sukarno promoted what he
called "guided democracy" in Indonesia, which the State Department
took as a code word for communism.[1]

In early 1958, a group of Indonesian colonels based on the Indonesian
island of Sumatra withdrew their allegiance from Sukarno. They demanded local autonomy for Sumatra, were more pro-Western than
Sukarno, and criticized his government as being Communist-influenced.[2]
Sukarno himself did not espouse communism; in fact, the Indonesian
Communist party, which had a strong local organization, was a for-
midable rival to Sukarno. The Communist party was popular because
in the 1940s, it led the move to force the Dutch to withdraw—a move
so popular that Sukarno felt he could not govern without the Communists'
cooperation.[3] So he drew Communists into his government, although
not into key posts.[4]

As the colonels conspired, Secretary of State Dulles removed John

75

Allison, our ambassador in Jakarta, calling the transfer a routine re-assignment. When reporters asked Dulles about the activity of the colonels on Sumatra, he replied, "The working out of these problems is primarily an internal problem for the Indonesian people and their Government. Actually, we observe what has gone on with interest, but we don't take any part in or interfere with these internal governmental problems."[5]

When the colonels soon after delivered an ultimatum to Sukarno, Dulles again had to comment, saying that we wanted in Indonesia a government that reflected "the real interest and desires of the people." Some reporters thought Dulles's statement implied that Sukarno's government did not fit the bill, and that we might be trying to remove it, but Dulles repeated that the conflict was "an internal problem for the Indonesian people."[6]

In February 1958, the colonels proclaimed themselves as the government of Indonesia, although they were far from being in actual control of the country; in Sumatra they controlled two major towns and a healthy chunk of that island, but they held no territory elsewhere in Indonesia. They had over 200,000 troops at their command, but no heavy weapons and no aircraft.[7] At an April 1 news conference, reporters again asked Dulles about U.S. policy. "The United States views this trouble in Sumatra as an internal matter," Dulles replied, reiterating his earlier position. "We try to be absolutely correct in our international proceedings and attitude toward it."[8]

The Sukarno government, however, began to level public charges that American pilots were flying bombing runs for the rebels. At an April 30 news conference, President Eisenhower was asked about the charge and, like Dulles, declared we were not involved. "When it comes to an intrastate difficulty anywhere, our policy is one of careful neutrality all the way through so as not to be taking sides where it is none of our business," Eisenhower argued. "As for any United States pilots, "every rebellion that I have ever heard of has its soldiers of fortune."[9] By "soldiers of fortune," Eisenhower meant free-lance fighters who sold their services; by using the term he was implictictly denying any involvement by military personnel at the behest of the U.S. government. The next day, when a reporter asked Dulles about Eisenhower's statement, Dulles denied knowing whether any Americans were active as soldiers of fortune in Indonesia; but, he added, "we have no legal obligation to control the activities of Americans of this character."[10]

By this time, the Soviet Union, too, was accusing us of having a hand in the Indonesian rebellion. Deputy Undersecretary of State Robert Murphy, testifying in Congress on Soviet anti-American actions around the world, responded to the charge by "Soviet propaganda" that we were "the major inspirer" of the Indonesia rebels and were giving them military aid. Murphy dismissed this charge as untrue.[11]

In May 1958, a rebel B-26 bomber targeting a government airfield mistakenly hit a crowded village marketplace instead, killing a number of residents who were on their way to church.[12] Although the B-26 was shot down over the airfield and caught fire, the crew managed to bail out. Indonesian authorities caught and arrested one pilot whose parachute had gotten tangled in a coconut tree. They were able to identify the pilot as Allen Lawrence Pope, an American, by documents he was carrying.

The day after this incident, Dulles was asked again by reporters whether the United States was involved with the rebels. And again Dulles replied that the rebellion was "an Indonesian matter" that should be handled "without intrusion from without."[13] But the following week Indonesian authorities brought Pope before the press in Jakarta, where they displayed his U.S. Air Force identification card, his post exchange-privilege card from U.S. Clark Air Force base in the Philippines, and a document connecting him to Civil Air Transport, a CIA-owned airline.[14] Relying on these documents, the Indonesian government charged that Pope was not a "soldier of fortune" but a CIA operative.

As CIA insiders later revealed, the Indonesian government was correct in its charge that the CIA was supplying both planes and pilots to the rebel colonels.[15] Pope, it turned out, had been contracted for the job by the CIA, which for several years had been plotting Sukarno's fall from power.[16] The CIA had spent a million dollars in the parliamentary elections of 1955 to back a Muslim party opposed to Sukarno, but the party did badly.[17]

The Communist party, on the other hand, did well in those elections, giving them a commanding role in the Indonesian government. That concerned Secretary Dulles and the CIA, who took the view that whenever a Communist party gained a role in government it would inevitably push out the other parties. The Americans thought they saw Moscow's hand in Indonesia and feared that the country would fall under Soviet influence, with the smaller countries of southeast Asia soon to follow.[18]

Within the State Department, Ambassador Allison disputed this analysis of Indonesian politics. Unlike Dulles and the CIA, Allison saw little connection to superpower rivalry in the wrangling among the Indonesian political parties. In his memoirs, Allison wrote that Al Ulmer, the CIA chief for the far east, had been "brainwashed" about a nonexistent "imminent Communist danger in Asia."[19]

The CIA's paramilitary operation against Sukarno was directed by CIA operative Joseph Burkholder Smith, who wrote in his memoirs that already by 1956 the CIA was exploring ways to destroy Sukarno's power.[20] In order to discredit Sukarno, it had planted a false press story that he was having an affair with a Soviet female intelligence agent, and that the Soviet government was blackmailing Sukarno over this.[21] The CIA thought that the story would shatter Sukarno's credibility, but the public paid little notice.

In 1957, the Sumatra-based colonels asked the CIA station in Indonesia for help, and it encouraged the colonels to organize and to make demands on the government.[22] To CIA headquarters in Washington, the Indonesian station fed information designed to get approval for a major operation in support of the colonels.[23] CIA headquarters agreed to send arms and instructors to teach the rebels how to to use them.[24] The CIA enlisted all three branches of the U.S. military in the venture: the army training rebel troops, the navy providing offshore backup, and the air force creating and operating a rebel air force.[25] The CIA hired 350 Americans, Chinese, and Filipinos to service and fly transport aircraft and B-26 bombers for rebel operations.[26] Using Singapore and the Philippines for planning and staging, the CIA airdropped supplies to the rebels.

CIA Director Allen Dulles ran the Indonesia operation, and his brother John Foster Dulles was the moving force behind it.[27] Even after Pope had been caught, the Eisenhower administration denied any American involvement, because the CIA had taken elaborate precautions to protect the secrecy of the operation. It had stripped the B-26s of markings that would identify them as ours and was counting on Pope not to disclose that he was CIA. Like all the CIA pilots, Pope had been instructed to say, if captured, that he was a soldier of fortune and unconnected with the U.S. government. To conceal the pilots' affiliation, CIA officers had instructed them not to carry personal documents that would compromise them.

But contrary to orders, Pope, like others of the CIA pilots in the Indonesia operation, kept official documents with him, figuring that he was less likely to be executed if he was seen to be formally connected to the U.S. government. When the Indonesians displayed Pope's identification cards to the press, his governmental affiliation became obvious and incriminating.[28] Still, Pope maintained that he was only a mercenary, while the American administration refused to acknowledge him or admit that it had promoted the rebellion.[29] Pope was court-martialed in an Indonesian court and sentenced to death, but was pardoned and released a few years later.[30]

John Allison, whom Secretary of State Dulles had fired as U.S. ambassador to Indonesia, had opposed the CIA operation all along and had tried to get the administration to work with Sukarno. That was why Dulles removed him and sent a new ambassador who would cooperate.[31]

Although it did not admit its role after Pope's capture, the administration called off the Indonesia operation.[32] The operation proved to be a fiasco: even with our aid, the rebels had made little progress against Sukarno,[33] and after we pulled out, the rebel colonels simply lost heart.[34] By the time they gave up, several thousand Indonesians had been killed in the fighting.[35]

The CIA was at least fortunate in being able to escape a large-scale reprimand for its actions. The Indonesian government did not raise the matter at the United Nations, while the American press, despite the evidence of the documents, accepted the story that Pope had been a soldier of fortune. In 1965, however, the CIA got its revenge in Indonesia, when conservative military officers forced Sukarno out of office. Once in power, the officers decided to kill Communist activists, but they did not know who all the Communists were. Our embassy and the CIA station, however, had compiled lists of local Communist party officials that included 5,000 names. As embassy and CIA officials revealed for the first time only in 1990, our ambassador, Marshall Green, allowed the lists be turned over to an Indonesian official, so that the army could track the Communists down.

"It really was a big help to the army," said Robert J. Martens, who served in our embassy's political section in Indonesia in 1965. "No one cared, so long as they were Communists, that they were being butchered," said Howard Federspiel, the Indonesia expert in the State

Department's bureau of intelligence and research. The Indonesian military found many other alleged Communists on its own, killing several hundred thousand Communists during this purge, in one of the largest political bloodlettings in history.

As the Indonesian army killed the Communists, our embassy kept tabs on its success. The army would report which people on the lists it had killed, while the embassy and CIA checked the names off, to see if the Communist party was being effectively eradicated. They concluded it was, and since 1965 the Communist party in Indonesia has remained dormant.[36]

Notes

1. John M. Allison, *Ambassador from the Prairie: or Allison Wonderland* (1973), p. 305.

2. Tillman Durdin, "Indonesia Rebels Proclaim Regime, Defying Jakarta," *New York Times,* February 16, 1958, p. A1, col. 8.

3. James Mossman, *Rebels in Paradise: Indonesia's Civil War* (1961), pp. 23–27.

4. Ibid., p. 37.

5. "Secretary Dulles' News Conference of February 11," DSB, vol. 38, p. 334 (1958).

6. "Doubt on Sukarno Voiced by Dulles," *New York Times,* February 12, 1958, p. A1, col. 2.

7. Tillman Durdin, "Indonesia Rebels Proclaim Regime, Defying Jakarta," *New York Times,* February 16, 1958, p. A1, col. 8; Mossman, *Rebels in Paradise,* pp. 104–111.

8. "Secretary Dulles' News Conference of April 1," DSB, vol. 38, p. 644 (1958).

9. "Transcript of the President's News Conference on Domestic and Foreign Matters," *New York Times,* May 1, 1958, p. A14, col. 1.

10. "Secretary Dulles' News Conference of May 1," DSB, vol. 38, p. 808 (1958).

11. Robert Murphy, "Review of Recent Anti-American Demonstrations," DSB, vol. 38, p. 960 (1958).

12. Joseph Burkholder Smith, *Portrait of a Cold Warrior* (1976), p. 247.

13. "Secretary Dulles' News Conference of May 20," DSB, vol. 38, p. 946 (1958).

14. Tillman Durdin, "Jakarta Reports U.S. Flier Downed," *New York Times,* May 28, 1958, p. A9, col. 1.

15. Leonard Mosley, *Dulles: A Biography of Eleanor, Allen, and John Foster Dulles and Their Family Network* (1978), p. 437.

16. Victor Marchetti and John Marks, *The CIA and the Cult of Intelligence* (1974), p. 29; Thomas Powers, *The Man Who Kept Secrets: Richard Helms and the CIA* (1979), p. 90; Richard Barnet, *Intervention and Revolution: The United States in the Third World* (1968), p. 236.

17. Smith, *Portrait of a Cold Warrior,* pp. 210–16.

18. Ibid., p. 214.

19. Allison, *Ambassador from the Prairie,* p. 307.

20. Smith, *Portrait of a Cold Warrior,* pp. 216–17.

21. Ibid., pp. 238–39.

22. Ibid., pp. 225–27, 233; Mossman, *Rebels in Paradise,* p. 174; Col. L. Fletcher Prouty, U.S. Air Force, Ret., *The Secret Team: The CIA and Its Allies in Control of the United States and the World* (1973), p. 323; Brian May, *The Indonesian Tragedy* (1978), p. 79.

23. Smith, *Portrait of a Cold Warrior,* p. 229.

24. Ibid., p. 242; Powers, *The Man Who Kept Secrets,* p. 90; Mosley, *Dulles: A Biography of Eleanor, Allen, and John Foster Dulles and Their Family Network,* p. 437.

25. Prouty, *The Secret Team,* pp. 323–24.

26. John Prados, *Presidents' Secret Wars: CIA and Pentagon Covert Operations Since World War II* (1986), pp. 140–42; Smith, *Portrait of a Cold Warrior,* p. 247. Powers, *The Man Who Kept Secrets,* p. 90; Prouty, *The Secret Team,* pp. 323–24.

27. Prados, *Presidents' Secret Wars,* p. 135.

28. Prouty, *The Secret Team,* pp. 325–26.

29. "U.S. Aide Sees Captive," *New York Times,* June 5, 1958, p. A12, col. 4; Mosley, *Dulles: A Biography of Eleanor, Allen, and John Foster Dulles and Their Family Network,* p. 438.

30. "Indonesia Sentences U.S. Flier to Death," *New York Times,* April 29, 1960, p. A4, col. 8; Robert F. Whitney, "Indonesia Frees American Flier," *New York Times,* August 23, 1965, p. A3, col. 4.

31. Allison, *Ambassador from the Prairie,* pp. 338–39; Smith, *Portrait of a Cold Warrior,* pp. 229–30, 240, 246.

32. Powers, *The Man Who Kept Secrets,* pp. 90–91.

33. Smith, *Portrait of a Cold Warrior,* p. 248; Mossman, *Rebels in Paradise,* pp. 135–87; Prouty, *The Secret Team,* p. 324.

34. Mossman, *Rebels in Paradise,* p. 225.

35. Smith, *Portrait of a Cold Warrior,* pp. 247–48.

36. Kathy Kadane, "U.S. Officials' Lists Aided Indonesian Bloodbath in '60s," *Washington Post,* May 21, 1990, p. A5, col. 1; Ralph McGehee, "The Indonesia File," *Nation,* September 24, 1990, p. 296.

8

Lebanon, Iraq, and Jordan: Cokes on the Beach

In Lebanon's recent stormy history, foreign armies have played a prominent role, with Syria, Israel, and the Palestine Liberation Organization controlling parts of Lebanon at various times. But the first foreign military intervention Lebanon experienced after its independence in 1943 was that of the United States.

The U.S. intervention resulted from a policy initiated by the Eisenhower administration that held that if Communists tried to take any country in the Middle East, we would stop them. Enshrined in a 1957 joint resolution of Congress, the policy, which came to be known as the Eisenhower Doctrine, was that

> the United States regards as vital to the national interest and world peace the preservation of the independence and integrity of the nations of the Middle East. To this end, if the President determines the necessity thereof, the United States is prepared to use armed forces to assist any such nation . . . requesting assistance against armed aggression from any country controlled by international communism.[1]

After Congress adopted the resolution, the Eisenhower administration approached Lebanon's president, Camille Chamoun, and asked him to "accept" the Eisenhower Doctrine, meaning that he would agree to military intervention if Lebanon were threatened by "international communism."

For better or worse, Chamoun conceded.[2] In a country sharply divided between Muslim and Christian communities, Chamoun's government was Christian-dominated, while Lebanon's Christian population had close ties to the West both culturally and politically.[3] But Lebanon's opposition, united as the National Front, was based in the Muslim community, which constituted the majority of Lebanon's population. At the time, the National Front strongly reflected Arab nationalism as espoused by Egyptian President Gamal Abdul Nasser.[4]

In 1956, Nasser had shocked the West by nationalizing the British- and French-owned Suez Canal. Then Syria, which shared Egypt's Arab nationalist attitude, merged with Egypt to form the United Arab Republic (UAR). The Eisenhower administration feared the spread in the region of anti-Western sentiment, which might attract Soviet support.

This anti-Western attitude, which rejected Western control of the economies and politics of the region, was understandable in light of the history of European involvement there. After World War I, Britain and France took control of the region following the fall of the Ottoman Empire, much to the chagrin of the Arabs, who had expected independence. After Britain and France gave most of the region its independence in the 1930s and 1940s, they continued a strong financial role, and in the 1950s the United States began to compete for its own controlling interest, as reflected in the Eisenhower Doctrine.

Chamoun's acceptance of the Eisenhower Doctrine put him at odds with both Egypt and Syria, as well as with Lebanon's own Nationalist Front, which immediately demanded that he renounce it.[5] But Chamoun refused, and to reward him, the CIA secretly funded pro-Chamoun candidates in parliamentary elections scheduled for 1957, resulting in a heavily pro-Chamoun majority.[6] Deprived of control of the parliament, the National Front was furious.[7] The most serious consequence of this defeat, from its standpoint, was that the new parliament would be selecting a president in July 1958, and Chamoun was seeking reelection. As Wilbur Crane Eveland, the CIA station chief in Beirut at the time, explained it, Chamoun was a shoo-in for the presidency, because the parliament had been "bought" for him by the CIA.[8]

Its frustration with this form of U.S.-bought control, which did not remain wholly secret, led the National Front to move against

Chamoun two months before the scheduled election. In May 1958, the Front mounted a military campaign against Chamoun and quickly gained control of most of Lebanon's territory.[9] Chamoun responded by seeking the aid of the United Nations Security Council, to whom he complained that the Front was being supplied and trained by the UAR.[10] After the UAR denied the charge,[11] the Council sent an observation mission "to ensure that there is no illegal infiltration of personnel or supply or arms or other matériel across the Lebanese borders."[12] The mission reported "substantial movements of armed men" in Lebanon, but said it could not determine whether they "had infiltrated from outside," or where they had obtained their arms. It said that of those involved against Chamoun in Lebanon, "the vast majority were in any case Lebanese."[13] Rejecting the UN mission's report, Chamoun and the Eisenhower administration pointed out that since the mission had not established good access to border areas, it might have missed acts of infiltration.[14]

Just at this point there was a new development in the region. On July 14, the solidly pro-Western government of Iraq was overthrown in a coup. The political complexion of the Iraqi coup makers was unclear, but because of the nationalist activity in Lebanon and the UAR, the Eisenhower administration feared that the Iraqi coup might be nationalist as well. Apart from what the Iraqi coup might portend for Iraq, President Eisenhower was concerned that this new development might encourage the Lebanese National Front to engage in a final offensive against Chamoun.

Concerned over both Iraq and Lebanon, Eisenhower decided to send troops into Lebanon. Quickly he landed a force of 10,000 Marines and airborne units, backed up by the 35,000-man Sixth Fleet offshore in the eastern Mediterranean.[15] Eisenhower's purpose was twofold: to keep the National Front from moving against Chamoun and to have troops close to Iraq in case a similar nationalist threat might emerge there.[16]

In the UN Security Council, U.S. Ambassador Henry Cabot Lodge justified the American intervention by explaining that our purpose in Lebanon was "to stabilize the situation brought on by the threats from outside."[17] President Eisenhower said that the rebellion in Lebanon was "supported by sizable amounts of arms, ammunition, and money and by personnel infiltrated from Syria to fight against the lawful authorities."[18] To bolster its case, the White House held that Lebanon's complaint to the Security Council had charged "indirect aggression."[19]

But Lebanon had not actually charged aggression, direct or indirect. In framing his complaint against the UAR, President Chamoun made the softer complaint that the UAR was creating a situation which "is likely, if continued, to endanger the maintenance of international peace and security."[20] This language derived from the United Nations Charter's Chapter 6 titled "Pacific Settlement of Disputes," while aggression involves more military action and is covered under Chapter 7 of the Charter. Thus, Lodge's charge against the UAR went beyond that made by Chamoun.

Two days after our Lebanon landing, the region's situation became more complicated still. At the request of Jordan, Britain landed troops in that country,[21] with Britain claiming to have intelligence information that a Syrian-backed coup would form that day in Jordan.[22] Like Lebanon, Jordan had a pro-Western government headed by King Hussein, who received regular subsidies from the CIA.[23]

To scare off the supposed coup plotters in Jordan, Eisenhower sent fifty U.S. jet fighters to fly over Jordan as a show of force.[24] At the UN we declared that we were supporting Britain's action "in the defense of Jordan's independence and integrity," and called our overflights "a justified exercise of the inherent right of nations to call for assistance when threatened."[25] Whether Syria was actually involved in an anti-Hussein plot was never clarified.

There was a legitimate reason, though, to doubt the Eisenhower administration's good faith in making charges against the Syrian government. As in Lebanon, we were anxious to suppress Arab nationalism in Syria. In 1956 and again in 1957, we paid Syrian military officers to overthrow Syria's leaders and replace them with less nationalistic types. In the 1957 attempt, the plotters turned themselves in and named two CIA officers, whom the Syrian government then expelled from the country.[26]

As for Lebanon, Ambassador Lodge explained that the UN mission there had "helped to reduce interference from across the border," but "with the outbreak of the revolt in Iraq, the infiltration of arms and personnel into Lebanon from the United Arab Republic in an effort to subvert the legally constituted Government has suddenly become much more alarming." The Iraqi coup, Lodge said, "coupled with persistent efforts over the past months to subvert the government of Jordan, must be a cause of grave concern to us all. They place in jeopardy both the independence of Lebanon and that of any Middle Eastern State which seeks to maintain its national integrity free from outside influences and pressures."[27]

The Iraqi coup and the supposed coup attempt in Jordan proved to Lodge that "there is, in the Middle East, a common purpose to take over everywhere, all at once. Clearly, there is a common purpose, masterminded from one source." As for the identity of that source, Lodge pinned the blame on the UAR. "You can read all about it in the Cairo newspapers," he said, "or listen to the incessant radio broadcasts from Cairo to other Arab countries."[28]

Lodge's charge of outside involvement in Lebanon had some basis in fact, as some arms likely were smuggled to the National Front from Syria;[29] but the Eisenhower administration could not prove aggression.[30] By mid-July, the UN mission had set up an extensive network of border checkpoints to watch for infiltration of arms and personnel.[31] Observing by air and on the ground, both during the day and at night, the mission reported on July 30 that infiltration of arms into Lebanon "cannot be on anything more than a limited scale, and is largely confined to small arms and ammunition." As for personnel, it said, "in no case have United Nations observers, who have been vigilantly patrolling the opposition-held areas and have frequently observed the armed bands there, been able to detect the presence of persons who have indubitably entered from across the border for the purpose of fighting."[32]

Whatever the facts about infiltration, the Lebanese conflict was, as the UN mission stated in its first report, of Lebanese, not Syrian or Egyptian, making. The United States, as we saw, was a catalyst for that conflict, because by drawing Chamoun into our orbit, and by skewing the makeup of the Lebanese parliament in his favor, we had aroused the National Front to action.

Beyond the alleged UAR involvement, President Eisenhower gave an additional reason for the Lebanon landing, namely, that U.S. citizens in Lebanon, whom he estimated at 2,500, were endangered by the hostilities and needed to be evacuated.[33] This justification, however, was a blatant pretext, because in June the State Department had already warned U.S. citizens against travel to Lebanon,[34] and in June and July it had evacuated most dependents of official U.S. personnel there.[35] By July 15, the date of the landing, most U.S. citizens resident in Lebanon were already gone.[36]

After the Marines landed, the administration seemed to have forgotten the issue, because the Marines did not organize an evacuation and the administration no longer mentioned any endangered citizens.

The Lebanon landing piqued the interest of reporters from the standpoint of U.S. Middle East policy. The Eisenhower Doctrine referred only to opposing communism, but the administration was not alleging any involvement in Lebanon by Communist countries or even by local Communists.[37] No matter, replied Secretary of State Dulles, the Eisenhower Doctrine could be expanded. The doctrine, he explained, meant "that the independence of these countries is vital to peace and the national interest of the United States," and "that is certainly a mandate to do something if we think that our peace and vital interests are endangered from any quarter."[38] With this sleight of hand, Dulles broadened our interventionist aims from opposing communism to opposing Arab nationalism.

One way in which the United States sought to curb nationalism in Lebanon was to make the Front come to terms with the government,[39] and by September, a political compromise was reached, with President Chamoun stepping aside and the head of the Lebanese army assuming the presidency. In Jordan and Iraq, all went well for us, too. In Jordan, King Hussein remained in power, his relation with the CIA unimpaired, while the new Iraqi government, contrary to expectations, turned out to be not nationalist but pro-Western.[40]

The Eisenhower administration's stated reasons for the Lebanon intervention, however, did not hold water. There was little to back up our claim of outside aggression,[41] and the asserted need to evacuate U.S. citizens was an obvious afterthought.*

When I visited Lebanon in 1977, it was recovering from the violent civil war of 1975–76 that again found pro-Western and nationalist elements contending, as they had done in 1958. Our intervention at the time had done nothing to resolve that conflict; if anything, we had

---

*One curious aside to the Lebanon intervention was that, once in Lebanon, our forces did little but sit in positions they had established on Lebanon's lovely Mediterranean beach. This deployment proved to be enough to intimidate the National Front from moving against Chamoun, so no military action was needed. Lebanese soft drink vendors on the beach, however, carried on a lively business with the Marines.

exacerbated it. I went to southern Lebanon, the scene of intense fighting during that civil war, where competing factions still held small pieces of territory. As I rode in a jeep on a dirt track, mortars exploded in front of the jeep, and we sped off out of range. Peace was hardly threatening to break out in Lebanon.

From the time of U.S. interventionism in 1958, Lebanon has found little respite from conflict. Had Lebanon been left to work out its domestic differences without the Eisenhower Doctrine, without the CIA, and without our troops, perhaps its recent history would have been less bloody. As we shall see in a later chapter, the same split between pro-Westerners and nationalists would again form the backdrop for us to intervene.

Notes

1. Joint Resolution to Promote Peace and Stability in the Middle East, H.J. Res. 117, U.S. Congress, *Statutes at Large,* vol. 71, p. 5 (1957), also in DSB, vol. 36, p. 481 (1957).

2. Richard Barnet, *Intervention and Revolution: The United States in the Third World* (1968), p. 142.

3. Thomas M. Franck, "Who Killed Article 2(4)? or: Changing Norms Governing the Use of Force by States," *American Journal of International Law* 64 (1970): 814.

4. Helena Cobban, *The Making of Modern Lebanon* (1985), pp. 84–85.

5. Wilbur Crane Eveland, *Ropes of Sand: America's Failure in the Middle East* (1980), p. 276.

6. Ibid., pp. 248–53; Jonathan Kwitny, *Endless Enemies: The Making of an Unfriendly World* (1984), p. 316.

7. Kwitny, *Endless Enemies,* p. 316.

8. Eveland, *Ropes of Sand,* p. 266.

9. Cobban, *The Making of Modern Lebanon,* p. 88.

10. SCOR, 13th yr., 823rd mtg., pp. 4–35, UN Doc. S/PV.823 (1958).

11. SCOR, 13th yr., 824th mtg., pp. 2–13, UN Doc. S/PV.824 (1958).

12. SCOR, 13th yr., 824th mtg., p. 23, UN Doc. S/PV.824 (1958); Res. 128, SCOR, 13th yr., *Resolutions and Decisions,* p. 5, UN Doc. S/INF/13/Rev.1 (1958).

13. "First Report of the United Nations Observation Group in Lebanon," July 3, 1958, SCOR, 13th yr., Supplement (July, August, September 1958), pp. 8–9, UN Doc. S/4040 (1958).

14. Eveland, *Ropes of Sand,* p. 279.

15. "Radio-TV Statement (White House press release dated July 15)," DSB, vol. 39, p. 183 (1958); Eveland, *Ropes of Sand,* p. 294.

16. Cobban, *The Making of Modern Lebanon,* p. 89.

17. SCOR, 13th yr., 827th mtg., p. 7, UN Doc. S/PV. 827 (1958).

18. "Message to the Congress," DSB, vol. 39, p. 182 (1958).

19. "Radio-TV Statement (White House press release dated July 15)."

20. SCOR, 13th yr., 823rd mtg., p. 4, UN Doc. S/PV.823 (1958), p. 184.

21. Drew Middleton, "British Land in Jordan, Backed by U.S. Jets," *New York Times*, July 18, 1958, p. A1, col. 8.

22. "Statement by MacMillan on Jordan," *New York Times*, July 18, 1958, p. A2, col. 4.

23. "Can Anyone Keep a Secret," and "Hussein on His CIA Money," *Newsweek*, March 7, 1977, p. 16; Bob Woodward, "CIA Paid Millions to Jordan's King Hussein," *Washington Post*, February 18, 1977, p. A1, col. 1.

24. Jack Raymond, "U.S. Jets Display Power in Jordan," *New York Times*, July 18, 1958, p. A1, col. 7.

25. "First Statement of July 17 (U.S./U.N. press release 2963)," DSB, vol. 39, p. 193 (1958).

26. Eveland, *Ropes of Sand*, pp. 253–54; "Syria Expelling 3 U.S. Diplomats," *New York Times*, August 14, 1957, p. A1, col. 7.

27. SCOR, 13th yr., 827th mtg., pp. 7–8, UN Doc. S/PV.827 (1958).

28. SCOR, 13th yr., 831st mtg., p. 10, UN Doc. S/PV.831 (1958).

29. Eveland, *Ropes of Sand*, pp. 275, 279.

30. SCOR, 13th yr., 831st mtg., p. 8, UN Doc. S/PV.831 (1958); Pitman B. Potter, "Legal Aspects of the Beirut Landing," *American Journal of International Law* 52 (1958): 727–28.

31. "Interim Report of the United Nations Observation Group in Lebanon," July 15, 1958, SCOR, 13th yr. Supplement (July, August, September 1958), p. 33, UN Doc. S/4051 (1958); "Second Interim Report of the United Nations Observation Group in Lebanon," July 17, 1958, SCOR, 13th yr., Supplement (July, August, September 1958), p. 34, UN Doc. S/4052 (1958).

32. "Second Report of the United Nations Observation Group in Lebanon," July 30, 1958, SCOR, 13th yr., Supplement (July, August, September 1958), p. 93, UN Doc. S/4069 (1958).

33. "Statement by President Eisenhower," DSB, vol. 39, p. 181 (1958); "Message to the Congress," DSB, vol. 39, p. 182 (1958).

34. "U.S. Issues Alert to Americans Traveling in Lebanon," DSB, vol. 39, p. 31 (1958).

35. "U.S. Dependents Authorized to Return to Lebanon," DSB, vol. 39, p. 688 (1958); Sam Pope Brewer, "Beirut Welcomes Marines; Second Contingent Ashore," *New York Times*, July 16, 1958, p. A1, col 6.

36. Eveland, *Ropes of Sand*, p. 276.

37. René-Jean Dupuy, "Agression indirecte et intervention sollicitée à propos de l'affaire libanaise," *Annuaire Français de Droit International* 5 (1959): 463.

38. "Secretary Dulles' News Conference of May 20," DSB, vol. 38, p. 945 (1957).

39. Mohammed Bennouna, *Le consentement à l'ingérence militaire dans les conflits internes* (1974), pp. 150, 178–79.

40. Cobban, *The Making of Modern Lebanon*, pp. 92–93.

41. Quincy Wright, "United States Intervention in the Lebanon," *American Journal of International Law* 53 (1959): 114.

9

Cuba: We Were Not Involved

It was not long after the Lebanon intervention that a situation closer to home attracted the interest of the Eisenhower administration. Little more than a year after a revolution in Cuba had overthrown longtime ruler Fulgencio Batista, the CIA began planning for military action there to overthrow the new government. It was headed by a former minor league pitcher named Fidel Castro, whom Eisenhower considered too far to the left. Castro eventually did attach his star to the Kremlin, but it was never clear whether this resulted from Castro's rejecting us or our rejecting him. During 1960, Castro and Eisenhower traded jabs, which led to a complete trade embargo with Cuba.

Once Eisenhower had decided on the need to get rid of Castro, the CIA set in motion a plan to infiltrate small groups of Cuban exiles, who would build up underground resistance units. Soon, however, the CIA shifted to a plan for a single major invasion, designed to spark a popular rebellion against Castro's government.[1] President Eisenhower approved the plan, and CIA operatives set about recruiting Cuban exiles living in Florida to form the invasion force.[2]

The State Department, skittish about the plan, insisted that no military training be done in the United States, lest word of it leak out.[3] So the CIA approached the Guatemalan government, which was in our debt politically after the 1954 coup. Guatemala's president in 1960 was Miguel Ydígoras Fuentes, who was one of the coup plotters in 1954. Castillo Armas, whom we had engineered into the presidency, was assassinated in 1957, and Ydígoras assumed office in his place. When approached by the CIA to provide training sites for the secret force of Cubans, Ydígoras was happy to return the favor. The CIA, therefore, set up shop at a remote location in Guatemala.[4]

Ydígoras's willingness, however, was almost his undoing, because soon after the training began, an armed rebellion broke out against him in the Guatemalan army. Once word about the training of the Cubans had leaked out in Guatemala, the rebels objected violently, arguing that Ydígoras was needlessly involving the country in a hostile action against a nearby country. In short order the rebels put together enough troops to pose a serious threat to Ydígoras, and took over the important Guatemalan port city of Puerto Barrios in addition to two army bases.[5]

President Eisenhower came to Ydígoras's defense, because if the Guatemala rebellion succeeded, the cover might be blown on the secret training of the Cubans. Eisenhower sent U.S. Navy ships from the Guantanamo naval base in Cuba to Guatemalan waters, announcing that the purpose was to "prevent intervention on the part of Communist-directed elements in the internal affairs of Guatemala."[6] By this Eisenhower meant to imply that Cuba was behind the Guatemala rebellion, although there was little evidence of that. From the information that exists on this point, the Guatemala army rebels who opposed Ydígoras were not sympathetic to Cuba, and Cuba, for its part, was not involved in their movement. The rebels merely objected to Ydígoras getting Guatemala involved in unnecessary conflicts.[7]

The U.S. Navy deployment around Guatemala was only for show, however. Eisenhower took more serious action to put down the Guatemala rebellion, permitting U.S. Air Force pilots who were training the Cubans at the CIA base to strafe the rebel headquarters. The rebels, who were no match for the U.S. Air Force, quickly surrendered.[8] The American press, while it had discovered that planes from the training base put down the revolt and that we were financing the training, did not learn that our own pilots had been involved. As for the purpose of the training, the press reported, although without coming to any conclusion, two contradictory stories: according to Ydígoras, it was to protect against a possible invasion by Cuba; the rebels, on the other hand, declared that the training was to prepare for an attack on Cuba.[9] After the rebellion failed, the Guatemalan government publicly thanked Eisenhower for the navy deployment but with no mention of the strafing.[10] Eisenhower, too, kept mum about it, so once again we had intervened in Guatemalan politics and no one was the wiser.

The Cuban government, however, did find out about the training in Guatemala. In January 1961, its foreign minister protested, charging that the objective was an invasion of Cuba.[11] *Time* magazine, reporting on the training in Guatemala, wrote that planes were flying in and out of an air base in Florida.[12]

Meanwhile, despite disclosures, the training of the Cuban exile force in Guatemala continued. When John F. Kennedy became president, he continued with the operation.[13] With Kennedy's approval, then, the CIA made final preparations for the invasion.[14] Lyman Kirkpatrick, CIA inspector general at the time, conducted an official post mortem on the operation in a book he wrote some years later explaining the details.[15] In preparation for landing on Cuba, the CIA built the Cuban exile force to a strength of 1,450 and provided all its financing and equipment.[16]

In April 1961, the CIA set the invasion plan in motion, sending Cuban pilots to bomb fighter aircraft on the ground at Cuban air bases in order to eliminate Cuba's air defense.[17] As a cover story, the CIA had the pilots land in Miami after the raids and say they were Cuban air force pilots defecting to the United States.[18] At the United Nations we repeated this story,[19] but it was full of inconsistencies and was quickly exposed by the press as a fabrication.[20]

After last-minute consultations with the Joint Chiefs of Staff and the State Department, the CIA then launched the Cubans by sea from a base in Nicaragua toward the Bay of Pigs on Cuba's southern shore, under the command of their CIA trainers.[21] Meanwhile, U.S. Navy destroyers waited offshore at the Bay of Pigs to offer logistical support, while pilots from the USS *Essex* flew strafing missions for the landing force.[22] As the exiles headed ashore in landing crafts, CIA instructors led them to the beaches.[23]

Despite all this effort, however, the landing force made little headway against the Cuban government. Contrary to expectations, the Cuban people did not rise up against their leader, and military resistance to the exile force was stiff. The Cuban military repelled the exiles, killing 114 of them in the process, and taking over a thousand prisoner.

Although the U.S. role in the affair was not public knowledge, it was widely suspected.[24] One reporter wrote that it "has been an open secret in Florida and Central America for months" that "the CIA planned, coordinated, and directed the operations that ended in the defeat on a beachhead in southern Cuba."[25] In a formal protest to President Kennedy, Soviet Premier Nikita Khrushchev charged that the invasion force had been "prepared, equipped, and armed in the United States." "The planes," he said, "which bomb Cuban towns belong to the United States of America, the bombs which they drop have been put at their disposal by the American Government."[26] In response to these charges of American involvement, President Kennedy expressed admiration for the Cubans but portrayed them as having acted on their own, not under our control.[27] Kennedy did not acknowledge that the CIA had organized the failed invasion.[28]

In the 1970s, the U.S. Senate set up a committee to investigate covert operations by the CIA, and for the first time in an official way acknowledged the CIA role in the Bay of Pigs, writing that "the President authorized the CIA to secretly direct and finance the military invasion" of Cuba. The operation, the committee said, may have amounted to "an act of war."[29] By acting covertly, the committee said, Presidents Eisenhower and Kennedy frustrated "the constitutional system of checks and balances" that is supposed to apply to military operations abroad. The Cuban operation ran the risk of full-scale war with Cuba, "on the sole authority of the President."[30]

The Bay of Pigs invasion nearly did bring war, not only with Cuba but also with the Soviet Union, which, like Cuba, was concerned that we might strike Cuba again.[31] In the months following the failed invasion, the CIA, far from backing off its efforts, fed the Cuban-Soviet fears by plotting to foment internal dissension in Cuba, and to assassinate President Fidel Castro. Its scheme, much like the plan that preceded the Bay of Pigs, was to send in Cuban exiles to organize underground cells. In addition, in what it dubbed "Operation Mongoose," the CIA installed raiding parties from Florida in Cuba in the summer of 1961, to sabotage sugar refineries and oil depots.[32]

To this activity the Soviet Union responded by giving Cuba missiles with nuclear warheads, apparently to deter another invasion. "We had to establish a tangible and effective deterrent to American interference," said Khrushchev in his memoirs. The "logical answer" to this problem "was missiles," he said. "We wanted to keep the Americans from invading Cuba, and, to that end, we wanted to make them think twice by confronting them with our missiles."[33]

Having discovered that Khrushchev was installing missiles in Cuba, Kennedy sent ships to intercept Soviet vessels entering Cuban waters.[34] Calling the operation a quarantine, Kennedy declared that if a Soviet ship refused to be searched, we would stop it by force. So the action risked military confrontation with the Soviet Union, a danger that Kennedy himself acknowledged. "This is a difficult and dangerous effort on which we have set out," he said; "no one can foresee precisely what course it will take or what costs or casualties will be incurred." The Soviet army could have moved against our forces in Europe, leading to general war. Kennedy warned, "Any hostile move anywhere in the world against the safety and freedom of peoples to whom we are committed will be met by whatever action is needed."[35]

If there were a confrontation on the seas around Cuba, we might invade it. I followed the moves by Kennedy and Khrushchev with fascination, having just finished a political science course at Harvard given by a young instructor named Henry Kissinger, who missed as many lectures as he gave, because he airhopped to Washington to consult at the National Security Council and the Arms Control and Disarmament Agency. Kissinger approached international relations as a chess master approaches the checkered board. Kissinger's playing surface was the globe, and the United States and the Soviet Union were the players.

Also being a U.S. Marine Corps reservist at the time of the Cuban missile crisis, I watched Kennedy announce the missile intercept with more than academic interest. Having been trained in amphibious landings, I wondered if I would be climbing down the side of a ship on a rope ladder to run up a Cuban beach.

When he ordered the missile interdiction, Kennedy said that we could not tolerate "offensive threats."[36] At the United Nations, Ambassador Adlai Stevenson alleged that the installation of missiles in Cuba gave clear evidence that the Soviet Union "has decided to transform Cuba into a base for Communist aggression."[37] The public, however, remained unaware that Eisenhower and Kennedy had organized the Bay of Pigs invasion, and it knew nothing of Operation Mongoose, so it viewed the Soviet action not as a defensive move but as Kennedy had portrayed it—an offensive, unprovoked act. The Bay of Pigs invasion, and the wraps under which the administration kept it, had brought the world to the brink of nuclear war. Fortunately, Khrushchev and Kennedy worked out a solution, Khrushchev removing the missiles in exchange for a promise by Kennedy not to invade Cuba.[38]

The press referred to the 1961 invasion of Cuba as a "fiasco," because it failed, and the episode makes only a footnote in our official postwar history. But in Cuba the failed invasion left a permanent stamp. On the island it is impossible to talk politics very long before someone brings up the Bay of Pigs. The threat of "Yankee invasion" left Cuba permanently militarized. Because Cuban exiles had formed the invasion force at the Bay of Pigs, the Cuban government became even more sensitive to dissent than it had already been. Successive American administrations castigated Cuba for violating human rights; however, if we had set a course of friendly relations, the internal situation in Cuba might have been far different.

Notes

1. Lyman B. Kirkpatrick, Jr., *The Real CIA* (1968), pp. 191–93.
2. Ibid., pp. 187–89, 200; Theodore C. Sorensen, *Kennedy* (1965), p. 295.
3. Kirkpatrick, *The Real CIA*, pp. 193–94.
4. Sorensen, *Kennedy*, p. 295.
5. "Guatemala Fights Revolt; State of Siege Is Imposed," *New York Times*, November 14, 1960, p. A1, col. 3.
6. "U.S. Positions Naval Units as Aid to Guatemala and Nicaragua," Statement by James C. Hagerty, Press Secretary to the President, November 17, 1960, DSB, vol. 43, p. 888 (1960).
7. Richard Gott, *Rural Guerrillas in Latin America* (1973), p. 70.
8. Ibid., pp. 71–72; Col. L. Fletcher Prouty, U.S. Air Force, Ret., *The Secret Team: The CIA and Its Allies in Control of the United States and the World* (1973), p. 41.
9. Paul P. Kennedy, "U.S. Helps Train an Anti-Castro Force at Secret Guatemala Air-Ground Base," *New York Times*, January 10, 1961, p. A1, col. 5.
10. "Guatemala Thanks United States for Naval Aid," DSB, vol. 43, p. 924 (1960).
11. "Cuban Charges Recalled," *New York Times*, January 10, 1961, p. A11, col. 5.
12. "Cuba: The Underground," *Time*, January 27, 1961, p. 26.
13. Arthur B. Schlesinger, Jr., *A Thousand Days* (1965), p. 257; Sorensen, *Kennedy*, pp. 295–96.
14. *Final Report: Foreign and Military Intelligence*, U.S. Senate, Select Committee to Study Governmental Operations with Respect to Intelligence Activities, Book I, 94th

Cong., 2d sess, April 26, 1976, p. 25; William Colby, *Honorable Men: My Life in the CIA* (1978), p. 172.

15. Kirkpatrick, *The Real CIA*, p. 189.

16. Ibid., p. 193; Sorensen, *Kennedy*, p. 294; *Final Report: Foreign and Military Intelligence*, p. 35.

17. Peter Wyden, *Bay of Pigs: The Untold Story* (1979), pp. 173–79.

18. Ibid., pp. 174–76, 186–90.

19. "U.S. Delegation Press Release 3697," April 15, 1961, DSB, vol. 44, p. 667 (1961).

20. Sorensen, *Kennedy*, p. 300.

21. Kirkpatrick, *The Real CIA*, pp. 195–98; Wyden, *Bay of Pigs*, pp. 163, 217–18.

22. Wyden, *Bay of Pigs*, pp. 214, 235–40, 261.

23. Ibid., pp. 216–20, 229.

24. Sorensen, *Kennedy*, pp. 300–301.

25. Tad Szulc, "C.I.A. Is Accused by Bitter Rebels," *New York Times*, April 22, 1961, p. A1, col. 3.

26. "Mr. Khrushchev to President Kennedy," April 18, 1961, DSB, vol. 44, p. 662 (1961).

27. Ibid., p. 661.

28. John F. Kennedy, "News Conference," April 12, 1961, DSB, vol. 44, p. 661 n. 2 (1961); John F. Kennedy, "The Lesson of Cuba," April 20, 1961, DSB, vol. 44 p. 659 (1961); "Text of Address by President to U.S. Editors," *New York Times*, April 21, 1961, p. A2, col. 2; "Transcript of the President's News Conference on World and Domestic Affairs," *New York Times*, April 22, 1961, p. A8, col. 1; "President's Remarks to Patriots of Cuba," *Washington Post*, December 30, 1962, p. A9, col. 1.

29. *Final Report: Foreign and Military Intelligence*, pp. 37–38; Richard A. Falk, "American Intervention in Cuba and the Rule of Law," *Ohio State Law Journal* 22 (1961): 568; Edwin C. Hoyt, *Law and Force in American Foreign Policy* (1985), p. 123.

30. *Final Report: Foreign and Military Intelligence*, pp. 37–38.

31. *Khrushchev Remembers*, Strobe Talbott, ed. (1970), p. 492.

32. *Alleged Assassination Plots Involving Foreign Leaders: An Interim Report of the Select Committee to Study Governmental Operations with Respect to Intelligence Activities*, U.S. Senate, 94th Cong., 1st sess., Report no. 94-465, November 20, 1975, pp. 139–70; Colby, *Honorable Men*, p. 190; Hoyt, *Law and Force in American Foreign Policy*, p. 123; Thomas Powers, *The Man Who Kept Secrets: Richard Helms & the CIA* (1979), p. 139.

33. *Khrushchev Remembers*, pp. 493–96.

34. "Interdiction of the Delivery of Offensive Weapons to Cuba, Presidential Proclamation," October 23, 1962, DSB, vol. 47, p. 717 (1962).

35. John F. Kennedy, "The Soviet Threat to the Americas," October 22, 1962, DSB, vol. 47, pp. 718–19 (1962).

36. Ibid., p. 716 (1962).

37. "U.N. Security Council Hears U.S. Charges of Soviet Military Buildup in Cuba," DSB, vol. 47, p. 733 (1962).

38. "President Kennedy's Message of October 27," DSB, vol. 47, p. 743 (1962); *Khrushchev Remembers*, pp. 498–99.

10

Laos: A Free-Fire Zone

When I arrived in Laos in 1978, it was enjoying its first peace in decades. From the time France had finally packed up its colonial bags and left the country in 1954, civil war, with substantial outside involvement, was Laos's fate until 1973. Seeing the Lao, however, I found it hard to imagine them at war. A Melanesian people, the Lao move harmoniously in their sarongs, a picture of grace. One oft-repeated tale, perhaps apocryphal, about the Laotian civil war is that once in Vientiane, the capital city, a battalion of government troops marched down a major street. In the opposite direction, on a parallel street, came a battalion of opposition troops. But neither commander was anxious to engage the other, so they pretended not to notice. The moral was that, if left to themselves, the Lao would not fight each other too strenuously.

In 1954, France lost a major battle at Dien Bien Phu in Vietnam, which led to independence talks in Geneva and to French withdrawal from all Indochina. After the French pullout, the leftist Pathet Lao organization enjoyed a great following and had a military force in the northeast part of the country. But the government of Laos was neutralist and sought to accommodate the Pathet Lao. Little concerned over superpower politics, the neutralist government desired only to keep the

97

peace and to improve the rice harvest. It was a reluctant participant in the internal conflict, content to leave the Pathet Lao alone.

The civil war in Laos might have remained a minor episode had Laos not been "blessed" by our strong interest in it. Just as in Korea, where leftists led the anti-Japan resistance, so in Laos did leftists lead the anti-France resistance. To the Eisenhower administration, imbued with the Korea mentality, however, Laos was a player on a global chessboard.[1] If communism won in Laos, it might spread to Cambodia, or Vietnam, or Taiwan. Secretary of State Dulles told the U.S. Senate that whether Laos and the rest of southeast Asia "can be kept out of Communist control depends very much on whether we build a dike around this present loss." By "loss," Dulles meant the French defeat at Dien Bien Phu. "The only thing we have to build that dike with is this money," he said, meaning the foreign aid money he was asking the Senate to appropriate for Laos. "It will be a domino business," Dulles continued, "unless we can bolster this situation up."[2] To keep friendly governments in the region on our side, Dulles organized them into the Southeast Asia Treaty Organization.

Walter Robertson, assistant secretary of state for Far Eastern affairs, told the House of Representatives that our "sole reason" for being involved in Laos was "to keep this little country from being taken over by the Communists." He said, "we are trying to keep Laos in the free world." Robertson called Laos "a finger pointing into the heart of Southeast Asia," which was "one of the prime objectives of the international Communists in Asia." So more than Laos was at stake: "Every time you lose a country, Robertson warned, "they become correspondingly stronger and the free world becomes weaker. . . . [I]t is happening all over the world, everywhere. We are engaged in a struggle for the survival of what we call a free civilization. The Communists probe first in Europe, then in the Middle East, in Africa, Taiwan, in Laos." He concluded, "this is an expansionist movement and they [the Communists] are dedicated to taking over the world."[3]

Robertson's deputy, J. Graham Parsons, like his boss, told the House that our aim was "to keep Laos this side of the Bamboo Curtain." In Parsons's estimate, the Laotian army, which we were financing, was "the principal bulwark of the country against Communist subversion."[4] Our goal in Laos thus was clear. Dulles viewed it as an advantage in the anti-Communist effort in Laos that the French were no longer in Indochina, because that put the anti-Communist fight on a higher moral plane. "We have a clean base there now, without a taint of colonialism," Dulles stated. "Dienbienphu was a blessing in disguise."[5]

The State Department's analysis of Laos, unfortunately, had little to do with the reality on the ground there. As they had done in Korea and Indonesia, our policy makers misread the situation because of their cold war mentality. At that point China, the Soviet Union, and Vietnam had little to do with Laos.[6] When neutralist Prime Minister Souvanna Phouma made a visit to China and the Soviet Union, however, the State Department decided he was "Communist-influenced." In fact, Phouma was trying to show his neutrality, in order to facilitate talks with the Pathet Lao. As in Indonesia, our policy makers worried that if Communists gained a role in a coalition government, they would push the other parties out.[7]

To prevent a role for the Communists, Eisenhower, starting in the mid-1950s, put pressure on Laotian politicians to exclude the Pathet Lao.[8] In 1956, the administration opened a military mission in Laos, to advise the Laotian army on how to defeat the Pathet Lao. In good bureaucratese, it named the mission the Program Evaluation Office, to disguise its true military purpose.[9] We gave generous aid, funding the entire military budget of Laos's army.[10] After National Assembly elections were scheduled in 1958, we became more generous still, in an effort to secure the election of conservative candidates. The Pathet Lao was strong in rural areas, but Souvanna Phouma's government paid little attention to rural development. So we mounted Operation Booster Shot to get economic aid to rural areas, to win hearts and minds for the government in time for the 1958 election.[11] To favored candidates we gave money, which they then distributed for high-visibility development projects.[12]

The booster shot did not take, however. Our candidates did poorly, while the Pathet Lao and one allied party won a majority in the National Assembly.[13] Despite the leftist victory, however, the executive branch of the Laotian government remained neutralist. But President Eisenhower feared the worst, namely that the Laotians were not serious about putting down the Pathet Lao. Therefore, if the Laotian army was not willing to fight the communists, the Eisenhower administration concluded, it must do the job itself. So under the code name Operation White Star, the CIA organized its own army, separate from the government's.[14]

CIA operatives covertly approached leaders of the Hmong, an ethnic minority in the mountains of northeast Laos, and asked them to fight the Pathet Lao. The Hmong, also known as the Meo, had fought on the side of France against the Lao, so they found it an easy transition to fight for the United States.[15]

The logistics were simple: the CIA had an airline called Air America, nominally a private cargo operation.[16] Air America was affiliated with Civil Air Transport, the CIA airline that operated in Indonesia during the 1958 rebellion; in Air America planes, the CIA men flew from one mountain village to another.[17] If the village would volunteer a few recruits, the CIA gave it money, guns, and rice. To the Hmong, whose livelihood was marginal at best, the offer was one they found hard to refuse. Moreover, if a village declined to contribute recruits, the CIA considered it pro-Pathet Lao, and made life difficult for it.[18] So most Hmong villages cooperated, for reasons either of gain or coercion, and the Hmong army began to attack Pathet Lao positions.

The CIA had one other economic lever to maintain Hmong loyalty. The area inhabited by the Hmong formed part of what was known as the Golden Triangle, famous for its opium; for the Hmong, opium was the major cash crop. But living in remote areas, the Hmong had difficulty getting their opium to market. Air America's supply flights into their villages provided the perfect solution:[19] the Hmong got their opium out of their villages as transport cargo onto Air America planes.[20] The CIA, while acknowledging that it knew the Hmong transported opium on Air America, claimed that it had tried to stop them.[21]

However, CIA pilots reported later that they were under orders from their superiors not to interfere with the shipments. The CIA was apparently concerned that opium might be detected on Air America flights landing outside Laos, so to help the Hmong get their opium out more quietly, the CIA set up a special airline for the Hmong army, called the Xieng Khouang airline. Xieng Khouang took opium to Vietnam, where some was used by our soldiers, with the rest going to the international opium market, which in turn led to our own shores. Some of the proceeds were used by the CIA and Hmong army leadership to pay Hmong soldiers. Thus we were running a secret war on opium profits.[22]

The press did not learn about Operation White Star and the Hmong army until some years later, however. When Kennedy assumed office, he stepped up operations in Laos, sending additional advisors to the Laotian army.[23] In March 1961, just at the time of the Bay of Pigs landing, the Pathet Lao seemed to be gaining the upper hand; Kennedy became so concerned about the threat of a Pathet Lao victory that he put Marines in Okinawa on alert and sent helicopters to Thailand for possible deployment in Laos.[24] Kennedy came close to sending the Marines in and reportedly would have done so except for the failure at the Bay of Pigs, which gave him pause concerning another landing. Kennedy later told an advisor, "Thank God the Bay of Pigs happened when it did. Otherwise we'd be in Laos by now, and that would be a hundred times worse."[25]

Kennedy also built up the ranks of the Hmong army. In a confidential report, Brigadier General Edward G. Lansdale stated that 9,000 Hmong had been trained and were operating "with considerable effectiveness in Communist-dominated territory in Laos." The Hmong army was commanded by the CIA station chief in Vientiane, while the Chief of our Military Assistance Advisory Group, which advised the Laotian army, played a consultative role.[26] Kennedy thought the Hmong army so effective that he ordered that 2,000 more Hmong be recruited.[27]

In 1962, when the Laotian political parties agreed at a Geneva meeting on the formation of a new government that would be free from foreign control and intervention, Kennedy was forced to withdraw American military advisors from the Laotian army. However, Kennedy continued secretly to fund the Hmong army, which let us keep pressure on the Pathet Lao without appearing to be involved.[28] In short order Kennedy built the Hmong army up to 30,000;[29] to augment it further, the CIA hired 20,000 members of the Thai army and brought them into Laos to fight the Pathet Lao. Because of the operation's size, the CIA had to inform a congressional committee, so that funds could be allocated. The CIA's chief for the Far East, William Colby, urged the committee to let him recruit even more Hmong.[30]

The secret war dragged on inconclusively, however, because the Hmong could not defeat the Pathet Lao. Soon after Lyndon Johnson assumed office, the CIA devised a new tactic, which was to send U.S. Air Force planes to bomb Pathet Lao positions on the Plain of Jars,*

---

*The plain derived its name from ancient vessels that archaeologists had found there.

its stronghold in northeast Laos. Johnson sent the first raids in May 1964,[31] and the air force started bombing in earnest in December.[32] The National Security Council oversaw the bombing operation, making sure to keep it secret; at a December 12, 1964, meeting, the Council decided not to make public statements about the bombing of the Plain of Jars, "unless a plane were lost." If that happened, the administration would claim that "we were merely escorting reconnaissance flights as requested by the Laotian government."[33]

In 1965, the U.S. Air Force built a secret radar station in northeast Laos to guide its planes bombing northern Vietnam.[34] North Vietnamese forces by then were operating in northeast Laos to support the Pathet Lao, and they overran the station, killing the dozen air force personnel who staffed it.[35]

Also in 1965, the air force and army began air and ground attacks in southeast Laos, an area it called the Ho Chi Minh trail, which was used by the Vietnamese to ferry supplies and personnel from the northern to the southern part of Vietnam.[36] To aid this bombing, the air force installed on the ground high-tech sensors that could detect movement. The sensors sent signals to airplanes, which then bombed the area of movement.[37] Since the sensors could not distinguish the type of movement, however, the targets might be civilians or farm animals. Like the bombing in northeast Laos, this operation was kept secret.

In 1966, the Johnson administration stepped up the bombing on the Plain of Jars, still keeping it quiet, even though by this time whole villages had been destroyed and thousands of inhabitants had been displaced.[38] George Chapelier, a Belgian UN official in Laos, reported that the bombing was so intense "that no organized life was possible in the villages."[39]

In November 1968, bowing to international pressure, President Johnson stopped heavy bombing over North Vietnam. But with the Laos bombing remaining unpublicized and, therefore, no international attention being focused there, Johnson was able to divert the bombers to the Plain of Jars.[40] The air force ran up to 800 bombing sorties a day, turning the plain, in military parlance, into a "free-fire" zone, to break the Pathet Lao's hold by making the Plain uninhabitable.[41] Chapelier described the impact: "The villagers moved to the outskirts and then deeper and deeper into the forest as the bombing climax reached its peak in 1969 when jet planes came daily and destroyed all stationary structures. Nothing was left standing. The villagers lived in trenches and holes or in caves. They only farmed at night."[42] In February 1970, the air force began using its giant B-52s, which can obliterate a large area through so-called "carpet bombing."[43]

A thirteen-year-old Laotian boy described the bombing of his village on the Plain of Jars. "The airplanes came bombing my ricefield until the bomb craters made farming impossible. And the village was hit and burned," he said. "And some relatives working in the fields came running out to the road to return to the village but the airplanes saw and shot them. . . . [W]e heard their screams, but could not go to help them. When the airplanes left, we went out to help them, but they were already dead."[44]

The Pathet Lao protested the bombing and the press reported the protests;[45] but the air force, in accordance with the 1964 National Security Council (NSC) decision, claimed it was only flying "armed reconnaissance" and kept the press from speaking to its Thailand-based pilots.[46] So the bombing still remained secret, even as it drove the Pathet Lao off the Plain of Jars, turning its towns to rubble and sending its inhabitants to refugee camps near Vientiane.[47]

When Richard Nixon became president in 1969, he continued the bombing of the Plain of Jars, but by then the official curtain of secrecy over the operation began to crumble, as reporters increasingly found out about the devastation.[48] "The rebel economy and social fabric," wrote one, had become "the main United States targets."[49] Senator Stuart Symington of Missouri held hearings on the Laos bombing and managed to uncover its scope. "We are fighting a big war in Laos," he concluded, yet "we are still trying to hide it not only from the people but also from the Congress." Symington continued, "we are telling Americans they must fight and die to maintain an open society, but not telling our people what we are doing."[50] With the Indochina war being controversial and divisive at home, the administration feared that if the public knew we were waging another major war in Laos, it might force an end to the whole project.

In 1970, with the Laos war now in its fourth presidential administration, reporters finally discovered the CIA's Hmong army and blew the lid off that aspect of the secret war. This revelation forced the president to make the Laos war public, with expenditures on Laos entering the official Pentagon budget.[51] Despite the press disclosures about the bombing on the Plain of Jars, President Richard Nixon still tried to conceal its true purpose, arguing that the air force was running only "combat-support missions for Laotian forces."[52]

Senator Edward Kennedy of Massachusetts took testimony from ranking officials and accused the administration of "saturation bombing" and "the forced evacuation of population from enemy held or threatened areas."[53] Kennedy found that the Plain of Jars was "almost completely depopulated" of its previous 150,000 inhabitants[54] and berated the administration for doing all this secretly, "to cover the expanding American involvement in Laos from the American people."[55]

In 1973, when peace talks were held for Indochina, Nixon ended operations in Laos, by which time the Air Force had dropped 1.5 million tons of bombs there, more than we used in all of World War II.[56] The CIA disbanded the Hmong army, and a new neutralist government took power in Vientiane, but was replaced within two years by a leftist government allied to North Vietnam. Our money, secret army, and bombing were not enough to keep Laos on our side of the "bamboo curtain." We had achieved, said Senator Frank Church of Idaho, "a hostile Laos," a country "that preferred the indigenous forces of communism to control imposed by Westerners."[57]

Notes

1. Charles A. Stevenson, *The End of Nowhere: American Policy Toward Laos since 1954* (1972), p. 37.

2. *Mutual Security Appropriations for 1955,* Hearings on H.R. 10051, an Act Making Appropriations for Mutual Security for the Fiscal Year Ending June 30, 1955, and For Other Purposes, Committee on Appropriations, U.S. Senate, 83rd Cong., 2d sess., p. 306 (1954).

3. *United States Aid Operations in Laos,* Hearings before a Subcommittee of the Committee on Government Operations, U.S. House of Representatives, 86th Cong., 1st sess., 1959, pp. 184–85.

4. *Mutual Security Appropriations for 1959,* Hearings before the Subcommittee of the Committee on Appropriations, U.S. House of Representatives, 85th Cong., 2d sess., 1958, p. 972 (testimony of J. Graham Parsons).

5. Quoted in Emmet John Hughes, *The Ordeal of Power: A Political Memoir of the Eisenhower Years* (1963), p. 208.

6. Stevenson, *The End of Nowhere,* p. 10.

7. Ibid., p. 41.

8. Ibid., pp. 44–45.

9. Walt Haney, "The Pentagon Papers and the United States Involvement in Laos," in Noam Chomsky and Howard Zinn, eds., *The Pentagon Papers: The Defense*

Department History of United States Decisionmaking on Vietnam (Senator Gravel ed., 1972), 5: 248, 251–52.

10. *U.S. Aid Operations in Laos,* Seventh Report by the Committee on Government Operations, U.S. House of Representatives, House Report 546, 86th Cong., 1st sess., 1959, p. 8; Stevenson, *The End of Nowhere,* pp. 26–27, 35–38. Andrew Tully, *CIA: The Inside Story* (1962), p. 217.

11. Haney, "The Pentagon Papers and the United States Involvement in Laos," in *The Pentagon Papers,* 5: 253.

12. Stevenson, *The End of Nowhere,* p. 47.

13. Tillman Durdin, "Leftists in Laos Prevail at Polls," *New York Times,* May 13, 1958, p. A7, col. 4.

14. James William Gibson, *The Perfect War: Technowar in Vietnam* (1986), p. 386; Stevenson, *The End of Nowhere,* p. 125.

15. John Prados, *Presidents' Secret Wars: CIA and Pentagon Covert Operations Since World War II* (1986), p. 269.

16. *Final Report: Foreign and Military Intelligence,* U.S. Senate, Select Committee to Study Governmental Operations with Respect to Intelligence Activities, Book I, 94th Cong., 2d sess., April 26, 1976, pp. 208–9, 219–27; William Colby, *Honorable Men: My Life in the CIA* (1978), p. 198.

17. Colby, *Honorable Men,* p. 195.

18. Gibson, *The Perfect War,* pp. 386–87.

19. Prados, *Presidents' Secret Wars,* p. 285.

20. Gibson, *The Perfect War,* p. 387; Alfred W. McCoy, *The Politics of Heroin in Southeast Asia* (1972), pp. 274–77.

21. *Final Report: Foreign and Military Intelligence,* pp. 228–30.

22. Transcript, "Frontline" Special, "Guns, Drugs and the CIA," WGBH, Public Broadcasting System (1988), pp. 4–18.

23. "National Security Action Memorandum No. 80," August 29, 1961, *United States-Vietnam Relations 1945–1967: Study Prepared by the Department of Defense* (1971), 11: 247–48; Haney, "The Pentagon Papers and the United States Involvement in Laos," in *The Pentagon Papers,* 5: 260, 263.

24. Haney, "The Pentagon Papers and the United States Involvement in Laos," in *The Pentagon Papers,* 5: 261; Stevenson, *The End of Nowhere,* pp. 146–53.

25. Theodore C. Sorensen, *Kennedy* (1965), p. 644.

26. Brig. Gen. Edward G. Lansdale, "Resources for Unconventional Warfare, S.E. Asia," July, 1961, in *The Pentagon Papers: The Defense Department History of United States Decisionmaking on Vietnam* (Senator Gravel ed., 1971), 2: 646.

27. "National Security Action Memorandum No. 80," August 29, 1961, *United States-Vietnam Relations 1945–1967: Study Prepared by the Department of Defense* (1971), 11: 247–48.

28. Haney, "The Pentagon Papers and the United States Involvement in Laos," in *The Pentagon Papers,* 5: 265–66.

29. Prados, *Presidents' Secret Wars,* p. 272; Stevenson, *The End of Nowhere,* p. 212; Victor Marchetti and John Marks, *The CIA and the Cult of Intelligence* (1974), pp. 31–32.

30. Ralph McGehee, *Deadly Deceits: My 25 Years in the CIA* (1983), p. 83.

31. Charles W. Corddry, "Communist Antiaircraft Batteries in Laos Attacked by U.S. Planes," *Washington Post,* June 14, 1964, p. A1, col. 1; Stevenson, *The End of Nowhere,* pp. 201–3; Haney, "The Pentagon Papers and the United States Involvement in Laos," in *The Pentagon Papers,* 5: 268; *Refugee and Civilian War Casualty Problems*

in Indochina, A Staff Report Prepared for the Use of the Subcommittee to Investigate Problems Connected with Refugees and Escapees of the Committee on the Judiciary, U.S. Senate, 91st Cong., 2d sess., September 28, 1970, p. 29.

32. Stevenson, *The End of Nowhere,* p. 207.

33. "Military Pressures Against North Vietnam, February 1964–January 1965," in *The Pentagon Papers,* 3: 253–54.

34. *Refugee and Civilian War Casualty Problems in Indochina,* pp. 21–22. Prados, *Presidents' Secret Wars,* pp. 281–82.

35. T. D. Allman, "12 Americans Died in Loss of Secret Laotian Outpost," *Washington Post,* March 16, 1970, p. A1, col. 1.

36. "The Air War in North Vietnam: Rolling Thunder Begins, February–June, 1965," in *The Pentagon Papers,* 3: 341–42; Colby, *Honorable Men,* p. 198; *Bombing in Cambodia,* Hearings before the Committee on Armed Services, U.S. Senate, 93rd Cong., 1st sess. (1973), pp. 492–93.

37. Gibson, *The Perfect War,* pp. 396–97.

38. *Refugee and Civilian War Casualty Problems in Indochina,* p. 29.

39. George Chapelier, "Plain of Jars: Social Changes Under Five Years of Pathet Lao Administration," excerpted in *War-Related Civilian Problems in Indochina. Part II: Laos and Cambodia.* Hearings before the Subcommittee to Investigate Problems Connected with Refugees and Escapees of the Committee on the Judiciary, U.S. Senate, 91st Cong., 1st sess., April 21–22, 1971, p. 92.

40. Stevenson, *The End of Nowhere,* p. 218.

41. *Refugee and Civilian War Casualty Problems in Indochina,* pp. 29–30; Jacques Decornoy, "Guerre oubliée au Laos," *Le Monde,* July 4, 1968, p. 2, col. 1; also in *War-Related Civilian Problems in Indochina. Part II,* p. 93.

42. Chapelier, "Plain of Jars," in *War-Related Civilian Problems in Indochina. Part II,* p. 92.

43. Gibson, *The Perfect War,* p. 395. William Shawcross, *Sideshow: Kissinger, Nixon and the Destruction of Cambodia* (1979), p. 211. John W. Finney, "U.S. Discloses Use of B-52's over Northern Laos," *New York Times,* May 4, 1971, p. A10, col. 4; *Bombing in Cambodia,* p. 489.

44. Fred Branfman, *Voices from the Plain of Jars* (1972), p. 45.

45. "Pathet Lao Cites U.S. Losses," *New York Times,* December 22, 1968, p. A3, col. 2; "Pathet Lao Complains U.S. Is Intensifying Its Bombing," *New York Times,* December 31, 1968, p. A6, col. 8.

46. John W. Finney, "U.S. Discloses Use of B-52's for Raids over Northern Laos," *New York Times,* May 4, 1971, p. A10, col. 4.

47. Gibson, *The Perfect War,* p. 392; Robert Shaplen, "Our Involvement in Laos," *Foreign Affairs* 48 (April 1970): 489; Branfman, *Voices from the Plain of Jars,* p. 23; *Refugee and Civilian War Casualty Problems in Indochina,* p. 24.

48. Daniel Southerland, "What U.S. Bombing Feels Like to Laotians," *Christian Science Monitor,* March 14, 1970, p. 1, col. 2.

49. Timothy D. Allman, "Support by U.S. Alters Laos War," *New York Times,* October 1, 1969, p. A9, col. 1.

50. *United States Security Agreements and Commitments Abroad: Kingdom of Laos,* Hearings before the Subcommittee on United States Security Agreements and Commitments Abroad, Comm. on Foreign Relations, U.S. Senate, 91st Cong., 1st sess., Part 2, October 20–28, 1969, p. 543.

51. Prados, *Presidents' Secret Wars,* pp. 290–94.

52. "Text of Statement Issued by President Nixon on U.S. Policy and Activity in Laos," *New York Times,* March 7, 1970, p. A10, col. 1.

53. *Refugee and Civilian War Casualty Problems in Indochina,* p. 19.

54. Ibid., p. 24.

55. Ibid., p. 19.

56. William S. Turley, *The Second Indochina War: A Short Political and Military History, 1954–1975* (1986), p. 87.

57. Frank Church, "Covert Action: Swampland of American Foreign Policy," *Bulletin of the Atomic Scientists,* February 1976, p. 11.

11

Vietnam: What Were Those Bleeps?

Our interest in Indochina was not limited to Laos. The Truman administration, as we saw earlier, used the Korean hostilities in 1950 as an occasion to start paying France's expenses to fight the Vietnamese insurgency. By the time France pulled out in 1954, following negotiations in Geneva, we were paying most of the bill for its war, and then it became our war. As in Laos, the leftists in Vietnam had been strong in fighting France, so their popularity was high.

The leftists set up an administration in Hanoi, while those Vietnamese who had not opposed France set up their own administration in Saigon. Under the agreement reached in Geneva, the two governments were separated by an imaginary line drawn at the 17th parallel. Importantly, however, the Geneva agreement called for national elections in 1956 to pick a single government for all Vietnam.

President Eisenhower, suspicious of the leftist administration in Hanoi, took the Saigon administration under his wing. Worried that if national elections were held, the popular president of the Hanoi administration, Ho Chi Minh, would win, Eisenhower told the Saigon administration it needn't go through with the elections scheduled for 1956, and as a result those elections were not held. This led to an exploration of other options to reunite the country, both by the Hanoi administration and by those Vietnamese living below the 17th parallel who viewed the Saigon administration as a foreign implant.

In 1963, the commanding officer of my Marine Corps reserve unit assigned me to give lectures to my unit on world affairs, especially on potential trouble spots. When I lectured on Vietnam, few of the Marines knew where it was, or what connection the United States had to it. I told them that Vietnam was important to the United States for strategic and economic reasons. The Communists, after all, were out to get it, I said. One Marine raised his hand to object. "I don't think we need to get in there; there's no reason to get into a war." I explained patiently that there was oil under Vietnam's continental shelf, that Vietnam's large population was an important market for our products, and that Vietnam commanded the sea route from the Middle East to the Far East.

By 1963, in fact, the Kennedy administration had military advisors in Vietnam, and in 1964, President Johnson decided on a major escalation to boost the Saigon administration's fortunes. We would bomb targets in the north to convince the Hanoi government to stop supporting the leftists in the south. Before starting the bombing raid, however, Johnson wanted to protect his political flank by securing Congress's blessing.[1] So he had his staff draft a joint resolution that Congress might pass to authorize a bombing campaign over North Vietnam.[2] At the time, however, Congress's attention was not focused on Indochina, and there was little hope it would go along.

Soon an opportunity for convincing Congress presented itself. On July 30, 1964, South Vietnamese naval forces under our direction raided two islands in the Gulf of Tonkin, which cuts into the Vietnamese coast north of the 17th parallel. At the same time, the destroyer USS *Maddox,* outfitted for electronic spying, sailed into the Gulf of Tonkin looking for intelligence information to use in bombing the north.[3] Several days later, the South Vietnamese naval forces raided again, and on August 3, North Vietnamese torpedo boats approached the *Maddox,* evidently thinking it was involved in the South Vietnamese raids. The *Maddox* frightened the torpedo boats off, and President Johnson ordered another destroyer, the USS *C. Turner Joy,* to provide protection for the *Maddox.* That same night, August 3, South Vietnamese PT boats attacked sites on the North Vietnamese shore.[4]

The next day, August 4, the *Maddox* reported being fired upon by North Vietnamese torpedo boats.[5] The report was based on sonar readings and by bleeps on the *Maddox*'s radar screen.[6] But the *C. Turner Joy,* which had more sophisticated sonar than the *Maddox,* did not detect any such firings, although it was watching the situation closely.[7] Neither of the two destroyers was hit, and their crews did not see any torpedo explosions. Navy pilot James B. Stockdale, who flew over the *Maddox* and *C. Turner Joy* that night looking for North Vietnamese action, saw no boats, no gunfire, and no torpedo wakes.[8]

The commander of the two ships quickly decided that the report of a firing on the *Maddox* had been erroneous. *Maddox* crew members had apparently mistaken sonar reflections of the *Maddox*'s own rudder for enemy torpedoes.[9] The commander immediately flashed an urgent message to Washington to withdraw the report.[10]

At the White House, the retraction message, curiously, was not accepted at face value. Instead it created "confusion over whether an attack on the destroyers had actually taken place."[11] Secretary of Defense Robert McNamara asked military commanders whether the first report might somehow have been accurate.[12] Despite the second report, the Defense Department publicly announced a "deliberate attack" on the two destroyers,[13] with President Johnson declaring that we would take reprisal strikes against North Vietnam.[14] In a televised address, Johnson said somberly, "It is my duty to the American people to report that renewed hostile actions against United States ships on the high seas in the Gulf of Tonkin have today required me to order the military forces of the United States to take action in reply." He accused the northern forces of "open aggression."[15]

Relying on the dubious intelligence he had received about the supposed attack, President Johnson redrafted his congressional authorization resolution for air strikes and submitted it for adoption.[16] In a Senate hearing on the draft resolution on August 6, Senator Wayne Morse of Oregon confronted Secretary McNamara with the information that the two destroyers had been associated with the South Vietnamese raids. McNamara denied that our commanders in Vietnam had been aware of these.

Senator Morse's misgivings notwithstanding, Congress accepted the false information about a firing on the *Maddox* and passed a joint resolution, solemnly intoning, "Whereas naval units of the Communist regime in Vietnam, in violation of the principles of the Charter of the United Nations and of international law, have deliberately and repeatedly attacked United States naval vessels lawfully present in international waters. . . ." On that basis, Congress "approved" the "determination of the President" to take "all necessary measures to repel any armed attack against the forces of the United States and to prevent further aggression." Congress said that the United States was "prepared, as the President determines, to take all necessary steps, including the use of armed force, to assist any member or protocol state of the Southeast Asia Collective Defense Treaty requesting assistance in defense of its freedom."[17] So certain was Congress of Johnson's information that the Senate passed the Gulf of Tonkin resolution 88 to 2, and the House 416 to 0.[18]

The Gulf of Tonkin incident as reported by President Johnson influenced not only Congress but the public, convincing it to back strong action against North Vietnam.[19] Whereas opinion polls before the resolution showed a 58 percent disapproval of Johnson's Vietnam policy, afterward it rose to a 72 percent approval rate, a remarkable overnight turnaround.[20] According to an administration report, the reprisal strikes that President Johnson ordered after the Gulf of Tonkin resolution "marked the crossing of an important threshold in the war, and it was accomplished with virtually no domestic criticism, indeed, with an evident increase in public support for the Administration."[21]

Undersecretary of State George Ball said later that while President Johnson knew that the information about a firing on the *Maddox* was shaky, being eager to attack North Vietnam, he used it anyway.[22] To make his case believable, President Johnson concealed from the public and from Congress the spy mission of the *Maddox,* the South Vietnamese raids in the vicinity, our support of those raids, and the commander's retraction of the initial report of a firing.[23]

Senator J. William Fulbright of Arkansas, who introduced the Gulf of Tonkin resolution in the Senate at Johnson's request, held hearings on the incident in 1968, by which time the facts were beginning to come out. Fulbright admitted then that had he known in 1964 about the actual communications from the commander, "I certainly don't believe I would have rushed into action." "I think I did a great disservice to the Senate," Fulbright said. "The least I can do . . . is to alert . . . future Senates that these matters are not to be dealt with in this casual manner."[24]

Having received his resolution from Congress, President Johnson in 1965 stepped up the bombing in North Vietnam and brought U.S. troops into South Vietnam. But something was still lacking in Johnson's ideological armor. The phantom assault in the Gulf of Tonkin provided a pretext for retaliation, but not a rationale for an all-out war. Johnson needed such a rationale in order to ensure the public's acceptance before he could use large numbers of troops in Vietnam.

The State Department took on the task, publishing a paper it titled *Aggression From the North: The Record of North Vietnam's Campaign to Conquer South Viet-Nam.*[25] For the duration of the Vietnam war, this document, which the press called the white paper on Vietnam, would be the administration's explanation of why we were fighting.

"South Viet-Nam," the white paper began, "is fighting for its life against a brutal campaign of terror and armed attack inspired, directed, supplied, and controlled by the Communist regime in Hanoi." The paper averred that "a Communist government [i.e., that of North Vietnam] has set out deliberately to conquer a sovereign people in a neighboring state [South Vietnam]."

North Vietnam's commitment to succeed, the paper said, "is no less total than was the commitment of the regime in North Korea in 1950." North Vietnam, according to the paper, had learned from North Korea's failure and did not attack openly, beginning instead "concealed aggression" against South Vietnam, hoping to take over the south before the world realized its aim.

As with the Korean war, our policy makers found Communist expansionism a key ingredient in rationalizing our purpose. Even before he became president, John Kennedy viewed Vietnam as "the cornerstone of the Free World in Southeast Asia, the keystone to the arch, the finger in the dike." "Burma, Thailand, India, Japan, the Philippines and obviously Laos and Cambodia," he said, would be threatened "if the Red Tide of Communism overflowed into Vietnam."[26] To stem this tide, Kennedy's staff worked out strategies for counterinsurgency efforts in "brush fire wars" in the Third World.[27]

Like Kennedy, President Johnson saw Vietnam as a cold war battleground. In 1961, while still vice president, Johnson visited Vietnam and reported back to Kennedy that "the battle against Communism" must "be joined in Southeast Asia with strength and determination to achieve success there—or the United States, inevitably, must surrender the Pacific and take up our defenses on our own shores."[28]

The white paper gave a scathing account of North Vietnam's tactics. The insurgency in South Vietnam that called itself the National Liberation Front, and which the Johnson administration called the Viet

Cong, was not genuine, charged the paper, but "was formed at Hanoi's order in 1960." The "principal function" of the Viet Cong was "to create the false impression that the aggression in South Vietnam is an indigenous rebellion against the established government." The Viet Cong was "directed by the Military High Command in Hanoi," the white paper said; its "hard core" was trained in North Vietnam and was "ordered into the South by Hanoi."

As evidence that the southern insurgency was being run from North Vietnam, the white paper averred that "many of the weapons and much of the ammunition and other supplies" were sent by North Vietnam, which had obtained this equipment from "Communist China and other Communist states." South Vietnam, the white paper continued, was merely fighting in self-defense. As for our own role, "the United States has responded to the appeals of the Government of the Republic of Vietnam for help in this defense of the freedom and independence of its land and its people." The white paper's bottom line was that we were in the right because South Vietnam was being attacked by an outside state, and under the United Nations Charter, a state may ask another state to help repel an aggressor. At the political level, the white paper's thrust was that a non-Communist nation was being blatantly attacked by a Communist country.

There was, to be sure, northern involvement in developments in the south of Vietnam. The Vietnamese Communist party had not split into southern and northern divisions after 1954, so party members in the north retained a voice in the party in the south.[29] This united party had, in fact, decided at a congress in Hanoi, in September 1960, to establish the National Liberation Front (NLF) in the south.[30] In 1961, the party's political bureau, referring to the north as a "source of support and a base area of the revolution to liberate the South," directed the NLF to step up military efforts against the Saigon administration in rural areas.[31]

This directive, however, did not necessarily impose policy on the southerners, as the white paper suggested it did. On the contrary, southern elements in the party pushed for a policy of starting military action against the Saigon administration. The core of the insurgency in the south were people who had long opposed French rule, and who viewed the Saigon administration as a continuation of Western control of Vietnam.[32] In 1960–61, these southerners saw military action as urgent, because legislative elections held in the south in 1959 had gone against Ngo Dinh Diem, who headed the Saigon administration; as a result, Diem began ruthlessly to suppress his opponents. The southerners feared that if they did not take the initiative against Diem, he would get them first.[33]

Although the Communist party's directive advocated stepping up military efforts, it did not call for a major military insurgency. The party in Hanoi was preoccupied with consolidating its rule in the north, and both the Soviet Union and China were reluctant to see armed action against the Saigon administration.[34] As at the start of the war in Korea, they were not anxious for a confrontation with the United States.

A major omission in the white paper was that it ignored the fact that the NLF had a following in the south. The NLF rose to prominence in the villages, where the Saigon administration was weak, and where Communist cadres succeeded in forcing out local Saigon officials and assuming authority themselves.[35] NLF military units, in fact, were militia that relied on the support of the villagers.[36] The NLF controlled over half the countryside,[37] collecting taxes in most of the villages of South Vietnam.[38] NLF control of the villages was so strong that the CIA initiated what it called its Phoenix Program, aimed at assassinating NLF village leaders.

The white paper exaggerated the north's role, leading the reader to think that the NLF obtained all its personnel and equipment from there; but these imports accounted for only a fraction of the NLF's strength. As for arms, some, indeed, were brought from the north, either by sea or over the Ho Chi Minh trail in Laos.[39] In 1962, the International Control Commission for Vietnam, which policed the 1954 Geneva agreement, found evidence "in specific instances" that "armed and unarmed personnel, arms, munitions and other supplies have been sent from the Zone in the North to the Zone in the South."[40] Most of the NLF's weapons, however, were manufactured in the south, or were bought or captured from the Saigon army. Adept at seizing weapons, the NLF, according to Pentagon figures for 1962–1964, captured 12,300 more weapons than it lost to the Saigon army.[41]

In an effort to demonstrate NLF dependence on the Communist world, the white paper included a statistical appendix on weapons produced in Communist countries that wound up in the NLF's hands.[42] The appendix, however, showed only one hundred weapons a year, mostly light rifles, a minuscule fraction of the total number of weapons the NLF held. When pressed by reporters, the Pentagon admitted that only 15–20 percent of the NLF's arms and equipment had come from North Vietnam.[43] Even to the extent that the NLF's weapons were Soviet or Chinese, this did not prove direct Soviet or Chinese aid, because these weapons were available on the international arms market.

As for personnel, the white paper stated in another appendix that the State Department could "confirm" 39,550 combatants who had joined the NLF from the north between 1959 and 1964, and estimated an additional 17,550 whom, it said, could not be "confirmed."[44] These figures, even if true, still could not reveal an impressive level of infiltration but, to the contrary, confirmed that most NLF recruits were local inhabitants in the south.[45] According to U.S. government figures for 1965, arrivals from the north accounted for only 10 percent of the total forces of the NLF, which was recruiting 3,500 men a month in the south.[46]

Of those who did travel south to join the NLF, most were people originally from the south, who had moved north after the demarcation line was drawn in 1954.[47] The white paper recognized this phenomenon and went to some pains to deal with it, charging that 75 percent of those coming south were actually natives of the north. But the white paper could give no firm evidence for this figure, reciting only a few case histories of individuals who went south, and most of these in fact involved Vietnamese who were natives of the south.[48] As for regular military units of native northerners entering the south, this began only after the Gulf of Tonkin resolution and President Johnson's bombing of the north; by the time of the white paper, these forces numbered only a few thousand.[49]

Beyond its weaknesses in showing levels of arms and personnel moving south, the State Department's white paper had a more fundamental flaw, because it did not explain the origin of the division between north and south in Vietnam. The white paper spoke of the north and south as if they were two separate countries, so that an attack by one on the other would constitute an act of international aggression, rather than a civil war; however, as we have seen, the 1954 demarcation line was *not* an international boundary.

The white paper's reference to Korea was instructive, however, because it gave the same false impression about Vietnam that the Truman administration had given about Korea in 1950. Korea and Vietnam were both single countries, but we tried to make them appear divided. Indeed, in Vietnam, the only major foreign element was the military presence of the United States, whom the International Control Commission criticized for bringing in military advisors, which, it said, violated the 1954 agreements.[50]

We were intervening militarily in a domestic dispute in Vietnam; and to cover that intervention, we portrayed a civil war as an act of international aggression. In the process, we lost 50,000 of our own forces, and overall two million were killed on both sides, the bulk of them civilians.[51] Had we not interfered, the Vietnamese would probably have settled their differences with far fewer casualties.

After the war ended, I visited Vietnam and witnessed the devastation. In the south alone, the bombs dropped by B-52s left an estimated 23 million craters, turning the land into swamp, and denuding nearly half of the south's forests.[52] Thousands of our explosive mines remained in the farmland, so that Vietnamese farmers continued to be killed and maimed by them.[53]

In downtown Hanoi I saw a neighborhood we had bombed in December 1972, because President Nixon said that bombing would convince North Vietnam to negotiate. Here thousands had been killed in a short time. There was no monument to the dead, but an exhibit had been set up with photographs of victims and demolished houses. An elderly man, a survivor of the bombing, was caretaker for the exhibit. As he showed it to me, I could see he was straining to avoid putting awkward questions to a guest whose country was responsible for the bombing. Finally he asked me, as politely as he could, how America could do this to his neighborhood. I had no answer.

Notes

1. *The Pentagon Papers As Published by the* New York Times (1971), pp. 253, 256, 259.

2. "Draft Resolution for Congress on Actions in Southeast Asia," May 25, 1964, in *The Pentagon Papers As Published by the New York Times,* p. 294.

3. *The Pentagon Papers As Published by the* New York Times, p. 267; Robert Scheer, "Tonkin—Dubious Premise for War," *Los Angeles Times,* April 29, 1985, p. A1, col. 1.

4. *The Pentagon Papers As Published by the* New York Times, pp. 267–68; Scheer, "Tonkin—Dubious Premise for War."

5. *The Pentagon Papers As Published by the* New York Times, p. 269; "The Tonkin Chronology," *Los Angeles Times,* April 29, 1985, p. A6, col. 5.

6. Scheer, "Tonkin—Dubious Premise for War."

7. Alan E. Goodman and Seth E. Tillman, "Debris from the Tonkin Resolution," *New York Times,* August 5, 1984, p. D21, col. 2.

8. Scheer, "Tonkin—Dubious Premise for War."

9. Ibid.

10. Joseph C. Goulden, *Truth Is the First Casualty: The Gulf of Tonkin Affair—Illusion and Reality* (1969), p. 152.

11. *The Pentagon Papers As Published by the* New York Times, p. 270.

12. Scheer, "Tonkin—Dubious Premise for War."

13. Arnold H. Lubasch, "Two Torpedo Vessels Believed Sunk in Gulf of Tonkin," *New York Times,* August 5, 1964, p. A1, col. 4.

14. Tom Wicker, "U.S. Planes Attack North Vietnam Bases; President Orders 'Limited' Retaliation After Communists' PT Boats Renew Raids," *New York Times,* August 5, 1964, p. A1, col. 8.

15. "The President's Address," *New York Times,* August 5, 1964, p. A1, col. 6.

16. *The Pentagon Papers As Published by the* New York Times, pp. 272–73.

17. Joint Resolution to Promote the Maintenance of International Peace and Security in Southeast Asia, August 10, 1964, U.S. Congress, *Statutes at Large,* vol. 78, p. 384, §§ 1–3 (1964).

18. *The Pentagon Papers As Published by the* New York Times, pp. 273–75.

19. Ibid., p. 277.

20. Scheer, "Tonkin—Dubious Premise for War."

21. *The Pentagon Papers As Published by the* New York Times, p. 278.

22. Scheer, "Tonkin—Dubious Premise for War"; Goodman and Tillman, "Debris from the Tonkin Resolution."

23. Goulden, *Truth Is the First Casualty,* pp. 239–40.

24. Scheer, "Tonkin—Dubious Premise for War."

25. Pub. no. 7839, DSB, vol. 52, p. 404 (1965).

26. John F. Kennedy, "America's Stake in Vietnam: The Cornerstone of the Free World in Southeast Asia," *Vital Speeches of the Day,* vol. 22, p. 618 (August 1, 1956).

27. William S. Turley, *The Second Indochina War: A Short Political and Military History, 1954–1975* (1986), p. 37.

28. *The Pentagon Papers: The Defense Department History of the United States Decisionmaking on Vietnam* (Sen. Gravel ed. 1971), 2: 57.

29. Turley, *The Second Indochina War,* pp. 19–21.

30. Ibid., p. 28; War Experiences Recapitulation Committee of the High-Level Military Institute, People's Army Publishing Hou e, Hanoi, *The Anti-U.S. Resistance War for National Salvation 1954–1975: Military Events,* in U.S. Government, Joint Publications Research Service no. 80968, June 3, 1982, p. 43.

31. Turley, *The Second Indochina War,* p. 28; *The Anti-U.S. Resistance War for National Salvation 1954–1975: Military Events,* pp. 45–46.

32. Turley, *The Second Indochina War,* p. 41.

33. Jean Lacouture, "Viet Cong. Who Are They, What Do They Want," *New Republic,* March 6, 1965, p. 21, at p. 22.

34. Turley, *The Second Indochina War,* p. 21.

35. Ibid., pp. 27, 30–31.

36. Ibid., pp. 40–41.

37. Lacouture, "Viet Cong. Who Are They, What Do They Want," p. 24.

38. Bernard B. Fall, *Viet-Nam Witness 1953–66* (1966), p. 284.

39. Turley, *The Second Indochina War*, pp. 43–45.

40. *Special Report to the Co-Chairmen of the Geneva Conference on Indo-China*, International Commission for Supervision and Control in Vietnam, Saigon, June 2, 1962, Command Paper 1755, in Great Britain, *Parliamentary Papers* (House of Commons and Command), Session 31 October 1961–25 October 1962, vol. 39, p. 7; "U.S. Comments on Report of Control Commission for Viet-Nam," DSB, vol. 47, p. 109 (1962).

41. I. F. Stone, "A Reply to the White Paper," in Marvin E. Gettleman, *Vietnam: History, Documents, and Opinions on a Major World Crisis* (1965), pp. 317–18.

42. Gettleman, *Vietnam: History, Documents, and Opinions on a Major World Crisis*, pp. 314–16.

43. Lacouture, "Viet Cong. Who Are They, What Do They Want," p. 24.

44. Gettleman, *Vietnam: History, Documents, and Opinions on a Major World Crisis*, p. 314.

45. Fall, *Vietnam Witness 1953–66*, p. 312; Turley, *The Second Indochina War*, p. 43.

46. Fall, *Vietnam Witness 1953–66*, p. 343.

47. Turley, *The Second Indochina War*, p. 42.

48. Stone, "A Reply to the White Paper," in Gettleman, *Vietnam: History, Documents, and Opinions on a Major World Crisis*, pp. 320–21.

49. Turley, *The Second Indochina War*, p. 58.

50. *Special Report to the Co-Chairmen of the Geneva Conference on Indo-China*, p. 10.

51. Richard Dean Burns and Milton Leitenberg, *The Wars in Vietnam, Cambodia, and Laos, 1945–1982: A Bibliographic Guide* (1984), p. xxiv.

52. Charles Piller and Keith R. Yamamoto, *Gene Wars: Military Control over the New Genetic Technologies* (1988), p. 70.

53. Burns and Leitenberg, *The Wars in Vietnam, Cambodia, and Laos, 1945–1982*, p. xxiv.

12

The Congo: Trouble Out East

Even as war was heating up in Indochina, the Johnson administration found reason for a more limited military action in the heart of Africa, and again there was more involved than met the public eye. An official brief by the State Department announced the landing at Stanleyville, capital of the Congo's eastern province, Orientale, of six hundred Belgian paratroopers transported by American planes, in late 1964:

A short time ago—early in the morning of November 24 in the Congo—a unit of Belgian paratroopers carried by United States military transport planes landed at Stanleyville in the Congo. The purpose of this action is to save the lives of innocent men, women, and children, both Congolese and citizens of at least 18 foreign countries. More than 1,000 civilians have been held as hostages by the Congolese rebels. They have been threatened repeatedly with death by their captors. The decision to send in a rescue force was taken only after the most careful deliberation and when every other avenue to secure the safety of these innocent people was closed by rebel intransigence. This decision was made jointly by the United States and Belgian Governments with the full knowledge and agreement of the legal Government of the Congo. The immediate mission is the rescue of innocent civilians and the evacuation of those who wish to leave the area. When this mission is accomplished, the rescue force will be withdrawn promptly.[1]

The landing was one more episode in the troubled history of the Congo, which had been pieced together by Belgium out of a huge area in central Africa. Although the Congo had gained independence from Belgium in 1960, it remained an unwieldy country, as it included half a dozen major nationalities that had no intrinsic reason to be united under a single flag. Various regions tried to split off, and in November 1964, Orientale province was controlled by an opposition group in rebellion against the central government, located in Leopoldville.

On the face of it, the paratrooper landing did appear to be a rescue mission, as the State Department announcement affirmed. The opposition group was holding hostage eight hundred foreigners of various nationalities, many of them Belgians and Americans, whom opposition leaders had threatened to kill. The opposition government had taken control not only of Orientale but of other parts of the Congo; at the time of the Belgian landing, however, the central government's forces were moving quickly to retake Stanleyville, and the opposition forces were no match for them. The apparent reason for the hostage-taking was that Belgium and the United States were giving military support to the central government in its efforts against the opposition group, which hoped that, by taking hostages, it could deter the expected central government attack on Stanleyville. The tactic worked for a time, since the government army held back. But then the Belgians landed, and simultaneously the central government forces moved into Stanleyville, wresting it away from the rebels.

The Organization of African Unity (OAU) condemned the landing as "an intervention in African affairs" and a threat to the peace of the African continent. In a letter to the UN Security Council, twenty-two countries, mostly African, declared that the OAU had been mediating between the two Congolese governments, and that it had kept Belgium and the United States apprised of its progress. The landing, they said, disrupted the OAU effort to resolve the situation.[2]

The American ambassador in Nairobi, Kenya, held negotiations there with the foreign minister of the opposition government, although the State Department was alleging that "the rebel representative was not concerned with the safety of the hostages."[3] The ambassador insisted on the release of the hostages as the only item for discussion, while the opposition government said it would release them if the central government army agreed not to attack. The ambassador, admitting that he was unable to speak for the Congolese army, broke off the talks.[4]

African countries charged that the purpose of the landing was not to rescue the hostages but to retake Stanleyville for the central government. "The objective of the imperialist aggressors," declared Guinea in the UN Security Council, "was none other than the fall of Stanleyville, the stronghold of popular resistance to foreign domination."[5] The saving of the hostages, alleged the other Congo, with its capital at Brazzaville, was merely a "pretext."[6] Guinea charged that the talks in Nairobi were a "travesty," whose only purpose was to provide an excuse to intervene.[7]

Whether the opposition government actually did plan to kill the hostages will never be known. It had mistreated them and had even threatened at various times to kill some of them, as it had killed foreigners elsewhere in its campaign against the central government—thirty-seven according to the Belgians.[8] On the other hand, the opposition had issued an order threatening to execute anyone who killed "a single white man"[9] among the hostages. It apparently feared that if hostages were killed, the central government troops would attack Stanleyville.

According to Belgium's foreign minister, Paul Henri Spaak, there was no way to prevent the central government from advancing on Stanleyville, so that the paratrooper landing was necessary. The opposition government, however, was not impressed with Spaak's logic, because the central government had collaborated closely, it said, with the United States and Belgium. By its lights, the United States bore direct responsibility if the central government decided to attack Stanleyville. The paratrooper landing was part of the assault on Stanleyville. Kenya, taking up this analysis, charged that U.S. and Belgian aid let the central government ignore calls for a cease-fire that might have resolved the civil war short of an assault on Stanleyville.[10]

Viewing the central army's assault as inevitable, Spaak told the UN Security Council that the central army "would have to start fighting as soon as it arrived outside Stanleyville. We thought that that was the time when the foreigners' lives would be in the greatest danger," the foreign minister reasoned. "That is why we chose that particular time for the parachute drop on the town."[11]

Viscount Étienne Davignon, of the Belgian foreign office, described what happened when the paratroopers arrived. As the U.S. troop transports approached Stanleyville airport, the opposition's commander led 250 hostages outside a hotel where they were being held, saying he intended to march them to the airfield, to trade them to the paratroopers for the safe exit of the opposition army. As the entourage reached the town square, firing could be heard from the airfield; those guarding the hostages became frightened and made the hostages crouch down. An opposition officer ran up shouting, "The paratroopers have come, shoot the whites." The hostages panicked and ran, and the guards fired on them, killing thirty of them.[12] In the Security Council, Ghana argued, "Was it not to be feared and foreseen that these tribesmen, faced with heavily armed soldiers dropping from the skies, would panic and, in a state of mass hysteria, would vent their wrath on the helpless hostages?"[13]

In the paratroopers' wake, the Fifth Brigade of the Congolese army entered Stanleyville and retook it.[14] A fact that provided some support for the OAU view that the central army force was beholden to Belgium and the United States, was that a combined force of Congolese and outside mercenaries, called the Fifth Brigade of the Congo Army, was commanded by Major Michael Hoare, a Briton. The paratrooper landing allowed the Fifth Brigade to enter Stanleyville; the paratroopers themselves were to rescue the hostages, thereby removing that obstacle to an assault on the town.[15] Together, the Fifth Brigade and the Belgian paratroopers took control of Stanleyville from the rebels,[16] and then evacuated upwards of a thousand foreigners.[17]

Belgian minister Spaak insisted that the paratroopers landed only to save the hostages, not to retake Stanleyville or to assist the Fifth Brigade,[18] but Uganda countered by charging that "it was obviously an operation in support of the one led by Major Hoare."[19] As some evidence for Uganda's view, the paratroopers did take pieces of territory in Stanleyville and turn them over to the Fifth Brigade.[20] The paratroopers, however, left before the fighting ended, as Spaak was quick to point out in reply.[21] Moreover, the "number of rebels killed by the Belgian troops," Spaak said, was "very small." The paratroopers fought only to the extent necessary to get the hostages out.[22]

That disclosure alone was incriminating. Whatever their intent, the paratroopers, by attacking the opposition forces, did help the Fifth Brigade take Stanleyville.[23] President Johnson, to justify our collaboration with Belgium, backed Spaak's position. "The United States has no political goals to impose upon the Congo," he said. "We have no narrow interest. We have no economic gain to be served in the Congo."[24] In the UN Security Council, our delegate, Adlai Stevenson, reiterated that by transporting the Belgian paratroopers to Stanleyville, the United

States had no interest other than to protect the hostages, and he denied that the United States was taking a military role in support of the central government in its battle with the opposition.[25]

Stevenson did, however, acknowledge that earlier in 1964, "the United States provided some military material and training assistance to the Congo," but with the qualifier that many African nations got such help from abroad. "There is not one of them, I dare say, that does not obtain military equipment or training or both from outside Africa." As the year wore on, the United States gave "additional equipment and transport." But, Stevenson affirmed, the United States "was not requested to, and it did not, undertake military operations in the Congo."[26]

Stevenson's statement, while it contained an element of truth, underplayed our role in the Congo. In 1963, the CIA began a paramilitary program there, enlisting South Africa's covert action organization, the Bureau of State Security, to help develop an army of mercenaries to function as part of the Congo's army.[27] In early 1964, the CIA used this paramilitary apparatus to put down a rebellion in Kwilu, another Congolese province; at the same time, it recruited Cuban exile pilots in Miami to fly missions for the central government.[28]

The State Department gave aircraft to the central government, as Stevenson acknowledged; then, as the Department affirmed, it sent pilots to fly them "in the eastern part of the Congo."[29] When confronted by reporters with the information that the pilots were recruited and supervised by the CIA, the State Department gave "no comment."[30]

In August 1964, after the opposition took Orientale province, President Johnson sent Undersecretary of State Averell Harriman, his top troubleshooter, to Brussels to coordinate Congo strategy with the Belgian government. According to the French daily *Le Monde,* Harriman asked the Belgians to help us in providing military support to the central government, to keep the Congo in the Western camp.[31] The central government was decidedly pro-Western, while the opposition government had befriended Soviet bloc countries, and President Johnson did not want a leftist government in the Congo any more than he did in Vietnam.[32]

After the Brussels meeting, the Johnson administration sent 106 U.S. military personnel, including 42 paratroopers; helicopters; and four C-130 transport planes, to help the central government. This deployment led Senator John Stennis of Mississippi to worry aloud that we might be drawn into "another undeclared war such as that in Vietnam."[33]

The administration, however, went ahead with its plans. Secretary of State Dean Rusk authorized an immediate effort, in conjunction with Belgium, to help the central government raise a mercenary force to hold government strong points, and to start a rebel rollback.[34] With that assistance, the central government recruited a mercenary force of 700, primarily from Belgium, South Africa, and Rhodesia; by September, this force had become the Fifth Brigade, the spearhead of the central government's army.[35] Flying the C-130 transports, U.S. pilots ferried Congolese troops, including the mercenaries, to battle areas. Johnson sent T-28 fighter bombers piloted by Cuban exiles, some of them veterans of the Bay of Pigs operation; these pilots strafed opposition positions in the eastern Congo. He also sent counterguerrilla advisors, who worked with central army combat units in the field.[36] When the Belgian paratroopers landed in Stanleyville, a force of Cubans was nearby with the mercenaries, to help out if needed.[37]

The involvement of the mercenaries on the central government's behalf was a major reason for the OAU's negative reaction to the Stanleyville landing, for the organization viewed the use of mercenaries in Africa as a continuation of colonial control. Unsuccessfully, it asked the Congo central government to send them home.[38] The UN Security Council, viewing mercenaries as a destabilizing influence, had earlier asked other countries to keep their citizens from becoming mercenaries.[39] At that time, European mercenaries were fighting for colonial governments in the Portuguese colonies and in Rhodesia, and many hopscotched from one war to another. Most African countries condemned the U.S.-Belgian intervention, because they viewed the opposition government as true nationalists, while the central government had allied itself with European governments.[40]

Notes

1. "Department Statement," November 24, 1964, DSB, vol. 51, p. 841 (1964).
2. UN Doc. S/6076, and Add. 1-5, December 1, 1964, SCOR, 19th yr., Supplement (October, November, December 1964), p. 198.
3. "Department Statement," November 24, 1964, DSB, vol. 51, p. 841 (1964).
4. SCOR, 19th yr., 1173rd mtg., p. 8, UN Doc. S/PV. 1173 (1964); SCOR, 19th yr., 1174th mtg., pp. 14-15, UN Doc. S/PV.1174 (1964).
5. SCOR, 19th yr., 1171st mtg., pp. 9-10, UN Doc. S/PV.1171 (1964).

6. SCOR, 19th yr., 1170th mtg., p. 15, UN Doc. S/PV.1170 (1964).

7. SCOR, 19th yr., 1171st mtg., p. 14, UN Doc. S/PV.1171 (1964).

8. SCOR, 19th yr., 1177th mtg., p. 12, UN Doc. S/PV.1177 (1964).

9. Pierre de Vos, "Les réfugiés rentrés à Bruxelles font des récits hallucinants sur les derniers jours de la capitale de la rébellion," *Le Monde,* November 28, 1964, p. 6, col. 1.

10. SCOR, 19th yr., 1175th mtg., p. 12, UN Doc. S/PV.1175 (1964).

11. SCOR, 19th yr., 1173rd mtg., p. 9, UN Doc. S/PV.1173 (1964).

12. Edward T. O'Toole, "Belgian Troops Start to Leave," *New York Times,* November 28, 1964, p. A3, col. 1.

13. SCOR, 19th yr., 1170th mtg., p. 29, UN Doc. S/PV.1170 (1964).

14. "Des troupes aéportées belges procèdent à l'évacuation des otages de Stanleyville," *Le Monde,* November 25, 1964, p. 1, col. 2.

15. Mohammed Bennouna, *Le consentement à l'ingérence militaire dans les conflits internes* (1974), p. 180.

16. Stephen R. Weissman, *American Foreign Policy in the Congo 1960-1964* (1974), p. 247.

17. SCOR, 19th yr., 1177th mtg., p. 16, UN Doc. S/PV.1177 (1964).

18. SCOR, 19th yr., 1173rd mtg., p. 3, UN Doc. S/PV.1173 (1964).

19. SCOR, 19th yr., 1177th mtg., p. 24, UN Doc. S/PV.1177 (1964).

20. Lloyd Garrison, "Refugee Airlift Halted in Congo," *New York Times,* November 29, 1964, p. A1, col. 7.

21. SCOR, 19th yr., 1173rd mtg., p. 10, UN Doc. S/PV.1173 (1964).

22. Ibid., p. 12.

23. Madeleine Kalb, *The Congo Cables* (1982), p. 378; Weissman, *American Foreign Policy in the Congo 1960-1964,* pp. 251-52.

24. "Statement by President Johnson," November 28, 1964, DSB, vol. 51, pp. 845-46 (1964).

25. SCOR, 19th yr., 1174th mtg., p. 12, UN Doc. S/PV.1174 (1964).

26. Ibid., p. 18.

27. John Stockwell, *In Search of Enemies: a CIA Story* (1978), pp. 34, 187-88.

28. Stephen R. Weissman, "CIA Covert Action in Zaire and Angola: Patterns and Consequences," *Political Science Quarterly* (Summer 1979): 271.

29. Max Frankel, "Flights in Congo Confirmed by U.S.," *New York Times,* June 17, 1964, p. A1, col. 5.

30. "U.S. Civilians Halt Congo Air Sorties," *New York Times,* June 18, 1964, p. A1, col. 7.

31. Pierre de Vos, "M. Harriman s'entretient avec M. Spaak de la situation au Congo," *Le Monde,* August 8, 1964, p. 1, col. 2.

32. "Intervention au Congo?" *Le Monde,* August 7, 1964, p. 1, col. 1.

33. M. S. Handler, "Revolt in Congo Termed 'Serious' by U.S. Officials," *New York Times,* August 15, 1964, p. A1, col. 8.

34. Weissman, "CIA Covert Action in Zaire and Angola," p. 271.

35. Ibid., p. 272. Lloyd Garrison, "20 to 30 Hostages Killed as Congo Rescue Begins; Stanleyville is Retaken," *New York Times,* November 25, 1964, p. A1, col. 8.

36. Handler, "Revolt in Congo Termed 'Serious' by U.S. Officials"; Tad Szulc, "Tide in Congo War Believed Turning in Regime's Favor," *New York Times,* October 5, 1964, p. A1, col. 1.

37. Weissman, *American Foreign Policy in the Congo 1960-1964,* p. 252.

38. SCOR, 19th yr., 1171st mtg., p. 4, UN Doc. S/PV.1171 (1964).

39. Res. 161, SCOR, 16th yr., *Resolutions and Decisions*, p. 2, UN Doc. S/INF/16/Rev.1 (1961).

40. SCOR, 19th yr., 1178th mtg., p. 9, UN Doc. S/PV.1178 (1964).

13

The Congo: Another Cuba?

American involvement in Congolese politics started well before 1964; indeed, we bore a certain responsibility for the outbreak of the rebellion in the first place. The opposition government based at Stanleyville was headed by Antoine Gizenga, who in 1960 had served as deputy prime minister of the Congo under Patrice Lumumba, the Congo's first prime minister. Lumumba, a strong nationalist who had given the Congolese a sense of self-identity as colonial rule ended, was eventually killed by opponents and subsequently held the status of a martyr for many Congolese.

Gaston Soumialot, another opposition leader active in the Stanleyville government, claimed Lumumba's mantle, declaring "I am the new Lumumba."[1] The political groups that paid homage to Lumumba were the most popular in the country.[2] To the opposition politicians, the deceased Lumumba was the bearer of true independence for the Congo, and those who killed him were out to feather their own nests by close ties with Belgium and the United States, which both had financial interests in the Congo. Thus, a major reason for the 1964 rebellion was that the Lumumbists chafed under the thought that they had been outmaneuvered by self-seeking political figures who were selling the country out.

Adlai Stevenson, hammering home his point that the United States had no ulterior motive in the Stanleyville landing, averred that we had never interfered in Congolese politics. "From the beginning," he said, referring to Congolese independence in 1960, "we have been opposed—and remain opposed—to foreign intervention in the internal affairs of the sovereign and independent state of the Congo."[3]

We were, however, hardly idle observers as the Congo forged a political system after independence in 1960. The Congo had no developed political parties, and our officials on the scene worried about whether the Congo might tilt toward the East. The CIA station chief in Leopoldville, Lawrence Devlin, cabled Washington that both he and our ambassador, Clare Timberlake, believed, "Congo experiencing classic Communist effort takeover government. . . . Whether or not Lumumba actually Commie or just playing Commie game to assist his solidifying power, anti-West forces rapidly increasing power Congo and there may be little time left in which take action to avoid another Cuba."[4]

CIA Director Allen Dulles cabled back, "In high quarters here it is the clear-cut conclusion that if [Lumumba] continues to hold high office, the inevitable result will at best be chaos and at worst pave the way to Communist takeover of the Congo. . . . Consequently we conclude that his removal must be an urgent and prime objective and that under existing conditions this should be a high priority of our covert action."[5]

Richard Bissell, the director of CIA covert actions, who at the time was gearing up the Bay of Pigs operation, later told Senate investigators that when CIA Director Dulles wrote "removal," he meant that President Eisenhower wanted Lumumba assassinated. Bronson Tweedy, who ran the CIA division for covert actions in Africa, said that the Dulles cable was an "authoritative statement" of a "policy consensus in Washington" that Lumumba should be removed by any means necessary, including assassination.[6]

Although Lumumba, elected prime minister in May 1960,[7] was, in Devlin's view, firmly in the Soviet camp, he had no clear political program; indeed, Lumumba had visited Washington and Ottawa shortly after independence to ask for American and Canadian economic aid.[8] At the same time, Lumumba signed a 50-year contract with a U.S. firm to develop the Congo's mining and hydroelectric resources.[9] These moves indicate that Lumumba wanted to form a compact with the West.

One other indication of Lumumba's leanings was that he was not reluctant to seek help from the United Nations, even though it was Western-dominated. When Congolese soldiers rebelled against their Belgian officers in July 1960, Belgian troops reentered the Congo and helped a secessionist movement in the mineral-rich province of Katanga. To counter them, Lumumba asked for UN intervention.[10] A few days later, Lumumba and Joseph Kasavubu, the Congo's president (a largely ceremonial post), sent a message to Soviet Premier Nikita Khrushchev, suggesting that they might be forced to ask for Soviet intervention if Belgium did not pull its troops out of the Congo.[11] This request drew only a noncommittal reply from Khrushchev but earned Lumumba a reputation in the Eisenhower administration of being pro-Soviet. The request was initially motivated by a fear that the UN might not act forcefully; but when the Security Council issued a strong demand to Belgium to withdraw, Lumumba said that he would no longer ask for Soviet intervention.[12]

Lumumba did, however, turn to the Soviet Union again the following month, when the issue of the secession of the province of Katanga came to the fore, and the UN refused to help the central government put it down. Lumumba asked the Soviet government for military aid and got it.[13]

Convinced by now of Lumumba's leftism and following through on the directive from CIA Director Dulles, Devlin and Timberlake explored ways to engineer a no-confidence vote against Lumumba in the Congolese parliament and encouraged Kasavubu to dismiss Lumumba.[14] Although the Congolese constitution did not give the president that power, Kasavubu did it anyway.[15] Lumumba, who enjoyed strong support in the parliament, responded by dismissing Kasavubu, and parliament voted to annul both dismissals.[16]

Since parliament would not fire Lumumba, Devlin approached Joseph Mobutu, a colonel who headed the Congolese army, promising financial support if Mobutu sided with Kasavubu against Lumumba.[17] Mobutu, like Kasavubu, was seen by Devlin as reliable for Western interests, and Mobutu was quick to respond: on September 14, he suspended parliament and took power from the prime minister in the name of the army. This move kept Kasavubu as president and sent Lumumba fleeing to Stanleyville, his political base.[18] Devlin, true to his promise to Mobutu, began giving him under-the-table subsidies.[19]

The next day, Mobutu arrested Lumumba, but Lumumba escaped.[20] To avoid re-arrest, Lumumba put himself in protective custody in a house guarded by UN troops. Soldiers from Mobutu's army tried to apprehend him, but the UN troops kept them out.[21]

Despite Lumumba's removal from power, the CIA still found him a threat. Devlin worried that Mobutu might let parliament meet again, and cabled to the CIA that "pressures for [Lumumba's] return will be almost irresistible."[22] To keep this from happening, Devlin worked behind the scenes to see that parliament was not reopened.[23] Devlin suggested to a "key Congolese leader" (the cable does not name him) to arrange the "arrest or other more permanent disposal of Lumumba, Gizenga, and Mulele."[24] Pierre Mulele, along with Gizenga, led Lumumba's supporters while Lumumba was in UN custody. Mobutu took up the suggestion, arresting Gizenga and making plans to hand him over to Katanga province authorities, who hated him and would likely have killed him. Gizenga was released, however, by sympathetic UN troops from Ghana, who managed to wrest him from Mobutu's men.[25]

With Lumumba still in UN custody, the CIA covert action department took to carrying out Director Dulles's order to kill him, enlisting a toxicology expert to prepare a poison that would produce a fatal disease, while giving the appearance, in the event of an autopsy, that Lumumba died from natural causes. CIA headquarters in Washington sent the toxicologist to Leopoldville, where he delivered the poison to Devlin with the message from Tweedy that he was to deliver the poison so that the Leopoldville station could "seriously incapacitate or eliminate Lumumba." The Leopoldville station then began looking for someone who could get Lumumba to take the poison.[26]

But it was difficult to slip anyone into the house where Lumumba lived, surrounded as he was by UN troops. After one person who had agreed to try was unable to "penetrate entourage," Tweedy cabled a more direct approach: "Possibility use commando type group for abduction [Lumumba], either via assault on house up cliff from river or, more probably, if [Lumumba] attempts another breakout into town."[27] Undersecretary of State C. Douglas Dillon said that this idea to abduct Lumumba from his UN-protected house had been approved at the highest level of the U.S. government.[28]

CIA station chief Devlin also urged Kasavubu to arrest Lumumba, cabling Director Dulles: "Station has consistently urged [Congolese] leaders arrest Lumumba in belief Lumumba will continue be threat to stability Congo until removed from scene."[29] It was clear that if the other leaders arrested Lumumba, they could not leave him alive and remain sure he would not make a comeback.

On the night of November 27, 1960, Lumumba decided that he had had enough of being protected and slipped past his UN guards toward Stanleyville.[30] Kasavubu immediately sent a team out to catch Lumumba, with the CIA station lending a hand. According to a CIA cable, "[Station] working with [Congolese government] to get roads blocked and troops alerted [block] possible escape route."[31]

Kasavubu's men soon found Lumumba and arrested him,[32] after which Gizenga set up an administration in Stanleyville to back Lumumba's claim to retain the prime minister's position.[33] With Lumumba in detention, Devlin pressed President Kasavubu to kill Lumumba, because he feared Lumumba might return to power. Devlin cabled Washington, "Station and embassy believe present government may fall within few days. Result would almost certainly be chaos and return [Lumumba] to power. . . . Refusal take drastic steps at this time will lead to defeat of [U.S.] policy in Congo."[34]

The next day, Kasavubu told the CIA he would send Lumumba to the town of Bakwanga, which was controlled by Lumumba opponents, in the expectation that these opponents would kill him. Three days later, Kasavubu had Lumumba put on a plane to Bakwanga; but while the plane was in the air, Kasavubu learned that UN troops were installed at the Bakwanga airfield. Since this would make it difficult for Lumumba's opponents there to seize him, Kasavubu diverted the plane to Elisabethville, capital of Katanga province, which was run by Moise Tshombe, another Lumumba opponent who could be counted on to kill him.

In Elisabethville, Lumumba was forced off the plane and quickly killed. A UN inquiry team found both the central and Katanga governments responsible for the death, concluding that Kasavubu turned Lumumba over to the Katangan authorities "knowing full well" that he was giving him over to his "bitterest political enemies."[35]

Devlin admitted that the CIA station had been in touch with the Congolese officials involved in the plan to ship Lumumba off to his death,[36] while U.S. Senate investigators found that the station was aware in advance of the plan to arrest Lumumba and to turn him over to his enemies.[37] One scholar reviewing the data concluded that the CIA was guilty of "complicity in murder."[38]

After Lumumba's death, the United States would not acknowledge the CIA role, voting in the UN Security Council in favor of a resolution that expressed "deep regret" over the killing of Lumumba and called it a "crime" likely to have "grave repercussions." In a paragraph that must have amused Devlin, the resolution spoke of "the imperative necessity for the restoration of parliamentary institutions in the Congo."[39]

Our collusion with President Kasavubu and Colonel Mobutu against Patrice Lumumba, as well as against parliamentary rule, was widely suspected in the Congo; one reason for the on-and-off rebellion throughout 1964 was that many Congolese viewed the central government as having cooperated with the United States in killing Lumumba and in obstructing parliament. Had we let Lumumba contend with the other political forces, the 1964 rebellion leading to the Stanleyville situation might never have broken out.

Unfortunately for the Congo, the Eisenhower, Kennedy, and Johnson administrations viewed this African nation from a cold war perspective. In addition, we had business interests there that caused the three administrations concern over the Congo's political future. During the Stanleyville events, Ambassador Stevenson denied that we were motivated by financial interests, but U.S. policy makers were not unaware of the Congo's rich deposits of copper, diamonds, and cobalt. The United States bought much of the Congo's cobalt for use as an alloy in the manufacture of jet engines.[40] During World War II, the Belgian mining company, Union Minière, had supplied us with Congolese uranium to build the atomic bomb.[41] In Katanga province, Moise Tshombe rebelled from the central government on a platform of giving free rein to foreign mining companies. One of the major foreign players was the Belgian-American billionaire Maurice Tempelsman, who had investments in Congo diamonds and copper. After retiring as Leopoldville CIA station chief, Devlin took a job as manager of Tempelsman's Congo interests.[42]

To protect the Congo government after the Stanleyville landing, the CIA kept its paramilitary operation in the Congo alive until 1967.[43] In 1965, it began to doubt Kasavubu's pro-Western credentials and helped Joseph Mobutu, from his army position, replace Kasavubu as president.[44] Mobutu retained close ties to the CIA, a fact that will be important when we get to our next African military operation.

Notes

1. Pierre de Vos, "M. Harriman s'entretient avec M. Spaak de la situation au Congo," *Le Monde,* August 8, 1964, p. 1, col. 2.

2. Stephen R. Weissman, "CIA Covert Action in Zaire and Angola: Patterns and Consequences," *Political Science Quarterly* (Summer 1979): 275.

3. SCOR, 19th yr., 1174th mtg., p. 17, UN Doc. S/PV.1174 (1964).

4. CIA cable, Leopoldville to Director, August 18, 1960, in *Alleged Assassination Plots Involving Foreign Leaders: An Interim Report of the Select Committee to Study Governmental Operations with Respect to Intelligence Activities,* U.S. Senate, 94th Cong., 1st sess., Report no. 94-465, November 20, 1975, p. 14 (the Committee referred to Devlin by the pseudonym "Victor Hedgman"); John Stockwell, *In Search of Enemies: A CIA Story* (1978), pp. 71, 136.

5. CIA cable, Dulles to Station Officer, Leopoldville, August 26, 1960, in *Alleged Assassination Plots,* p. 15.

6. *Alleged Assassination Plots,* p. 16.

7. Madeleine Kalb, *The Congo Cables* (1982), p. xxv.

8. Ibid., pp. 36, 41.

9. Henry Tanner, "Congo Signs Pact with U.S. Concern to Tap Resources," *New York Times,* July 23, 1960, p. A1, col. 5.

10. Kalb, *The Congo Cables,* pp. 9-10.

11. Joseph Kasavubu and Patrice Lumumba, "To His Honor the Chair of the Council of Ministers of the Soviet Union," *Pravda,* July 16, 1960, p. 1, col. 5; "Text of Congolese Leaders' Appeal to Premier Khrushchev and His Reply," *New York Times,* July 16, 1960, p. 3, col. 2.

12. Res. 145, SCOR, 15th yr., *Resolutions and Decisions,* p. 6, UN Doc. S/INF/15/Rev.1 (1960).

13. Kalb, *The Congo Cables,* pp. 56, 60.

14. *Alleged Assassination Plots,* p. 15; Andrew Tully, *CIA: The Inside Story* (1962), p. 221; Kalb, *The Congo Cables,* p. 61.

15. *Alleged Assassination Plots,* p. 16.

16. Henry Tanner, "Leopoldville's Parliament Rejects Ousters—Step Helps Lumumba," *New York Times,* September 8, 1960, p. A1, col. 8.

17. Kalb, *The Congo Cables,* p. 93; Tully, *CIA: The Inside Story,* p. 222.

18. Weissman, "CIA Covert Action in Zaire and Angola," pp. 267-68; *Alleged Assassination Plots,* p. 16.

19. Kalb, *The Congo Cables,* p. 96.

20. Weissman, "CIA Covert Action in Zaire and Angola," pp. 268-69.

21. Jonathan Kwitny, *Endless Enemies: The Making of an Unfriendly World* (1984), pp. 66-67.

22. CIA cable, Leopoldville to Director, October 26, 1960, in *Alleged Assassination Plots,* p. 18.

23. *Alleged Assassination Plots,* p. 17.

24. CIA cable, Leopoldville to Director, September 20, 1960, in *Alleged Assassination Plots,* p. 18.

25. Weissman, "CIA Covert Action in Zaire and Angola," p. 268.

26. *Alleged Assassination Plots,* pp. 21-22, 23, 28.

27. Ibid., p. 32.

28. Ibid., p. 42.

29. CIA cable, Leopoldville Station Officer to Director, October 11, 1960, in *Alleged Assassination Plots,* p. 42.

30. Kalb, *The Congo Cables,* p. 157.

31. CIA cable, November 28, 1960, in *Alleged Assassination Plots,* p. 48.

32. Paul Hoffman, "Lumumba Seized in Congo," *New York Times,* December 3, 1960, p. A1, col. 8.

33. Paul Hoffman, "Pro-Red Lumumba Aide Claims Authority to Rule," *New York Times,* December 14, 1960, p. A1, col. 4.

34. CIA cable, Leopoldville CIA station to Director, January 13, 1961, in *Alleged Assassination Plots,* p. 49.

35. "Report of the Commission of Investigation established under the terms of General Assembly resolution 1601 (XV) of 15 April 1961," November 11, 1961, UN Doc. S/4976, SCOR, 16th yr., Supplement (October, November, December 1961), p. 118.

36. *Alleged Assassination Plots,* p. 51.

37. Ibid., p. 48.

38. Weissman, "CIA Covert Action in Zaire and Angola," p. 269.

39. Res. 161, SCOR, 16th yr., *Resolutions and Decisions,* p. 2, UN Doc. S/INF/16/Rev.1 (1961).

40. Kalb, *The Congo Cables,* p. 349.

41. Ibid., p. xxii.

42. Kwitny, *Endless Enemies,* pp. 9, 58; Weissman, "CIA Covert Action in Zaire and Angola," p. 275.

43. Weissman, "CIA Covert Action in Zaire and Angola," pp. 272–73.

44. Ibid., p. 273; Kalb, *The Congo Cables,* p. 379.

14

The Dominican Republic: Bullets in the Embassy Window

In 1965, the Johnson administration intervened much closer to home, in the midst of turmoil in the Dominican Republic. Juan Bosch, elected president in 1963, was soon overthrown by the military, which set up a ruling junta. He was a left-of-center nationalist, but not hostile to the United States. Bosch spent his exile living in Puerto Rico, a U.S. territory, after leaving the Dominican Republic in 1963. The junta officers, however, were closer politically to the United States. In April 1965, military and civilian elements revolted against the junta to restore Bosch to office, and, after sometimes intense street fighting, they quickly had the junta on the run.[1] On the evening of April 28, President Johnson sent in a military force, which he built up over several days to 23,000 troops.[2] After several weeks of fighting, the pro-Bosch forces were defeated, and a new military junta friendly to the United States assumed power.

When President Johnson sent in the first contingent of troops, he said his aim was to rescue U.S. citizens. We had "been informed," Johnson explained, "by military authorities in the Dominican Republic that American lives are in danger. These authorities are no longer able to guarantee their safety and they have reported that the assistance of military personnel is now needed for that purpose."[3]

The "military authorities" to whom Johnson referred were Dominican Air Force Colonel Pedro Benoit and a group of other air force officers including General Elias Wessin y Wessin, who had led the 1963 overthrow of Bosch.[4] Headquartered at the San Isidro air base east of Santo Domingo, the capital city, these officers had simply declared themselves to be a junta, after prompting in that direction from U.S. embassy officials and the CIA.[5] The junta represented the number of troops it could control, which at that point were very few.[6] Johnson's reference to the junta officers as "military authorities" made it sound as if they were in control of the country, although they were not. So when he argued that the officers could not protect our citizens, it was not because of any overriding danger, but because the officers were out of power.

In a plea for American help, Benoit phoned U.S. Ambassador Tapley Bennett to tell him that the officers at San Isidro were weeping, and that one was hysterically urging a retreat.[7] Their only hope for gaining power against the pro-Bosch forces, Benoit pleaded, was direct U.S. intervention. Knowing which buttons to press with the Johnson administration, Benoit told Bennett that the return of Bosch would "convert the country into another Cuba,"[8] whereupon Bennett immediately cabled Washington and recommended military intervention to prevent "another Cuba."[9]

The State Department, however, denied this request. Bennett then advised Colonel Benoit that it would be more politic to ask for assistance on the grounds that he could not protect U.S. citizens, because this would provide a more publicly acceptable rationale.[10] In making a second request for intervention, Benoit duly stressed the supposed danger to Americans residing in the Dominican Republic, and on that basis Johnson sent in a contingent of Marines.[11]

At the time, there were nearly 2,000 U.S. citizens in the Dominican Republic. Of these, one thousand lived in Santo Domingo, the only scene of hostilities.[12] On April 27, the day preceding the intervention, 1,172 of them were evacuated by ship and helicopter by the U.S. Navy, without the landing of troops.[13] On April 28, but before the Marines arrived, another 684 were evacuated by the same means.[14] In all, then, 1,856 Americans had already been evacuated before the intervention.

A few weeks later, Secretary of State Dean Rusk declared that overall we had evacuated 1,800 U.S. citizens from the Dominican Republic, counting those evacuated both before and after the intervention.[15] But with 1,856 evacuated prior to the intervention, that left none to be evacuated by the time the Marines arrived. Even more remarkably, President Johnson claimed on May 2 that 1,500 of our citizens in the Dominican Republic were still desperate to be saved, thus giving him the excuse to send in more Marines.[16]

Even if there were American citizens in the Dominican Republic desiring to leave after April 28, they could have been evacuated without a military intervention and occupation. Residential areas occupied by Americans in Santo Domingo were free of hostilities, and all the major Dominican factions had agreed to facilitate the evacuation of any foreigners who wanted to leave.[17] Nevertheless, President Johnson claimed that the Marines were fired upon as soon as they arrived: "We had 20 of our boys killed by the rebels, who fired first and who tried to keep us from evacuating these people." This was patently untrue. Johnson continued to elaborate, however; in a public statement he announced that Ambassador Bennett "had a thousand American men, women, and children assembled in the [Embajador] hotel who were pleading with their President for help to preserve their lives."[18] But as we have seen, U.S. citizens wanting to get out had been evacuated *prior* to American military intervention.

Secretary Rusk, like President Johnson, characterized the sending in of troops as a "rescue operation," in which the Marines arrived "just in time to avoid a major calamity."[19] Our citizens, Rusk said, "were actually under fire" on April 28, the date of the intervention. He elaborated the scene at the hotel described by Johnson: "[H]undreds were gathered in the Embajador Hotel, and there were people running around the hotel, shooting it up with tommyguns, and so forth. There were large numbers of people gathered on the Polo Grounds [near the hotel] who were then apparently under fire. When the Marines got there at 7 o'clock [April 28], or thereabouts, they in fact found that these people were under fire."[20]

There was little truth in Rusk's account, either: while some shooting had occurred at the Embajador Hotel on April 28, no U.S. citizens were under fire when the Marines arrived. Rusk's reference may have been to an incident that occurred not on April 28 but the day before, when armed pro-Bosch elements entered the Embajador Hotel looking for a rightist opponent. A few shots were fired, for reasons that are not clear; but none of these was directed at foreigners, and the evacuation proceeded smoothly.[21]

In another vivid but equally fallacious account, President Johnson reported firing on the U.S. embassy building in Santo Domingo on April 28, while inside Ambassador Bennett was making frequent telephone calls to Washington: "As we talked to our ambassador to confirm the horror and tragedy and the unbelievable fact that they [the rebels] were firing on Americans and the American Embassy," Johnson said, "he was talking to us from under a desk while bullets were going through his windows."[22] Whatever may have been the source of Johnson's information, Bennett denied that he had hidden under his desk while bullets flew through the windows.[23] Nor had there been any firing on U.S. citizens, either at the embassy or anywhere else. During the entire episode, from what can be gathered, no American was ever harmed by a Dominican.[24] The only U.S. citizens injured during the conflict were two newsmen shot and seriously wounded by "friendly fire" from U.S. Marines.[25]

During the crisis, both Ambassador Bennett and top U.S. military officers gave press briefings full of atrocities that later turned out to be untrue.[26] The distortions, in fact, became so obvious to the press that one reporter called these briefings "an important part of the whole picture of misleading newsmen and, through them, public opinion about what the United States was doing or planning to do in the Dominican Republic."[27]

President Johnson kept elaborating the horrors, stating that as of May 4, "1,000 to 1,500" Dominicans were lying "dead in the street" in Santo Domingo, many of them beheaded.[28] But reporters never saw more than a few bodies in the streets.[29] Although several hundred Dominicans were killed in street fighting,[30] there were no reports of beheadings, or execution-style killings.[31] One reporter called President Johnson's public statements about the Dominican Republic "hyperbolic."[32]

A journalist covering the U.S. embassy during the Dominican crisis wrote that the decisive element in its recommendations to the State Department was "the ebb and flow of rebel fortunes, rather than the degree of danger to U.S. or other foreign nationals."[33] In Congress, Johnson's claim of intervention to protect our citizens was seriously questioned.[34] Senator J. William Fulbright, who conducted closed hearings into the Dominican situation, said flatly that "the danger to American lives was more a pretext than a reason."[35] Senator Joseph Clark of Pennsylvania added, "It is all very well to talk about protecting American lives, but the real reason that the Marines went in there was to prevent a Communist takeover."[36]

Notes

1. "Dominican Coup Deposes Regime; Rebels Are Split," *New York Times*, April 26, 1965, p. A1, col. 8.

2. "Johnson Charges Red Plotters Took Over Dominican Uprising; Increases U.S. Forces to 14,000," *New York Times*, May 3, 1965, p. A1, col. 8; "U.S. Acts to Meet Threat in Dominican Republic, White House press release," April 28, 1965, DSB, vol. 52, p. 738 (1965); Abraham F. Lowenthal, *The Dominican Intervention* (1972), p. 112; Tad Szulc, *Dominican Diary* (1965), p. 149.

3. "U.S. Acts to Meet Threat in Dominican Republic, White House press release," April 28, 1965, DSB, vol. 52, p. 738 (1965).

4. Szulc, *Dominican Diary*, p. 15.

5. John Bartlow Martin, *Overtaken by Events: The Dominican Crisis from the Fall of Trujillo to the Civil War* (1966), p. 655; Szulc, *Dominican Diary*, p. 85; *Congressional Record*, vol. 111, p. 24242, September 17, 1965 (statement of Sen. Joseph Clark).

6. Theodore Draper, *The Dominican Revolt: A Case Study in American Policy* (1968), pp. 117-18.

7. Martin, *Overtaken by Events*, p. 656.

8. Ibid., p. 656; *Congressional Record*, vol. 111, p. 23857, September 15, 1965 (statement of Sen. J. William Fulbright).

9. Martin, *Overtaken by Events*, pp. 656-57.

10. *Congressional Record*, vol. 111, p. 23857, September 15, 1965 (statement of Sen. J. William Fulbright); Philip Geyelin, *Lyndon B. Johnson and the World* (1966), p. 252.

11. Draper, *The Dominican Revolt*, pp. 119-21; Philip Geyelin, "Dominican Flashback: Behind the Scenes," *Wall Street Journal*, June 25, 1965, p. 8, col. 3.

12. Charles Mohr, "President Sends Marines to Rescue Citizens of U.S. from Dominican Fighting," *New York Times*, April 29, 1965, p. A1, col. 8; David Atlee Phillips, *The Night Watch* (1977), pp. 147-50; Piero Gleijeses, *The Dominican Crisis: The 1965 Constitutionalist Revolt and American Intervention* (1978), p. 241.

13. Captain James A. Dare, "Dominican Diary," *U.S. Naval Institute Proceedings*, December 1965, pp. 41-42; Martin, *Overtaken by Events*, p. 652; Tad Szulc, "Dominican Revolt Fails After a Day of Savage Battle," *New York Times*, April 28, 1965, p. A1, col. 3.

14. Lowenthal, *The Dominican Intervention*, p. 103; Szulc, *Dominican Diary*, p. 42; Dare, "Dominican Diary," p. 42. Gleijeses, *The Dominican Crisis*, p. 397.

15. "Secretary Rusk's News Conference of May 26," DSB, vol. 52, p. 938 (1965).

16. "Statement by President Johnson," May 2, 1965, DSB, vol. 52, p. 746 (1965), also in "Remarks by President Johnson," May 4, 1965, DSB, vol. 52, pp. 820-21 (1965).

17. Draper, *The Dominican Revolt*, p. 62; Phillips, *The Night Watch*, p. 147; Gleijeses, *The Dominican Crisis*, p. 237.

18. Lyndon B. Johnson, "An Assessment of the Situation in the Dominican Republic," DSB, vol. 53, p. 20 (1965).

19. "Secretary Discusses Situation in Dominican Republic," May 8, 1965, DSB, vol. 52, p. 842 (1965).

20. "Secretary Rusk's News Conference of May 26," DSB, vol. 52, p. 941–42 (1965).

21. Geyelin, "Dominican Flashback: Behind the Scenes"; Gleijeses, *The Dominican Crisis*, p. 397; Lowenthal, *The Dominican Intervention*, p. 204 n. 27; Szulc, *Dominican Diary*, p. 33.

22. Johnson, "An Assessment of the Situation in the Dominican Republic."

23. David Wise, *The Politics of Lying: Government Deception, Secrecy, and Power* (1973), p. 43; Draper, *The Dominican Revolt*, p. 116; Frank Cormier, *LBJ: The Way He Was* (1977), p. 188; Szulc, *Dominican Diary*, p. 45.

24. *Congressional Record*, vol. 111, p. 23855, September 15, 1965 (statement of Sen. J. William Fulbright); *Congressional Record*, vol. 111, p. 24973, September 23, 1965 (statement of Rep. Armistead Selden); Lyndon B. Johnson, "The Search for a Durable Peace in the Dominican Republic," May 28, 1965, DSB, vol. 52, p. 990 (1965).

25. James Deakin, *Lyndon Johnson's Credibility Gap* (1968), p. 34; Szulc, *Dominican Diary*, p. 150.

26. Draper, *The Dominican Revolt*, p. 94.

27. Szulc, *Dominican Diary*, p. 102.

28. "Remarks by President Johnson," May 4, 1965, DSB, vol. 52, p. 822 (1965).

29. Draper, *The Dominican Revolt*, pp. 92-93.

30. Martin, *Overtaken by Events*, p. 655.

31. Lowenthal, *The Dominican Intervention*, p. 207, n. 50; Merle Miller, *Lyndon: An Oral Biography* (1980), p. 427.

32. Geyelin, *Lyndon B. Johnson and the World*, p. 238.

33. Ibid., p. 246.

34. Mohammed Bennouna, *Le consentement à l'ingérence militaire dans les conflits internes* (1974), p. 180.

35. *Congressional Record*, vol. 111, p. 23857, September 15, 1965 (statement of Sen. J. William Fulbright).

36. Ibid., p. 24242, September 17, 1965 (statement of Sen. Joseph Clark).

15

The Dominican Republic: Seeing Red

According to his critics, Lyndon Johnson's purpose in the Dominican Republic was not to rescue American citizens but to prevent President Juan Bosch from returning to office. Indeed, four days after the initial landing on April 28, 1965, Johnson announced that he was sending in additional Marines because, as he put it, Communists were participating on Bosch's side. "Our goal," Johnson said, "is to help prevent another Communist state in this hemisphere."[1] Dean Rusk concurred that "the Communists had captured the revolution according to plan, and the danger of a Communist takeover was established beyond question."[2]

Johnson and Rusk did not withdraw their rescue rationale, but said that while they were carrying out the rescue, Communists were assuming a new and prominent government role on the pro-Bosch side. "What began as a popular democratic revolution, committed to democracy and social justice," Johnson said on May 2, was "seized and placed into the hands of a band of Communist conspirators."[3] As we saw in the last chapter, however, the Dominican Air Force officers *first* requested intervention to prevent "another Cuba"; before sending the first units, Johnson mentioned to congressional leaders his own concern about communism in the Dominican Republic.[4] As Senator Fulbright said, from the beginning of the crisis the administration's policy "was directed against the return of Bosch and against the success of the rebel movement."[5] Johnson saw the junta as being firmly in the U.S. camp, while Bosch remained, for Johnson, too independent-minded. He argued that "very close to the beginning of the [pro-Bosch] revolution, U.S. policymakers decided that it should not be allowed to succeed."[6] Indeed, two days before the initial intervention, the American embassy in Santo Domingo sent the State Department a cable proposing intervention to keep Bosch out of office. "All members of the country team," the cable read, "feel Bosch's return and resumption of control of the government is against U.S. interest in view of extremists in the coup and Communist advocacy of Bosch return."[7]

By the time this embassy cable was sent, the pro-Bosch forces had already pulled off a virtually bloodless coup; moreover, street crowds, made up largely of poor people, supported both the coup and Bosch's return to office.[8] If we had done nothing, Bosch would have been restored as the lawfully elected president.

According to a cable sent to the State Department by our chargé d'affaires in Santo Domingo, the Dominican Republic's officers asked him whether the United States would back them if they started fighting against the pro-Bosch forces. The chargé "reluctantly agreed to the de los Santos-Wessin [two Air Force officers] plan even though it could mean more bloodshed." His cable continued, "Our attachés have stressed to the three military leaders, Rivera, de los Santos and Wessin, our strong feeling everything possible should be done to prevent a Communist takeover."[9] Buoyed by the promise of U.S. support, the Dominican Air Force began to strafe the National Palace on April 25.[10] It was this strafing that resulted in most civilian casualties in the Dominican fighting.[11]

Although the administration claimed to favor neither the anti-Bosch nor pro-Bosch forces,[12] Ambassador Bennett encouraged the pro-Bosch forces to give up,[13] while our embassy's military attachés plotted military strategy with the Dominican officers,[14] urging them to take up the fight after the pro-Bosch units appeared to have won.[15]

Our embassy also provided material support, granting a request by the Dominican Air Force officers for walkie-talkies, just prior to the intervention; in addition, Ambassador Bennett gave them food and other equipment.[16] To hinder the Bosch elements, U.S. military intelligence jammed radio broadcasts of the pro-Bosch forces to keep them from getting their message to the public.[17] To cover salaries for the junta's troops, the U.S. embassy gave the junta a reported $750,000.[18]

Once the Marines landed, they assisted the Dominican officers against the pro-Bosch units. Fearing that a direct U.S. attack on the Bosch partisans might backfire, Johnson secretly instructed the Joint Chiefs of Staff to ensure that the pro-Bosch forces were defeated not by outright assault but by attrition.[19] At press briefings in Santo Domingo, American military officers referred to the anti-Bosch forces as "friendlies" and to the pro-Bosch units as "unfriendlies."[20] The Marines set up a perimeter to confine the pro-Bosch forces to a small downtown area, thereby preventing them from advancing and making it easier for the junta forces to attack them.[21]

U.S. Army airborne units coordinated efforts with the Marines. Landing at the air force officers' headquarters located on the San Isidro air base, airborne units secured it for them and moved toward downtown Santo Domingo, where they seized a key bridge from the pro-Bosch forces in heavy fighting.[22] They then occupied part of the downtown area itself and, after linking up with the Marines, began to patrol downtown Santo Domingo.[23] There the combined American forces made little pretense of neutrality, setting up checkpoints jointly with the Dominican junta to check suspected Bosch supporters for weapons,[24] and on occasion exchanging fire with pro-Bosch forces.[25] The American military stopped the delivery of supplies, the aim being, as one of our officers later told a reporter, to starve the Bosch supporters into submission. The Marines and airborne units helped the junta forces capture the pro-Bosch radio station and do a house-by-house sweep in order to find pro-Bosch combatants.[26] Thus, U.S. units played a key role in helping the anti-Bosch forces consolidate power.[27]

While the Johnson administration was apparently motivated by anti-communism, it never made a solid case that the Dominican strife had much to do with the East-West split, or that leftists controlled the pro-Bosch forces.[28] Johnson claimed to the press that U.S. intelligence had identified fifty-eight "Communists and Castroites," whom he called "evil persons who had been trained in overthrowing governments and in seizing governments and establishing Communist control."[29] But the list contained so many factual errors that reporters quickly discredited it; indeed the administration had no evidence whatsoever that the persons listed were even active in the revolt, much less in charge of it.[30]

Leftists, in fact, played only a minor role in the Dominican conflict.[31] Of the Dominican Republic's three leftist parties, the Dominican Communist party (pro-Soviet), the Dominican Popular Movement (pro-China), and the June 14 Party (pro-Cuba), none was involved in planning the pro-Bosch coup;[32] as events unfolded, the three parties could not even agree among themselves how to react.[33]

Once fighting began, leftists did go into the streets in support of the pro-Bosch faction, but leadership remained squarely with both the military and politicians across the political spectrum.[34] Senator Fulbright, who took evidence on this issue, found "little basis" for "the assertion that the rebels were Communist-dominated or certain to become so; on the contrary, the evidence suggests a chaotic situation in which no single faction was dominant at the outset and in which everybody, including the United States, had opportunities to influence the shape and course of the rebellion."[35]

Fulbright told the Senate that U.S. policy "throughout the whole affair" had been "characterized by a lack of candor."[36] Administration officials in both Washington and Santo Domingo operated from a cold war mindset that led them to interpret events in an East-West framework.[37] The State Department, stung by having "lost" Cuba, was perhaps predisposed to find a Cuban hand.[38] Johnson's aim from the beginning of the intervention in the Dominican Republic was ideological;[39] when he could no longer pretend to be saving U.S. citizens, he gave a public airing to what had been his true motive all along—a fear that the Dominican Republic would go Communist.[40]

Was the fight against communism worth the candle? Was it worth concocting stories that kept the public and Congress from assessing what a president was doing? I was beginning to have doubts, not so long after my pronouncements in my Marine reserve unit of the need to stop communism in Indochina. About that time I got a chance to view life from the other side, after Eisenhower and Khrushchev negotiated a university student exchange program. Each probably thought he would get more useful information than the other, which he could then use to advantage in the cold war. But I had a different idea. If the United States were to buy Soviet products, I thought, and sell them ours, perhaps we would develop a mutual interest in the other's continued existence.

To promote this trade, I found a place for myself, in 1966, in the

Eisenhower-Khrushchev exchange program, to do research at Moscow University. I would study the Soviet system of export and import and write an explanation of it from the technical side, so that people at home could understand how to buy and sell there. Then trade would flourish, and perhaps peace would break out.

My room in Moscow was in a severe-looking skyscraper dormitory on the city's outskirts. The view I had from my window of the Kremlin, with the sun reflecting off the gold cupolas of its cathedrals, was so splendid that it made getting up on below-zero mornings almost a pleasure. The subway took me downtown, where I pored over trade laws and yellowing documents in a reading room across the street from the Kremlin itself. And all the while missiles in silos in Nebraska or Oklahoma were pointed at my head. I knew that Soviet missiles were aimed at our cities as well, but it seemed ironic to be living in the prime target zone of our own missiles. Would the war start while I was there, and would I be hit by one of our missiles?

The friends I made in Moscow were also in the prime target zone. They were not, however, the faceless "Soviets" whose history I had studied but real people, with names, personalities, character flaws, senses of humor. And they were suffering from the cold war more than we were, because even with a smaller economy they were building a military to match ours.

The cold war entered my life in Moscow in another way, although I did not learn of it until later. During those years the CIA routinely opened mail coming from the Soviet Union. As part of this mail cover, they intercepted the letters I wrote home. A few years later, after the CIA program was revealed, Congress, in legislation against government secrecy, required agencies to turn over documents they had collected about individuals. So I wrote the CIA, which sent me photocopies of all my letters. I don't know if my letters yielded anything valuable. Several recounted my difficulty coping with the ancient electric washing machines in which I did my laundry at Moscow University. But if the CIA was concerned about a "laundry gap" between the two countries, I may have provided valuable information.

Notes

1. "Statement by President Johnson," May 2, 1965, DSB, vol. 52, pp. 744–47 (1965).

2. "Secretary Discusses Situation in Dominican Republic," May 8, 1965, DSB, vol. 52, p. 842 (1965).

3. "Statement by President Johnson," May 2, 1965, DSB, vol. 52, p. 745 (1965).

4. David Wise, *The Politics of Lying: Government Deception, Secrecy, and Power* (1973), p. 42; Tad Szulc, *Dominican Diary* (1965), pp. 50–51.

5. *Congressional Record*, vol. 111, p. 23858, September 15, 1965 (statement of Sen. J. William Fulbright).

6. Ibid., p. 23855.

7. Theodore Draper, *The Dominican Revolt: A Case Study in American Policy* (1968), pp. 60–61.

8. Piero Gleijeses, *The Dominican Crisis: The 1965 Constitutionalist Revolt and American Intervention* (1978), pp. 161, 176, 182, 185, 187, 208, 212–13, 224.

9. Draper, *The Dominican Revolt*, p. 61.

10. Ibid., pp. 60–61. Gleijeses, *The Dominican Crisis*, pp. 191–95.

11. Draper, *The Dominican Revolt*, p. 95. Abraham F. Lowenthal, *The Dominican Intervention* (1972), pp. 78, 89–90.

12. Szulc, *Dominican Diary*, p. 79.

13. John Bartlow Martin, *Overtaken by Events: The Dominican Crisis from the Fall of Trujillo to the Civil War* (1966), pp. 653–54.

14. Martin, *Overtaken by Events*, p. 658; Lowenthal, *The Dominican Intervention*, p. 119; Szulc, *Dominican Diary*, pp. 56, 243.

15. Draper, *The Dominican Revolt*, pp. 74–76.

16. *Congressional Record*, vol. 111, p. 23855, September 15, 1965 (statement of Sen. J. William Fulbright); Martin, *Overtaken by Events*, p. 655; Draper, *The Dominican Revolt*, pp. 99–102, 123.

17. Lowenthal, *The Dominican Intervention*, p. 205; Szulc, *Dominican Diary*, p. 177.

18. Szulc, *Dominican Diary*, p. 200.

19. Lowenthal, *The Dominican Intervention*, pp. 116–18.

20. Szulc, *Dominican Diary*, p. 124.

21. Lowenthal, *The Dominican Intervention*, pp. 114, 131, 139; Draper, *The Dominican Revolt*, pp. 132, 185–86.

22. Lowenthal, *The Dominican Intervention*, p. 115; Szulc, *Dominican Diary*, p. 78.

23. Lowenthal, *The Dominican Intervention*, pp. 120, 127; Szulc, *Dominican Diary*, pp. 79, 109.

24. Szulc, *Dominican Diary*, pp. 104, 158; James Nelson Goodsell, "Dominican Role of U.S. Clouded," *Christian Science Monitor*, May 18, 1965, p. 1, col. 4.

25. Tad Szulc, "14 Marines Are Wounded; 4 Army Men Are Also Hit," *New York Times*, May 1, 1965, p. A1, col. 6; *Congressional Record*, vol. 111, p. 23857, September 15, 1965 (statement of Sen. J. William Fulbright); Szulc, *Dominican Diary*, pp. 80–81, 187, 195, 214; David Atlee Phillips, *The Night Watch* (1977), p. 159.

26. Barnard L. Collier, "Dominican Junta Gets U.S. Help," *Washington Post*, May 20, 1965, p. A1, col. 8.

27. Szulc, *Dominican Diary*, p. 256.

28. Robert A. Caro, *The Years of Lyndon Johnson: Means of Ascent* (1990), p. xxv; Draper, *The Dominican Revolt*, p. 65.

29. Max Frankel, "Red Role in Rising Grows," *New York Times*, May 2, 1965,

p. A1, col. 5; "Remarks by President Johnson," May 4, 1965, DSB, vol. 52, pp. 821–22 (1965). Draper, *The Dominican Revolt,* p. 91.

30. Frank Cormier, *LBJ: The Way He Was* (1977), p. 188; Philip Geyelin, *Lyndon Johnson and the World* (1966), p. 253; Draper, *The Dominican Revolt,* pp. 141–43; Szulc, *Dominican Diary,* p. 70.

31. Szulc, *Dominican Diary,* pp. 82–83, 108; Gleijeses, *The Dominican Crisis,* p. 207; Lowenthal, *The Dominican Intervention,* p. 48.

32. Draper, *The Dominican Revolt,* pp. 66–68, 87; Lowenthal, *The Dominican Intervention,* pp. 40, 56–57; *Congressional Record,* vol. 111, p. 23857, September 15, 1965 (statement of Sen. J. William Fulbright).

33. Martin, *Overtaken by Events,* p. 651; Gleijeses, *The Dominican Crisis,* p. 211.

34. Gleijeses, *The Dominican Crisis,* pp. 224, 229–30, 251; Draper, *The Dominican Revolt,* pp. 68–71; *Congressional Record,* vol. 111, pp. 23857–58, September 15, 1965 (statement of Sen. J. William Fulbright).

35. *Congressional Record,* vol. 111, p. 23859, September 15, 1965 (statement of Sen. J. William Fulbright).

36. Ibid., p. 23855.

37. Geyelin, *Lyndon B. Johnson and the World,* p. 254.

38. Lowenthal, *The Dominican Intervention,* pp. 25–26, 31.

39. Szulc, *Dominican Diary,* p. 19.

40. Phillips, *The Night Watch,* p. 144.

16

Cambodia: Fish in the Craters

Flying over Cambodia in 1979, I was puzzled by what appeared to be large ponds, all perfectly circular, across the countryside. Since cultivation of fish is a major Cambodian industry, the Cambodians, I thought, must have gone to great pains to cut the ponds so precisely. But I kept seeing more. Could they have so many fish ponds?

Once in Phnom Penh, I learned that the holes were not the product of Cambodian handiwork, but craters from bombs dropped by American B-52s. From 1969 to 1975, the air force dropped half a million tons on Cambodia, not as much as in Laos or Vietnam, but still enough to alter the character of the countryside.[1] My first guess had not been completely wrong, however, because once the craters filled with water, the Cambodians did use them to cultivate fish.

Our military action in Cambodia came first as an outgrowth of the action in Vietnam. Beginning in 1967, our commanders there decided that the National Liberation Front (NLF) must have a central command post. After failing to find one in South Vietnam, they crossed the border into Cambodia to look for something suitable.[2] When that effort failed to turn up the desired command post, the commanders, beginning in 1969, asked for permission to bomb in Cambodia, both to find the command post and to destroy other suspected NLF bases. President Nixon approved but insisted that the operation remain secret, because Congress had not authorized action in Cambodia. With opposition to the Vietnam war building in the United States, Nixon could not risk public discussion of our forces operating in still another country of Indochina.

In March 1969, the air force began using B-52s for bombing raids over Cambodia.[3] The bombing was heavy, and the Cambodian government was quick to complain. Cambodian Prince Norodom Sihanouk told the press that the bombs were hitting not Communist soldiers, but "peasants, women and children in particular."[4] The press, however, all but ignored Sihanouk's protests, while the American public remained unaware of the Cambodia bombing.

In May 1970, Nixon sent a large troop force into Cambodia, announcing the operation publicly as one aimed at finding the NLF command post.[5] Lon Nol, who by then was the Cambodian leader, and also a U.S. ally, complained that the invasion violated Cambodian sovereignty.[6] There was little evidence that the NLF used Cambodia to any significant extent;[7] even if a command post did exist, a short-term operation could destroy it but could not prevent it from being reestablished. The press, skeptical of Nixon's "official" rationale, questioned whether he had some other, secret motive for the Cambodia invasion.[8]

In any event, Nixon kept the troops in Cambodia only a few weeks, declaring, as he pulled them out, that they had "completed successfully the destruction of enemy base areas" on the Cambodian side of the border with Vietnam.[9] Ellsworth Bunker, our ambassador in Vietnam, declared the invasion "perhaps the most successful of the war."[10] Vice-President Spiro Agnew said that the operations resulted in "the cleaning out of the sanctuaries."[11]

Beyond these statements from official Washington, however, there was little to indicate that our troops had actually found any NLF bases. All that could be said for sure was that our troops had destroyed a number of Cambodian villages, apparently to keep any enemy forces from using them.[12]

After the ground invasion, the Nixon administration continued the aerial bombardment of Cambodia, no longer keeping it secret; Nixon did not acknowledge, however, that we had bombed prior to the incursion.[13] It was not until July 1973, in fact, that the Defense Department admitted that it had bombed Cambodia before May 1970.[14]

It was then revealed that from March 1969 to May 1970, American B-52s dropped 108,000 tons of bombs on Cambodia.[15]

When the Senate armed services committee finally learned that we had carried on secret bombing, it called in Defense Department officials to explain and to provide details. The air force had filed reports with the committee in 1969 on bombing activity in Indochina, but those reports reflected no raids over Cambodia. Senator Harold Hughes of Iowa, outraged at the omission, called it "official deception."[16]

What came out at the Senate hearings was that the air force kept the pre-1970 bombing a secret by failing to keep records of the raids.[17] When it bombed in Cambodia, the air force reported instead that it had bombed in South Vietnam, specifying some locations that had in fact not been touched.[18] Air force Major Hal Knight, who supervised the crews, told the committee that when he asked his superiors why he should falsify reports, they replied that it was for political reasons.[19]

Since Prince Sihanouk already knew that Cambodia was being bombed before 1970, Senator Hughes said that the only people the air force deceived "were the people of the United States of America."[20] Senator Stuart Symington of Missouri, referring to the power given to Congress to declare war, called the secret bombing unconstitutional, and bemoaned the fact that the air force "dropped a hundred thousand tons" on Cambodia, "and I had no idea you dropped one ton."[21] Stuart Symington determined that the bombing had "accomplished very little" from a military standpoint.[22]

As for the bombing in Cambodia after May 1970, President Nixon announced on June 30, 1970, that the sole purpose of further bombing raids would be to stop "enemy efforts to move supplies and personnel through Cambodia toward South Viet-Nam and to reestablish base areas relevant to the war in Viet-Nam."[23] But on June 13, 1970, a secret cable drafted by the Joint Chiefs of Staff authorized bombing in Cambodia "in any situation which involves a serious threat to major Cambodian positions."[24] By this the Joint Chiefs meant that bombing was to be done to support the government of Cambodia, which faced a strong guerrilla insurgency in rural areas of the country. Thus, contrary to what President Nixon had announced publicly, the bombing was meant to support the government of Lon Nol, which was sympathetic to the United States and a recipient of American military aid.[25] The opposition was a leftist insurgency led by the Khmer Rouge—Khmer being the predominant ethnic group of Cambodia, while Rouge ("red" in French) stood for their socialist philosophy.

The Joint Chiefs' directive was not made public, however, and the administration continued to deny that it was intervening in Cambodia's civil war. It denied, in fact, that there even was a civil war, claiming instead that the hostilities in Cambodia were between the Cambodian government on the one side, and the NLF and North Vietnamese forces on the other. Vice-President Agnew declared in 1970, "this is not a civil war in Cambodia"; the fighting there was the result of "outrageous aggression by the North Vietnamese."[26] When in 1975 the Khmer Rouge marched into Phnom Penh and took over the country, it became obvious that the administration's story had been false.

As Congress debated Cambodian policy in 1970, the administration played down the extent of its bombing in Cambodia.[27] In 1971, however, a Government Accounting Office (GAO) study of the Cambodia bombing found that two million Cambodians, of a total population of six million, had been forced to abandon their home areas. The air force's bombing, the GAO concluded, had wrought immense civilian casualties and was "a very significant cause of refugees."[28] As in Laos, the bombing was aimed at beating back a leftist insurgency by depriving it of a population within which to operate. If, as Mao Tse-tung said, guerrillas must swim like fish in the sea, the air force would then dry up the sea.

In 1972, President Nixon stopped the bombing of Cambodia;[29] but when the January 1973 peace agreement for Vietnam ended our bombing campaign in that country, the Air Force redirected its B-52s to Cambodia, bombing as much there in the first half of 1973 as it had done from 1969 to 1972.[30] As on the Laotian Plain of Jars, farming became impossible in much of Cambodia, with peasants streaming into cities to escape.[31] Under pressure from Congress, the air force finally put an end to the Cambodia bombing in August 1973.[32]

The bombing of Cambodia, first totally secret and then partially secret, led to enactment of the War Powers Resolution, requiring a president to notify Congress if he sends troops abroad for combat, and establishing a procedure for Congress to stop the operation if it disagrees.[33] It was under this law that President Bush notified Congress when he sent troops to Saudi Arabia in August 1990.

Our support for Lon Nol's government, as it turned out, was to no avail. As in Laos, the bombing did nothing to stop the rural insurgency that was its target. If anything, the bombing helped the insurgents, because the Khmer Rouge called for a self-reliant, peasant-based society, which would build up Cambodia's economy without foreign investment or extensive export or import. A high level of discipline would be required, in addition to hard physical work. The Khmer Rouge planned new and extensive peasant communities; the bombing only reinforced the Khmer Rouge's arguments of the futility of relying on the Western world.

Moreover, the mass influx of refugees into Phnom Penh as a result of the bombing provided an ideal jumping-off point for the Khmer Rouge's project. Peasants lived in shanties on the outskirts of Phnom Penh, where the city could not provide them with services, and where disease was rampant. But for the Khmer Rouge, these migrants formed the base for new peasant communities. Since many existing villages had already been emptied because of the bombing, the Khmer Rouge could shuffle the population at will.

Implementing its plan after taking Phnom Penh in April 1975, the Khmer Rouge drove out nearly the entire population, forcing the people to new locations to work in highly disciplined farming brigades. On any who protested, the Khmer Rouge inflicted harsh treatment, killing large numbers of people in an effort to stamp its mold on the population. The Khmer Rouge held power until 1979, when Vietnam sent troops to Cambodia and helped to power a dissident faction of the Khmer Rouge that opposed its harsh policies.

As for Phnom Penh, from 1975 to 1979 it was a ghost town. When I saw the city in 1979, I could tell that it had once been an attractive, sleepy colonial capital of broad, well laid-out avenues showing the influence of the French who built it. But now houses stood empty and old Renaults, abandoned and inoperable, blocked driveways, where their owners had left them four years before.

I was in Phnom Penh as an expert witness at a trial organized by the new Cambodian government against the top two Khmer Rouge leaders, Pol Pot and Ieng Sary. Since they were both off in the Thailand-Cambodia border area leading the remnants of the Khmer Rouge against the new government, the trial was held without them. The charge against Pol Pot and Ieng Sary was genocide, a crime that had been defined by the 1948 Genocide Convention, drafted in the wake of the mass killings in Europe during World War II.

For four days, witnesses, whose testimony could be corroborated by other sources, told of mass murder, and many instances of individual and small-group killings by Khmer Rouge cadres. Some of the killings were aimed at officials of the prior governments, others at persons who opposed the forced employment in highly disciplined agriculture. A parade of witnesses described how members of their own families had been killed; few could complete their testimony without losing their composure.

After the witnesses had completed their testimony, I gave the court an explanation of the law on genocide, describing how it was defined under the Genocide Convention, and giving my opinion that if the evidence presented at the trial were accurate, genocide had indeed been committed. I also mentioned the bombing of Cambodia by the U.S. Air Force, which, I said, "destroyed much of the Cambodian countryside through its bombing. The mass influx of people into Cambodia's cities as a result of that bombing led to shortage and disease in the cities." Those conditions, I concluded, set the stage for the genocide that followed.[34]

The air force's bombing of Cambodia left physical and moral scars that will continue to haunt the country for years to come, all done by a president who officially denied it. The public had no basis on which to object, because until 1970 it did not know the bombing was occurring, and from 1970 to 1973, it did not have knowledge of the bombing's full scope.

The bombing, however, was not the last chapter in our military action in Cambodia. In a bizarre postscript, barely a month after the Khmer Rouge came to power in April 1975, a naval vessel of the new Khmer Rouge government seized a U.S.-registered merchant vessel with an American crew. The SS *Mayaguez* was stopped and led to Koh Tang Island, off the Cambodian coast, where it was forced to anchor.[35] The reasons for the seizure were not made clear, as the *Mayaguez* was apparently on an ordinary commercial run, but the Khmer Rouge government, only just installed in power, may have suspected it of electronic surveillance of the Cambodian coast.

In any event, the Ford administration decided to retake the ship, and after demanding its return, sent U.S. Navy vessels to positions near

Koh Tang island. President Gerald Ford said that the deployment was to prevent the Cambodian navy from taking U.S. sailors to the mainland. On May 14, Cambodian authorities met Ford's demands, turning over to the navy first the *Mayaguez,* at 9:00 P.M., EDT, and then its crew, at 11:30 P.M., EDT.

The return of the *Mayaguez* and its crew did not end the episode, however; in the early hours of May 15, a force of U.S. Marines led an assault on Koh Tang Island. In an official statement President Ford declared that its purpose was "to search out and rescue such other Americans as might still be held there." In addition, our jet fighters strafed a military airfield and other military targets on the Cambodian mainland, in order "to prevent reinforcement or support from the mainland of the Cambodian forces detaining the American vessel and crew."[36]

As this sequence shows, by the time we assaulted the island and bombed the mainland, we had already recovered both the *Mayaguez* and its crew.[37] Navy officials, when asked to explain, acknowledged that it was unnecessary to attack; however, they claimed they had not gotten word of the return of the vessel and crew soon enough to call off the raids, which, they said, had been planned prior to the return.

Several hours, in fact, had elapsed before the navy's subsequent raid. The assault on and bombing of the island, skeptics speculated, were a reprisal by an administration still smarting from the recent fall of its allied governments in both Cambodia and South Vietnam. Some thought the United States was trying to show that it was still tough even after its losses.[38]

Indeed, administration officials substantiated these suspicions when they described the operation as a warning to North Korea and other communist countries that the United States, in the wake of the Vietnam war, "still stood ready to meet force with force to protect its interests."[39] Officials speaking on background said that the incident provided "a test of American determination in Southeast Asia." Demonstrating that determination was important after the collapse of the Cambodian and South Vietnam governments.[40] So it was not, as the navy argued, that we could not stop a raid already set in motion. We strafed and assaulted Cambodian territory to make a point to someone else.

Notes

1. William S. Turley, *The Second Indochina War: A Short Political and Military History, 1954–1975* (1986), p. 87.

2. *Bombing in Cambodia,* Hearings before the Committee on Armed Services, U.S. Senate, 93rd Cong., 1st sess. (1973), pp. 231–48, 493.

3. James William Gibson, *The Perfect War: Technowar in Vietnam* (1986), pp. 404–5; *Bombing in Cambodia,* pp. 80, 98, 104, 132, 279–80, 347, 482.

4. *Bombing in Cambodia,* pp. 158–59.

5. Robert B. Semple, Jr., "Nixon Sends Combat Forces to Cambodia to Drive Communists from Staging Zone," *New York Times,* May 1, 1970, p. A1, col. 8.

6. William Shawcross, *Sideshow: Kissinger, Nixon and the Destruction of Cambodia* (1979), p. 149.

7. Edward S. Herman and Noam Chomsky, *Manufacturing Consent: The Political Economy of the Mass Media* (1988), pp. 268–69.

8. Haynes Johnson, "The Irreconcilable Conflict between Press and Government: 'Whose Side Are You On?' " in Thomas M. Franck and Edward Weisband, eds., *Secrecy and Foreign Policy* (1974), pp. 165, 173.

9. Richard Nixon, "A Report on the Conclusion of the Cambodian Operation," DSB, vol. 63, p. 65 (1970).

10. Ellsworth Bunker, "A Review of Progress and Problems in Vietnam," DSB, vol. 64, p. 207 (1971).

11. "News Conference, September 1, San Clemente, California," DSB, vol. 63, p. 385 (1970).

12. Shawcross, *Sideshow,* pp. 150–52.

13. *Bombing in Cambodia,* p. 40.

14. Edgar O'Ballance, *The Wars in Vietnam, 1954–1980* (1981), p. 155; *Bombing in Cambodia,* p. 496.

15. *Bombing in Cambodia,* p. 487.

16. Ibid., p. 38.

17. Ibid., p. 11.

18. Ibid., pp. 98, 132, 352, 358, 483.

19. Ibid., p. 5.

20. Ibid., p. 160.

21. Ibid., p. 101.

22. Ibid., p. 180.

23. Richard Nixon, "A Report on the Conclusion of the Cambodian Operation," DSB, vol. 63, p. 72 (1970).

24. Shawcross, *Sideshow,* p. 214.

25. "U.S. and Cambodia Sign Agreement Regulating Military Assistance," DSB, vol. 63, p. 387 (1970).

26. "News Conference, September 1, San Clemente, California," DSB, vol. 63, p. 386 (1970).

27. Shawcross, *Sideshow,* p. 214.

28. Terence Smith, "Refugee Problem in Cambodia Laid to Allied Bombs," *New York Times,* December 5, 1971, p. A1, col. 3.

29. Shawcross, *Sideshow,* p. 218.

30. "Pentagon's Statistics Underscore Intensity of Cambodia Bombing," *New York Times,* June 22, 1973, p. A2, col. 3.

31. Shawcross, *Sideshow,* p. 319.

32. *Bombing in Cambodia,* p. 482.

33. U.S. Code, vol. 50, §1541.

34. Statement of John Quigley, Professor of Law, U.S.A., People's Revolutionary Tribunal Held in Phnom Penh for the Trial of the Genocide Crime of the Pol Pot-Ieng Sary Clique, August 15–19, 1979 (unpublished).

35. "Statement by White House Press Secretary," May 13, 1975, DSB, vol. 72, p. 719 (1975).

36. "Statement by President Ford," May 15, 1975, 12:27 A.M., E.D.T., DSB, vol. 72, p. 721 (1975); Letters (identical) from Gerald Ford to the President Pro Tempore, U.S. Senate, and to the Speaker, U.S. House of Representatives, May 15, 1975, DSB, vol. 72, pp. 721–22 (1975).

37. "Secretary Kissinger's News Conference of May 16," DSB, vol. 72, p. 760 (1975); "A Chronology of the *Mayaguez* Episode," *New York Times,* May 16, 1975, p. A14, col. 2; Bob Woodward, *The Commanders* (1991), p. 175.

38. "Secretary Kissinger's News Conference of May 24," DSB, vol. 72, p. 802 (1975).

39. Bernard Gwertzman, "U.S. Sees Foray for Ship as Signal to Communists," *New York Times,* May 16, 1975, p. A14, col. 7.

40. "Thailand Reports Marines' Arrival in Ship's Seizure," *New York Times,* May 14, 1975, p. A1, col. 8.

17

Angola: A Global Monroe Doctrine

In 1975, President Ford capitalized on the backing that earlier administrations had given to Colonel Mobutu in the Congo, which by then had been renamed Zaire. Mobutu, who remained our close ally, was aspiring by the mid-1970s to extend his influence elsewhere in Africa. Mobutu found support for these ambitions in Washington, where CIA Director William Colby viewed Zaire as "a future regional big power."[1] Both Colby and Secretary of State Henry Kissinger looked to Mobutu to oppose Soviet influence in Africa, and in particular to support us in Angola, where we were involved in a push-pull with the Soviet Union.[2]

Angola was of particular interest to Mobutu; an enclave called Cabinda, located on Zaire's Atlantic coast but belonging to Angola, had a huge pool of oil that Gulf Oil was busily tapping.[3] For Kissinger, Angola was of interest because in 1975 it was to gain independence from Portugal, following the overthrow of the long-time Portuguese dictatorship in 1974 and Lisbon's subsequent decision to free its African colonies. In Angola three independence groups that had fought Portugal were vying for control: the Popular Movement for the Liberation of Angola (MPLA), the National Front for the Liberation of Angola (FNLA), and the National Union for the Total Independence of Angola (UNITA). Although the three did not differ markedly in outlook, the

157

MPLA was more critical than the others of the United States' support for Portugal during the years it refused to grant Angola independence.[4] All three had received Soviet-bloc aid, but the MPLA had tighter relations than the others with the Soviet Union. The FNLA had close ties to President Mobutu, as it was based in Zaire, where it enjoyed Mobutu's encouragement.

Secretary Kissinger, smarting over losing Indochina to communism and determined not to let leftists win elsewhere, saw Angola as a cold war battlefield.[5] The Soviet Union had been giving arms to the MPLA when it was fighting Portugal, but ended that aid in 1973.[6] However, when the Soviets resumed arms aid in the fall of 1974, Kissinger feared that an MPLA-led Angola would become a Soviet beachhead in Africa.[7]

Kissinger's connection to U.S. policy on Angola went beyond his role as secretary of state, because in addition Kissinger headed the so-called Forty Committee, an interagency body that oversaw American covert operations around the world. In January 1975, the Forty Committee authorized aid to the FNLA to help it against the MPLA, its main rival in Angola.[8] From bases in Zaire the FNLA attacked Angola in an effort to take territory around Luanda, the Angolan capital.[9] The Soviet Union responded in March 1975 by sending the MPLA a new quantity of arms.[10]

With Portugal scheduled to leave Angola in November 1975, Nathaniel Davis, assistant secretary of state for African affairs, proposed to Kissinger that the United States promote negotiations among the three rival parties. Unlike Kissinger, Davis thought that Angola was "basically an African problem," not an East-West confrontation.[11] Along with Davis, other administration officials opposed Kissinger's approach of trying to "face off the Russians" in Angola.[12]

Kissinger, however, rejected these suggestions; in June and July 1975, he got the Forty Committee to approve another arms shipment to the FNLA and, for the first time, to supply arms as well to UNITA, which also opposed the MPLA and which seemed to lean to the West.[13] On the basis of the Forty Committee decision, President Ford signed a secret order authorizing the aid to both groups.[14]

In August, the aid began in earnest, when the CIA set up a task force in Washington to run the Angola operation. First the task force planned a propaganda-information campaign for the FNLA and UNITA. CIA propaganda experts in Zaire planted (true) stories in the wire services to expose Soviet arms shipments and (false) stories that Cuban soldiers operating with the MPLA had raped Angolan girls. CIA publicists also wrote position papers for the FNLA, which it used at the United Nations.[15]

The task force generated a flurry of activity: a CIA team flew to Zaire, where it briefed the FNLA and UNITA on tactics and set up radio systems for FNLA communications inside Angola. CIA cables flew between Zaire and Washington, as CIA officers brought in weapons and equipment and trained the FNLA and UNITA on their use.[16] In September, the administration allocated a new round of aid to the FNLA and UNITA; in November, it gave more aid.[17]

The Forty Committee set up a special supervisory group to oversee the CIA's handling of the Angola operation, with representatives from the State Department, Defense Department, and White House.[18] From Zaire, CIA personnel visited FNLA and UNITA positions in Angola to check on operations.[19] What they found convinced them that they needed to train and supervise the FNLA and UNITA more closely; therefore, more CIA personnel went into combat areas in Angola.[20] There they advised and organized, drawing up battle plans and helping the FNLA and UNITA figure out how to put them into operation.[21] When Assistant Secretary Davis testified on Angola policy before the Senate Subcommittee on Africa on July 14, he gave no hint of any American assistance to UNITA or FNLA.[22] Davis, however, so opposed the Angola operation that he resigned in protest shortly after testifying.[23] Kissinger replaced him with William Schaufele, who shared Kissinger's perspective on Angola.[24]

The CIA operation was not enough to put the FNLA and UNITA over the top, however, because the two groups needed more combatants. So the CIA recruited and hired mercenaries, mainly Portuguese and French, and sent them to FNLA and UNITA units in Angola.[25] The administration also convinced Mobutu to send in Zairian troops to help against the MPLA; Mobutu quickly obliged,[26] but his troops did so poorly that they were soon withdrawn.[27] For a time the operation made progress. CIA Director Colby later took credit for "completely reversing" the momentum away from the MPLA. The MPLA had to ask for more help from the Soviet Union and approached Cuba, which sent several thousand troops to fight on its side.[28] For all the CIA activity in Angola, Congress and the public remained in the dark, as the Ford administration kept the Angola operation under close wraps; even the media could not penetrate its veil of secrecy.

Over the summer a new factor emerged in the Angola picture: South Africa entered the war, sending a small troop force into southern Angola in mid-August.[29] The press reported South Africa's role in Angola, even while it remained unaware of our own. South Africa's entry, however, brought political risks for the administration, which did not want to appear to be collaborating with the apartheid government, for no one would believe that South Africa had Angola's interests at heart. When asked at a press conference in November about South Africa's role, Kissinger replied, "the South Africans are not engaged officially; that is, they are not engaged with their own military forces."[30] But even as Kissinger spoke, South African regular troops were fighting alongside UNITA forces, as he well knew.[31] In October, South Africa sent a large force into central Angola to support UNITA,[32] while two South African armored columns accompanied UNITA almost to the outskirts of Luanda.[33]

Kissinger's answer to the press, then, obscured the fact that we were effectively allied with South Africa in supporting the FNLA and UNITA.[34] UNITA was obtaining arms and training from South Africa, and the FNLA was getting South African heavy artillery.[35] CIA Director Colby, concerned that if our collusion with South Africa became known, our reputation in independent Africa would plummet, claimed later that the CIA "stayed well away from" South Africa.[36] But CIA officials consulted regularly with South Africa's Bureau of State Security to coordinate Angolese operations.[37] Under cross-examination in the U.S. Senate, Deputy Assistant Secretary of State for African Affairs Edward Mulcahy acknowledged that after South African forces entered Angola, we had "routine exchange of intelligence" with South Africa and that this included discussion of its troop movements in Angola.[38] South African officials even claimed that they entered Angola with our blessing.[39]

It was not only the South Africa connection that concerned the administration, however; after Vietnam, public sentiment would not have backed a war of any kind in Angola, and the administration knew it. So it went to great pains to keep the public from finding out about the CIA support to the FNLA and UNITA.[40] Kissinger publicly criticized the Soviet Union for helping the MPLA but gave no hint that the Soviet aid of March 1975 had come only in response to our own.[41] "Events in Angola have taken a distressing turn, with widespread violence," Kissinger said. "We are most alarmed at the interference of extracontinental powers who do not wish Africa well and whose involvement is inconsistent with the promise of true independence. We believe a fair and peaceful solution must be negotiated, giving all groups representing the Angolan people a fair role in its future."[42]

To the public the administration denied providing any arms to the FNLA or UNITA, but to Congress, in secret briefings, CIA Director Colby admitted that arms were being sent, although he denied any involvement by CIA personnel.[43] The administration's secrecy ultimately doomed the operation, however, because there was no way to respond to the Soviet and Cuban counteraid without higher visibility. The operation came apart at the seams in late 1975, when the press finally exposed our activities, giving details on what the CIA was doing.[44] As pressure built in Congress to end the operation, Kissinger continued to view it in apocalyptic terms: if Congress forced termination, the Soviet Union and other countries might not take our warnings seriously in other parts of the world. Kissinger, invoking a doomsday scenario, claimed that Syria might invade Israel, with Soviet support.[45]

Hearings on Angola were called in the Senate, and Kissinger was summoned to testify. The senators wanted to know who had started the arms aid to Angola, the United States or the Soviet Union. Dissembling, Kissinger told the senators that our aid to the FNLA and UNITA began only in August 1975, making it seem like a response to the increase in Soviet aid to the MPLA in March.[46] But Schaufele, Kissinger's new assistant secretary, told the senators the truth, i.e., that we had begun funding the FNLA in January.[47]

Kissinger kept insisting that we were "responding" to "Soviet military moves" in Angola, to "outside interference initiated by the Soviet Union." Moreover, we were maintaining strict neutrality regarding the three Angola factions. "We are not opposing any particular faction," Kissinger argued. "In Angola we have consistently advocated a government representing all three factions . . . [and] never opposed participation by the Soviet-backed Popular Movement for the Liberation of Angola, the MPLA." Kissinger also denied that we collaborated with South Africa.[48]

Kissinger and other State Department officials who testified in the Senate, and in the House as well, did not disclose the existence of the CIA Task Force, or the fact that CIA operatives operating out of Zaire worked with the FNLA and UNITA in the field in Angola. They denied that the CIA recruited mercenaries.[49] Senator John Tunney of California, who accepted Schauffele's version of events, decried the coverup, stating, "There is a pattern of American orchestration and involvement that goes far beyond what the administration has admitted."[50]

Senator Joseph Biden of Delaware objected that the administration twice changed the reason for its involvement in Angola. First, the CIA told him in a private briefing that the aim was to respond to a request from Zambia and Zaire, because they feared the MPLA. Then administration officials said that strategic issues were involved—the Atlantic sea lanes and the possibility of the spread of revolution to Brazil. But Kissinger gave the Senate a third reason as well—global considerations related to keeping the Soviet Union from dabbling in the Third World. Biden called Kissinger's concept of responding anywhere to the Soviet Union a "global Monroe Doctrine."[51]

A House committee also looking into the Angola operation decided that the CIA prompted Soviet and Cuban aid, not vice versa. The committee found that those two countries acted in "reaction to U.S. efforts," and that the aid we had given the FNLA in January 1975 "panicked the Soviets" into new aid to the MPLA in March.[52]

Disgusted over the administration's deception and opposed to the CIA operation, Congress ended the Angola operation in February 1976 by passing a statute that prohibited any expenditure of funds in Angola for paramilitary operations.[53] By then the House Appropriations Committee was so suspicious of the administration that it did not trust the CIA to comply with this law, so it sent a special team of auditors to the CIA to make sure the agency would not cheat.[54]

With the CIA out of the picture, the FNLA soon collapsed, and UNITA withdrew to the southern reaches of Angola.[55] The Senate select committee on intelligence examining the operation complained that President Ford had not given Congress or the public a chance to assess the reasons for what it called "a large-scale covert paramilitary operation in Angola." The president had made a major foreign policy decision without telling anyone outside the administration, in an operation initiated, the committee said, "without any effort on the part of the executive branch to articulate, and win public support for, its overall policy in Africa."[56]

The Senate committee concluded that Secretary of State Kissinger had needlessly turned Angola into a cold war confrontation. The three Angolan factions, it said, were just three parts of an anticolonial movement trying to get Portugal to leave. But the East-West confrontation scenario was the world as Kissinger had presented it in his lectures on world affairs that I still remembered. In Kissinger's world, there were only two players. I understood why he viewed Angola as he did.

Notes

1. Leslie Gelb, "Should We Play Direct Tricks in the World?" *New York Times Magazine,* December 21, 1975, p. 15.
2. Leslie Gelb, "U.S., Soviet, China Reported Aiding Portugal, Angola," *New York Times,* September 25, 1975, p. A1, col. 1; Bernard Gwertzman, "US Seeks Rapid Aid to Zaire but Congress Is Wary," *New York Times,* October 16, 1975, p. A2, col. 4; Michael T. Kaufman, "The U.S.-Zaire Connection: Substantial," *New York Times,* January 4, 1976, p. D2, col. 3.
3. *Angola,* Hearings before the Subcommittee on African Affairs of the Committee on Foreign Relations, U.S. Senate, 94th Cong., 2d sess., 1976, pp. 109–10 (statement of Stephen Weissman).
4. John Marcum, "Lessons of Angola," *Foreign Affairs* 54 (April 1976): 410–12; *United States Policy on Angola,* Hearing before the Committee on International Relations, U.S. House of Representatives, 94th Cong., 2d sess., 1976, p. 8 (statement of Asst. Secretary of State William Schaufele).
5. John Stockwell, *In Search of Enemies: A CIA Story* (1978), p. 43; Nathaniel Davis, "The Angola Decision of 1975: A Personal Memoir," *Foreign Affairs* 57, no. 1 (Fall 1978): 124.
6. Stockwell, *In Search of Enemies,* p. 68.
7. Marcum, "Lessons of Angola," p. 413.
8. *Final Report: Foreign and Military Intelligence,* U.S. Senate, Select Committee to Study Governmental Operations with Respect to Intelligence Activities, Book I, 94th Cong., 2d sess., April 26, 1976, p. 151; Seymour Hersh, "Early Angola Aid by U.S. Reported," *New York Times,* December 19, 1975, p. A1, col. 2; Stephen R. Weissman, "CIA Covert Action in Zaire and Angola: Patterns and Consequences," *Political Science Quarterly* 94, no. 2 (Summer 1979): 282.
9. Stockwell, *In Search of Enemies,* p. 67; Marcum, "Lessons of Angola," p. 415.
10. Stockwell, *In Search of Enemies,* p. 68.
11. Davis, "The Angola Decision of 1975," p. 112.
12. Seymour Hersh, "Angola Aid Issue Opening Rifts in State Department," *New York Times,* December 14, 1975, p. A1, col. 4.
13. William Colby, *Honorable Men: My Life in the CIA* (1978), p. 422; Seymour Hersh, "Angola Aid Issue Opening Rifts in State Department," *New York Times,* December 14, 1975, p. A1, col. 4.
14. *Final Report: Foreign and Military Intelligence,* p. 152.
15. Stockwell, *In Search of Enemies,* pp. 72, 194–96.
16. Ibid., pp. 86–87.
17. *Final Report: Foreign and Military Intelligence,* p. 152.
18. Stockwell, *In Search of Enemies,* p. 94.
19. Ibid., pp. 121, 128, 138.
20. Ibid., p. 177.

21. Ibid.

22. "Department Discusses Situation in Angola," DSB, vol. 73, p. 212 (1975).

23. Seymour Hersh, "Angola Aid Issue Opening Rifts in State Department," *New York Times,* December 14, 1975, p. A1, col. 4; Davis, "The Angola Decision of 1975," p. 117.

24. *United States Policy on Angola,* p. 2.

25. Stockwell, *In Search of Enemies,* pp. 182–84, 220–25.

26. David B. Ottoway, "Zaire Conflict Poses Dilemma for U.S.," *Washington Post,* May 18, 1978, p. A18, col. 4; *Angola,* p. 165 (statement of Sen. John Tunney).

27. Madeleine Kalb, *The Congo Cables: The Cold War in Africa From Eisenhower to Kennedy* (1982), p. 382.

28. Colby, *Honorable Men,* p. 422; Marcum, "Lessons of Angola," p. 416.

29. *United States Policy on Angola,* pp. 22, 83.

30. "Secretary's News Conference of November 28," DSB, vol. 73, p. 897 (1975).

31. Stockwell, *In Search of Enemies,* p. 185; Fred Bridgland, "S. African Regulars Fight Inside Angola," *Washington Post,* November 23, 1975, p. A18, col. 1.

32. *Angola,* p. 165 (statement of Sen. John Tunney), 176 (statement of Asst. Secretary of State Schaufele).

33. David B. Ottoway, "Angola: Charges Prompt New Look at U.S. Role," *Washington Post,* May 10, 1978, p. A12, col. 1; Davis, "The Angola Decision of 1975," p. 122.

34. Gregory F. Treverton, *Covert Action: The Limits of Intervention in the Postwar World* (1987), p. 148.

35. Ottoway, "Angola"; *United States Policy on Angola,* p. 22 (statement of Deputy Secretary of State for African Affairs Edward Mulcahy).

36. Colby, *Honorable Men,* p. 422.

37. Stockwell, *In Search of Enemies,* pp. 187–88.

38. *Angola,* p. 187.

39. Marcum, "Lessons of Angola," p. 422.

40. Stockwell, *In Search of Enemies,* pp. 55, 170–71.

41. "Secretary's News Conference of November 28."

42. Henry Kissinger, "The United States and Africa: Strengthening the Relationship," DSB, vol. 73, p. 574 (1975).

43. Stockwell, *In Search of Enemies,* pp. 200, 227–30.

44. Ibid., p. 202; Hersh, "Angola Aid Issue Opening Rifts in State Department."

45. Bernard Gwertzman, "Kissinger Said to Warn Allon of Angola Danger," *New York Times,* January 9, 1976, p. A3, col. 3.

46. *Angola,* Hearings, pp. 10, 17.

47. Ibid., p. 185.

48. Ibid., pp. 7–13, 20, 53.

49. Ibid., p. 27 (statement of Secretary of State Kissinger).

50. Ibid., p. 166.

51. Ibid., pp. 45–46.

52. *Report,* Select Committee on Intelligence, U.S. House of Representatives, 94th Cong., 2d sess., as published in *Village Voice,* February 16, 1976, p. 85.

53. U.S. Congress, *Statutes at Large,* vol. 90, p. 166 (1976).

54. Stockwell, *In Search of Enemies,* p. 242.

55. Ibid., p. 234.

56. *Final Report: Foreign and Military Intelligence,* p. 445.

18

Shaba: A Congolese Reprise

In 1978, we again got involved in the Congo (Zaire), after a rebellion against U.S.-backed President Joseph Mobutu in Shaba, the new name for Katanga province. Following the turmoil the country experienced in the 1960s, which we reviewed in earlier chapters of this book, Zaire remained a fragile construct into the 1970s. The 1978 anti-Mobutu rebellion was led by former Shaba Province residents living in exile across the border in Angola; they were members of the Lunda tribe, whose territory extended across the Zaire-Angola border. This was one of many cases in which colonial borders had been drawn without regard to those who lived on the land. The rebels called themselves the Congo National Liberation Front, and their stated aim was to overthrow Mobutu.

Mobutu depicted the rebels as an outside group, which, from a nation-state standpoint, they were. When the rebellion broke out, Mobutu claimed that this outside contingent numbered between 3,000 and 4,000, but that estimate could not be verified.[1]

The situation was all the stickier because many of these Lunda rebels had fought for Katangan independence in 1960 when they still lived in the province. At that time, they fought alongside the Belgian mercenaries then employed by Moise Tshombe, who headed Katanga's government. After the Katanga secession failed, they, like the Belgian

165

mercenaries, took refuge in Angola, which was still a Portuguese colony. Angola was friendly territory for pro-Tshombe soldiers, since Tshombe was the champion of the Western mining companies.

After taking refuge in Angola, these Lunda fought on behalf of Portugal against the Zaire-based National Front for the Liberation of Angola (FNLA). When Portugal withdrew from Angola, the Lunda kept fighting the FNLA, but now on behalf of the Popular Movement for the Liberation of Angola (MPLA).[2] In 1977, there was a short-lived anti-Mobutu rebellion staged by Lunda in Shaba province; after it ended, many of those on the losing side joined their brethren in Angola, augmenting their numbers.[3]

The Lunda in Shaba province had ample reason to rebel against President Mobutu, because their province held the country's major mineral deposits, making it a particular focus of Mobutu's attention. The Lunda were upset because Mobutu took that wealth out of the province and put it into the national treasury. But worse, it was common knowledge that Mobutu used the proceeds less for the welfare of Zaire than to line his own pockets. From the copper, cobalt, and uranium of Shaba, Mobutu had amassed a fortune, much of which he kept in bank accounts abroad. At the expense of Shaba province, Mobutu became one of the world's wealthiest men.

After entering Shaba province, the Front quickly captured the key mining town of Kolwezi, where several thousand North Americans and Europeans, mainly Belgians, lived and worked. Mobutu, who could not handle the rebels with his own army, asked for outside intervention and found receptive ears. Belgian Prime Minister Leo Tindemans claimed that the Front was engaged in a "hunt against whites" in Shaba,[4] and one news report called it "the worst massacre of Europeans in modern African history."[5] The extent to which these American and European expatriates were victims of the violence remained unclear; but Belgium and France organized paratrooper forces, and the Carter administration agreed to fly in ammunition, trucks, and fuel for them.[6]

President Jimmy Carter expressed "abhorrence and distress over the violence and the killing that resulted from the Katangan invasion from Angola into Zaire. As great as the human tragedy was, it could have been much worse for the European nationals and for the Zairians, and the consequences much more severe for that country, if we had not joined with our allies in a common effort."[7]

Ignoring the fact that the Front rebels were Lunda natives of Shaba province, the administration picked up Mobutu's claim that the Shaba rebellion was an outside job. Even with no evidence that Angola's government was actually inciting the Lunda, Secretary of State Cyrus Vance defended U.S. involvement because Shaba had been invaded from Angola.[8]

"The Government of Angola," Carter said, "must bear a heavy responsibility for the deadly attack which was launched from its territory, and it's a burden and a responsibility shared by Cuba. We believe that Cuba had known of the Katangan plans to invade and obviously did nothing to restrain them from crossing the border. We also know that the Cubans have played a key role in training and equipping the Katangans who attacked."[9]

According to National Security Advisor Zbigniew Brzezinski, "the invasion of Katanga or Shaba from Angola could not have taken place without the full knowledge of the Angolan Government," or "without the invading parties having been armed and trained by the Cubans and, indeed, perhaps also the East Germans." "[W]e have sufficient evidence to be quite confident in our conclusion that Cuba shares the political and the moral responsibility for the invasion," Brzezinski said, "indeed, even for the outrages that were associated with it." When a reporter pointed out that no Cubans participated directly, Brzezinski replied, "there is a difference between direct involvement and responsibility. Direct involvement," he said, would mean "direct participation in the fighting, in command and control, presence on the ground." Brzezinski was charging Cuba with something different, responsibility for "a violation of territorial integrity, which in fact is a belligerent act," even though it was others who had physically entered Zaire: "[T]he Cuban Government and in some measure the Soviet Government bear the responsibility for this transgression."[10]

Thus, by the administration's account, European and American forces were on a rescue mission to save endangered Europeans and to drive out foreign invaders who were sponsored by Soviet-bloc countries. While there was some truth in this, it was not the whole truth. The administration had failed to mention that some of the participants in the rebellion were Lunda who still lived in Shaba province. Indeed, many local Lunda had joined their Angola-based brethren.[11]

Brzezinski and Carter argued that Angola and Cuba had known

of the Lunda plans; indeed, in a message to Carter, Cuban president Fidel Castro admitted he did know in advance of the Lunda plan but that he had tried to stop them.[12] Angolan President Agostinho Neto said that his government had not trained or equipped the Lunda, and that neither the Soviet Union nor Cuba had done so in Angola.[13] Meanwhile the Front denied having received any Soviet or Cuban assistance.[14] There was little evidence of a Soviet or Soviet-bloc role in the Shaba rebellion. All that could be said for certain was that Angola was tolerating the Front's presence in its territory. In reply, Carter merely charged that Cuba could have done more to stop the invasion.[15]

The Belgian foreign minister, Henri Simonet, noted that Zaire was still aiding the FNLA, and that the FNLA was still active in northern Angola. If the Angolan government were aiding the Front, it would have been as a counterweight to the FNLA.[16]

Mobutu, for all his peccadilloes, was still "our man." We saw earlier how the Eisenhower, Kennedy, and Johnson administrations helped him to power, as someone who would side with the West. Thus, the Americans' role in suppressing the Shaba rebellion was a payback to Mobutu. We were also, of course, protecting our own position in Zaire, keeping it on our side in the cold war. While Brzezinski and Carter accused Angola and Cuba of responsibility, we bore responsibility ourselves. Had we not helped Mobutu gain power and helped keep him there over the years, despite his corruption, there might have been no cause for a rebellion in Shaba in 1978.

Secretary of State Vance gave justifications for our role that went beyond the protection of the Europeans. "We cooperated with other nations to rescue those trapped in the fighting," he said, but also, "to help preserve Zaire's territorial integrity, and to help prevent its economic collapse."[17] To talk of preventing Zaire's economic collapse when it was being pillaged by Mobutu personally must have made the words stick in Vance's throat. The United States had contributed to Zaire's sorry economic situation by promoting Mobutu, and protecting him against the Shaba rebellion only perpetuated Zaire's misery.

Mobutu was even more imaginative than the Carter administration in describing the Shaba events, claiming that Cuban troops had entered Zaire along with the Shaba natives.[18] Castro, however, denied the charge, and no evidence ever surfaced to back it.

As for Carter's professed concern over the safety of Europeans in Shaba, there was scant evidence of rebel atrocities. After the rebels took Kolwezi, the European community there was reported calm.[19] The Front denied targeting Europeans,[20] and even offered to cooperate with foreign governments to evacuate their nationals.[21]

One hundred thirty Europeans were killed during the Kolwezi fighting, which was heavy, resulting in 500 Zairian deaths.[22] But it was not clear that the Europeans would have been harmed if the paratroopers had stayed out. According to the rebel leader, most of the European deaths resulted from the occupation of European residential areas by French paratroopers. When that occurred, the rebels counterattacked, and residents were caught in the cross-fire.[23] Reports did emerge that a small number of French were killed intentionally by the rebels.[24] The best explanation that surfaced was that these killings were in reprisal for the landing of the French paratroopers.[25]

Within a short time the French and Belgian paratroopers drove the rebel forces out of Kolwezi.[26] As in Stanleyville in 1964, the paratroopers combined rescue with helping the central government regain control. The Carter administration acknowledged this second goal when it said that one aim of the landing had been to preserve Zaire's territorial integrity.

The French and Belgian paratroopers evacuated most of the Europeans from Kolwezi. Some doubtless left from fear, but others apparently departed simply because the fighting had so disrupted Kolwezi that making a living there became problematic. The United States citizens in Kolwezi were evacuated prior to the arrival of the paratroopers by the company for which they worked. As for France and Belgium, the French daily Le Monde suggested that a concern for French and Belgian investments prompted them to act.[27] Mobutu had been scrupulously respectful of their financial interests in Shaba.[28]

Speaking on background, administration officials acknowledged other motives for the Shaba action. Our decision to help Belgium and France had been motivated, they said, by concern over Soviet activity elsewhere in Africa, specifically Ethiopia. Showing a willingness to intervene in Shaba might curb the Soviet Union in other African countries. If this sounds like Kissinger's rationale for intervening in Angola in 1975, it was.

Carter was also concerned that he had acquired a reputation of being indecisive as the leader of the Western alliance.[29] He had not intervened abroad as aggressively as his predecessors, therefore putting his cold war credentials in doubt. A modest intervention in Shaba provided a low-cost way for Carter to show the flag.

The Carter-Brzezinski rationale for the intervention gave the public the impression that Zaire was being invaded by an outside force having only a marginal connection to Zaire, and that Angola, and perhaps the Soviet Union and East Germany, were pulling the strings. Like previous administrations dealing with conflict situations, Carter exaggerated the role of the Soviet bloc. By depicting an event of local significance as a move on the cold war chessboard, he gave himself a pretext for an intervention whose real aim was to protect the loyal, if larcenous, Mobutu, and to enhance his own anti-Communist credentials.

Notes

1. David B. Ottoway, "GIs on Alert as Fears Mount over Zaire War," *Washington Post,* May 17, 1978, p. A1, col. 1.

2. Jean Pierre Langellier, "Les anciens 'gendarmes katangais' ne jouent plus qu'un rôle mineur parmi les rebelles du Shaba," *Le Monde,* May 21–22, 1978, p. 3, col. 1; David B. Ottoway, "Zaire Conflict Poses Dilemma for U.S.," *Washington Post,* May 18, 1978, p. A18, col. 4; *Angola,* Hearings before the Subcommittee on African Affairs of the Committee on Foreign Relations, U.S. Senate, 94th Cong., 2d sess., 1976, p. 183 (statement of Deputy Asst. Secretary of State for African Affairs Edward Mulcahy).

3. David B. Ottoway, "Zaire Says Rebels Backed by Angola Invade the South," *Washington Post,* May 15, 1978, p. A1, col. 5; "En 1977: Deux cent vingt mille Zaïrois se sont réfugiés en Angola," *Le Monde,* May 20, 1978, p. 3, col. 5.

4. William Claiborne and Don Oberdorfer, "Zaire Rescue Mission Launched," *Washington Post,* May 19, 1978, p. A1, col. 4.

5. David B. Ottoway, "Death & Destruction in a Terrorized City in Zaire," *Washington Post,* May 21, 1978, p. A1, col. 2.

6. Claiborne and Oberdorfer, "Zaire Rescue Mission Launched"; David B. Ottoway, "French Troops Parachute into Zaire," *Washington Post,* May 20, 1978, p. A1, col. 4.

7. "News Conference, May 25," DSB, vol. 78, pp. 17–18 (July 1978).

8. "The Secretary: U.S. Relations with Africa," DSB, vol. 78, p. 12 (August 1978).

9. "News Conference, May 25," pp. 17–18.

10. "National Security Adviser Brzezinski on 'Meet the Press,' " DSB, vol. 78, p. 26 (July 1978).

11. Pierre de Vos, "La France a une politique africaine qui n'est pas la nôtre," *Le Monde,* May 23, 1978, p. 3, col. 1.

12. David Binder, "Castro Says He Told U.S. He Tried to Halt Invasion into Zaire," *New York Times,* June 11, 1978, p. A1, col. 6; Jon Nordheimer, "Castro Says Carter Was 'Deceived' on Cuban Role," *New York Times,* June 13, 1978, p. A8, col. 1.

13. "Angola to Disarm Zaire Rebels," *New York Times,* June 11, 1978, p. A6, col. 5.

14. David B. Ottoway, "Zairians, Rebels Reportedly Battle in Mining Center," *Washington Post,* May 16, 1978, p. A1, col. 5.

15. "Transcript of the President's News Conference on Foreign and Domestic Matters," *New York Times,* June 15, 1978, p. A18, col. 1.

16. de Vos, "La France a une politique africaine qui n'est pas la nôtre."

17. "The Secretary: U.S. Relations with Africa," DSB, vol. 78, p. 12 (August 1978).

18. David B. Ottoway, "Zaire Says Rebels Backed by Angola Invade the South," *Washington Post,* May 15, 1978, p. A1, col. 5.

19. "Des parachutages ont été effectués par les gouvernementaux près de Kolwezi," *Le Monde,* May 17, 1978, p. 6, col. 1.

20. "Le sort de la communauté étrangère de Kolwezi reste très préoccupant," *Le Monde,* May 18, 1978, p. 4, col. 1.

21. René Lefort, "Dès que les parachutistes auront quitté Kolwezi nous serons capables de reprendre la ville rapidement, affirme un porte-parole du F.N.L.C.," *Le Monde,* May 23, 1978, p. 3, col. 1.

22. Paul Lewis, "French Troops Land in Zaire Battle Zone; U.S. Sees Cuban Role," *New York Times,* May 20, 1978, p. A1, col. 6.

23. "Le chef des rebelles affirme que des contacts avaient été établis pour assurer la sécurité des Européens," *Le Monde,* May 25, 1978, p. 3, col. 1.

24. David B. Ottoway, "French, Zairian Troops Patrol an Empty, Corpse-Strewn City," *Washington Post,* May 23, 1978, p. A1, col. 1.

25. David B. Ottoway, "French, Belgian Get all Whites Out of Zaire City," *Washington Post,* May 22, 1978, p. A1, col. 5.

26. "Troops End Rebels' Hold on Zaire City," *Washington Post,* May 21, 1978, p. A1, col. 6; Jacques Isnard, "Une opération en trois temps," *Le Monde,* May 21–22, 1978, p. 3, col. 4.

27. Philippe Decraene, "Qui sauver?" *Le Monde,* May 20, 1978, p. 3, col. 1.

28. Jean Pierre Langellier, "Les intérêts belges demeurent considérables dans l'ancien Congo," *Le Monde,* May 20, 1978, p. 3, col. 2.

29. Bernard Gwertzman, "Washington Acts to Show It Is Ready to Check Havana and Moscow in Africa," *New York Times,* May 20, 1978, p. A1, col. 5.

19

Iran: Hostages Will Die

In Iran a U.S. military operation of a most unusual kind was mounted in response to a most unusual situation. In November 1979, a group of Iranians entered the American embassy in Tehran and took members of the staff hostage. Governments are normally protective of foreign embassies, but Iran's government refused to step in to help the embassy staff; on the contrary, it applauded the action. After fruitless demands on Iran, the Carter administration took legal action in the International Court of Justice, which ordered Iran to release the hostages. But Iran still took no action.

To free the hostages, President Carter decided on direct action, devising a plan that sounded as if it were taken from the plot of a spy novel. Carter would fly a handpicked team of ninety military personnel into Iran on eight helicopters from an aircraft carrier, while six C-130 transport planes flew into Iran from a base in Egypt. The helicopters and the C-130s would converge at a designated point in the Iranian desert, 200 miles from Tehran. From there the helicopters would fly to a site near Tehran, where they would be met by U.S. agents who had already entered Iran clandestinely. These agents would assemble a fleet of small vehicles, in which the team would drive into Tehran, where they would get a night's sleep in prearranged hideouts.

The next day the team would drive to the American embassy, and to several other locations to which some of the hostages had been removed. They would free the hostages from their guards, and the helicopters would fly in and pick up both team members and hostages.

The C-130s, meanwhile, would have flown to a location near Tehran; the helicopters would fly from the embassy to that location, where both team members and hostages would board the C-130s. The helicopters would be abandoned, and the entourage would fly out of Iran in the planes.[1]

On April 24, 1980, Carter put the plan into operation. The C-130s, as projected, arrived at the desert rendezvous point. But the helicopters were not so lucky: they encountered an intense desert dust storm, and several experienced mechanical problems. Of the eight helicopters, only six reached the rendezvous; once there, one of the six developed a mechanical problem. That left only five helicopters, the minimum number necessary to accommodate the hostages and the team members. However, using just five helicopters was risky, because it left no margin for error.

Soon another problem emerged: the point chosen for the rendezvous was close to a highway, and while the team was on the ground a bus with fifty passengers happened by. Realizing that the passengers had gotten a good look at the transport planes and the helicopters, the team decided it could not risk the possibility that the passengers might inform authorities; therefore, it seized the bus and detained the passengers. Then a truck came along, followed by an automobile. Again concerned about being detected, team members fired at the truck, trying to stop it. Its driver, however, jumped out and climbed into the automobile, which sped off into the desert.[2]

All this time the team was in communication with Washington, with President Carter being informed of each mishap as it arose. The team had been detected, and with only five operating helicopters, any more mechanical problems would spell disaster. Moreover, they were holding fifty bus passengers and had no idea what to do with them. At that point, Carter decided to cancel the mission, deciding that the chances of success had become too remote.

So the helicopters and C-130s prepared to leave Iran; but as they were taking off, one of the helicopters flew into a C-130, bursting into flames, killing eight team members and severely injuring several others. Fearful of more problems with helicopters, the team abandoned them, leaving behind as well the bodies of the eight dead team members, and flew off in the remaining transport planes.[3]

Carter's decision to abort the mission in the desert probably averted further disaster. If the team had reached Tehran, it might have been detected before it arrived at the embassy. With the embassy in a downtown location, slipping in unnoticed would not have been easy. Police or military forces might have confronted the team, and if that happened, the chances of getting the hostages out safely were truly remote.

During the planning of the mission, in fact, some of the participants thought the odds on succeeding were poor; indeed, U.S. Marine Corps Commandant Robert Barrow expressed serious doubts.[4] It was anticipated, in particular, that the team would have to confront at least the armed Iranian civilians who guarded the hostages. Colonel Charles Beckwith, the operation commander, told Deputy Secretary of State Warren Christopher that the team planned to kill most or all of these guards. Beckwith also thought that some of the hostages and some team members would be killed when the shooting started.[5] Thus, even if the operation had been carried out as planned, it would probably not have saved all the hostages.

Had the hostages been under threat of death, the risks might have been worth running. But from what was known at the time, the Iranian captors had no intention of killing the hostages. Secretary of Defense Harold Brown thought there was a potential danger to the hostages from "the deteriorating security situation in Iran," because of disorder in the streets, and tensions between Iran and Iraq.[6] But there was no reason to think the hostages were in immediate danger.

For President Carter, it was difficult to deal with the hostage situation without considering its political impact. Facing reelection in November 1980, Carter saw his popularity plummeting as the hostage crisis dragged on; therefore, he was under great pressure to get a speedy release. Many suspected there was a kernel of truth in the statement by the Soviet government, which criticized the raid and accused Carter of being prepared to sacrifice the lives of American citizens for "his election interests."[7] Even after the raid failed, the administration did not explain to the public the risks that made success unlikely.

Even as the hostage-taking continued, Carter was reluctant to discuss prior U.S. policy in Iran, and that refusal may have reduced the chances of a peaceful resolution. The context of the hostage-taking was that many Iranians harbored deep grievances against the United States for our attempts to control Iran's political life. In 1953, the CIA, in one of its most spectacular covert operations, collaborated with the shah of Iran, a figurehead monarch, to depose the prime minister and to assume power himself. The prime minister, Mohammed Mossadegh, an elderly land-owner described by Secretary of State Dean Acheson as "rich, reactionary, [and] feudal-minded," had nationalized a major British firm, the Anglo-Iranian Oil Company.[8] Anglo-Iranian's parent company in the United States had once been represented by the law firm of Secretary of State Dulles, and President Eisenhower said that Mossadegh was not offering enough compensation.[9] Beyond the nationalization issue, Eisenhower worried that Iran might fall to the Soviet camp.

The shah had already tried once to dismiss Mossadegh, but street demonstrators supported Mossadegh and forced the shah to back down. The top CIA operative in Iran, Kermit Roosevelt, a grandson of President Theodore Roosevelt, urged the shah to try again, promising that the CIA would organize pro-shah street demonstrations.

Encouraged by Roosevelt, the shah declared Mossadegh fired. When, as expected, pro-Mossadegh crowds took to the streets, Roosevelt's recruits demonstrated for the shah. Roosevelt also encouraged the army to back the shah; when a pro-shah general named himself prime minister, Mossadegh resigned in fear.[10] The grateful shah gave our oil companies part of the British monopoly and oriented Iran's economy to the West; the political relationship, in fact, became so cozy that the CIA built up an Iranian security police organization. The reputation it developed for brutality became a major Iranian grievance against the United States.[11]

Iran declared that the United States would have to "repent" for its misdeeds before the hostages were returned, but President Carter refused to discuss the matter with Iran and did not indicate to the American public that there was any truth to the points the Iranian government was raising.[12] Carter's silence is all the more enigmatic in light of the fact that in 1979, Kermit Roosevelt published his book explaining how he had engineered the overthrow of Mossadegh in 1953. Therefore, our prior interference in Iranian politics could not be disputed.[13]

In reaction to the past American interference, the Iranian government also asked the United States to "make a pledge and a promise that from now on she will in no way interfere, either directly or indirectly, politically or militarily, in the affairs of the Islamic Republic of Iran."[14] Carter did not respond to this demand, although a statement pledging noninterference would not have been difficult.

In the midst of the anti-shah uprising in 1979, I happened to be flying home from the Far East via Tehran, where I had a scheduled stopover before continuing to New York. Knowing the history of our support for the shah, however, I was not anxious to be an American in Tehran while the shah was being overthrown.

When the plane's doors opened on the ground in Tehran, my fears were confirmed, as Americans flocked into the plane to get out of the country. I pled with the steward to let me keep my seat to New York. The plane soon filled, but the steward somehow found me a seat. As we took off, I was happy to see the lights of Tehran fade in the distance.

Notes

1. George C. Wilson and Michael Getler, "Raid Team Had Hoped to Surprise Hostage Captors in Ground Assault," *Washington Post,* April 26, 1980, p. A1, col. 5.

2. Richard Harwood, "Series of Mishaps Defeated Rescue in Iran," *Washington Post,* April 26, 1980, p. A1, col. 1.

3. "Secretary Brown's News Conference," April 25, 1980, DSB, vol. 80, p. 39 (June 1980).

4. David Martin and John Walcott, *Best Laid Plans: The Inside Story of America's War Against Terrorism* (1988), p. 32.

5. Ibid., p. 4.

6. "Secretary Brown's News Conference," April 25, 1980, p. 40.

7. Harwood, "Series of Mishaps Defeated Rescue in Iran."

8. Dean Acheson, *Present at the Creation* (1969), p. 504.

9. "Text of the Letters by Mossadegh and Eisenhower," *New York Times,* July 10, 1953, p. A4, col. 3.

10. Kermit Roosevelt, *Countercoup* (1979), pp. 150–97; John Prados, *Presidents' Secret Wars: CIA and Pentagon Covert Operations Since World War II* (1986), p. 97; Andrew Tully, *CIA: The Inside Story* (1962), pp. 88–99.

11. Jonathan Kwitny, *Endless Enemies: The Making of an Unfriendly World* (1984), p. 12.

12. "Iran Chronology, September 1980," DSB, vol. 80, p. 55 (November 1980).

13. Roosevelt, *Countercoup.*

14. "Iran's Proposals for Release of American Hostages," DSB, vol. 80, p. 46 (December 1980).

20

Nicaragua: Who Is Contra?

Not long after the helicopter crash in the Iranian desert, another curious U.S. military action was taking shape in Central America. In the 1970s, a movement formed in Nicaragua to oppose long-time strongman Anastasio Somoza Debayle; it called itself Sandinista, after Augusto Sandino, a Nicaraguan general who had waged a guerrilla campaign against American Marines when they occupied Nicaragua in the 1920s. The Marines spearheaded an actively interventionist policy by the United States in Nicaragua which sought to orient Nicaragua's economy in our direction and to protect our companies operating there. To keep the peace after the Marines left in 1933, we organized a National Guard for Nicaragua, to be headed by Anastasio Somoza García. As head of the Guard, Somoza came to control the government, and his rule was heavy-handed. In the 1970s, that style was continued by his son, Anastasio Somoza Debayle.

All this time relations between the Somozas and the United States remained close. Recall that in 1961, President Kennedy launched the Bay of Pigs invasion from Nicaragua. In 1979, the Sandinista party waged war against Somoza and overthrew him, despite President Carter's unsuccessful attempt to organize a military force from the Organization of American States to prop Somoza up. When the Sandinistas took power, much of Somoza's National Guard fled Nicaragua and regrouped in neighboring Honduras, from which it started military raids back into Nicaragua. A committee of Nicaraguans who had fled to Miami assumed control of this effort and began to speak as a kind of government in exile. The media dubbed the force the Contras, Spanish for "against," because they opposed the new Nicaraguan government.

There was more to all this than met the eye, however. The Contras had not developed spontaneously. In 1981, President Ronald Reagan allocated funds for CIA covert operations in Central America, and one major project was to organize an army to fight the Sandinista government of Nicaragua.[1] In Honduras the CIA forged the National Guard remnants into a fighting force. The committee in Miami had not formed by itself, therefore, but was a product of the CIA.[2]

One of the Miami Nicaraguans picked by the CIA, Edgar Chamorro, explained in a *New Republic* article that a CIA operative had told the Nicaraguans that the purpose of forming this leadership group was to deceive Congress. The reasoning was that while Congress was unlikely to fund the National Guard remnants, it might support an anti-Sandinista movement headed by respectable businessmen who did not bear the taint of an affiliation with Somoza, even if the Guard remnants remained the fighting force. The CIA men organized a press conference in Miami to announce the formation of the leadership group, after one of them briefed the Nicaraguans on what to say. The Nicaraguans followed their script well, denying any connection to the United States, denying even that their aim was to overthrow the Nicaraguan government. Although the Miami group announced itself as the political arm of the National Guard, it gained little control over the Guard. That remained the province of the CIA and its station in Honduras.[3]

For the Contras, the CIA set up training bases in Florida, Texas, and California, paid the soldiers' salaries, and planned their missions. Under the cover of military exercises, U.S. Army engineers built command posts for the Contras in Honduras. The CIA produced for the Contra soldiers a pamphlet explaining how to operate in Nicaragua, and including suggestions on how to assassinate local officials in order to show that the government could not rule effectively.[4] Eventually a second Contra group sprang up in Costa Rica, also organized by the CIA.

All this, of course, was done on the quiet, which meant that, without any public debate, the administration had started a war.[5] As with the

Cuban exiles in 1961, the CIA tried against all odds to keep its role unseen. However, in 1982, reporters found out that the Contras were a CIA product, and a congressional committee called in CIA Director William Casey to explain. Casey told the committee that, yes, the CIA was aiding the Contras, but the aim was only to stop arms shipments from Nicaragua to insurgents in El Salvador, where a civil war was in progress. Casey denied that we were trying to bring down the Nicaraguan government or put the Somoza forces back in power.[6]

Other administration officials said—although not for attribution—that, indeed, overthrowing Nicaragua's government was our express aim.[7] Outraged, Congress wrote an amendment into a foreign appropriations bill that "none of the funds provided in this Act may be used by the Central Intelligence Agency or the Department of Defense to furnish military equipment, military training or advice, or other support for military activities, to any group or individual, not part of a country's armed forces, for the purpose of overthrowing the Government of Nicaragua."[8] That law did not stop the operation, however, because the administration found ways to keep the Contras in business.

The fall of 1983 and the winter of 1984 witnessed a series of spectacular military operations against Nicaragua. Aircraft bombed Nicaraguan economic installations; speedboats raided the Nicaraguan coast, blowing up oil depots; and undersea explosive mines appeared in the waters off Nicaragua's major port.[9] Ten ships were hit—ships registered in Nicaragua, the Netherlands, Liberia, Panama, and the Soviet Union. Nicaragua reported that the mines had killed two crew members and injured fourteen, and it temporarily closed its ports. When asked by reporters whether our government had done the mining, government officials said no.[10]

In Moscow, Soviet Foreign Minister Andrei Gromyko called in our chargé d'affaires and called the mining "an act of banditry and piracy," asserting we had done it using "mercenaries and terrorists." The State Department replied, "We note that anti-Sandinista forces have widely advertised that certain Nicaraguan ports have been mined. We have no further information on the incident." The Department expressed regret for "any injury to mariners or shipping," but blamed tensions leading to the mining on "Soviet encouragement of conflict in Central America and the Caribbean."[11] So not only were we uninvolved, but the blame rested with the Soviet Union.

Meanwhile, the Contras announced they had done the mining, when in fact, they had not. Contra leader Chamorro, who served as Contra publicity director, admitted later that the CIA gave him a Spanish-language press release proclaiming Contra responsibility for the mining, which Chamorro read over a CIA-funded Contra radio station in Honduras.[12] Soon, however, the administration's story unraveled, with evidence surfacing that the CIA had organized the operation.[13] The press even obtained a classified CIA report that gave dates and places of CIA speedboat attacks and the mining.[14] These activities were carried out by Latin American mercenaries recruited by the CIA, and called, in CIA shorthand, unilaterally controlled Latino assets (UCLAs). CIA trainers launched the UCLAs into small boats from "mother ships," to take the mines in and plant them.[15]

Once Congress realized that the administration had kept it in the dark concerning the entire operation, Capitol Hill simmered with rage.[16] The Senate, 84 votes to 12, adopted a resolution "that no funds heretofore or hereafter appropriated in any act of Congress shall be obligated or expended for the purpose of planning, executing or supporting the mining of the ports or territorial waters of Nicaragua."[17]

During the summer following these raids, I inspected the oil depots that the UCLAs had hit at Corinto, Nicaragua's largest port; children played in the charred remains of huge Esso tanks that had been the main repositories of fuel supplies for the country. The port director told me the tanks burned for three days.

Nicaragua reacted to the attacks as Carter had to the hostage-taking in Iran, by suing in the International Court of Justice. The court found that the United States had, as Nicaragua charged, organized the Contras, the raids, and the mining, and ruled in Nicaragua's favor, calling our attacks on Nicaragua acts of international aggression.[18]

In 1984, a presidential election was held in Nicaragua, and I happened to be in Managua the day the Sandinista party opened its election campaign in a downtown shopping center. While Daniel Ortega waited for the ceremonies to begin, my wife struck up a conversation with Ortega, who called me over. To my surprise, Ortega immediately raised a serious topic. He said that by its war the United States was making life unbearable for Nicaraguans, yet the public in the United States was letting it happen. "What will it take to make the public in North

America pay attention?" he asked. Although Congress opposed the war, the administration kept it going.

Thinking through the history of our military actions abroad, I had to tell Ortega the bad news: that the public usually gives the president free rein. It habitually believes what the president tells it, even when that story doesn't match the facts. Only when wars drag on too long, and our casualties are too high, does the public seriously ask itself whether to fight on, as happened in Korea or Vietnam. But in the Nicaraguan war, we were not suffering casualties.

My answer held little comfort for Ortega, and he never found a way to get the American public aroused. In 1984, however, Congress tightened the screws on Reagan by passing a law that "no funds available to the Central Intelligence Agency, the Department of Defense, or any other agency or entity of the United States involved in intelligence activities" could be used to support "directly or indirectly, military or paramilitary operations in Nicaragua."[19] That sounded like the death knell for Contra funding; but Reagan evaded even this law, by approving a National Security Council directive to create a surrogate network, nominally private, to finance and train the Contras.[20] The funding was creative, as administration officials convinced not only private citizens to contribute, but the governments of Saudi Arabia and Brunei. They even asked Israel to contribute weapons, which it did.[21] The administration quietly sold arms to Iran and gave the Contras the proceeds.[22] It collected privately contributed equipment in the United States, while a CIA-owned airline, Southern Air Transport, ferried it to the Contras.[23]

On the return legs of some of these flights, Southern Air carried Contra cocaine and marijuana for the U.S. drug market, as still another way to add to the Contra coffers. When Drug Enforcement Administration agents confirmed the contents, the pilots told them that they had White House protection for the drug-running.[24] George Morales, who had recently been convicted of drug smuggling, had directed the pilots who flew arms to the Contras from southern Florida. Morales told the Senate Subcommittee on Terrorism, Narcotics, and International Operations that on return trips, he carried cocaine and marijuana under CIA protection.[25] Getting these drugs into our market gave the Contras the financial means for buying weapons and paying salaries.[26]

The CIA apparently had no more qualms about running cocaine and marijuana from Central America than it had transporting opium in Laos for the Hmong a generation before. Once the Medellín cartel in Colombia saw that the Contras had an easy route for getting drugs into the United States, it began renting space from the Contras on the CIA planes. So the CIA shipped cartel drugs into the United States, generating even more revenue for the Contras.[27]

As part of its effort to bring down Nicaragua's government, the Reagan administration cut off trade with Nicaragua and imposed strict economic sanctions that made it difficult for Nicaraguans to get essential commodities. Then, in a major political coup, the White House turned Congress around in 1985 and got it to fund the Contras.[28] All this put heavy pressure on Nicaragua; with thousands being killed in Nicaragua in Contra attacks, the economy could not generate goods, and so markets stood half empty. In the 1990 presidential election, Nicaraguan voters turned Ortega and the Sandinista party out, preferring a coalition of parties that included some sympathetic to the Contras.[29] Nicaraguans could not stand the pressure of the war, the constant privation. They wanted a normal life, which was impossible while the Yankees were trying to do them in. The only way, therefore, to get rid of the Yankees was to vote out the Sandinistas. So Reagan and the Contras won.

Notes

1. David Ignatius and David Rogers, "Why the Covert War in Nicaragua Evolved and Hasn't Succeeded," *Wall Street Journal,* March 5, 1985, p. 1, col. 1.

2. Leslie H. Gelb, "State Dept. Aides Said to Question Acts in Nicaragua," *New York Times,* April 7, 1983, p. A1, col. 1; Bob Woodward, *Veil: The Secret Wars of the CIA 1981–1987* (1987), pp. 229–30, 263.

3. Edgar Chamorro, "Confessions of a 'Contra,' " *New Republic,* August 5, 1985, pp. 18–19.

4. Peter Kornbluh, "The Covert War," in Thomas Walker, ed., *Reagan versus the Sandinistas: The Undeclared War on Nicaragua* (1987), pp. 23–27; Bob Woodward, "Middle-Level CIA Officials Cleared Manual," *Washington Post,* October 24, 1984, p. A1, col. 1.

5. "Should the U.S. Fight Secret Wars?" *Harper's Magazine,* September 1984, p. 45 (statement of Morton Halperin, former member of National Security Council).

6. Philip Taubman, "Moynihan Questions C.I.A.'s Latin Role," *New York Times,* April 1, 1983, p. A3, col. 4; Woodward, *Veil,* pp. 225–26.

7. Gelb, "State Dept. Aides Said to Question Acts in Nicaragua."

8. U.S. Congress, *Statutes at Large,* vol. 96, p. 1865 (1982).

9. David Rogers and David Ignatius, "How CIA Aided Raids in Nicaragua in '84 Led Congress to End Funds," *Wall Street Journal,* March 6, 1985, p. 1, col. 1.

10. "U.S. Denies Responsibility," *New York Times,* March 22, 1984, p. A4, col. 1.

11. Ibid.

12. Chamorro, "Confessions of a Contra," p. 22; Kornbluh, "The Covert War," in *Reagan versus the Sandanistas,* p. 30.

13. Philip Taubman, "Americans on Ship Said to Supervise Nicaragua Mining," *New York Times,* April 8, 1984, p. A1, col. 6.

14. David Rogers and David Ignatius, "CIA Internal Report Details U.S. Role in Contra Raids in Nicaragua Last Year," *Wall Street Journal,* March 6, 1985, p. 20, col. 1.

15. Woodward, *Veil,* p. 281; Kornbluh, "The Covert War," in *Reagan versus the Sandanistas,* p. 29.

16. Woodward, *Veil,* p. 320.

17. Martin Tolchin, "Senate, 84–12, Acts to Oppose Mining Nicaragua Ports; Rebuke to Reagan," *New York Times,* April 11, 1984, p. A1, col. 6.

18. Case concerning Military and Paramilitary Activities in and against Nicaragua (*Nica.* v. *USA*), International Court of Justice, *Reports,* pp. 46–51 (1986).

19. U.S. Congress, *Statutes at Large,* vol. 98, p. 1935 (1984).

20. Kornbluh, "The Covert War," in *Reagan versus the Sandanistas,* p. 31.

21. Senate Select Committee on Intelligence, *Report on Preliminary Inquiry,* January 29, 1987, p. 49; President's Special Review Board, *Report of the Special Review Board,* February 26, 1987 (Tower Commission Report), p. B-123.

22. Kornbluh, "The Covert War," in *Reagan versus the Sandanistas,* p. 32.

23. Ibid., pp. 32–33.

24. Joel Brinkley, "Contra Arms Crews Said to Smuggle Drugs," *New York Times,* January 20, 1987, p. A1, col. 4.

25. Keith Schneider, "Smuggler Ties Contras to U.S. Drug Network," *New York Times,* July 16, 1987, p. A13, col. 5.

26. Leslie Cockburn, *Out of Control* (1987), pp. 152–88.

27. Transcript, "Frontline" Special, "Guns, Drugs and the CIA," WGBH, Public Broadcasting System (1988), pp. 23–24.

28. U.S. Congress, *Statutes at Large,* vol. 100, p. 3341-299 (1986).

29. "Nicaraguan Opposition Routs Sandinistas; U.S. Pledges Aid, Tied to Orderly Turnover," *New York Times,* February 27, 1990, p. A1, col. 6.

21

El Salvador: A Textbook Case

For the Reagan administration, Nicaragua and El Salvador were closely linked. As we have seen, it claimed to be helping the Contras not to overthrow the Nicaraguan government, but to stop arms from Nicaragua to El Salvador insurgents. The administration justified aid that it gave to the government of El Salvador on the same basis, namely, that the El Salvador insurgents were getting arms from outside, especially through Nicaragua. For a time at least, the administration made the public believe that our Contra funding was aimed at dealing with the civil war in El Salvador.

That war began in 1980, but it was a continuation of a conflict that had plagued the tiny Central American nation for generations. The name the Spanish colonists had given the country—"the Savior"—held more than a little irony. As of 1980, El Salvador was still waiting to be saved. Its economy was controlled by a small number of powerful families who had established large plantations in the nineteenth century. The vast majority of the Salvadoran population who did not own land lived in poverty unrivaled in the region. Babies died of malnutrition at alarming rates, and unemployment reached staggering levels.

The government and military in El Salvador were the domain of the small landowning group. When the peasants rebelled in 1932, the army killed them by the thousands. That kept the peasants quiet until the 1970s, when political agitation resumed. Political parties supporting land reform contested national elections; but even when they did win at the polls, the army stepped in and kept them from taking office.

In 1980, when civil protest picked up, with political marches and general strikes being waged, the government reacted harshly, killing or jailing protesters. Off-duty police and soldiers formed "death squads" that kidnapped and executed opponents. Finally, the opposition decided that it would not succeed through the political process, so it took to the hills and started a civil war.[1] One of the insurgency leaders, Guillermo Ungo, had been a vice-presidential candidate from whom the military stole an election in 1972.

To help it suppress the insurgency, the Carter administration began modest aid to the government of El Salvador. The landowning group that the Salvadoran government represented were the people in the country to whom we were linked, politically and financially. The night Ronald Reagan was elected to succeed Jimmy Carter, champagne flowed in the homes of El Salvador's elite, because they knew they would get even more help from him.

Reagan did not disappoint the Salvadoran establishment, immediately giving more military equipment and training to Salvadoran military personnel at bases in the United States and Panama. Beyond that, it sent military advisors, who were deployed at strategic locations to plan counterinsurgency strategy with Salvadoran commanders.[2] El Salvador's archbishop, a respected figure in the country, denounced the aid, arguing that it only encouraged the government to be repressive. Many Roman Catholic clergy advanced so-called liberation theology, which viewed the poor as victimized by the rich, while the government viewed them as merely subversive, and thus ripe targets for death squads.

The Reagan administration justified its aid and advisors to the Salvadoran government as a response to the aid the El Salvador insurgents were receiving from abroad. We were not interfering in a civil war, the administration argued, but protecting El Salvador from external interference. When this analysis was questioned by reporters, the State Department published a "white paper" to document its case.

The white paper made bold charges, stating that the El Salvador insurgents got arms and ammunition from Cuba, East Germany, Vietnam, Bulgaria, the Soviet Union, Hungary, Ethiopia, Czechoslovakia, and Nicaragua. One of the paper's key items of evidence was a document supposedly captured from the insurgents listing armaments received from Ethiopia, Bulgaria, Czechoslovakia, and Hungary. The paper concluded that "the insurgency in El Salvador has been progressively transformed into a textbook case of indirect armed aggression by Communist powers through Cuba."[3]

The white paper, whose arguments were similar to those of the Vietnam white paper of 1965, brought a round of firm denials from Nicaragua and the Soviet Union.[4] The insurgents themselves claimed that the white paper's documents were forged, and that their arms were captured from the government, or else purchased abroad.[5]

One weakness of the white paper was that it focused entirely on the Salvadoran Communist party, which was only one of five groups making up the insurgency.[6] Later the Bush administration acknowledged that the Soviet Union had no connection with the other four.[7]

The information relating to the Communist party drew criticisms as well, based as it was on documents supposedly captured from the party. The State Department, however, was hard pressed to prove the authenticity of the documents. When challenged, it refused to make the documents available to the public, although it did let several reporters review them and interview the paper's drafters.

Reporters found that several documents attributed by the white paper to insurgency leaders were obviously not written by them.[8] According to the *Washington Post,* many documents that the white paper identified by author and date contained no markings to indicate either date or author.[9] The white paper's principal author, Jon D. Glassman of the State Department, who had personally collected the documents in El Salvador, acknowledged to the *Wall Street Journal* that the intelligence analysts who examined them had to make guesses about their meaning. Glassman admitted that even the Salvadoran government expressed concern to the State Department about the white paper's accuracy; their message was, "You guys have made some mistakes."[10] Glassman admitted that the white paper contained errors and inconsistencies on basic points, and that parts were "misleading" and "overembellished."

At the time the white paper was written, the U.S. ambassador in El Salvador was Robert White. White, who was removed from his post over policy differences with the Reagan administration, said the white paper did not give a credible presentation and "tries to prove more than the evidence warrants"; White called its conclusions "bizarre" and "tendentious." According to the *Wall Street Journal,* the white paper's authors "were making a determined effort to create a 'selling' document, no matter how slim the background material."[11]

The most important document in the white paper was one it identified as a report by Shafik Handal, head of the Salvadoran Communist party. The document, the white paper said, described a visit by Handal to Soviet-bloc countries; the white paper, therefore, used the document as evidence that Handal had obtained commitments for arms shipments to the insurgents. The reporters, however, found that nowhere in the document did Handal's name appear, nor could they confirm that Handal was the person to whom the document related. In its English translation of this document, the State Department deleted a sentence that said that a particular shipment of arms "will leave in our ship the fifth of August." Since the Salvadoran Communist party had no ships, the author of the document could not have been one of the Salvadoran insurgents. By deleting the sentence, the white paper's drafters apparently hoped to mask this inconsistency. Further research on the document showed it was actually written in Cuba; moreover, at the time of its writing, Handal was not in Cuba. When pressed by the *Wall Street Journal,* Glassman finally admitted that Handal could not have authored the report.

One of the white paper's most significant conclusions was that the Soviet Union was involved in the arms shipments to the insurgents. The paper claimed "definitive evidence of the clandestine military support given by the Soviet Union, Cuba and their Communist allies to Marxist-Leninist guerrillas now fighting to overthrow the established government of El Salvador." The white paper reported that Handal had received a commitment from Soviet officials to transport arms, which were to be made available by Vietnam. But the *Washington Post* found that while the documents did reflect discussions about arms, they said nothing about a Soviet commitment. Since this oblique reference to the Soviet Union was the only one made in any of the documents, there was in fact nothing in them to substantiate Soviet involvement in arms shipments.

As for the quantity of arms supposedly received from abroad, the captured documents were reported to show the delivery to El Salvador of "nearly 200 tons of arms, mostly through Cuba and Nicaragua."

But Glassman, when pressed by reporters, conceded that the documents did not bear out that figure, for which the Department apparently had no basis.[12]

Another of the white paper's claims of outside arms shipments was that the insurgents met in Managua with Yassir Arafat, head of the Palestine Liberation Organization, and that he "promised military equipment, including arms and aircraft." As Glassman acknowledged to the *Wall Street Journal*, however, the document said only that a meeting with Arafat occurred, with no mention of arms.

The *Washington Post* concluded from its review "that on several major points, the documents do not support conclusions drawn from them by the administration." After the criticisms were published, the State Department defended the paper's overall conclusion but did not reply point by point.[13]

The white paper also suffered from omission: in focusing on possible arms shipments, it ignored the causes of the Salvadoran civil war, failing to indicate the human rights violations and poverty that led to discontent, or that the opposition took to the hills only after electoral victory had been snatched from it by the military. The absence of such analysis made it appear that El Salvador was a happy country in which Cuba, Nicaragua, and the Soviet Union were stirring up trouble.[14]

The question of whether Nicaragua sent arms to the Salvadoran insurgency came up as well in the lawsuit Nicaragua filed against the United States in the International Court of Justice. The Reagan administration defended its military action against Nicaragua by arguing that Nicaragua was committing aggression against El Salvador, through aid to its insurgents, and that we were merely defending El Salvador against this aggression. On this point the court decided that there had been "an intermittent flow of arms" from Nicaragua to the insurgents from late 1980 to early 1981, but no evidence to show that the government of Nicaragua promoted it. The court denied that the shipment of some arms from Nicaragua to the El Salvador insurgents meant that the Nicaraguan government was responsible.[15] The Court found no evidence of arms shipments after early 1981.

Neither in the white paper nor later did the administration make its case of massive outside arms shipments to the Salvadoran insurgents. It drew major conclusions from questionable data, in order to convince the public and Congress to fund the government of El Salvador. It did nothing to refute the insurgents' claim that they had obtained arms by purchase abroad and by capturing, stealing, or buying them from government troops.[16]

Even after the white paper's flaws were exposed, Reagan used the supposed arms shipments from Nicaragua to justify funding the Contras and aiding the Salvadoran government. He put out more public information, but none of it any more convincing than the white paper.[17] In 1983, David MacMichael, a CIA official responsible for analyzing data on El Salvador resigned in protest, saying that the administration had "exaggerated the amount of arms" from Nicaragua to the insurgents, "to justify our covert aid to the contras." MacMichael called the administration's hyperbole "plain prevarication."[18]

As the civil war in El Salvador dragged on, Congress from time to time challenged the administration over the Salvadoran government's sweeping measures to suppress opposition, as death squads continued to roam the country killing government opponents. Congress would allow the administration to send the aid only if the president periodically certified that El Salvador was improving its human rights record. Reagan duly gave the required certification, despite evidence of continuing brutality, and the aid still flowed.

In addition to human rights, Congress was concerned over the Salvadoran government's military tactics, particularly in 1983, when it began what appeared to be saturation bombing in rebel-held provinces, not unlike what the U.S. Air Force had done in Indochina.[19] Peasants reported apparently random aerial attacks on villages.[20]

Denying that the Salvadoran air force was bombing indiscriminately, or to drive the population from rebel-held areas, administration officials averred that the bombing was done with "surgical precision." Even though some members of Congress accused the administration of lying, Congress nonetheless continued the funding.[21]

Our support probably kept the Salvadoran government in power, and doubtless kept the war going. As the war intensified, the American embassy in San Salvador assumed the demeanor of a modern-day armed fast, with concrete barriers and heavy wire fencing protecting it from potential assaults.

The civil war in El Salvador took its toll, as thousands of combatants and noncombatants were killed and injured. Humanitarian organizations in the United States became concerned over the situation of wounded insurgent combatants who could not get medical attention. Insurgent field hospitals were rudimentary, but the wounded avoided government hospitals for fear of being killed. The archbishop intervened, and several times the government allowed small numbers of seriously wounded to leave the country for medical treatment abroad, mostly amputees and others too seriously wounded to fight again. Finally an agreement was reached for the government to let the International Committee of the Red Cross evacuate all the seriously wounded; however, the agreement broke down, and one hundred seriously wounded insurgents were left hiding in the bush. Some members of Congress expressed concern.

I was invited by the humanitarian organizations to try to convince the Salvador government to let the evacuation proceed. When, along with several other Americans, I visited military headquarters in San Salvador, the minister of defense was cordial and, to our delight, agreed to let the seriously wounded leave. Eventually, the president, Napoleon Duarte, also agreed, announcing that he was giving the order for the evacuation. But with Duarte dying of cancer, conservative members of parliament objected that letting the wounded leave would help the insurgents. So the order was canceled, Duarte died, the conservatives won the Salvadoran presidency, and the wounded remained in the field to fend for themselves.

Notes

1. James Petras, "Blots on the White Paper: The Reinvention of the 'Red Menace,' " in Marvin Gettleman et al., eds., *El Salvador: Central America in the New Cold War* (1986), p. 327.

2. Michael McClintock, *The American Connection* (1985), pp. 332–37; Reps. Jim Leach and George Miller, Sen. Mark Hatfield, "U.S. Aid to El Salvador: An Evaluation of the Past, a Proposal for the Future—A Report to the Arms Control and Foreign Policy Caucus," in Marvin Gettleman et al., eds., *El Salvador: Central America in the New Cold War* (1986), p. 231.

3. "Communist Interference in El Salvador," February 23, 1981, U.S. Dept. of State, Special Report no. 80.

4. Kevin Kose, "Soviets Deny Supply Weapons to Marxist Guerrillas in El Salvador," *Washington Post,* February 26, 1981, p. A30, col. 1.

5. Stephen Weeks, "International News," Reuters, February 26, 1981, AM cycle.

6. Robert G. Kaiser, "White Paper on El Salvador Is Faulty; Flaws in Salvador White Paper Raise Questions about Its Analysis," *Washington Post,* June 9, 1981, p. A1, col. 2.

7. Clifford Krauss, "U.S. and Soviets Jointly Urge Settlement in El Salvador," *New York Times,* October 19, 1990, p. A3, col. 3.

8. Jonathan Kwitny, "Apparent Errors Cloud U.S. 'White Paper' on Reds in El Salvador," *Wall Street Journal,* June 8, 1981, p. A1, col. 6.

9. Robert G. Kaiser, "White Paper on El Salvador Is Faulty."

10. Kwitny, "Apparent Errors Cloud U.S. 'White Paper' on Reds in El Salvador."

11. Ibid.

12. Ibid.

13. Kaiser, "White Paper on El Salvador Is Faulty."

14. Petras, "Blots on the White Paper," in *El Salvador,* pp. 327–28; Raymond Bonner, *Weakness and Deceit: U.S. Policy and El Salvador* (1984), pp. 259–60.

15. Case concerning Military and Paramilitary Activities in and against Nicaragua (*Nica.* v. *USA*), International Court of Justice, *Reports,* p. 86, § 160 (1986).

16. Bonner, *Weakness and Deceit,* pp. 267–68.

17. Ibid., p. 261.

18. "Should the U.S. Fight Secret Wars?" *Harper's Magazine,* September 1984, p. 44.

19. Mary Jo McConahay, "Living under El Salvador's Air War," in Gettleman et al., *El Salvador,* p. 235.

20. James LeMoyne, "Salvador Air Role in War Increases," *New York Times,* July 18, 1985, p. A1, col. 3.

21. Reps. Leach and Miller, Sen. Hatfield, "U.S. Aid to El Salvador," in *El Salvador,* p. 367.

22

Lebanon: Death on the Beach

In August 1982, the American Marines returned to the beaches of Beirut, as the Reagan administration sent a force to Lebanon into a civil war that pitted the pro-Western government representing Lebanese Christians against Muslim-based Arab nationalists. If this scenario sounds familiar, it was the same political lineup as that at the time of our intervention in Lebanon in 1958, and on the same side.

This intervention was precipitated by Israel's invasion of Lebanon in June 1982. Israel's aim was twofold: to drive the Palestine Liberation Organization (PLO) out of Lebanon and to install in that country a government friendly to Israel.[1] Lebanon by this time had been rent by internal war for so long that it was in no position to repel Israel's attack; therefore, the Israeli army was able quickly to push northward to Beirut.

Once Israel's army was in occupation, the Lebanese parliament held a presidential election and chose Bashir Gemayel, of the rightist Phalange party. The Phalange, based in Lebanon's Christian population, was a rival for the Christian vote to the party of the more moderate Camille Chamoun, who had been president in 1958.[2] The Phalange party was founded in the 1930s by Bashir Gemayel's father, Pierre Gemayel, who named it after the fascist movements in Italy and Spain, which he admired.[3] More than Chamoun's party, the Phalange was prone to use force against its opponents, and it commanded a strong militia.

President Reagan, however, called the election of Bashir Gemayel a positive development.[4] From Reagan's perspective, Gemayel presented advantages, because for some time he had been close to the United States, particularly to the CIA.[5] Indeed, the United States had given military aid to the Phalange militias and put Gemayel in contact with Israel;[6] since the mid-1970s, Israel and the Phalange had forged a virtual military alliance to oppose their common enemy, the PLO.[7] Israel also gave the Phalange military aid,[8] in return for which the Phalange provided Israel with intelligence information about Palestinians in Lebanon.[9] When Israel invaded Lebanon, Gemayel welcomed it, because he wanted the PLO out.[10]

Israel hit the PLO's stronghold, West Beirut, with massive bombardment, until the PLO agreed to withdraw from the country. The Reagan administration, working with several other countries, sent troops to oversee the PLO evacuation as well as to protect the Palestinian refugees living in Beirut, who had relied on the PLO for protection against the Phalange.[11]

The PLO departed Beirut in early September,[12] and the Marines left one week later.[13] Calm, however, was not to return to Lebanon. Israel and the Phalange suspected that PLO combatants had stayed behind and hidden in Palestinian refugee camps in Beirut; therefore, they made plans for a Phalange search expedition into the camps.[14]

There was another reason for the joint Phalange-Israeli action: just a few days after the Marines left, Bashir Gemayel was assassinated.[15] Soon the Israeli army sealed off the Palestinian refugee camps in Beirut and let Phalange militiamen enter, ostensibly to search for PLO combatants. Once in the camps, however, the Phalange soldiers began killing Palestinian civilians indiscriminately.[16] Estimates of the dead ranged from 700 to 3,000.[17]

Gemayel's brother Amin was elected president by the parliament,[18] and President Reagan sent 1,200 Marines back into Beirut.[19] Reagan declared that this second landing would "assist the Government of Lebanon in reasserting authority over all its territory. Foreign forces and armed factions have too long obstructed the legitimate role of the Lebanese Government's security forces."[20] This was a longer-term and more complex objective than the August landing.

While Reagan tried to portray the U.S. function as neutral, i.e., to help restore Lebanon to the elected government, his backing of the "Lebanese Government's security forces" could only mean opposing the Arab nationalists. Like Eisenhower in 1958, Reagan hoped to shore up the pro-Western government against a variety of nationalist militia forces that were arrayed against it.[21]

As president, Amin Gemayel cooperated with the United States and Israel.[22] In May 1983, he helped negotiate an agreement for an Israeli pullback from central Lebanon, which still left Israel in occupation of southern Lebanon.[23] This agreement foresaw a close military and intelligence partnership with Israel.[24] Reagan pressured Gemayel to hold conciliation talks with the other Lebanese militia in order to broaden the base of his government, but factionalism in Lebanon remained strong; on October 19, 1983, Gemayel suspended the talks.[25]

On October 23, 1983, with the U.S. Marines in Beirut just over a year, a member of a Shia Muslim militia drove a truck laden with explosives to the door of an apartment building that served as a Marine barracks in Beirut, not far from the waterfront. The explosives detonated, the driver was blown up, and the building collapsed, killing 241 of the Marines inside.[26] Administration officials called the bombing an act of terrorism, while the press covered the killing as a senseless act against men who were trying to help Lebanon. From the standpoint of the Shia militias, however, the Marines in Lebanon were the enemy, because we sided with the Phalange. We were backing the element in Lebanon that had traditionally been pro-Western and allied to the United States. To make matters worse, we were consolidating power for a Lebanese government that worked hand in glove with Israel, which was strongly disliked by the nationalists for depriving the Palestinians of nationhood.

Even after the bombing of the Marines barracks, Reagan continued to back the Gemayel government. Since Syria had troops in the country arrayed against the Phalange, Reagan ordered the navy to shell Syrian positions in villages in central Lebanon from the USS *New Jersey*.[27] This angered the nationalists even more, because the shelling killed civilians. In February 1984, Reagan withdrew the Marines from Lebanon but kept the ships offshore.[28]

Throughout the Lebanon episode, the Reagan administration was successful in selling its version of the events, so Congress and the public did not realize that the Marines were acting not in a neutral but in a distinctly partisan role, which is what led to the bombing of the barracks. If our true objectives had been understood, the administration might have been forced to take an evenhanded approach, or simply leave Lebanon. As it was, this second expedition of the Marines to the Lebanese beaches ended in disaster.

Notes

1. David K. Shipler, "Israel and Lebanon Sign Agreement at 2 Ceremonies," *New York Times,* May 18, 1983, p. A16, col. 1.

2. John Kifner, "Lebanon Assembly Elects a Rightist to the Presidency," *New York Times,* August 24, 1983, p. A1, col. 6; Joe Stork, "Report from Lebanon," *MERIP Reports* 13, no. 8 (October 1983): 4.

3. Edward A. Gargan, "Bashir Gemayel Lived by the Sword," *New York Times,* September 15, 1982, p. A8, col. 1.

4. Bernard Gwertzman, "Washington Hails Lebanon Outcome," *New York Times,* August 24, 1980, p. A6, col. 1.

5. Bob Woodward, *Veil: The Secret Wars of the CIA 1981-1987* (1987), p. 204.

6. Ibid., pp. 205, 217-18.

7. David K. Shipler, "Israeli Inquiry into Beirut Massacre to Focus on 2 Key Questions," *New York Times,* October 10, 1982, p. A14, col. 1.

8. Woodward, *Veil,* p. 203; "Maronist Leader Says He Started Israeli Link," *New York Times,* June 20, 1982, p. A12, col. 1.

9. Woodward, *Veil,* p. 249.

10. Gargan, "Bashir Gemayel Lived by the Sword."

11. Bernard Gwertzman, "Reagan Orders Marines to Beirut to Oversee Withdrawal by P.L.O.," *New York Times,* August 21, 1982, p. A1, col. 1; Helena Cobban, *The Making of Modern Lebanon* (1985), p. 185.

12. Colin Campbell, "Last Guerrillas Quit West Beirut," *New York Times,* September 2, 1982, p. A1, col. 5.

13. Colin Campbell, "U.S. Marines Leave Lebanese Capital," *New York Times,* September 11, 1982, p. A5, col. 1.

14. Shipler, "Israeli Inquiry into Beirut Massacre to Focus on 2 Key Questions."

15. Colin Campbell, "Gemayel of Lebanon Is Killed in Bomb Blast at Party Offices," *New York Times,* September 15, 1982, p. A1, col. 6; John Laffin, *The War of Desperation: Lebanon 1982-85* (1985), p. 169.

16. Thomas L. Friedman, "Christian Militiamen Accused of a Massacre in Beirut Camps; U.S. Says the Toll Is at Least 300," *New York Times,* September 19, 1982, p. A1, col. 6; Laffin, *War of Desperation,* pp. 170-71.

17. Linda A. Malone, "The Kahan Report, Ariel Sharon and the Sabra-Shatilla Massacres in Lebanon: Responsibility Under International Law for Massacres of Civilian Populations," *Utah Law Review* (1985): 396.

18. Colin Campbell, "Amin Gemayel Elected President in a Display of Unity by Lebanese," *New York Times,* September 22, 1982, p. A1, col. 4.

19. Steven R. Weisman, "Reagan Says U.S. Will Keep Its Marine Force in Lebanon Till Israelis and Syrians Go," *New York Times,* September 29, 1982, p. A1, col. 6;

"Ambassador Dillon's Letter," September 25, 1982, DSB, vol. 82, p. 51 (November 1982); Cobban, *The Making of Modern Lebanon,* p. 190.

20. "President's Statement," September 20, 1982, DSB, vol. 82, p. 49 (November 1982).

21. Cobban, *The Making of Modern Lebanon,* pp. 199–202; Jonathan Randal, *The Tragedy of Lebanon: Christian Warlords, Israeli Adventurers and American Bunglers* (1983), p. 277; Francis A. Boyle, "International Law and Organizations as an Approach to Conflict Resolution in the Middle East," in Thomas Buergenthal, ed., *Contemporary Issues in International Law: Essays in Honor of Louis B. Sohn* (1984), p. 532; Stork, "Report from Lebanon," pp. 3–4, 12–13.

22. Stork, "Report from Lebanon," p. 4.

23. Ibid., p. 3; Shipler, "Israel and Lebanon Sign Agreement at 2 Ceremonies."

24. Shipler, "Israel and Lebanon Sign Agreement at 2 Ceremonies."

25. Cobban, *The Making of Modern Lebanon,* p. 202.

26. Ibid., pp. 202–3; Thomas L. Friedman, "Beirut Death Toll at 161 Americans," *New York Times,* October 24, 1983, p. A1, col. 6.

27. Joseph B. Treaster, "Battleship's Guns Shell Syrian Sites in Lebanese War," *New York Times,* December 15, 1983, p. A1, col. 6.

28. Cobban, *The Making of Modern Lebanon,* p. 205; Steven R. Weisman, "President Asserts Marines in Beirut Still Have a Role," *New York Times,* February 23, 1984, p. A1, col. 6.

23

Grenada: An Ocean Venture

On a Saturday evening in October 1983, I was at a dinner party with close friends, where the conversation turned to the Caribbean. In the tiny island nation of Grenada, with a population of 100,000, a leftist government was in crisis. One faction within the ruling party had just overthrown and killed the leader, a man named Maurice Bishop; in the ensuing fighting, seventeen others were killed. News broadcasts that Saturday aired rumors that the Reagan administration might move against Grenada, which, because of its close relations with Cuba, was a thorn in the administration's side. President Reagan had campaigned in 1980 on a platform of fighting communism, but after two years in office, he still had no victory to show. The political weakness in Grenada that had been created by the internal dissension now provided an ideal opportunity to strike. On that very evening, in fact, the Joint Chiefs of Staff were ordering Admiral Wesley McDonald, commander in chief of the U.S. Atlantic command, to land Marines and Army Ranger paratroopers in Grenada.[1] Grenada had attracted Reagan's interest early on in his administration. In 1981, he had the Atlantic command run a training exercise off the coast of Puerto Rico,[2] which the navy called Ocean Venture 1981. The exercise was based on a hypothetical invasion of an island country code-named "Amber and the Amberines." Grenada's full name, as it happens, is Grenada and the Grenadines. In Grenada, there was a location called Amber; in the exercise, Amber was being supported by a country called Orange, which in turn was supported by Red. Orange represented Cuba, and Red the Soviet Union. The commander of Ocean Venture 1981 explained at a press briefing that Amber was "exporting terrorist activities to neighboring islands." His forces would, therefore, rescue "twenty U.S. citizens held hostage there after negotiations with the Amber Government had broken down." The objective of Ocean Venture 1981, then, was to capture Amber and install a "government friendly to America."[3]

Grenada was featured in a speech President Reagan gave in March 1983 on U.S. military policy. Prominently displayed behind the president was an aerial photograph of a new airport under construction in Grenada; Reagan used this as an ominous sign that Grenada was preparing to let Cuba or the Soviet Union land military aircraft for military invasions in the Caribbean. "On the small island of Grenada," Reagan said, "the Cubans, with Soviet financing and backing, are in the process of building an airfield with a 10,000-foot runway. Grenada doesn't even have an air force. Who is it intended for?" The president then elaborated:

> [T]he Caribbean is a very important passageway for our international commerce and military lines of communication. More than half of all American oil imports now pass through the Caribbean. The rapid build-up of Grenada's military potential is unrelated to any conceivable threat to this island country of under 110,000 people, and totally at odds with the pattern of other eastern Caribbean States, most of which are unarmed. The Soviet-Cuban militarization of Grenada, in short, can only be seen as power projection into the region.[4]

While the map made for good television, the president's analysis was dubious. Reagan said that the airport was for Communist military aircraft, but the Grenada government claimed it was for tourism. Other Caribbean island nations had airports that could accommodate large passenger jets on direct flights from New York and Miami. Grenada's only airport had been a mountain airstrip that could not take the big planes.

Since Cuba contributed construction workers to do the heavy work on the airport, Cuba was, in fact, building the airport. The general contractor on the job, however, wore no red star; it was Plessey, Ltd., a British contracting firm, whose executives explained to the press that they had designed the airport for civilian use. The buildings had not been reinforced to withstand shelling, nor had side-runways or bunkers been built to protect military aircraft from attack.[5] As for lines of communication, U.S. vessels did, as Reagan averred, use the Caribbean for transit, but Cuba was much larger and closer to our shores, and we never had trouble sailing around it.

On October 25, 1983, Ocean Venture 1981 was played out in the real world, in an invasion so remarkably similar to the exercise that the *Times* of London, in retrospect, called Ocean Venture a "rehearsal."[6] Admiral Wesley McDonald carried out President Reagan's orders, landing 6,000 troops in Grenada. Charging that Grenada was about to export revolution elsewhere in the Caribbean, Reagan purported to be rescuing American citizens who, he said, were in danger of being taken hostage by the Grenadian government. In fighting that lasted four days, McDonald defeated the Grenada army, captured Grenada's leaders, and asked a Grenadian official friendly to the United States—a man named Sir Paul Scoon, who held the post of governor general*—to serve as caretaker until a new government could be formed.

Thus, the script of Ocean Venture 1981 was carried out to the letter. While the military action achieved its aim, however, the political fallout of the action was treacherous. At the United Nations, the General Assembly called the assault on Grenada a "flagrant violation of international law," and a denigration of Grenada's "independence, sovereignty and territorial integrity."[7] The administration argued in justification that we had been invited into Grenada by the Organization of Eastern Caribbean States, a regional association of island nations, and also by Governor General Scoon.[8] According to the State Department, Scoon made a request on October 23 for our intervention—not directly but via the Organization of Eastern Caribbean States (OECS).[9]

Scoon confirmed to the press that he had made such a request, but not on October 23. Rather, Scoon sent a request letter on October 24 to the OECS, addressed to Barbados Prime Minister Tom Adams.[10] While the time discrepancy could perhaps have been explained away, there was a more serious problem with Scoon's statement. Prime Minister

---

*In Grenada the governor general was a liaison officer with Great Britain, which ruled Grenada until 1974.

Adams could not confirm having received any letter from Scoon prior to the invasion; Adams's press officer, when queried by the media, replied that Adams received no such letter from Scoon, before or after the invasion.

A request letter with Scoon's signature was later made public by the State Department, despite denials from Adams and his press officer. The press officer thought that the letter had been composed by someone outside Grenada and hand-delivered to Scoon for his signature by U.S. paratroopers. As for who had ghostwritten the request letter, no one ever found out for sure; but press speculation centered on the country most anxious to have the request, the United States.[11]

From available evidence, it is unlikely that Scoon wrote and sent a request letter prior to the invasion. Although he had been in communication with regional officials in the days preceding the intervention, there is no indication that he had specifically requested it.[12] Britain's foreign secretary, Geoffrey Howe, affirmed that a British diplomat spoke with Scoon in person the day before the invasion, but Scoon did not mention that he had made a request or was planning one. Prime Minister Margaret Thatcher concurred. Since these meetings were private, Scoon would have had no concern about his security in revealing he had sent a request letter.[13] As for any contact with the United States before the invasion, Scoon denied there was any, direct or indirect. He said, in fact, that he had no idea the United States was involved until U.S. paratroopers knocked on his door.[14]

Whatever the true story about a request from Scoon, the decision to land troops in Grenada had been made on October 22, three days before the actual landing.[15] So under any version of the alleged request by Scoon, Reagan ordered the intervention prior to any request.

The administration, however, did not rely only on a request from Scoon as justification for the Grenada landing; it also claimed that we had been invited to Grenada by the OECS under its own authority.[16] Grenada was a member of the OECS, whose treaty had provisions about military intervention; therefore, on the face of it, the argument was plausible. And the OECS did ask us to intervene. At its meeting in Barbados on October 21, the OECS decided on intervention; what is more, it asked the United States to do it.

But while that much of the administration's statement was true, it was not the whole story. The OECS treaty allowed military intervention only in case of "external aggression" against one of the member countries, the idea being that the OECS countries would unite to help a member state if it was invaded from outside the area. Grenada, however, had not been invaded by a state outside the area or by any other state. Documents like the OECS treaty give a regional organization only certain powers; therefore, the OECS countries did not have the right to intervene absent an invasion. Nor did they have the right under the treaty to become involved in the domestic politics of one of the member countries, regardless of what they thought of the government in power.

The administration's reliance on the OECS treaty faced one other serious obstacle. The treaty specified that before taking any military action to stop "external aggression," a unanimous vote of all the member countries was required. This was designed to prevent military action in a member country without its consent. Grenada was notably absent, however, from the October 21 OECS meeting in Barbados, which meant that the other members could not vote for military action without violating the treaty. But this is precisely what they did.[17]

If the OECS did not have the right to intervene in Grenada, then it could not ask us to do so on its behalf. But why would the OECS so blatantly violate its own treaty? From all evidence, Washington's gentle hand was at work. When the trouble started in Grenada, the State Department geared up, making plans for a Grenada intervention and approaching Caribbean leaders to sound them out on the subject.[18] Officials in Jamaica, one of the countries we approached, reported that the State Department pressured them to endorse a U.S. intervention to replace the government of Grenada.[19] While the State Department acknowledged that it had held talks about the Grenada situation with Caribbean leaders, it denied having encouraged them to make such a request.

While OECS members met on October 21, Charles Gillespie, our deputy assistant secretary of state for Caribbean affairs, sat in an anteroom outside the meeting chamber.[20] According to reporters, Gillespie was too high an official to spend several hours sitting outside someone else's meeting, unless he had some role to play. In all probability, Gillespie was there either to make sure the delegates voted for intervention, or at least to let them know that if they requested our intervention, they would get it.[21] Since the OECS countries had no military forces to speak of, they could not themselves have intervened in Grenada, which did have an army. The OECS decision to intervene, therefore, made sense only if it already knew that we would carry out the intervention.

When he announced the invasion, however, President Reagan gave the impression that the initiative had come from the OECS. We "acceded," Reagan said, "to the request to become part of a multinational effort with contingents from Antigua and Barbuda, Barbados, Dominica, Jamaica, St. Lucia, St. Vincent and the Grenadines and the United States. . . . Early this morning, forces from six Caribbean democracies and the United States began a landing."[22]

Reagan stressed here the collective nature of the operation. Before the Organization of American States, too, our delegate took up this theme, saying that "a collective security force, made up of contingents from four member states of the OECS—Antigua and Barbuda, Dominica, St. Lucia, and St. Vincent and the Grenadines, supplemented by units from Barbados, Jamaica, and the United States—disembarked on Grenada yesterday [October 25] at dawn."[23]

These statements not only made the Grenada landing sound like an action to which we agreed only after being asked, but they depicted the invasion as having been carried out by a joint force of troops from a number of countries. That was simply not true; the assault was done by U.S. troops alone, Marines and army paratroopers. After the American forces landed, they brought in 300 Jamaicans and Barbadans, not for combat but to guard prisoners and patrol the streets.[24]

In convincing the OECS countries to ask for our help, however, we did not have to twist arms overly hard. Like the Reagan administration, the OECS governments, all right of center, worried about the leftists in Grenada. Already leftists in other OECS countries were looking to Grenada as a model; therefore, putting down Grenada would stop the virus before it spread. After the landing, in fact, OECS governments cracked down on leftists in what was described as a "climate of militant anti-radicalism."[25]

Notes

1. Lt. Col. Michael J. Byron, U.S. Marine Corps, "Fury from the Sea: Marines in Grenada," 110/5/975 *U.S. Naval Institute Proceedings*, p. 124 (May 1984); "Ten Days of Urgent Fury," *All Hands* (U.S. Navy), p. 34 (May 1984).

2. Fred Hiatt, "U.S. Says Situation Still Unclear as Naval Force Nears Grenada," *Washington Post,* October 23, 1983, p. A24, col. 1.

3. Christopher Searle, *Grenada: The Struggle Against Destabilization* (1983), pp. 37–38.

4. "President's Speech on Military Spending and a New Defense," *New York Times,* March 24, 1983, p. A20, col. 1.

5. Rodney Cowton, "Plessey Say New Airport Not Military," *Times* (London), November 1, 1983, p. 6, col. 5; "L'aéroport de Point-Salines," *Le Monde,* November 1, 1983, p. 3, col. 1; "Firm Dismisses Claim Airport Was Military," *Toronto Globe and Mail,* November 2, 1983, p. 14, col. 1.

6. Nicholas Ashford, "U.S. Staged 'Invasion Rehearsal' in 1981," *Times* (London), November 7, 1983, p. 5, col. 1.

7. Res. 38/7, GAOR, 38th yr., *Resolutions and Decisions,* Supplement No. 47, p. 19 (1983).

8. Letter from Davis R. Robinson, Legal Adviser, U.S. Dept. of State, to Prof. Edward Gordon, Chairman, Committee on Grenada, Section on International Law and Practice, American Bar Assn., February 10, 1984, in *International Lawyer* 18 (1984): 381.

9. Letter from Davis R. Robinson, p. 381.

10. Alex Brummer, "Scoon Tells of Rescue by Paras," *Guardian* (Manchester), November 1, 1983, p. 1, col. 6.

11. Alan George, "Did Washington Ghost-Write Scoon's Appeal?" *New Statesman,* November 11, 1983, p. 5.

12. Latin America Bureau, *Grenada: Whose Freedom?* (1984), p. 88.

13. Ian Aitken and Martin Wainwright, "Hurt Thatcher Widens Breach with Reagan," *Guardian* (Manchester), October 31, 1983, p. 1, col. 1.

14. Alex Brummer, "Scoon Tells of Rescue by Paras."

15. "D-Day in Grenada," *Time,* November 7, 1983, p. 27.

16. Letter from Davis R. Robinson, p. 381.

17. Treaty Establishing the Organization of Eastern Caribbean States, June 18, 1981, art. 8, *International Legal Materials* 20 (1981): 1166.

18. Patrick E. Tyler, "State Dept. Denies Reports that U.S. Sought Pretext for Invasion," *Washington Post,* October 28, 1983, p. A10, col. 1.

19. Juan Williams, "Jamaicans Indicate U.S. Signaled Will to Invade," *Washington Post,* October 27, 1983, p. A20, col. 1; Tyler, "State Dept. Denies Reports that U.S. Sought Pretext for Invasion."

20. Ralph Kinney Bennett, "Grenada: Anatomy of a 'Go' Decision," *Reader's Digest,* February 1984, p. 74.

21. Bob Woodward, *Veil: The Secret Wars of the CIA 1981–1987* (1987), p. 290.

22. "Grenada: Collective Action by the Caribbean Peace Force," DSB, vol. 83, p. 67 (December 1983).

23. "Grenada: Collective Action by the Caribbean Peace Force," p. 72.

24. Fred Halliday, "An Ambiguous Turning Point: Grenada and Its Aftermath," in *North American Congress on Latin America Report on the Americas,* November–December 1984, p. 21.

25. Dennis Volman, "Antileftist Feeling Is Rising in Caribbean," *Christian Science Monitor,* November 28, 1983, p. 11, col. 1.

24

Grenada: Saving Our Students

The Reagan administration had one other pretext for the Grenada landing: to protect American citizens residing there.[1] If true, this might not justify overthrowing Grenada's government, although it might at least justify getting a foot in the door. And there were, in fact, U.S. citizens in Grenada, most of them students at a medical college run from New York. President Reagan said that it was "of overriding importance" to intervene to protect "innocent lives, including up to a thousand Americans, whose personal safety is, of course, my paramount concern."[2]

These students had not, however, come to any harm, nor had they been threatened. But administration officials still alleged that the Grenadians who overthrew Maurice Bishop might take these students hostage.[3] One official, who wished to remain anonymous, told reporters that the United States found documents in Grenada showing a government plan to seize some of the students. "It is clear from these documents and other information we now have," said the official, "that serious consideration was being given to seizing Americans as hostages and holding them for reasons that are not entirely clear, but seem to involve an effort to embarrass the United States and, more immediately, to forestall American military action in Grenada."[4] The administration, however, never disclosed these putative documents, even though the media pressed for them.[5]

But prior to the invasion the administration did have information about the situation in Grenada. James Budeit, one of several State Department officials sent to Grenada two days before the invasion to talk to Grenadian officials and to the medical students, found no reason to believe that the Grenada government would harm the students.[6] Violence had occurred on October 19, but on October 20 the new government imposed a curfew, and from that time Grenada was quiet. The situation was calm enough that Leon Cornwall, a member of the new Grenadian government, invited Budeit to spend the evening at a disco. Although Cornwall "seemed a nice enough guy," Budeit said, he declined the invitation, explaining later, "I can't go to discos with them. Our president called them a gang of leftist thugs."[7]

The administration could not present a logical explanation why the Grenadian government might take hostages; indeed, that government had good reasons to treat the students well. The medical school was a prime source of foreign exchange for the tiny nation, a key element in its economy. A government that lost the medical school would not likely survive. The school's vice-chancellor, Geoffrey Bourne, in fact, received a visit soon after the anti-Bishop coup from the head of the new government, who asked if the students were doing well and who gave Bourne his home telephone number to call in case of any difficulties.[8]

When he announced the invasion, President Reagan gave as one reason for thinking the students were in danger the fact that "we'd been informed of several hundred who wanted to leave."[9] The number given by State Department officials in Barbados on October 24 was 300.[10]

On October 22 and 23, however, according to Budeit and the vice-chancellor, only 100 to 150 students wanted to leave, and their fear was prompted by the threat of a U.S. attack.[11] On the evening of October 23, radio stations from neighboring islands broadcast "rumors" that we would invade Grenada and, according to the vice-chancellor, "this scared the students very much."[12] Understandably, they did not want to be caught in Grenada during an invasion. This concern was shared back in the United States by the students' parents, five hundred of whom sent President Reagan a telegram on October 24, asking him not to invade Grenada, because they did not want their children endangered.[13] Meanwhile, State Department officials in Barbados told the medical students that while the Grenadian government would likely not harm them, there could perhaps be a counter-coup against the new government, which might be a source of danger. Budeit, who actually believed there might be a counter-coup, "scared the hell out of those people," leaving the wives of some of the students in tears.[14]

But no evidence surfaced of any Grenadian group in formation to stage a counter-coup, and even if there had been, there was no reason to believe the students would be harmed. In the fighting that accompanied the overthrow of Bishop, no medical students were injured; none were even reported to be in the fray, since most of the students lived some distance from the downtown area where the violence occurred.

The State Department took one other tack to create the appearance of danger to the students. Peter Bourne, a professor at the medical school and son of the vice-chancellor, happened to be in the United States at the time, when he got a phone call from a member of the school's board of trustees. The board member told Bourne that State Department officials were telephoning the school officials in New York and pressing them to state publicly that the students were in danger.[15] The medical school issued no such statement. Nor did the school officials see any danger until they heard that the United States would invade.

There was one other flaw in President Reagan's position that an invasion was necessary to save the students. Even if there were a danger of a hostage-taking by the Grenadian government, or else of a counter-coup in which the students might be caught up, it remained unclear why a Marine landing was needed. There were no hostilities, and the Grenadian government was not preventing the students from leaving.

On October 22 and 23, in fact, State Department officials from Barbados talked with the Grenadian government about possible ways to evacuate the students. But according to Secretary of Defense Caspar Weinberger, while "attempts were made to get Americans out," the Grenadian government "failed to live up to its assurances that the airport would be opened on October 24 and foreigners would be free to leave. Therefore, the U.S. was unable to get any Americans out on charter flights prior to the U.S. invasion."[16] Thus, in Weinberger's version of events, the Grenadian government had made it impossible to get the students out by normal means, making an invasion necessary. Deputy Secretary of State Kenneth Dam made the same allegation: "Charter flights were not allowed in."[17]

Weinberger was referring not to the new airport under construction, but to the existing smaller airport called Pearls, which was, in fact, open and functioning on October 24. By chance, a retired federal official, Robert J. Myers, who had been chief actuary in the Social Security Administration, was in Grenada at the time; he reported taking a flight out of Grenada from Pearls Airport on October 24.[18]

Four charter flights, in fact, flew into and out of Pearls Airport that day. A fifth had been scheduled, but was canceled at the last minute by the charterer, Leeward Islands Air Transport, which was owned jointly by several Caribbean island countries collaborating in the invasion.[19] Leeward Islands canceled the flight because the Caribbean Community, a regional economic group, decided on October 22 to ban all flights to Grenada as an economic sanction.[20]

State Department officials apparently made no effort to get the medical students on these flights, or to organize others. The Grenadian government, far from obstructing an evacuation, contacted the vice-chancellor by phone on October 21, to ask whether any students wanted to leave and to offer cooperation in transport arrangements if they did. Cornwall told State Department officials that charter flights could use Pearls to evacuate students; however, the State Department declined, claiming that the runway at Pearls was too short to accommodate large planes, and that the road to Pearls was poor. The State Department proposed sending a battleship for the students, but Grenadian officials, fearing an invasion, insisted that any ships be civilian.[21] U.S. Officials then told Cornwall that a Cunard cruise liner, the SS *Countess,* was scheduled to dock in Grenada October 25, and Cornwall agreed that any students wishing to leave could board. This plan was scotched in Washington, however, because the invasion was already set for October 25.[22]

The State Department had been purposly avoiding options for a peaceful evacuation. *Time* magazine reasoned that evacuation would have been better than invasion, "if their [the students'] safety was [our] primary concern."[23] "There was no evidence," wrote another observer, "that the Americans could not have been evacuated without military action."[24] The medical students, in fact, were part of the administration's plan for invading Grenada. It needed the appearance of their being in danger as a pretext to remove Grenada's government.

On October 25, as the invasion began, reporters were keen to know the fate of the students. When they asked President Reagan whether the students were safe, he replied, "As far as we know, the citizens are safe. We have been monitoring that very closely."[25] Two days later, on October 27, Reagan said in a televised speech, "Almost instantly our military seized the two airports, secured the campus where most of our students were and they're now in the mopping-up phase."[26] In fact, our forces had not located many of the medical students. Incredibly, no one had even told the commanders where to find them.

The first U.S. forces to arrive in Grenada were airborne U.S. Army Ranger units that parachuted into the new airport under construction at Point Salines. Next door was a campus where one hundred of the medical students lived. There was a second campus at a location called Grand Anse, where over two hundred students lived, and a residential area called Lance aux Épines, which housed two hundred more. Still other students lived in private apartments scattered around St. George's, the capital. Secretary of Defense Weinberger, when asked in a House hearing whether "operation commanders were not aware that the Medical School in Grenada had two separate campuses," answered, "Initially it was not known that the medical school had two campuses."[27] One of the commanders, Major General Norman Schwarzkopf, who in 1990 would lead U.S. forces in the Persian Gulf, confirmed that the commanders had been told only about the campus at Point Salines. Schwarzkopf called the commanders' ignorance of the Grande Anse campus or the Lance aux Épines residential area a failure of intelligence.[28]

Admiral McDonald, the overall commander, recorded the snafu in his "after-action" report: "Evacuee locating information was not available except that they were generally located in the St. George area [i.e., St. George's]. During execution of the operation, interviews with the first evacuees provided location information for other potential evacuees."[29] The commanders themselves had information about the whereabouts of only one hundred out of nearly one thousand students.

The reason for this is that the Grenada landing was not a rescue mission; its purpose was to remove Grenada's government. This so-called intelligence failure, however, could have turned the Grenada "rescue" from low comedy to high tragedy: Grenada, after all, had an army, and fighting went on for four days. Just as their parents feared, the students wound up caught in a war zone.

Incredibly, the U.S. forces did not try, once they arrived, to rescue those students whose location they did know. Although the commanders knew about the Point Salines campus, the Rangers landing at the Point Salines airport did not immediately approach it. They landed at 5:30 A.M.

but did not enter the campus until 10:30 A.M.—five hours later—even though it was only a few yards away.[30] More incredibly still, after the Rangers reached that campus, they did not arrange an evacuation, even though fighting was continuing in the immediate area. Only on the following day did they begin to arrange transportation for the students.[31]

At the Point Salines campus, the firing was intense. The Grenadian army had gun emplacements around the airport construction site, and some of the Cuban airport workers living in dormitories nearby had rifles. The Rangers attacked both groups by calling in helicopter gunships. Approaching from the sea, the gunships flew directly over the campus en route to Grenadian positions and the dormitories, where they inflicted heavy casualties.[32]

Seeing the helicopters firing overhead, the students were frightened out of their wits. Several students had ham radios; one broadcast that there was "quite a bit of fire" coming directly into the campus from the gunships.[33] Another student reported that shells fired by the gunships landed "less than 50 meters from our building on the campus,"[34] while still another claimed that a bullet struck the pillow on his bed.[35] One frantic student sent out a message by radio to our forces, pleading that they divert the helicopters from the campus.[36] If these students were being rescued, this was a strange way to go about doing it. When the medical school chancellor in New York received word that firing was occurring close to the campus, he replied if any students were hurt, President Reagan "should be held accountable."[37]

Meantime, our forces were still in the process of recovering the other nine hundred medical students. The next group to be reached were those at the Grand Anse campus, but that did not occur until the afternoon of October 26, thirty-five hours after the landing. Grand Anse was close to St. George's, in an area well defended by the Grenadian army; to take those Grenadian positions, our bombers had to strafe heavily near the Grand Anse campus, in particular releasing what reporters called a "devastating barrage" that leveled two hotels near the campus.[38] To assault this area, Marines piloted the helicopters ferrying in Army Rangers. The return fire against the helicopters was so intense that some of the Marine pilots refused to land, hovering just above the ground, and forcing the Rangers to jump.[39]

While the fighting with the Grenada units near the Grand Anse campus continued, the Marines took helicopters in to evacuate the students. But these helicopters, too, met heavy fire, with students reporting that as they ran to the helicopters, "shots whizzed about them."[40] According to the Marine Corps "after-action" report, four helicopters were hit during the evacuation operation, although no one was injured. "Liftoff" with the Grand Anse campus students, the report said, "commenced at 1600" (4:00 P.M.) on October 26. "In less than an hour, 224 students were evacuated under fire without any friendly casualties. Three helicopters were damaged in the assault with one helicopter destroyed. There were no losses to passengers or crew."[41]

Our forces did not reach the students at the Lance aux Épines residential area until October 28, three days after landing in Grenada.[42] All this time these students had remained behind Grenadian army lines. The same was true of those students who lived in private housing around St. George's, where our forces called in air strikes on Grenadian army positions.[43] One of the air strikes demolished, apparently by accident, a mental hospital, killing seventeen patients.[44] Fortunately, in the bombing of St. George's, no students were hit.

Robert Pastor, who had been a Latin American specialist in the National Security Council during the Carter administration, was doubtless correct when he told a House committee that "U.S. citizens were more likely to have been endangered by the invasion than by the Grenada Government."[45] While there was little reason to expect harm from the Grenadian government, a full-scale military invasion with one thousand United States civilians in the line of fire was extremely hazardous. An army analyst wrote that had the Grenadian forces been so inclined, they could easily have retaliated against the students for the invasion.[46]

Reporters understood that the administration had invented facts to justify the Grenada landing. The *New York Times* wrote that the administration put out "deliberate distortions and knowingly false statements of fact."[47] *Time* magazine called the administration "disingenuous in its public explanations," and said that "American aims" went "well beyond those stated."[48]

Most media coverage, however, accepted the administration statements at face value. The television networks broadcast and rebroadcast scenes of the medical students kissing the ground at U.S. airports after their return flights, giving the impression that our forces had saved them from certain danger. The networks did not elaborate on who had put the students in danger initially, and just how lucky they were to arrive home alive.

Notes

1. Letter from Davis R. Robinson, Legal Adviser, U.S. Dept. of State, to Prof. Edward Gordon, Chairman, Committee on Grenada, Section on International Law and Practice, American Bar Assn., February 10, 1984, in *International Lawyer* 18 (1984): 385.

2. "Grenada: Collective Action by the Caribbean Peace Force," DSB, vol. 83, p. 67 (December 1983).

3. Ibid., p. 80.

4. Philip Taubman, "U.S. Reports Evidence of Island Hostage Plan," *New York Times,* October 28, 1983, p. A14, col. 5.

5. John Quigley, "The United States Invasion of Grenada: Stranger than Fiction," *University of Miami Inter-American Law Review* 18 (1986–87): 281.

6. Jonathan Kwitny, *Endless Enemies: The Making of an Unfriendly World* (1984), p. 417.

7. Ibid., p. 416.

8. *U.S. Military Actions in Grenada: Implications for U.S. Policy in the Eastern Caribbean,* Hearing before the Subcommittees on International Security and Scientific Affairs and on Western Hemisphere Affairs of the House Committee on Foreign Affairs, 98th Cong., 1st sess. (1983), pp. 187–91.

9. " 'U.S. Had to Act Strongly, Decisively,' " *Washington Post,* October 26, 1983, p. A7, col. 1.

10. Michael T. Kaufman, "50 Marines Land at Barbados Field," *New York Times,* October 25, 1983, p. A1, col. 1.

11. Kwitny, *Endless Enemies,* p. 413.

12. *U.S. Military Actions in Grenada,* p. 193.

13. Michael T. Kaufman, "50 Marines Land at Barbados Field," *New York Times,* October 25, 1983, p. A1, col. 1.

14. Kwitny, *Endless Enemies,* p. 414.

15. P. Bourne, "Was the U.S. Invasion Necessary?" *Los Angeles Times,* November 6, 1983, p. IV3, col. 4.

16. *Situation in Lebanon and Grenada,* Hearing Before a Subcommittee of the House Committee on Appropriations, 98th Cong., 1st sess. (1983), p. 58.

17. *The Situation in Grenada,* Hearing before the Senate Committee on Foreign Relations, 98th Cong., 1st sess. (1983), p. 6.

18. Hedrick Smith, "Ex-U.S. Official Cites Ease in Leaving Grenada Day Before Invasion," *New York Times,* October 29, 1983, p. A7, col. 3.

19. "Ottawa Probing if Grenada Flights Purposely Scuttled," *Toronto Globe and Mail,* November 12, 1983, p. 1, col. 2.

20. Christopher Thomas, "Marines Sent to Three Islands near Grenada," *Times* (London), October 25, 1983, p. 1, col. 2.

21. *U.S. Military Actions in Grenada,* p. 193.

22. Hedrick Smith, "Reagan Aide Says U.S. Invasion Forestalled Cuban Arms Buildup," *New York Times,* October 27, 1983, p. A1, col. 3; Kwitny, *Endless Enemies,* p. 413.

23. "Now to Make It Work," *Time,* November 14, 1983, p. 19.

24. Edwin C. Hoyt, *Law and Force in American Foreign Policy* (1985), p. 144.

25. " 'U.S. Had to Act Strongly, Decisively.' "

26. "Transcript of Address by President on Lebanon and Grenada," *New York Times,* October 28, 1983, p. A10, col. 1.

27. *Situation in Lebanon and Grenada,* Hearing Before a Subcommittee of the House Committee on Appropriations, 98th Cong., 1st sess. (1983), p. 56.

28. Edward Cody, "Estimates of Casualties in Grenada Are Raised," *Washington Post,* November 9, 1983, p. A1, col. 6.

29. Commander in Chief, U.S. Atlantic Command, *Operation Urgent Fury Report* (1984), p. II-9.

30. U.S. Marine Corps Development and Education Command Newsletter: *Operational Overview,* January–March 1984, p. 12.

31. Quigley, "The United States Invasion of Grenada," p. 296.

32. Drew Middleton, "Operation on Grenada: How Forces Performed," *New York Times,* October 28, 1983, p. A12, col. 1.

33. Judith Valente, "Beltsville Ham Operator Monitors Eyewitness Reports on Invasion," *Washington Post,* October 26, 1983, p. A10, col. 1.

34. Ward Sinclair, "Medical Students Recount Tale of Tense Escape from Grenada," *Washington Post,* October 28, 1983, p. A17, col. 1.

35. "D-Day in Grenada," *Time,* November 7, 1983, p. 23.

36. "Under Fire, Ham Radio Operators Describe Invasion," *New York Times,* October 26, 1983, p. A20, col. 2.

37. John T. McQuiston, "School's Chancellor Says Invasion Was Not Necessary to Save Lives," *New York Times,* October 26, 1983, p. A20, col. 5.

38. "Battle for Grenada," *Newsweek,* November 7, 1983, p. 72.

39. *U.S. Military Actions in Grenada,* p. 83.

40. "D-Day in Grenada," *Time,* November 7, 1983, p. 25.

41. *Operational Overview,* p. 18.

42. Cody, "Estimates of Casualties in Grenada Are Raised."

43. Sinclair, "Medical Students Recount Tale of Tense Escape from Grenada."

44. B. Drummond Ayres, Jr., "U.S. Concedes Bombing Hospital in Grenada, Killing at Least 12," *New York Times,* November 1, 1983, p. A1, col. 1; "Pentagon Account of Attack," *New York Times,* November 1, 1983, p. A16, col. 3.

45. *U.S. Military Actions in Grenada,* p. 73.

46. Charles Doe, "Grenada: Will Its Lessons Be Taught?" *Army Times,* November 5, 1984, p. 32.

47. Stuart Taylor, Jr., "In Wake of Invasion, Much Official Misinformation by U.S. Comes to Light," *New York Times,* November 6, 1983, p. A20, col. 1.

48. "Weighing the Proper Role," *Time,* November 7, 1983, p. 48.

25

Grenada: The Cubans Were Ferocious

One other aspect of the Grenada operation found the administration anxious to press its version of events. As we saw, Cuban workers were housed in dormitories near the Point Salines airport site. The administration alleged that they were in fact a military unit masquerading as construction workers, and that they fought in alliance with the Grenadian army to repel our attack.[1]

The Cuban workers, at least some of them, did fight against the Army Rangers who parachuted into Point Salines, but it is less clear how that fighting started. The Defense Department claimed that it did not intend to engage the Cubans, and that the Cubans fired first.[2] According to Secretary of Defense Caspar Weinberger, "we broadcast to the Cubans as quickly as possible that we were not attacking Cubans, and that they should not shoot at us, because our aim was to liberate the American students—American civilians there, and that we were dealing only with the Grenadian Armed Forces. They didn't heed that, and as a result, we had to use force." The Cubans, to whom Weinberger referred as "the Cuban forces," had been readied to "resist a landing" by our forces.[3]

Other U.S. officials painted a similar picture. Admiral Wesley McDonald called the Cubans "well-trained professional soldiers" who

213

were impersonating construction workers.[4] Deputy Secretary of State Kenneth Dam said they were "organized Cuban units. These were not just construction workers helping out the poor Grenadian people to build a little airfield."[5] At first the Defense Department estimated that there were 1,100 Cubans in Grenada but later reduced the number to 750, which was close to the number of 784 given by the Cuban government.[6]

The version of events provided by Cuban sources, however, was quite different from the Defense Department's. Within a few hours after the landing, Cuba sent a diplomatic note to the United States, charging that the Rangers had assaulted the workers without provocation.[7] At the United Nations, Cuba called it a "cowardly surprise attack."[8] The Cuban government acknowledged that the workers—who were only civilians, after all—had fired back at the Rangers but only in self-defense.

During a visit to Cuba the following spring, I decided to talk to the construction workers to see what I could learn, because our media had not interviewed them. They were still employed, as they had been in Grenada, by the National Union of Enterprises (Caribbean), a parastatal construction firm. I found them in a little town called Puerto Escondido, just east of Havana, where they were at their first post-Grenada job, building a swimming pool. The only visible sign of their Grenada experience was a display they had set up in a makeshift building of portrait photographs of the twenty-four crew members killed in Grenada.

From the Defense Department accounts, I expected the workers to be brawny young specimens, but the men and women I met at Puerto Escondido did not look like a match for Army Rangers. Some were middle-aged, and many were overweight. Quite a few were female clerical workers, while others were female schoolteachers, who taught high school equivalency classes for crew members. Looking at this crew, I could not imagine the "well-trained professional soldiers" described by Admiral McDonald. Some had rifles, they told me, although not all, not even a majority. They had made preparations to defend their dormitories if attacked, but not to initiate fighting in order to repel the invading Rangers.

After returning to the United States, I checked accounts of the Grenada operation by our military officers—what the Defense Department calls "after-action" reports—to see if they might shed light on the character of the Cubans they confronted. "After-action" reports are written for use within the military to assess their strategy, and they are more frank than the public statements the Pentagon issues. What I found in these reports was a picture of the Cubans quite different from Secretary Weinberger's and Admiral McDonald's.

One Marine Corps report admitted to "the low state of training on the part of the Cuban troops (actually only construction workers)."[9] One of the operation's intelligence officers, Captain Thomas A. Brooks, wrote that the Cubans were but lightly armed with personal weapons, and that there were only "three to four dozen Cuban Army regulars" in Grenada. These "were not organized into a regular military unit, but were primarily advisers and instructors to the Grenadian military."[10]

These assessments were more in line with my own observations of the Cubans. Clearly they were not a combat unit, or even a military construction unit. I found out that the medical students had gotten on well with the Cubans, who were their neighbors at Point Salines. Professor Peter Bourne of the medical school said that the students and the workers played softball together.[11]

I asked the workers at Puerto Escondido how the fighting with the Rangers started. Roberto Abreu Cruz, a 38-year-old bricklayer, told me that the Rangers "landed on the airstrip we had built. We thought they would go to the end of it where the U.S. university was. Instead they surrounded our camp." In a Cuban newspaper, I found a similar account by another bricklayer, Alberto Díaz, who said that the Rangers "occupied a hill and took up attack positions. I was watching them and I thought they were doing this to take the U.S. students away, but they advanced to where we were."[12] What did the Rangers do next? They started shooting, several of the workers told me, and they "took over the whole area. They took our bulldozers and construction tools."

I found more information on the fighting between the Rangers and the workers in a diplomatic note the United States sent to Cuba during the fighting. Curiously, the notes that the two countries exchanged— and there were several—had not been published in the United States, but in Cuba they had been reprinted in a book on Grenada.

Even before receiving the Cuban protest note on October 25, the United States sent a note to Cuba, through John Ferch, who headed the U.S. diplomatic office in Havana. The note, delivered at 5:00 P.M., October 25, urged Cuba to have the workers stop fighting. It said that the United States "regrets the armed clashes between men from the two countries and considers that they have occurred due to confusion and accidents brought about by your men's proximity to the area of operations of the multinational troops."[13]

That was tantamount to an apology, almost an acknowledgement that the Rangers had started the fighting, although it seemed to excuse the Rangers for shooting at the workers while the Rangers were engaging the Grenada forces. The administration, however, never published this or any of the other communications between the United States and Cuba during the Grenada hostilities. It did not even inform the press that Cuba had contacted us during the crisis. So was this text authentic as published in Cuba, or could it have been a forgery to make the United States look bad?

When I visited Havana, I wondered if Ferch could authenticate the message texts, which, according to the Cuban account, all went through his hands. Therefore, I made an appointment to meet with him. Ferch's office was in a large building that had been under construction as a new embassy when President Eisenhower broke diplomatic relations with Cuba. To carry on contacts at a minimal level, the State Department arranged with the Swiss government to have this office be considered a part of its embassy in Havana, and we dubbed it the U.S. interests section of the Swiss embassy. In Washington, Cuba did the same, using the Czech embassy. The building in Havana was now completed, and the interests section moved in on two upper floors. Otherwise the building stood empty, which lent it an eerie quality. Ferch's office had a window with a northern exposure, at which he kept a telescope trained on Miami.

When I asked Ferch about the diplomatic notes as published in Cuba, he readily affirmed their accuracy. While he could not be sure of every word, he said, the Spanish translation had not changed the essential meaning. This meant that what the Defense Department told the American public about the encounter with the Cubans was substantially different from what the State Department admitted privately to Cuba.

Although the press had not focused on the details of the encounter with the Cubans, one Ranger commander had been interviewed, and his version of events had us initiating the action. Major Jim Holt, who arrived at Point Salines on the morning of October 25 as a battalion executive officer, told a reporter that it was part of the Rangers' battle plan to seize the Cuban dormitory area. The first objective Holt's unit was assigned after landing was to seize the Cuban workers' living area.[14]

More light was shed on the question when Congress became interested in the technical side of the Grenada operation. William S. Lind, an aide to Senator Gary Hart of Colorado, wrote a report critical of many aspects of our tactics in Grenada. The Joint Chiefs of Staff, over the signature of Chairman John W. Vessey, Jr., sent a point-by-point rebuttal to the House Armed Services Committee.

One of Lind's charges was that the Rangers attacked the Cubans frontally, whereas, he said, they should have attacked from the flanks. The Joint Chiefs responded:

> B Co., 1st Ranger Battalion, 75th Infantry, on the western flank of the runway, started rolling up the flank of the Cuban defensive position from west to east by 0700. The company first sergeant led a three-man team to assault a Cuban position, killing two Cubans and capturing 28 more. B Co. rolled up the Cuban defenses until they reached the main Cuban camp. Ranger snipers took Cuban mortar positions under fire and killed or wounded 18 Cubans at ranges of 600–1,000 meters.[15]

So the Joint Chiefs were saying in effect that the Rangers did not attack the Cubans frontally but from the western flank. Implicitly, however, the Joint Chiefs' account acknowledged that it was the Rangers who had initiated the attack on the Cuban workers. The Joint Chiefs admitted, in fact, that although "the principal military mission" was "to rescue U.S. citizens and other foreign nationals," "in order to achieve this objective, Cuban and Grenadian forces would have to be neutralized and a stable situation on the island achieved." As for the Cuban workers housed at Point Salines, "the plan called for the capture of the two airfields on Grenada to include the immediate neutralization of Cuban forces at Point Salines Airfield." This confirmed Major Holt's statement that his unit had been ordered to take the Cuban dormitory area. Moreover, the Joint Chiefs acknowledged that the Rangers had succeeded in this aim: "The surprise airborne assault on Point Salines Airfield by the Rangers effectively neutralized Cuban forces at the outset and led to the capture of several hundred Cubans despite stiff resistance."[16]

I asked the workers at Puerto Escondido how their twenty-four fellow workers had been killed at Point Salines. They were shot, I was told, "at different times during the day, mostly in the afternoon. Most were shot from helicopters." News accounts confirmed that the Cubans had been killed by "naval guns, land-based artillery, Cobra helicopter gunships, AC130 gunships and jets from the carrier."[17] The Rangers, anxious to avoid close combat, called in jets and helicopter gunships to strafe the workers. The gunships "operated with impunity, destroying, with heavy casualties, the main Cuban position at the Point Salines airfield."[18]

Early reports on the Ranger-Cuban fighting were that it was heavy, reinforcing the impression the Defense Department was suggesting, that the Cubans were part of the defense of Grenada. But the *Washington Post* wrote later that "early impressions and reports on the scale and intensity of the action" were "exaggerated by the military, by the news media whose information initially was limited to what the Pentagon provided, and by pre-invasion reports by the Grenadian junta of a coming bloodbath, coupled with post-invasion Cuban propaganda about the fighting."[19]

Why did the Defense Department exaggerate the numbers and ferocity of the fighting by the Cuban workers? Military action that could be attributed to Cuba supported the administration's claim that Cuba was indeed building up Grenada as a bastion to export revolution. The Cuban government did, to be sure, order the workers to fire back if fired upon, and a Cuban colonel even went to Grenada shortly before the invasion to help the workers plan a defense. Cuban leader Fidel Castro, when he learned that a U.S. armada was approaching Grenada, sent the workers a message dated October 22, which he made public at a press conference:

> If the United States intervenes, we must vigorously defend ourselves as if we were in Cuba . . . in our camp sites and our work places close by, but only if we are directly attacked. I repeat: only if we are directly attacked. We would thus be defending ourselves, not the Government or its deeds. If the Yankees land on the runway section near the university or on its surroundings to evacuate their citizens, fully refrain from interfering.[20]

This message had been apparently conveyed to the workers as well, because the NBC television program "First Camera," which aired on October 30, interviewed Dr. Raul Jimenez, an instructor at the medical school, who said he encountered a Cuban worker near the Cuban dormitories early in the morning of October 25, just before the Rangers landed. Dr. Jimenez saw that the Cubans had taken up positions with weapons; when he asked one of them what they were doing, the worker replied that the United States was going to land, but that the Cubans "would not fire unless they were fired upon."

Castro's statement that the Cubans should defend themselves but "not the Government or its deeds" seems curious at first blush, but is understandable in the context of the complex politics of the situation. Castro had been close to Maurice Bishop, the assassinated Grenadian leader, and he was appalled at Bishop's overthrow and death. The new Grenadian leaders, who, like Castro, knew we were about to attack, asked Castro to help defend them, at least by having the construction workers participate in the defense of Grenada alongside the Grenadian army. Castro refused, however, telling them, "the political situation created inside the country due to the people's estrangement on account of the death of Bishop and other leaders, isolation from the outside world, etc., considerably weakens the country's defense capabilities."[21]

The administration had tried to make it appear that Cuba was the major support behind the new Grenadian government, suggesting that those who overthrew Bishop were even more in the Cuban camp than Bishop himself had been.[22] But Cuba was not willing to defend the new Grenadian government from an invasion. Castro reasoned that because the Grenadian people were not supportive of this new leadership group, "the present military and political conditions are the worst for organizing a firm and efficient resistance against the invaders, an action which is practically impossible without the people's participation."[23] Recalling the Bay of Pigs, and how Cubans rushed to the beach to defend it, Castro did not expect Grenadians to do the same. Disgusted with the new Grenadian leaders, Castro began to withdraw technical aid personnel.[24]

Although Castro was unwilling to defend Grenada, he did not want U.S. forces to capture the Cuban workers. In a message to Ferch on October 22, the first in the series of communications the two sides would exchange, Castro expressed his concern about the construction workers to the United States. Like the other notes, it was not published, or publicly acknowledged, by the administration. In the note, Castro said he wanted to avoid any confrontation between the Cuban workers and our forces if they invaded Grenada. Castro was aware of the administration's "concern about the numerous U.S. residents there," adding, "we are also concerned about the hundreds of Cuban cooperation personnel working there in different fields and about the news that U.S. naval forces are approaching Grenada." Castro advised that Cuba and the United States should "keep in touch on this matter, so as to contribute to solve favorably any difficulty that may arise or action that may be taken relating to the security of these individuals, without violence or intervention in the country."[25]

Thus, Castro offered to remain in communication with the United States in order to avert any conflict with the workers. The administration did not reply to that message, however. When I asked Ferch why, he told me that he thought Castro's message was "bizarre," and that it did not require a response. Although his answer puzzled me, Ferch did not elaborate.

While it told the workers not to defend Grenada, the Cuban government did advise them to fire back if fired upon. That seemed to me a foolhardy decision, given the overwhelming firepower of the U.S. forces. I asked Cuban Deputy Foreign Minister Ricardo Alarcón about this when I was in Havana, and he told me what he had said in a published interview: the defense was "intended to have a demonstration effect. The Americans now have to think of how many thousands of battalions they would need to subjugate Cuba or Nicaragua if all their technical and logistical strength hasn't enabled them to take Grenada."[26] So Cuba had not forgotten the Bay of Pigs.

Early in the invasion, the Defense Department claimed that up to five hundred Cuban workers fled from their dormitories into mountainous areas to take up a Che Guevara-style guerrilla campaign against the U.S. forces, and for several days after the invasion the press carried these reports. Later the Defense Department acknowledged that it never had information about such a guerrilla campaign; however, it failed to explain why the story had been released in the first place. During the fighting, however, these stories reinforced the impression that Grenada was a Cuban bastion.[27]

While the fighting continued, the Defense Department excluded the press from Grenada, giving the administration "full opportunity to manage the news to its best advantage," as one reporter complained: the administration distorted events to create "the impression conveyed to the world that the bulk of the fighting was done by Cuban troops and that Grenadian resistance had been minimal."[28]

Another black mark against Cuba was accounts of large caches of arms in Grenada. According to President Reagan, we had found "weapons and ammunition . . . enough to supply thousands of terrorists."[29] These weapons must have come from Cuba. Since Grenada did not need such weaponry for defense, Reagan inferred that it must have been planning to invade other Caribbean islands. According to an assessment later by the CIA, however, the arms were too few and too outdated for much offense.[30] When reporters were allowed to see them in a warehouse in Grenada, they concurred with the assessment. Later the Defense Department displayed captured weapons at Andrews Air Force Base near Washington, but soon closed the exhibit because no one was impressed.

After the Grenada invasion, the new government completed the Point Salines airport, which began handling tourist flights, while the CIA provided money to organize elections to ensure a process that would end with a government friendly to us.[31] That was hardly necessary, however, because most Grenadians welcomed the invasion. Had we invaded while Bishop was alive, Grenadians would have objected; but when we did strike, they were, as Reagan well knew, angry over the assassination of Bishop and the violence that accompanied his overthrow. Once we were in occupation, Grenadians hoped we would take the tiny country under our wing and pour in investment and aid. Perhaps they had struck it rich. A year passed, however, and then two and three, without much investment or aid. The glow began to fade.

Notes

1. John Quigley, "Parachutes at Dawn: Issues of Use of Force and Status of Internees in the United States-Cuban Hostilities on Grenada, 1983," *University of Miami Inter-American Law Review* 17 (1986): 199.

2. Stuart Taylor, Jr., "Treatment of Prisoners Is Defended," *New York Times,* October 29, 1983, p. A7, col. 1.

3. *Situation in Lebanon and Grenada,* Hearings Before a Subcommittee of the House Committee on Appropriations, 98th Cong., 1st sess. (1983), pp. 39–40.

4. Taylor, "Treatment of Prisoners Is Defended."

5. *Situation in Grenada,* Hearings Before the Senate Committee on Foreign Relations, 98th Cong., 1st sess. (1983), p. 16.

6. Fred Hiatt and David Hoffman, "U.S. Drops Estimate of Cubans on Island," *Washington Post,* October 30, 1983, p. A1, col. 5.

7. Editorial de Ciencias Sociales (Havana), *Grenada: The World Against the Crime* (1983), p. 41.

8. "Situation in Grenada," *UN Chronicle* 20 (December 1983): 18.

9. U.S. Marine Corps Development and Education Command Newsletter: *Operational Overview,* January–March 1984, p. 31.

10. William Berry, "Ten Days of Urgent Fury," *All Hands,* May 1984, p. 23.

11. P. Bourne, "Was the U.S. Invasion Necessary?" *Los Angeles Times,* November 6, 1983, p. IV3, col. 4.

12. "National and Foreign Press Interview Cuban Wounded in Grenada," *Granma Weekly Review,* November 13, 1983, p. 7, col. 1.

13. *Grenada: The World Against the Crime,* p. 41.

14. "Grenada: Now the American Model," *Los Angeles Times,* November 6, 1983, p. A1, col. 5.

15. "JCS Replies to Criticism of Grenada Operation," *Army,* August 1984, p. 32.

16. Ibid., pp. 29–30.

17. Richard Harwood, "Tidy U.S. War Ends: 'We Blew Them Away,' " *Washington Post,* November 6, 1983, p. A1, col. 4.

18. Drew Middleton, "Operation on Grenada: How Forces Performed," *New York Times,* October 28, 1983, p. A12, col. 1.

19. Harwood, "Tidy U.S. War Ends: 'We Blew Them Away.' "

20. *Grenada: The World Against the Crime,* p. 34; "Cuba Says Troops End Resistance," *Washington Post,* October 27, 1983, p. A1, col. 6.

21. *Grenada: The World Against the Crime,* pp. 34–35.

22. Jonathan Kwitny, *Endless Enemies: The Making of an Unfriendly World* (1984), p. 409.

23. *Grenada: The World Against the Crime,* pp. 34–35.

24. Kwitny, *Endless Enemies,* p. 417.

25. *Grenada: The World Against the Crime,* pp. 35–36.

26. Alma Guillermoprieto, "Havana Seeks to Turn Loss in Grenada into a Moral Victory," *Washington Post,* October 30, 1983, p. A10, col. 1.

27. Hugh O'Shaughnessy, *Grenada: Revolution, Invasion and Aftermath* (1984), p. 210.

28. Ibid., p. 204.

29. Ronald Reagan, "America's Commitment to Peace," October 27, 1983, DSB, vol. 83, p. 4 (December 1983).

30. Bob Woodward, *Veil: The Secret Wars of the CIA 1981–1987* (1987), p. 299.

31. Ibid., p. 300.

26

Libya: Qaddafi's Air Conditioner

On the night of April 14, 1986, thirty-three American bombers lit up the skies over Libya. While navy jets flying from an aircraft carrier in the Mediterranean bombed two military bases near the city of Benghazi, air force F-111 bombers flying from Great Britain hit three targets in Tripoli, the capital city. President Reagan described the targets as "terrorist facilities," by which he meant that they were connected with terrorist attacks abroad by Libya. The Tripoli targets, said the White House, were command and control systems intelligence-gathering, communications, and logistics and training facilities.[1]

The Libyan government said the bombing killed 37 people and wounded 93.[2] Hit, apparently by accident, was a residential district of Tripoli near the French embassy, which accounted for many of the casualties.[3]

As justification for the raid, the administration accused Libya of arranging an explosion, on April 5, 1986, in a West Berlin nightclub, killing an American serviceman and a Turkish woman and wounding two hundred other patrons.[4] The White House also claimed to have intercepted a message between Libya and the Libyan mission in East Berlin acknowledging the Libyan government's role in the bombing.[5] The intercepts reportedly had unnamed persons in Berlin transmitting to Libya on April 4 that "we have something planned that will make you happy," and several hours later, "an event occurred. You will be pleased with the result."

Secretary of Defense Caspar Weinberger and Secretary of State George Shultz claimed that only minutes prior to the explosion at the nightclub, police, acting on the basis of the intercepts, were on the streets in Berlin and nearly prevented the explosion.[6] But this was denied by the deputy chief of West Berlin's military police, who said the information in the intercepts was too general for any such operation. Nor was there any police activity of the type Weinberger and Shultz claimed.[7]

Libya, for its part, denied that it had had anything to do with the nightclub bombing, and objective verification was hard to find. The West German government, although it knew what information we had, could not trace a Libyan hand.[8] The chief of Germany's anti-terrorist police doubted any Libyan involvement.[9]

Other governments, too, were dubious. In the United Nations Security Council, most delegates criticized the U.S. raid and expressed doubts about its putative evidence. A Security Council resolution to condemn the United States for aggression received nine votes out of fifteen; but it was vetoed by France, Great Britain, and the United States.[10] In November, the UN General Assembly passed a resolution condemning the raid.[11]

Even some administration officials apparently doubted the information. Journalist Seymour Hersh reported that a number of them, although refusing to speak for attribution, expressed skepticism. The intercepted messages were vague, they said, and they doubted that Libya would target the particular nightclub, because it was frequented by many black GIs. In addition, the intercepts were speeded from the National Security Agency, which first obtained them, to the White House, without being evaluated by experts. Normal procedure is to analyze such information carefully before using it publicly. But the administration, evidently too anxious to wait for an evaluation, rushed the information to the press, as President Johnson had done with the Gulf of Tonkin.[12] Whether the administration actually believed it had evidence or was using the nightclub bombing merely as a pretext, it never gave any convincing confirmation of its charge.[13]

Subsequent information suggested a Syrian connection to the nightclub bombing. In 1988, West German police arrested a woman on suspicion of involvement in the bombing, saying she acted on orders of a Palestinian man implicated in another bombing in which Syria was involved. The Palestinian, however, also had a Libyan connection, and so the State Department continued to maintain that Libya was responsible for the nightclub bombing.[14]

As additional justification for the Libya raid, the administration claimed that Libyan planned to attack thirty U.S. targets in various countries. Libyans, it said, had surveilled embassies and commercial installations in Africa, Europe, the Middle East, and Latin America. For security reasons, however, the White House could not give any details about these plans.[15] The media did not press the matter, and no evidence either to prove or disprove this charge ever surfaced.

Skepticism about the administration's information abounded, however, because of our long-standing efforts to get rid of the Libyan leader, Colonel Moammar Qaddafi. For several years, the CIA had encouraged Libyan exile groups to overthrow Qaddafi, and to kill him if necessary.[16] In 1985, the Reagan administration asked Egypt to invade Libya to overthrow Qaddafi, but Egyptian President Hosni Mubarak declined.[17]

Some evidence that the nightclub bombing was a makeweight reason comes from the fact that in January 1986, Donald Fortier, an aide to National Security Advisor John Poindexter, told *Newsweek* magazine that the administration was preparing military action against Libya; it was merely waiting for a pretext to strike. At the same time, Libyan assets in the United States were frozen and U.S. citizens ordered out of Libya, so that they would not be hurt during an attack.[18] In January 1986 also, the administration claimed Libyan responsibility for the shootings at the ticket counters of the Israeli El Al airline at the Vienna and Rome airports the previous December. The shootings left twenty dead, including five American citizens. It was apparently immediately after the Rome and Vienna incidents that the White House geared up for the attack it launched on April 14.[19]

In early 1986, apparently to lay a foundation for the planned raid, Secretary of State Shultz argued that the United States had a right to use military force against states that support terrorism, and in particular to deter anticipated terrorist attacks. State Department lawyers elaborated on Shultz's argument, setting the legal groundwork for a military attack on Libya. At the same time, to better monitor its communications, the administration sent a new spy satellite into orbit over Libya.[20]

In February and March 1986, the administration positioned planes and ships near Libya in a campaign of pressure. On March 24, it sent a guided missile cruiser into waters claimed by Libya, accompanied overhead by jet fighters.[21] The alleged message about the nightclub bombing was intercepted March 25.[22] If Libya was indeed responsible for the nightclub bombing, it might have acted in response to what it considered provocative military action by the United States.

Suspicions were heightened when four months after the raid, the administration released reports that Libya was increasing terrorist activity, and that we might attack again, or else that Colonel Qaddafi might be overthrown. The stories were "plants," in the jargon of the propaganda business, as the administration knew that Libya was not increasing terrorist activity, nor did it have any information that Qaddafi was about to be toppled from power. According to a memorandum that John Poindexter sent to President Reagan, the idea was to mount a "disinformation program" (Poindexter's term) to make Colonel Qaddafi think that internal opposition to him was growing, that key aides were disloyal, and that we would move against him militarily. This would make Colonel Qaddafi "paranoid and ineffective" and "embolden" forces in Libya that might overthrow him.[23] The administration said that its purpose was to deceive Qaddafi, not to deceive the public. However, the fact that it had planted false stories regarding Libyan terrorism cast earlier accusations against Libya in a new light.

For several years, in fact, the Reagan White House had been making questionable allegations against Qaddafi. In 1981, CIA Director William Casey was the intelligence officer for a secret task force the administration had set up on Libya. Casey told the task force he had information that Libya was organizing "hit teams" to assassinate administration officials, and stories, apparently based on leaks from the administration, that such teams had arrived in the United States began to appear in the press. Some members of the task force suspected that Casey had fabricated the information, and no evidence came to light to confirm it.[24]

In January 1986, when the administration imposed economic sanctions on Libya, it allegedly had "irrefutable evidence" that Libya was behind the recent shootings at the Vienna and Rome airports. When asked to describe his evidence, President Reagan replied, "There are things that should not be revealed." While the perpetrators had not been Libyan, Reagan said, "these murderers could not carry out their crimes without the sanctuary and support provided by regimes such as Col. Qaddafi's in Libya."[25]

It appeared from other sources that the "evidence" the administration had on the Rome and Vienna operations was three passports found on the Vienna attackers. One passport had been lost in Libya eight years before by a Tunisian laborer, and the other two had been seized by Libyan authorities from Tunisians earlier in 1985. The interior ministers of Italy and Austria said at a joint news conference that they did not think that this or other evidence established Libyan involvement in the Rome or Vienna incidents.[26] The White House urged the foreign ministers of Greece and Germany to make formal accusations against Libya, but they both refused.[27] The fact that other governments with an interest in finding the perpetrators did not take the administration's information strongly suggests that it was overplaying its evidence.

Responsibility for the Rome and Vienna attacks was never determined; however, some proof did emerge that they were carried out by Palestinians recruited by the organization of Abu Nidal, who were from the refugee camps in Beirut where the Lebanese Phalange militia killed Palestinian civilians during Israel's 1982 invasion.[28] As we saw earlier, Palestinians held the United States partly to blame for those killings, because it did not protect the refugees after the PLO withdrew from Beirut, and because our officials were aware of the massacre as it started. The Palestinians reportedly trained in the Bekaa Valley of Lebanon, a territory under the occupation of Syria, the country in which the Abu Nidal group is based.[29]

Besides using dubious information to justify the April 14 raid, the administration was less than candid about what our bombers hit. It said that we were going after "terrorist infrastructure," and announced three targets in Tripoli and two in Benghazi.

Of these five targets, the one to which the administration directed the greatest firepower was the El-Azziziya barracks in Tripoli. Although the White House did not admit this publicly, this barracks contained the family compound of Colonel Qaddafi. The administration denied that it was trying to kill Qaddafi,[30] but circumstances suggested the contrary. According to one official, "we hoped we would get him, but nobody was sure where he would be that night."[31] Seymour Hersh, who interviewed seventy administration officials about the raid, concluded that Qaddafi was the primary target.[32]

The administration sent nine F-111s to bomb the El-Azziziya barracks, the highest number of planes for any of the five targets. In the planning for the raid, President Reagan picked El-Azziziya at the last minute from a list of potential targets. While El-Azziziya was not favored as a target by the Defense Department because it had minimal military significance and was in a crowded downtown area of Tripoli,[33] hitting it would send a message to Colonel Qaddafi. Of the nine planes slated to hit El-Azziziya, two were to target Colonel Qaddafi's house, aiming for an air conditioning unit on the roof that was visible from the air.[34] Although the F-111s did not manage a direct hit on Qaddafi's residence, they landed several bombs within a few yards of it, injuring several family members and killing an adopted daughter.[35]

Whatever the targets, the Libya raid was structured in a way that made it almost certain there would be civilian casualties. One target was a command post in a densely populated area of downtown Benghazi, while the El-Azziziya barracks was located in a densely populated section of Tripoli.[36]

It was one of the F-111s aiming for El-Azziziya, in fact, that hit the neighborhood near the French embassy. The administration called this a mistake, and Secretary Shultz "regretted" any casualties.[37] Secretary of Defense Caspar Weinberger, however, denied that it was the F-111s that had killed civilians near the French embassy, claiming instead that the deaths could have been caused by Libyan anti-aircraft missiles falling to earth.[38]

Given the way in which the raid was carried out, civilian casualties were all but certain. The administration planned the raid for nighttime hours, because it expected Libyan anti-aircraft defenses to be down. Operating at night, however, made visibility more difficult and made it more likely that some bombs would miss their targets. The F-111s were to bomb while flying at 600 m.p.h., so that any timing error would put a bomb off its target. The fact that El-Azziziya was chosen as a target only a few days before the raid meant that there was no time for precision planning.[39]

During the early months of 1986, the air force trained a small number of highly experienced pilots for the Libya raid, giving them practice on long-range flights from England to Turkey. Late in the preparations, however, when the White House learned it would not be able to use French airspace to fly from England to Libya, it decided to increase the number of F-111s from six to eighteen. This meant that the air force had to use less experienced pilots who had not been trained for the mission. This change increased the chance of bombing errors.[40] Bombing at night, at high speed, in congested areas, by pilots with inadequate training, meant that mistakes and civilian casualties were highly likely in the Libya raid. But they were a cost the administration was willing to pay.

Notes

1. "Announcement by Speakes," *New York Times,* April 15, 1986, p. A13, col. 5.
2. "Pentagon Details 2-Pronged Attack," *New York Times,* April 15, 1986, p. A1, col. 5.
3. Seymour Hersh, "Target Qaddafi," *New York Times,* February 22, 1987, p. F17, col. 1.
4. "Announcement by Speakes."
5. Bob Woodward, *Veil: The Secret Wars of the CIA 1981–1987* (1987), pp. 444–45.
6. "Joint News Conference by Secretary Shultz and Secretary Weinberger, April 14, 1986," DSB, vol. 86, p. 5 (June 1986).
7. Bill Schaap, "Disinforming the World on Libya," *Covert Action Information Bulletin,* No. 30 (Summer 1988): 71.
8. Bernard Gwertzman, "Plots on Global Scale Charged," *New York Times,* April 15, 1986, p. A1, col. 3.
9. Hersh, "Target Qaddafi."
10. SCOR, 41st yr., 2682nd mtg., p. 43, UN Doc. S/PV.2682 (1986).
11. Res. 41/38, GAOR, 41st yr., Supplement No. 53, p. 34, UN Doc. A/41/53 (1987).
12. Hersh, "Target Qaddafi."
13. Schaap, "Disinforming the World on Libya," p. 76.
14. Serge Schmemann, "German Is Seized in Disco Bombing," *New York Times,* January 12, 1988, p. A3, col. 1.
15. Gwertzman, "Plots on Global Scale Charged."
16. Hersh, "Target Qaddafi."
17. David Martin and John Walcott, *Best Laid Plans: The Inside Story of America's War against Terrorism* (1988), pp. 265–66; Bob Woodward and Don Oberdorfer, "State Dept. Acted to Block U.S.-Egypt Attack on Libya; White House Envisioned Aiding a 1985 Invasion," *Washington Post,* February 20, 1987, p. A1, col. 1.
18. Harry Anderson, "Get Tough: The Reagan Plan: Clearing the Way for Military Action—If Necessary," *Newsweek,* January 20, 1986, p. 16.
19. Martin and Walcott, *Best Laid Plans,* p. 268; Bill Keller, "State Dept. Study on Terror Group Cites Libyan Link," *New York Times,* January 1, 1986, p. A1, col. 3.

20. Hersh, "Target Qaddafi."

21. Martin and Walcott, *Best Laid Plans,* pp. 279–81.

22. Ibid., p. 289.

23. Bob Woodward, "Gadhafi Target of Secret U.S. Deception Plan; Elaborate Campaign Included Disinformation that Appeared as Fact in American Media," *Washington Post,* October 2, 1986, p. A1, col. 2.

24. Hersh, "Target Qaddafi."

25. "President's News Conference on Foreign and Domestic Issues," *New York Times,* January 8, 1986, p. A6, col. 1.

26. Loren Jenkins, "Airport Terrorists Reportedly Trained in Syrian-Controlled Area," *Washington Post,* January 11, 1986, p. A1, col. 2.

27. John Tagliabue, "West Germans Decline U.S. Bid to Join in Moves against Libya," *New York Times,* January 22, 1986, p. A4, col. 1 (Germany); Paul Lewis, "The French Offer a Pledge on Libya," *New York Times,* January 23, 1986, p. A6, col. 1 (Greece).

28. Lou Cannon and Don Oberdorfer, "U.S. Seeks to Temper Response by Israel," *Washington Post,* December 29, 1985, p. A1, col. 6; Martin and Walcott, *Best Laid Plans,* p. 267.

29. Martin and Walcott, *Best Laid Plans,* pp. 268, 289.

30. "Joint News Conference by Secretary Shultz and Secretary Weinberger, April 14, 1986," DSB, vol. 86, p. 4 (June 1986).

31. George C. Wilson, "Qaddafi Was a Target of U.S. Raid," *Washington Post,* April 18, 1986, p. A1, col 6.

32. Hersh, "Target Qaddafi."

33. Martin and Walcott, *Best Laid Plans,* pp. 287–88.

34. Ibid., pp. 293–95.

35. Bernard Weinraub, "U.S. Jets Hit 'Terrorist Centers' in Libya," *New York Times,* April 15, 1986, p. A1, col. 6; Martin and Walcott, *Best Laid Plans,* p. 310.

36. Martin and Walcott, *Best Laid Plans,* p. 287.

37. " 'Worldnet' Interview with Secretary Shultz, April 16, 1986," DSB, vol. 86, p. 9 (June 1986).

38. Martin and Walcott, *Best Laid Plans,* p. 309.

39. Ibid., pp. 286–87.

40. Ibid., p. 293.

27

The Philippines: Shoring Cory

While the United States has used force a number of times to remove a government, it has rarely done so to keep one in power. That, however, is what the President George Bush did in December 1989, when elements of the Filipino army mounted a coup attempt against the new and fragile government of President Corazon Aquino. The Reagan administration had helped facilitate Aquino's accession to power to replace former strongman Ferdinand Marcos, and Bush was anxious to keep her from being removed. Shortly after the coup plotters made their move, Bush ordered jet fighters at our Clark Air Force Base in the Philippines into the air to shoot down any rebel planes that might get off the ground.

At that point, the rebels had not used any aircraft, and Bush wanted to make sure they did not strafe ground troops loyal to Aquino. The tactic worked: the rebels did not get any planes into the air, and quickly the coup attempt folded.[1] While our jet scrambling predictably drew a favorable reaction from the Aquino government, a number of Manila newspapers criticized our intervention as an interference in internal Philippines affairs.[2] A former spokesperson for the late President Ferdinand Marcos said President Aquino's "most urgent and nearly exclusive concern is her physical and political survival, and only Washington's

231

continued support can ensure it," by which he meant that Aquino's request for U.S. protection revealed a shaky political posture.[3]

The White House explained why we decided to get involved. At President Aquino's request, President Bush had "authorized U.S. military assistance to the government of the Philippines in defending itself against a coup attempt," adding, "This assistance is intended to allow the democratically elected government of the Philippines to restore order. The President also is determined to protect the lives of Americans in the Philippines."[4] Thus, the stated aims were two: to protect an elected government and to protect U.S. citizens.

President Bush was, indeed, trying to keep President Aquino in power; like Reagan before him, Bush viewed the Aquino government as one that would protect U.S. interests without being as authoritarian as the Marcos government had been. In particular, the administration thought that Aquino could more effectively combat a long-standing leftist insurgency in the Philippines that might threaten American investments and other commercial interests. In addition, Bush viewed Aquino as being favorable to our continued use in the Philippines of two large military bases.

As for the second reason for intervening, the White House statement did not explain in any detail how our intervention would protect "the lives of Americans." The administration did not indicate what danger our citizens might be in, or how the jet overflights or the defeat of the rebels might avert it. Bush did not organize an evacuation of American citizens or take any measures to protect them in the places where they lived and worked.

There was, to be sure, street fighting in a commercial district of Manila that included hotels and apartments occupied by Americans. The administration might have been concerned that the rebels would harm our citizens, but the rebels were politically to the right of President Aquino. Their political position was not hostile to the United States; to allay fears—and probably in the hope of stopping U.S. intervention—they issued a statement that "the United States of America is not our enemy."[5] If the rebels did harbor any grievance against the United States, it was because we were intervening to put them down.

Because of the street fighting, there was a potential danger that U.S. citizens might be caught up in it; indeed, at one point in the fighting, the rebels took over Manila's commercial district. Had the Aquino government tried to retake it by force, civilians might have been trapped in the cross fire. However, that danger never came to pass, because on December 5, a truce was negotiated to allow foreign nationals to leave, including those from the United States.[6]

Even if there had been a real danger, flying jets overhead was not likely to help, since overflights would not get American citizens out of the commercial district. Bush might have thought that by helping to put down the rebellion, Manila would more quickly become safer for our citizens; but at the same time, intervening ran the risk of turning the rebels against us. From what information is available, it seems unlikely that protecting Americans residing in the Philippines was, after all, a genuine aim of the intervention. As we have seen, however, prior administrations sending troops abroad have invoked the need to protect U.S. citizens, a rationale that always strikes a sympathetic chord with the public. Presidents seem unable to resist using this reason when there is a chance it will be believed.

Beyond shoring up the Aquino administration, there was another likely motivation for the intervention that Bush did not mention. In 1989, the United States and the Philippines were about to begin negotiations to extend the lease in the Philippines on the Clark Air Force Base and the Subic Naval Base.

These two bases were the largest U.S. military facilities outside the United States, and in the Philippines they were a political hot potato. Many Filipinos objected to the bases and wanted the leases terminated, seeing in them an unnecessary militarization of their country. In addition, some feared that, just as with the 1989 coup attempt, the United States would interfere in Philippines politics by using the forces it had stationed at these bases. Even if the United States did not actually use the troops, their presence was an ever-present threat looming over the Philippines' political scene.

The bases themselves were the product of prior military intervention in the Philippines. During the Spanish-American war, we drove Spain out as ruler of the Philippines. The Filipinos, happy to be free from Spanish control, expected us to leave as well. When we did not, Filipino guerrillas waged a bloody campaign against us. We put it down, however, inflicting several hundred thousand casualties on the Filipinos, and then we turned the Philippines into a colony. In 1946, we finally withdrew; but as a condition of our leaving, we made the Philippines give us leases for military bases.

Filipino critics of the bases charged that by asking for our help to put down the 1989 coup attempt, President Aquino jeopardized her bargaining position regarding the bases.[7] The *New York Times,* viewing the matter from the U.S. standpoint, saw the situation that way, too: the intervention "created a new atmosphere for negotiations on the future of United States military bases in the Philippines."[8] Rep. Stephen Solarz, chair of the House foreign affairs subcommittee on Asia and the Pacific, said that our intervention would put the base negotiations "in an entirely different context," because it showed the Filipinos that we could intervene quickly to protect democracy.[9] By saving President Aquino from the coup, the Bush administration increased her dependence on the United States and thus strengthened its hand in the base negotiations.

The differences between the United States and the Philippines on the bases issue were quite sharp. While Philippines Foreign Secretary Raul Manglapus called for our departure from Clark Air Force Base by late 1991, and from Subic Naval Base by 1996 to 1998, U.S. negotiator Richard Armitage insisted that we keep both bases until 2001 or 2003, with a continued lower-level presence indefinitely into the future.[10]

In December 1989, of course, neither the Bush administration nor the Aquino government could know that a volcanic eruption would hit Clark Air Force Base in 1991, leading the United States to decide unilaterally to pull out. The distance between the positions of the Aquino government and the Bush administration as of 1989 showed the importance of any pressure we might be able to put on the Aquino government. By intervening on President Aquino's behalf, Bush gained significant leverage over her government.

Notes

1. Criselda Yabes, "Manila Turns Back Coup Bid with Help of U.S. Air Power," *Washington Post,* December 2, 1989, p. A1, col. 6; Bob Woodward, *The Commanders* (1991), pp. 146–52.

2. Sheila Coronel, "Coup Fails, Manila Says amid Fighting," *New York Times,* December 4, 1989, p. A16, col. 1.

3. Jeremy Clift, "U.S. and Philippines Far Apart on Future of Bases," Reuters, September 21, 1990, BC cycle.

4. "Bush OKs Military Aid for Aquino; U.S. Jets Fly over Filipino Bases," *Chicago Tribune,* December 1, 1989, p. A1, col. 2.

5. David E. Sanger, "Cease-Fire in Manila Allows for Evacuation of Foreigners," *New York Times,* December 6, 1989, p. A1, col. 1.

6. Bob Drogin and Mark Fineman, "Foreigners Evacuated under Truce in Manila," *Los Angeles Times,* December 6, 1989, p. A1, col. 3.

7. "Philippine Bases Negotiator Defends U.S. Military Help," *Reuter Library Report,* BC cycle, December 17, 1989.

8. Robert Pear, "The U.S. Stake in the Philippines," *New York Times,* December 17, 1989, p. D3, col. 3.

9. David B. Ottoway, "U.S. Bases Rarely Used to Save Host Government; Effect on Philippine Negotiations Unclear," *Washington Post,* December 3, 1989, p. A30, col. 5.

10. Fernando Del Mundo, "Philippines Favors Extension of Subic Lease," UPI, November 15, 1990, BC cycle.

28

Panama: Slaying a Monster

Lifting huge tankers up over the hills that separate the Atlantic Ocean in the west from the Pacific Ocean in the east—Yes, in Panama, the Atlantic is west of the Pacific; check your atlas—the Panama Canal is an engineering marvel. The canal is all the more remarkable because it was built between 1904 and 1914, before the era of modern earth-moving equipment. A French crew had tried to build a canal across Panama in the 1880s, but was decimated by malaria and gave up. Our own crew overcame malaria before it could overcome the earth and rock. The canal's construction was also a feat of human endurance.

On the political side, however, we did not match our human and engineering accomplishment. To obtain the right to build the canal, we wrested the territory away from Colombia, of which Panama was a part. First we negotiated with Colombia and got its government to sign a treaty to let us build a canal across Panama.[1] But Colombia's Senate called the treaty a giveaway because it granted us virtual sovereignty for the area of a canal; therefore, the treaty was turned down.[2]

At that point the administration of Theodore Roosevelt approached some of Panama's most prominent citizens, professional people of Spanish ancestry, who had aspirations to independence from Colombia. We told them that if they rebelled, our destroyers would stand by offshore to neutralize the Colombian navy.[3] A rebellion was soon staged, and Colombia, as expected, sent ships to put it down. As the Colombian fleet approached Panama, however, they were met by American destroyers. The Roosevelt administration was true to its word.

The saga of how the U.S. Navy came out to meet the Colombian navy is omitted from many history books, but to me it was a familiar childhood story. My grandfather, as a seventeen-year-old orphan, ran away to join the navy in 1903, lying about his age. His first ship was the USS *Wyoming*. Thin and agile, he could scamper up the ship's tall masts, a feat he was happy to recount to me. (I had no reason to doubt his word, because even in his eighties he could still climb the apple trees in his yard.) My grandfather was also fond of describing the ship's mortars, which he obviously had studied and practiced hard to master.

In November 1903, before my grandfather had time to adjust fully to life on board ship, the *Wyoming* was dispatched to Panama as part of the armada being sent by President Roosevelt. When the *Wyoming* came within sight of the Colombian ships, my grandfather was at the ready by his mortar. He was ordered to fire and did it, just as he had learned. The sounds and smells were as real to him as an old man as they had been when he stood on the ship's deck. He described the measurements of the mortar, how he aimed, and how the Colombian ships backed off.

The political issues, understandably, did not attract my grandfather's attention at the time; but when the *Wyoming* and the rest of our fleet had accomplished their mission, Colombia decided there was nothing it could do to keep Panama, and so overnight a new country was born.[4] Not unexpectedly, President Roosevelt found Panama more willing than Colombia to meet our terms. We drafted a treaty called the Isthmian Canal Convention. While the treaty did not quite give us the territory outright to build a canal, it came close: Panama granted the United States the rights it would have "if it were sovereign" within a ten-mile-wide strip of Panama, "to the entire exclusion of the exercise by the Republic of Panama of any such sovereign rights, power or authority."[5]

This deal was even better than the one Colombia had initially rejected, and Roosevelt could not have been more pleased. Over the next few years, we built the canal within our "sovereign" zone, and some years later we found that we had enough room there for military bases as well. In the 1960s, these bases became the headquarters of the U.S. Southern Command, which used them as a center of operation for military action elsewhere in Latin America. We also used the bases to train Latin American troops in counterinsurgency tactics.

If the treaty deal seemed too good to be true, in the long run it turned out to be just that, since it left an undercurrent of resentment in Panama. In the 1960s, with anti-colonialist sentiment sweeping Africa, Asia, and Latin America, some Panamanians, largely from the lower (mixed-race) classes—not the professional classes on whom we had relied—took to the streets to protest our control of the canal and the zone.[6] The United Nations, now including a number of African, Asian, and Latin countries as members, pressured us to give the zone back to Panama.

In 1977, President Carter, seeing the handwriting on the wall, signed two new treaties to redesign our relation with Panama. One was the Panama Canal Treaty, by which we gave the zone back to Panama immediately and agreed to phase out our control of the canal, turning it over completely to Panama on December 31, 1999.[7] The other agreement was the Treaty Concerning the Permanent Neutrality and Operation of the Panama Canal, which stipulated that Panama and the United States would jointly keep the canal open to world shipping, even after 1999, and that after 1999 we would close our military bases.[8]

For a time, all went well under the new treaties. In the 1980s, Panama's leader was General Manuel Noriega, a man with whom we could deal. Throughout his early career Noriega had moonlighted from his military post by providing U.S. intelligence agencies with information on leftist activities in Panama.[9] Once in power, General Noriega helped us fight the insurgency in El Salvador, and gave the CIA sensitive information about Nicaragua to help in our attacks there.[10]

Most important, General Noriega lent a hand with our Contra army, helping the CIA set up the second Contra army in Costa Rica and allowing Contras to train in Panama.[11] He also cooperated with the Drug Enforcement Administration (DEA), which was trying to stop cocaine from being smuggled through Panama from South America. The DEA learned, however, that even while General Noriega was helping us in anti-drug efforts, he was making a tidy profit for himself in the cocaine traffic.[12] Cuban accountant Ramón Milian Rodríguez, who was convicted of cocaine possession and drug-money laundering, testified before the

Senate Foreign Relations Committee's Subcommittee on Terrorism, Narcotics, and International Operations that he delivered to General Noriega money from both the CIA and the Colombian drug cartel.[13]

Since, however, General Noriega was helping with the Contras, he was "our man" in Panama, because the Contras were our top priority.[14] When anyone in Washington raised concerns about General Noriega, CIA Director William Casey intervened to mention the Contras, which effectively ended the discussion.[15] And as we saw in our chapter on Nicaragua, the CIA itself was involved in the cocaine traffic as part of the aid package to the Nicaraguan Contras. Casey was not letting Noriega do anything he was not prepared to do himself.

Eventually, however, General Noriega apparently balked at some of the things we asked him to do. After the Contra southern front against Nicaragua in Costa Rica collapsed, the CIA wanted to reopen it; when the agency asked Noriega to help, he declined.[16] By 1986, in fact, the relationship with General Noriega had begun to sour.[17] When Noriega reportedly threatened to blow the lid off the CIA drug trafficking, a federal prosecutor in Florida indicted him *in absentia* in 1988 for cocaine smuggling.[18]

Concerned over a leader in a key country who now seemed recalcitrant, we huddled with Panamanian military officers who wanted to overthrow General Noriega.[19] To put pressure on Noriega, and hopefully to secure either his resignation or removal, the Reagan administration froze Panamanian government assets in American banks[20] and instructed U.S. citizens and companies in Panama not to pay their taxes there.[21] Although these sanctions put a severe crimp in Panama's economy, General Noriega remained in power.

Unlike Carter, Reagan had reservations about giving up the canal and our military bases in Panama in 1999. In 1987, J. Edward Fox, assistant secretary of state for legislative and intergovernmental affairs, thought that the State Department might try to renegotiate the 1977 treaties, in particular to continue our base rights after 1999. Fox stated that the domestic political situation in Panama might threaten stability in Central America, and that "steps should be taken to bring about the resignation of General Noriega," replacing him with other military officers committed to "the safeguarding of U.S. strategic interests."[22] Thus, to the State Department, General Noriega had become an obstacle to renegotiating the canal treaties.

In May 1989, a presidential election was held in Panama, and a candidate loyal to General Noriega was challenged by Guillermo Endara, around whom most opposition groups stood united. By then our economic sanctions were causing havoc in Panama's economy, and voters knew that if Endara were elected, we would lift them. Toward the end of the presidential campaign, the press reported that President Bush had issued a secret finding to the CIA to funnel $10 million to Endara.[23] Although Bush himself refused to comment on the report, administration officials, speaking not for attribution, disclosed that the president approved the plan in February 1989 as part of his effort to bring Noriega down. Endara denied that he had received the funds.[24]

As Panamanians voted to choose a president in May 1989, international observers flooded the isthmus to watch the vote tally. Almost to a person, the observers said that Endara had won. General Noriega, however, declared the elections null, citing the reports of CIA funding to Endara.[25] The Bush administration then asked the Organization of American States (OAS) to approach General Noriega on the matter,[26] and over a period of months the OAS repeatedly urged Noriega to yield authority to Endara.[27]

Relations with Panama went from bad to worse, as our military personnel stationed there experienced run-ins with Panamanian soldiers. Some of our civilian personnel working at the canal experienced harassment as well, and we complained to the UN Security Council.[28] We also continued political pressure on General Noriega, taking our case to the OAS that he had turned Panama into a "haven for drug traffickers."[29]

As an object lesson to General Noriega, and perhaps to provoke him, the U.S. Southern Command conducted highly visible military maneuvers in Panama, sending armored personnel carriers rumbling through city streets.[30] The Panamanian administration called this a provocation, an attempt to intimidate Panama, and complained to the Security Council that the maneuvers created "a state of imminent war" between Panama and the United States.[31] Despite its efforts to convince General Noriega to resign, the Organization of American States criticized our maneuvers as "inopportune."[32]

Conflict also developed over the administration of the canal. Under the Panama Canal Treaty, a Panamanian was to replace a U.S. citizen as canal administrator on January 1, 1990.[33] But the State Department refused to accept a canal administrator appointed by General Noriega; nor would we recognize the administration that took office in September 1989, since General Noriega had annulled the May presidential election. President Bush would accept no diplomatic correspondence from the Panamanian administration, including correspondence about the appointment of a canal administrator.[34] By refusing, therefore, to accept a Noriega-appointed administrator, Bush hoped to bring down the Panamanian administration.[35]

As a further means of undermining Noriega, President Bush issued an order to halt the import into the United States of Panamanian sugar.[36] When an insurgent group formed among Panamanian military officers in neighboring Costa Rica to overthrow General Noriega, the CIA lent a hand.[37] In October, some Panamanian officers tried to raise a coup against General Noriega, and we helped them by blocking some roads; but the coup failed.[38]

At that point, however, the Pentagon had begun final planning for a full-scale invasion of Panama to overthrow Noriega, and during November 1989, the assigned units rehearsed.[39] On December 1, Bush stopped up the economic pressure by announcing that we would not let Panama-registered ships dock at U.S. ports.[40] This was a major blow, because Panama turned a tidy profit by letting out its flag to foreign shippers as a "flag of convenience."[41] Viewing this as one more hostile act, Panama's National Assembly of District Representatives passed a resolution on December 15 "that the Republic of Panama is in a state of war while there is aggression against the people of Panama from the United States of America."[42] By "aggression," the Assembly meant our military maneuvers and economic sanctions.[43]

On December 16, a shooting incident occurred in Panama City. According to the Defense Department's account, four unarmed off-duty U.S. military officers driving in an automobile had been out for dinner and gotten lost on their way home. Not knowing where they were, the officers drove up to a military checkpoint at the headquarters of the Panamanian army, called the Panama Defense Force (PDF). PDF soldiers pointed weapons at them and reached into the automobile in a menacing fashion. In fear, the driver started up the car and drove through the checkpoint, with the PDF soldiers firing after the car, killing one of the officers and wounding another.[44]

The PDF, however, gave a different version of the shooting incident.

According to its communique, the four U.S. officers were armed, and it was they who fired first, wounding two Panamanian civilians and one soldier.[45] Neither version of the story could be confirmed. The PDF said there were witnesses who could back up its version but did not produce any. The Defense Department's version was shaky as well, because before arriving at the checkpoint, the four officers had to drive past two other barricades that should have alerted them that they were in a restricted area.

As it happened, a U.S. Navy officer and his wife were near the checkpoint and saw the incident. Some other PDF soldiers were nearby, reportedly intoxicated.[46] They stopped the officer and his wife and took them off to a nearby building where they questioned them both for four hours. In the process, according to the Defense Department account, the PDF soldiers beat the officer and threatened his wife with sexual attack.[47]

President Bush called the checkpoint shooting and the treatment of the navy officer and his wife an "outrage"; the president's spokesperson said that this, together with the December 15 Panamanian resolution about a state of war with the United States, created a "climate of aggression."[48] Although the PDF did not consider its soldiers at fault for the incident, it reportedly told U.S. representatives that the incident had not been intended.[49] While not an apology, this appeared at least to be an expression of mild regret, as well as a statement that the incident had not been a result of high-level policy.

In any event, shortly after the checkpoint incident President Bush decided to put the invasion plan into action. With 12,000 troops already stationed in Panama, on December 20, Bush sent an equal number to make an invasion force of 24,500 that took over Panama in several days of fighting.[50] We contacted Endara and asked him to assume the presidency.[51]

U.S. forces suffered 26 dead and 300 wounded in the invasion; but the invasion had taken a far more severe toll on Panama. A prime target of our forces was the PDF headquarters in Panama City, located in a densely populated lower-class district. In bombing the headquarters, our planes leveled several city blocks of nearby housing, killing many residents.[52] Overall, several thousand Panamanians were hospitalized for injuries suffered during the invasion.[53] The Red Cross reported that hospitals in Panama City were "inundated with civilian and military casualties," that "over 800 people were treated during the first few days," and that "medicines and medical material were in short supply." The Red Cross brought in two planeloads of medical supplies to make up the shortfall.[54]

As for deaths, Deputy Secretary of State Lawrence Eagleburger estimated 400 Panamanians killed, a figure that most observers considered far too low.[55] The overthrown government estimated 7,000 killed, but that figure could not be substantiated.[56] According to a Red Cross official, there were "at least two thousand killed; the morgues of the hospitals are overflowing and there is no more room." He accused the United States of covering up a massacre.[57]

In Panama City shortly after the invasion, I spoke with survivors of the bombing in the neighborhood around the PDF headquarters. For them it was a night of horror, with houses in flames all around, uncertainty over whether they would be hit, and worry over relatives living nearby. Survivors of the bombing told of psychological trauma and of children who became frantic at the sound of a helicopter.

A year after the invasion, I sat as a hearing officer in Panama on an inquiry panel organized by Panamanian human rights organizations, to assess responsibility for the damage suffered by Panama's civilian population. The case files prepared by investigators recounted bombing deaths and fatal shootings of civilians by U.S. soldiers.

One reason why the number of fatalities was not immediately apparent was that our forces sealed off the heavily damaged area around the PDF headquarters for the first four days, keeping out the media and the Red Cross. They forced the residents out of the houses, which they then demolished. When I visited the area, there were no standing structures at all in the area. Mass graves discovered months after the invasion led to the revelation that U.S. forces had collected bodies in the streets and carted them off without identifying them. Some Panamanians reported seeing our soldiers incinerating bodies in the streets with flame throwers.[58] The apparent aim of all this activity was to hide the human and material damage caused by the bombing. Under pressure from Panamanian human rights groups, the Endara government exhumed from the mass graves many bodies, some of which could be identified.

Once in occupation, our soldiers set up roadblocks to try to identify members of the PDF; since they had trouble distinguishing friend from foe, all were rendered suspect. At roadblocks, the soldiers might hear a shot and fire in return, not knowing where the shot originated. A number of passersby were killed in this way.

In one well-documented case, our forces pulled five young Panamanian men out of their van and shot them execution-style as they lay face down on the ground; it was unclear whether the soldiers suspected the young men of hostile activity. In many cases of civilians killed by shooting, the Panamanian courts conducted a coroner's inquest and determined that the person had been shot by an American soldier, who could not, however, be identified. Despite requests, U.S. officials in Panama refused to determine the circumstances or the identity of the soldier, and the Panamanian courts had no access to U.S. military personnel.

In its early statements after the invasion, the Bush administration painted a picture of normalcy in Panama, but several newspapers told a different story: "North American Invasion Leads to Total Chaos in Panama," screamed the headline of the Madrid daily *El País*.[59] "Looting and Bombs Turn Panama into a No Man's Land," said Argentina's *La Prensa*.[60] "Chaos Grips Streets," said the *Los Angeles Times*.[61] Looters emptied shops, as Panama City experienced a wave of robbery and violence perpetrated by ordinary criminal elements.[62] One reason for the chaos was that American forces had disbanded the existing police force without immediately substituting any other security measures.[63] Damage from the bombing and looting combined was estimated at $1 billion.[64] After several weeks of direct military rule, our forces turned control over to Endara, although we maintained advisors in government departments as a kind of shadow administration.[65]

Notes

1. Construction of a Ship Canal (Herran-Hay Treaty), January 22, 1903, *Unperfected Treaties of the United States of America: 1776-1976* (1977), 3: 447.

2. Antonio Jose Uribe, *Colombia, Estados Unidos y Panamá* (1976), pp. 90-98; Manuel Arteaga Hernandez and Jaime Arteaga Carvajal, *Historia política de Colombia* (1986), p. 501. German Cavelier, *La política internacional de Colombia* (1960), 2: 305-7.

3. Uribe, *Colombia, Estados Unidos y Panamá*, pp. 103-5; Cavelier, *La política internacional de Colombia*, 2: 308-9.

4. John Bassett Moore, *Digest of International Law* (1906), 3: 46; Uribe, *Colombia, Estados Unidos y Panamá*, p. 105; Arteaga and Arteaga, *Historia política de Colombia*,

p. 502; David Howarth, *Panama* (1966), p. 235. Albert Edwards, *Panama: The Canal, the Country, and the People* (1912), p. 471.

5. Isthmian Canal Convention, art. 3, November 18, 1903, Treaty Series 431, U.S. Congress, *Statutes at Large,* vol. 33, p. 2234 (1904).

6. "Panama Suspends U.S. Tie and Charges Aggression After Riot in Canal Zone," *New York Times,* January 10, 1964, p. A1, col. 8.

7. Panama Canal Treaty, arts. 2–3, September 7, 1977, TIAS No. 10030, in *International Legal Materials,* vol. 16, p. 1022 (1977).

8. Treaty Concerning the Permanent Neutrality and Operation of the Panama Canal, arts. 1, 5, September 7, 1977, TIAS No. 10029, in *International Legal Materials,* vol. 16, p. 1040 (1977).

9. Frederick Kempe, "Ties That Blind: U.S. Taught Noriega to Spy, but the Pupil Had His Own Agenda," *Wall Street Journal,* October 18, 1989, p. A1, col. 1.

10. Seymour Hersh, "Panama Strongman Said to Trade in Drugs, Arms and Illicit Money," *New York Times,* June 12, 1986, p. A1, col. 1.

11. "A Man, a Plan, a Canal, Panama," *Economist,* January 6, 1990, p. 17; Stephen Engelberg, "U.S. Said to Ignore Noriega Drug Role," *New York Times,* April 5, 1988, p. A1, col. 1; Stephen Engelberg, "Officials Say Bush Heard '85 Charge Against Noriega," *New York Times,* May 8, 1988, p. A1, col. 4; David Johnston, "Papers Seized from Noriega Could Help Iran-Contra Case," *New York Times,* January 12, 1990, p. A8, col. 1.

12. Hersh, "Panama Strongman Said to Trade in Drugs, Arms and Illicit Money"; Transcript, "Frontline" Special, "Guns, Drugs and the CIA," WGBH, Public Broadcasting System (1988), p. 22.

13. Dennis Volman, "Money Courier Tells of Services for CIA," *Christian Science Monitor,* July 16, 1987, p. 3, col. 2.

14. Connie Bruck, "How Noriega Got Caught and Got Away," *American Lawyer,* July–August 1988, p. 35.

15. Transcript, "Frontline" Special, "Guns, Drugs and the CIA," p. 23.

16. Milton Martinez, *Panama 1978-1990: Una Crisis sin Fin* (1990), p. 97; Independent Commission of Inquiry on the U.S. Invasion of Panama, *The U.S. Invasion of Panama: The Truth Behind Operation 'Just Cause'* (1990), p. 22.

17. "The OAS and the Panama Crisis," DSB, vol. 89, p. 72 (November 1989).

18. Philip Shenon, "Noriega Indicted by U.S. for Links to Illegal Drugs," *New York Times,* February 6, 1988, p. A1, col. 2.

19. Neil A. Lewis, "U.S. Withholds a Canal Payment in New Steps to Oust Panamanian," *New York Times,* March 12, 1988, p. A1, col. 4.

20. "Prohibiting Certain Transactions with Respect to Panama," Exec. Order. 12635, April 8, 1988, *Federal Register,* vol. 53, p. 12134 (April 12, 1988); Lewis, "U.S. Withholds a Canal Payment in New Steps to Oust Panamanian," *New York Times,* March 12, 1988, p. A1, col. 4; Julie Johnson, "Reagan Halts All Payments to Panamanian Government," *New York Times,* April 9, 1988, p. A1, col. 5; "Contemporary Practice of the United States Relating to International Law: Economic Sanctions," *American Journal of International Law* 82 (1988): 573.

21. "Prohibiting Certain Transactions with Respect to Panama"; Johnson, "Reagan Halts All Payments to Panamanian Government."

22. Letter of J. Edward Fox to Sen. Jesse Helms, March 26, 1987, reprinted in Independent Commission of Inquiry on the U.S. Invasion of Panama, p. 20.

23. "Taking Aim at Noriega: Will CIA Campaign Funds Topple a Dictator in Panama's Election?" *U.S. News & World Report,* May 1, 1989, p. 40.

24. Stephen Engelberg, "C.I.A. Funnels Aid to Noriega's Election Foes," *New York Times,* April 23, 1989, p. A14, col. 4.

25. Lindsey Gruson, "Noriega Stealing Election, Carter Says," *New York Times,* May 9, 1989, p. A1, col. 6; Bernard Weinraub, "Bush Urges Effort to Press Noriega to Quit as Leader," *New York Times,* May 10, 1989, p. A1, col. 6; "Transcript of Bush's News Conference on the Panama Vote," *New York Times,* May 10, 1989, p. A10, col. 1.

26. Robert Pear, "Hemispheric Group Asks Noriega to Yield Power," *New York Times,* May 18, 1989, p. A8, col. 3.

27. Larry Rohter, "O.A.S. Draws Latin Fire for Stand on Panama," *New York Times,* June 4, 1989, p. A10, col. 1; Robert Pear, "Latin Envoys Report No Progress in Their Effort to Dislodge Noriega," *New York Times,* June 20, 1989, p. A8, col. 1; Robert Pear, "Diplomats Urge Noriega to Resign by September 1," *New York Times,* July 20, 1989, p. A6, col. 4; Robert Pear, "Washington Talk; Diplomacy," *New York Times,* August 22, 1989, p. A20, col. 5. Robert Pear, "U.S. Is Faulted on Military Maneuvers in Panama," *New York Times,* August 24, 1989, p. A3, col. 1.

28. "Panama, United States Again Before Council," *UN Chronicle* 26 (December 1989): 20.

29. Robert Pear, "U.S. Renews Attack on Noriega, Offering Evidence of Ties to Drugs," *New York Times,* September 1, 1989, p. A1, col. 1.

30. Bob Woodward, *The Commanders* (1991), pp. 92, 99–100.

31. "Panama, United States Again Before Council"; Paul Lewis, "Panama Urges U.N. to Send Observers," *New York Times,* August 12, 1989, p. A3, col. 4; Pear, "U.S. Is Faulted on Military Maneuvers in Panama," p. A3, col. 1.

32. Pear, "U.S. Is Faulted on Military Maneuvers in Panama," p. A3, col. 1.

33. Panama Canal Treaty, art. 3(3)(c).

34. Robert Pear, "Aide to Noriega Is Sworn In: U.S. Won't Recognize Him," *New York Times,* September 2, 1989, p. A3, col. 5.

35. John Pearson, "Panama," *Business Week,* December 25, 1989, p. 70.

36. "U.S. Severs Diplomatic Contact with Noriega Regime," DSB, vol. 89, p. 69 (November 1989); "Economic Measures Against Panama," Department Statement, September 12, 1989, DSB, vol. 89, p. 69 (November 1989); "U.S. Expands Its Sanctions Against Panama," *New York Times,* September 13, 1989, p. A5, col. 1.

37. Tony Avirgan, "Panama Contras?" *Nation,* September 18, 1989, p. 263; Mark A. Uhlig, "An Untold Guerrilla War: Noriega Foes Rule Border," *New York Times,* January 10, 1990, p. A8, col. 5.

38. Stephen Engelberg, "Bush Aides Admit a U.S. Role in Coup, and Bad Handling," *New York Times,* October 6, 1989, p. A1, col. 6; Woodward, *The Commanders,* pp. 119–24.

39. Woodward, *The Commanders,* pp. 132–45.

40. "U.S. Imposes Ban on Ships under Panamanian Flag," *Wall Street Journal,* December 1, 1989, p. B2, col. 5.

41. Don A. Shanche, "Rivals Try to Flag Down Panama Ship Business," *Los Angeles Times,* December 19, 1989, p. A8, col. 1.

42. Andrew Rosenthal, "U.S. Forces Gain Wide Control in Panama; New Leaders Put In But Noriega Gets Away," *New York Times,* December 21, 1989, p. A1, col. 6.

43. William Branigin, "Noriega Appointed 'Maximum Leader'," *Washington Post,* December 16, 1989, p. A21, col. 1; William Branigin, "Noriega's 'State of War' Seen as Quest for Backing," *Washington Post,* December 20, 1989, p. A32, col. 1.

44. "Excerpts from U.S. Account of Officer's Death in Panama," *New York Times,* December 18, 1989, p. A8, col. 3.

45. William Branigin, "U.S. Assails Panama in Killing of GI," *Washington Post,* December 18, 1989, p. A1, col. 6.

46. Walter Pincus, "Pair of Incidents Pushed Bush Toward Invasion," *Washington Post,* December 24, 1989, p. A16, col. 2.

47. "Excerpts from U.S. Account of Officer's Death in Panama."

48. Andrew Rosenthal, "President Calls Panama Slaying a Great Outrage," *New York Times,* December 19, 1989, p. A1, col. 1.

49. Ibid.

50. Molly Moore and Ann Devroy, "Officials Say Panama Taking More Time and Troops Than Expected," *Washington Post,* December 23, 1989, p. A6, col. 6.

51. Rosenthal, "U.S. Forces Gain Wide Control in Panama; New Leaders Put In But Noriega Gets Away."

52. Brook Larmer, "With the Dictator Disabled, Panama Looks to Rebuild," *Christian Science Monitor,* December 27, 1989, p. 1, col. 4.

53. Brook Larmer, "In Invasion's Wake, Disorder Reigns in Panamanian Capital," *Christian Science Monitor,* December 22, 1989, p. 1, col. 1 (report that over 1,000 wounded).

54. "U.S. Military Intervention in Panama," *International Committee of the Red Cross Bulletin,* No. 169 (February 1990): 2.

55. J. D. Gannon, "Invasion Took Its Toll in Deaths, Human Suffering," *Christian Science Monitor,* December 29, 1989, p. 3, col. 1; Andrew Rosenthal, "No More Panamas, Bush Aides Predict," *New York Times,* January 8, 1990, p. A9, col. 1; David E. Pitt, "The Invasion's Civilian Toll: Still No Official Count," *New York Times,* January 10, 1990, p. A9, col. 3.

56. "Panamá sumida en el caos y Noriega continua prófugo," *La Prensa* (Buenos Aires), December 23, 1989, p. 1, col. 3.

57. "Acusan a EE.UU. de esconder una matanza," *La Prensa* (Buenos Aires), December 26, 1989, p. 2, col. 3.

58. Independent Commission of Inquiry on the U.S. Invasion of Panama, pp. 41–43.

59. "La invasión norteamericana provoca el caos total en Panamá," *El País* (Madrid), December 25, 1989, p. 1, col. 2.

60. "Panamá sumida en el caos y Noriega continúa prófugo"; "Saqueos y bombas han convertido a Panamá en 'tierra de nadie,' " *La Prensa* (Buenos Aires), December 23, 1989, p. 3, col. 1.

61. "Noriega Loyalists Hit Back at U.S. Military as Chaos Grips Streets," *Los Angeles Times,* December 24, 1989, p. A1, col. 5.

62. William Branigin, "Looters Lay Waste to Panama City Shops," *Washington Post,* December 23, 1989, p. A1, col. 1; Michael R. Gordon and David E. Pitt, "Panama Crime Wave Shakes Faith in Police," *New York Times,* February 2, 1990, p. A10, col. 1.

63. Larmer, "With the Dictator Disabled, Panama Looks to Rebuild"; Brook Larmer, "Panama Forges Police Force From Members of Noriega's Military," *Christian Science Monitor,* December 28, 1989, p. 1, col. 1.

64. Larmer, "With the Dictator Disabled, Panama Looks to Rebuild"; Douglas Waller and John Barry, "Inside the Invasion," *Newsweek,* June 25, 1990, pp. 29–31.

65. Independent Commission of Inquiry on the U.S. Invasion of Panama, p. 49.

29

Panama: Explaining Why

In the words of the White House statement announcing the Panama invasion, "Last Friday [December 15, 1989], Noriega declared a state of war with the United States. The next day, the P.D.F. [Panama Defense Force] shot to death an unarmed American serviceman, wounded another, seized and beat another serviceman and sexually threatened his wife. Under these circumstances, the President decided he must act to prevent further violence."[1] President Bush affirmed that these incidents showed that "the lives of American citizens were in grave danger," and that the December 15 resolution was a declaration of war which clearly showed that Panama planned to attack American citizens.[2] In addition, Secretary of State James Baker said that we had information that General Noriega was preparing "an urban commando attack on American citizens in a residential neighborhood" in Panama City, although Baker acknowledged that he could not prove this information. Baker said that he received it only after President Bush had ordered the invasion.[3]

How solid was the administration's information? Did it provide, as the administration argued, a "just cause" for invasion? As for the December 15 National Assembly resolution, it was not Panama's first reference to a "state of war" with the United States. In August 1989, as we saw, Panama's government declared that our military maneuvers created "a state of imminent war," although Bush did not make much of this statement.[4] The December 15 resolution was, according to the *Christian Science Monitor,* more a statement that the United States had initiated an economic war than one of Panamanian intent to initiate a shooting war.[5] Since we had 12,000 troops stationed in Panama at the time, it would have been foolhardy for Panama to start anything.

Why, in fact, did the National Assembly pass the resolution, and why did it refer to a "state of war"? In all likelihood, the motive was to rally the population behind General Noriega by showing the United States trying to bring him down through military pressure and financial sanctions. The resolution thus appealed to Panamanian patriotism; to say that we had instigated a "state of war" was a strong and eloquent way of denouncing our actions.

The notion of war by economic means is a common one in hemispheric relations: one of the perennial fears of the Latin states is that the United States may use its economic clout against them. To stop this, in fact, they wrote a provision into the Charter of the Organization of American States (OAS) that equates economic sanctions with war. The provision reads, "No State may use . . . coercive measures of an economic . . . character in order to force the sovereign will of another State."[6]

That the December 15 resolution was aimed at rallying the Panamanian population behind General Noriega appears clearly from the fact that the resolution also named General Noriega "chief of government" and "maximum leader of national liberation" to oppose the United States. The pronouncement about a state of war was a basis for giving General Noriega these new titles.[7] The Bush administration kept close enough watch on Panamanian politics for it to understand that this was the import of the December 15 resolution. While the administration knew that the resolution was not a formal declaration of war, it seized on the opportunity to take the phrase "state of war" out of context, in order to find a pretext to invade.

Beyond the matter of the December 15 resolution, the White House relied as well, as we have seen, on the checkpoint incident of the following day, to prove that the Panamanian administration was carrying out its "declaration of war" by attacking U.S. citizens. But the circumstances indicated that the incident was not part of any overall plan to attack Americans in Panama, even if the U.S. version were accurate. Since the four American officers drove up to the checkpoint unannounced, the attack could not have been planned in advance. As for the treatment of the navy officer and his wife, the Defense Department conceded that the PDF soldiers responsible were intoxicated, which strongly suggests that the incident was not part of a general plan.

Although President Bush insisted that the invasion was prompted by the "declaration of war" and the checkpoint incident, he had been planning it for months. Military officers posing as tourists had spread through Panama to reconnoiter locations they planned to attack. Fred Hoffman, a former Pentagon official, referring to classified planning documents for the invasion, said the administration "had a plan" and was "just waiting for an excuse to use it."[8]

The Bush administration gave three other justifications for the invasion. One objective, according to Secretary of State Baker, was "to seize and arrest an indicted drug trafficker"—a pointed reference to General Noriega and his indictments in Florida.[9] The army did capture General Noriega and take him to Florida for trial; however, the United States had known of Noriega's drug involvement even during the years we befriended him. Therefore, the impression that the administration was trying to give of coming down hard on a cocaine trafficker was disingenuous at best.

The second justification was given by President Bush, who said that we invaded "to defend democracy in Panama."[10] Secretary Baker averred that "in taking the actions that we've taken, we consulted the legitimate, democratically elected government of Panama, which welcomed our actions."[11] This suggested that Guillermo Endara had specifically asked for the intervention, or at least that his opinion had been sought. However, Endara said that the administration never asked him if he *wanted* an invasion; the White House only informed him when the invasion was imminent and told Endara that he should get ready to take over as president. Endara's UN representative also said that Endara had not requested or authorized the invasion, calling it a unilateral decision by the U.S., in which the Endara government had no part.[12]

Was Bush truly moved by a desire for democracy in Panama in his decision to invade? In Latin America, the rationale was met with skepticism, because the United States has often supported undemocratic governments, particularly in Latin America, if they were safely in our camp. In the Dominican Republic, as we have seen, the Johnson administration intervened *against* an elected president to keep him from reclaiming his office. In Chile in 1973, we helped overthrow a democratically elected government. Our history has been to favor governments on the basis of national interest, not on the basis of democracy. Perhaps this time the leopard had changed its spots, but there was little reason to believe it.

A third justification given by the administration is that we invaded Panama to protect our interests in the Panama Canal; as Secretary of State Baker put it, "to defend the integrity of United States' rights under the canal treaties."[13] The smooth functioning of the canal, Baker argued, was at stake, because Panama was harassing canal workers and attacking our military personnel who were there to defend the canal. Baker declared that "the United States has both the right and . . . the duty to protect and defend the Canal under Article 4 of the Panama Canal Treaty."[14] Article 4 states that Panama and the United States should defend the canal, in particular "to meet the danger resulting from an armed attack or other actions which threaten the security of the Panama Canal or of ships transiting it."[15]

Baker, referring to "the continuing pattern of harassment that we've seen going on down there against Americans in the exercise of our treaty rights," said that we "anticipated that there might be problems with respect to the canal if Noriega continued to retain power illegitimately."[16] Baker's statement focused less, however, on the impact of those incidents on canal operations than on a concern that the incidents might increase in the future, in which case they could affect the operation. Similarly, in congressional testimony a month earlier, Michael G. Kozak, deputy assistant secretary of state for inter-American affairs, indicated that the harassment incidents had not yet adversely affected the canal: "Despite regime efforts to change U.S. nonrecognition policy by harassing U.S. and Panamanian employees of the U.S. forces and the Panama Canal Commission, Noriega has seemingly sought to avoid a direct threat to the canal or a direct challenge to the proper exercise of U.S. rights." Like Baker, however, Kozak saw a possible future threat: "Nevertheless, it becomes clearer each day that Noriega's continuation in power is a threat not only to the interests and freedom of his own people, but also to the canal."[17]

Despite the problems between General Noriega and the Bush administration, wrote the *New York Times,* "ship traffic on the canal was hardly disrupted."[18] "The security of the canal," according to the *Economist,* "was

not at stake" in the administration's confrontation with Noriega.[19] Ships
were going through, and the prospects were that they would continue
to go through. "There is no evidence," wrote Madrid *El País,* "that might
prove that Noriega or his forces had any intention of attacking the installations of the waterway."[20] Even after the invasion began, our forces showed
no concern that the canal might be sabotaged, and while they took no
precautions to protect the canal, the PDF made no moves against it.[21]

Of the long list of reasons Bush gave for invading Panama, none
withstood scrutiny, and although the American public did not raise much
objection, the administration's rationale for intervening in Panama did
not play well abroad.[22] The OAS, which had repeatedly urged General
Noriega to give up power, issued a resolution in which it "deeply deplored"
the invasion and called the American action a violation of "the right
of the Panamanian people to self-determination without outside interference."[23] The OAS resolution was adopted by a vote of 20 to one,
the only negative vote being our own.[24]

In the UN Security Council, a majority voted a condemnation, but
we vetoed it, along with Britain and France.[25] The UN General Assembly
"strongly deplored" the intervention and demanded the immediate withdrawal of U.S. forces from Panama. This resolution passed 75–20, and
most of the states that voted against it agreed that the invasion was
unjustified; however, they wanted the resolution to mention the misdeeds
by General Noriega.[26] The Bush administration had anticipated the
negative reaction abroad but decided it could live with it.[27]

International condemnation was so strong because the Bush administration's various rationales for the Panama invasion did not ring
true. But if these were not the real reasons, why then did we invade
Panama? The drug-trafficking angle may have been a factor, but not
quite for the reason the administration gave. As vice-president, Bush
had been responsible for drug policy, and as president he declared a
"war on drugs"; but he had registered no major successes against drug
trafficking.[28] Much of the cocaine from Colombia was being shipped
to the United States, and Panama was a transit point.[29] A high-visibility
move like arresting General Noriega might appear to be a victory in
the "war on drugs."

Another possible factor in the administration's decision to invade
was its war in Nicaragua, because at the time it was still financing the

Contras. With elections scheduled in Nicaragua for February 1990, Bush may have hoped, by an invasion of Panama, to reemphasize to Nicaragua's voters that you can't cross Uncle Sam. The anti-Sandinista candidate, Violeta Chamorro, whom we supported, promised close relations with the United States; since Chamorro won, perhaps this strategy had worked after all.[30]

In London, the *Economist* theorized along a different line: "Robbed of a plausible threat in the shape of the Evil Empire [a term President Reagan had used for the Soviet Union], the United States Defence Department needs new enemies to take on. Who better than beastly drug runners like General Noriega?"[31] With the cold war ending, the administration was being put under pressure to justify its arms budget, which had nearly doubled during the 1980s. One weapon the Defense Department used in Panama was the "stealth" bomber, which, said the *Economist,* "reinforced the impression that the Pentagon is treating Panama as a playground in which to practise its new arts."[32] Defense Department critics charged that the only reason we used the stealth bomber at all in Panama was to buttress the case for buying more of them, even in the face of serious congressional opposition.[33] The suspicion heightened when it was revealed that the Defense Department had lied about the number of stealth bombers it used in Panama. At first the Department acknowledged only two, but later Army Lieutenant General Carl Stiner, who commanded the invasion, revealed there were six.[34]

The canal may indeed have been a factor in the United States' decision to invade, although not quite for the reason the administration gave. As we saw, Panama was to have the right, beginning January 1, 1990, to appoint the canal administrator, and Bush did not want a Noriega appointee. Invading ten days before that deadline let the administrator be appointed by a Panamanian government friendly to American interests.

Also, the Panama Canal Treaty called for the complete transfer of the canal and the withdrawal of U.S. troops by December 31, 1999; however, that treaty had been controversial, and in 1989 some in Congress still thought we should keep the canal.[35] They wanted to ask Panama to renegotiate, but with General Noriega in power, that was not likely. On the other hand, a Panamanian government that owed us its position might be more amenable. Although President Bush reaffirmed our commitment to turn the canal over on schedule,[36] he did not rule out the possibility of renegotiation. The press reported from inside sources that renegotiation had indeed figured in the administration's thinking about the invasion.[37]

Endara was also more likely to cooperate because he represented the white upper stratum of Panamanian society, the group we had approached in 1903 to separate Panama from Colombia. That group ruled until 1968, when a military coup brought in an administration oriented to lower-class black and brown Panamanians, and who were more nationalistic, more concerned about Yankee domination. It was they who rioted in 1964 to demand that we turn over the canal. General Noriega, although he collaborated with us early in his career, drew his support from the lower class. When Endara took office, he showed his colors by appointing a cabinet almost entirely from the upper class.

While some of these factors could have been behind the Panama invasion, we may have to wait for memoirs by Bush administration insiders to find out the real reasons. All I know for sure is that I still have my grandfather's sailor hat from the USS *Wyoming*. "Wyoming" is emblazoned, still brightly, on the bill.

Notes

1. "Text of Statement by Fitzwater," *New York Times,* December 21, 1989, p. A19, col. 2.
2. "A Transcript of Bush's Address on the Decision to Use Force in Panama," *New York Times,* December 21, 1989, p. A19, col. 1.
3. Andrew Rosenthal, "U.S. Forces Gain Wide Control in Panama; New Leaders Put In But Noriega Gets Away," *New York Times,* December 21, 1989, p. A1, col. 6; "Excerpts from Statement by Baker on U.S. Policy," *New York Times,* December 21, 1989, p. A19, col. 3.
4. Paul Lewis, "Panama Urges U.N. to Send Observers," *New York Times,* August 12, 1989, p. A3, col. 4; "Panama, United States Again Before Council," *UN Chronicle* 26 (December 1989): 20.
5. Lucia Mouat, "U.S. Policy of Grinding Down Noriega Stalls," *Christian Science Monitor,* December 20, 1989, p. 1, col. 4.
6. Charter of the Organization of American States, 1948, art. 16, *United States Treaties and Other International Agreements,* 2: 2394; *United Nations Treaty Series,* 119: 3.
7. William Branigin, "Noriega Appointed 'Maximum Leader,' " *Washington Post,* December 16, 1989, p. A21, col. 1; William Branigin, "Noriega's 'State of War' Seen as Quest for Backing," *Washington Post,* December 20, 1989, p. A32, col. 1.
8. Douglas Waller and John Barry, "Inside the Invasion," *Newsweek,* June 25, 1990, pp. 29–31.

9. "Excerpts from Statement by Baker on U.S. Policy."

10. "A Transcript of Bush's Address on the Decision to Use Force in Panama."

11. "Excerpts from Statement by Baker on U.S. Policy."

12. Ethan Schwartz, "World Criticism of U.S. Intervention Mounts," *Washington Post,* December 22, 1989, p. A29, col. 2.

13. "Excerpts from Statement by Baker on U.S. Policy."

14. Ibid.

15. Panama Canal Treaty, art. 4, September 7, 1977, entered into force October 1, 1979, TIAS No. 10030, in *International Legal Materials* 16 (1977): 1022.

16. "Excerpts from Statement by Baker on U.S. Policy."

17. "Panama Canal: The Strategic Dimension," U.S. Dept. of State, Current Policy No. 1226, p. 3 (November 1989) (statement before Subcommittee on Panama Canal and Outer Continental Shelf, Committee on Merchant Marine and Fisheries, U.S. House of Representatives, November 2, 1989).

18. David E. Pitt, "Challenge for Panamanians: A Canal in Transition," *New York Times,* January 29, 1990, p. A11, col. 1.

19. "A Man, a Plan, a Canal, Panama," *Economist,* January 6, 1990, p. 17.

20. "George Bush, contra reloj," *El País* (Madrid), December 25, 1989, p. 2, col. 1.

21. Peter Grier, "U.S. Forces Strike Panama in Bid to Oust Strongman," *Christian Science Monitor,* December 21, 1989, p. 1, col. 4.

22. Schwartz, "World Criticism of U.S. Intervention Mounts"; Bill McAllister, "U.S. Cites Self-Defense; Legal Scholars Skeptical," *Washington Post,* December 21, 1989, p. A36, col. 3; "Generalizada condena a la intervención estadounidense," *La Prensa* (Buenos Aires), December 22, 1989, p. 3, col. 1.

23. "La OEA deplora la invasión y exige un cese del fuego," *La Prensa* (Buenos Aires), December 23, 1989, p. 4, col. 1.

24. "Criticism of U.S. Action Is Supported in 20–1 Vote," *New York Times,* December 23, 1989, p. A15, col. 5; John M. Goshko and Michael Isikoff, "O.A.S. Votes to Censure U.S. for Intervention," *Washington Post,* December 23, 1989, p. A7, col. 5.

25. Paul Lewis, "Two Delegates Vying to Be the Voice of the New Government," *New York Times,* December 29, 1989, p. A12, col. 1.

26. Ethan Schwartz, "U.N. Assembly Blasts Invasion of Panama," *Washington Post,* December 30, 1989, p. A17, col. 1.

27. Bob Woodward, *The Commanders* (1991), p. 170.

28. Richard L. Berke, "Bush Endorses Outline of Plan for Drug Battle," *New York Times,* August 16, 1989, p. A1, col. 5.

29. Ann B. Wrobleski, "Presidential Certification of Narcotics Source Countries," DSB, vol. 88, pp. 47–50 (June 1988).

30. "Nicaraguan Opposition Routs Sandinistas; U.S. Pledges Aid, Tied to Orderly Turnover," *New York Times,* February 27, 1990, p. A1, col. 6.

31. "A Man, a Plan, a Canal, Panama," p. 17.

32. Ibid., p. 18.

33. "Stealth Fighter's Mission Reported Marred by Error," *New York Times,* April 4, 1990, p. A1, col. 2.

34. "Panama Alerted to Attack, General Says," *New York Times,* February 27, 1990, p. A7, col. 1.

35. "Combat in Panama," *Los Angeles Times,* December 21, 1989, p. A9, col. 1.

36. Ibid.

37. "Quayle Trip: Resentment Dramatized," *New York Times,* January 31, 1990, p. A16, col. 4.

30

Liberia: Just in Case

Just as the U.S. invasion of Panama got underway, a civil war broke out in the west African nation of Liberia, and the Bush administration's antennae went up. After five months of watching from a distance, on May 31, 1990, as the fighting continued, we sent up to Liberia's coast a flotilla of six battleships with 2,100 U.S. Marines aboard carrying tanks, helicopter gunships, and vertical takeoff jet fighters. According to a Defense Department spokesperson, Commander David Thomas, as the ships cast anchor offshore, they were under orders to "be prepared to evacuate American citizens" from Liberia. When the civil war began, there were about 5,000 American citizens in Liberia; however, by the time the flotilla arrived, all but about 1,200, including one hundred embassy personnel and dependents, had left.[1]

The Defense Department was concerned, it said, with the possible danger to U.S. citizens in Liberia, where two separate rebel forces were challenging the government of President Samuel Doe. Pete Williams, another Defense Department spokesperson, explained the Marines' presence "as a precaution to take up a position in international waters in the event they are needed to help American citizens and other non-combatants who need to leave and cannot do so by commercial means."[2]

Liberia was a nation in which the United States had long had a

256

substantial interest. Unique among African countries, Liberia was founded in the nineteenth century by emancipated slaves from the American south; it had for a long time been our closest ally in west Africa. American companies were heavily invested there, and we gave Liberia substantial aid.[3] Indeed, during the early 1980s, Liberia was the largest per capita recipient of U.S. foreign aid in sub-Saharan Africa.[4]

One reason for our generosity was that Liberia let us maintain vital facilities there. On Liberian territory we had set up a navigation station to guide nuclear-powered missile launching submarines in much of the Atlantic Ocean. We also had sophisticated communications equipment there that relayed all CIA and State Department radio messages to and from sub-Saharan Africa. The Voice of America radio station had its transmitter for sub-Saharan Africa there as well;[5] officials put the value of the facilities at $200 million.[6] None of these facilities had been damaged or immediately threatened by the fighting, but they were not under military guard and could have been entered by troops, many of whom were not under tight discipline.

In its explanation of why it sent the flotilla, the Bush administration did not mention these facilities, or say why it needed so many well-equipped ships to rescue a small number of civilians. This led one skeptical reporter to ask whether the communications facilities might be the reason for the deployment, and whether we might land troops or launch aircraft from the flotilla to protect those facilities. Herman Cohen, assistant secretary of state for African affairs, did not deny the possibility, answering, "I wouldn't want to reject any options." Cohen acknowledged that "they are important installations," and that "it would be difficult and very expensive to move them to another country."[7]

As the flotilla rested offshore, the civil war reached Monrovia, Liberia's capital; small numbers of American citizens were evacuated to the ships from time to time, while others continued to leave Liberia on their own. By early August, only 300 Americans remained in the country. As the fighting intensified, the Liberian death toll mounted, and Monrovia was left with little water, electricity, or food. Prince Johnson, the commander of the smaller of the two rebel groups, threatened to arrest foreign nationals, apparently as a way of bringing about international intervention in the civil war.[8]

On August 5, Johnson seized a dozen foreigners, including one American, from a Monrovia hotel;[9] thereupon, President Bush, citing "an increased threat to our embassy and its facilities" from the fighting, ordered 225 of the Marines from the flotilla to helicopter into Monrovia. The helicopters carried back to the flotilla personnel from the embassy, from the Voice of America station, and from a communications facility— eighty persons in all.[10]

Charles Taylor, the leader of the larger rebel group, protested the landing, one of his aides charging that it created "a situation where an accident will be caused and someone will blame us."[11] Cuba also protested the landing, fearing we might help the government forces of President Doe.[12]

Several members of Congress suspected that the administration had organized the Liberia landing for reasons other than rescue. As it happened, Iraq had invaded Kuwait just three days before, leaving many U.S. citizens under Iraqi occupation there, with Iraq's intentions uncertain. Representative Les Aspin of Wisconsin called the Liberia landing "a marvelous opportunity for George Bush to send a message to [Iraqi president] Saddam Hussein."[13] The *New York Times* editorialized that the action "sends a useful signal about America's willingness to use appropriate military force in defense of clear national interests."[14] The Liberia landing might well have been intended as an object lesson to Iraq that we can protect our citizens.

After the Marines landed, they took up positions around the American embassy but stayed clear of the civil hostilities and, in particular, did not assist President Doe.[15] They remained for several months, however, evacuating from time to time small numbers of U.S. citizens. In January 1991, the Defense Department removed the flotilla, leaving only a handful of Marines at the embassy, by which time they had evacuated 224 United States citizens, a figure that included eighty official personnel.[16]

Therefore, most of the 1,200 Americans still in Liberia at the flotilla's arrival left the country while it sat offshore, with only about 224 using its services, nearly a third of whom were official personnel. During the Liberian hostilities, only one U.S. citizen was killed, and that occurred outside Monrovia in April 1990, before the deployment of the flotilla.[17]

Although few private citizens used the flotilla, it remained off Liberia's coast for over seven months. When the Defense Department finally removed the flotilla, spokesperson Pete Williams gave the operation a curious epitaph, calling it the "longest evacuation of its kind in U.S. naval history."[18] The fact that the flotilla stayed so long with no evidence of harm or threatened harm to U.S. citizens cast doubt on the administration's characterization of the effort as a rescue. If our citizens had been desperate to leave, they would have gotten to the flotilla as soon as it arrived.

Rescue, even in serious civil turmoil, can usually be done without putting military forces in a country. We saw that done in the Dominican Republic, prior to the Marine landing. Similarly, during a civil war in Somalia in 1991, we flew in helicopters from offshore ships to evacuate eighty American citizens, and Marines who flew in on the helicopters to protect the evacuation flew out with the evacuees.[19]

But for Liberia we sent six large ships with sophisticated assault equipment and left them there for seven months. Into Liberian territory we sent 225 Marines who stayed for five months. All that was hardly necessary to provide an exit route. Our aim, in short, was less to rescue our citizens than to be on hand in case the civil war threatened our facilities. By January 1991, no harm had come to the installations. With the outbreak of the Persian Gulf war we needed the ships elsewhere, so we left.

Notes

1. "Liberian Rebels Gain; U.S. Forces Poised," *Los Angeles Times,* June 2, 1990, p. A6, col. 1.

2. Patrick E. Tyler, "U.S. Sends Ships to Liberia, Orders Most Personnel Out," *Washington Post,* June 1, 1990, p. A1, col. 5.

3. J. Gus Liebenow, *Liberia: The Quest for Democracy* (1987), pp. 135–37.

4. Gordon C. Thomasson, "Liberian Disaster: Made in the U.S.A.," *New York Times,* July 14, 1990, p. A21, col. 2.

5. Liebenow, *Liberia,* p. 137; Thomasson, "Liberian Disaster."

6. Clifford Krauss, "U.S. Worried Over Safety of Americans in Liberia as Crisis Grows," *New York Times,* June 2, 1990, p. A3, col. 1.

7. Clifford Krauss, "Strategic Interests Tie U.S. to Liberia," *New York Times,* June 13, 1990, p. A3, col. 1.

8. John W. Mashek, "Marines Evacuate Americans from Liberia amid Rebel Threats," *Boston Globe,* August 6, 1990, p. A1, col. 1.

9. Eric Schmitt, "Liberian Rebel Seizes Foreigners, Including American," *New York Times,* August 7, 1990, p. A3, col. 3.

10. "Department of State Statement," August 5, 1990, *Foreign Policy Bulletin* 1, no. 2 (1990): 30; Michael A. Hiltzik, "Marines Fly Americans from War-Torn Liberia," *Los Angeles Times,* August 6, 1990, p. A1, col. 2.

11. Mashek, "Marines Evacuate Americans from Liberia amid Rebel Threats."

12. "Cuba's Castro Condemns U.S. Marine Landing in Liberia," *Reuter Library Report,* August 6, 1990.

13. Hiltzik, "Marines Fly Americans from War-Torn Liberia."

14. "The Uses of Force," *New York Times,* August 6, 1990, p. A12, col. 1.

15. "Department of State Statement," p. 30.

16. "Defense Department Briefing," Federal Information Systems Corp., January 10, 1991.

17. Krauss, "U.S. Worried Over Safety of Americans in Liberia as Crisis Grows."

18. "Defense Department Briefing."

19. "Americans Are Evacuated from Somalia," *Los Angeles Times,* January 6, 1991, p. A16, col. 1.

31

Why Not Tell the Truth?

The military actions we have described do not exhaust the field, but they are the major episodes in U.S. military intervention abroad since World War II. With covert operations, the pattern is fairly uniform. An operation is undertaken clandestinely, and once word leaks to the press, the administration typically puts itself in a "deniability" situation, giving the press an apparently plausible statement that disguises its true purpose. One example of this is the Eisenhower-Dulles cover story for the Indonesia operation, namely, that the U.S. personnel were "really" private mercenaries. The story is usually believed at least long enough for the operation to be completed, and even if not everyone buys the "official version" of what happened, any negative public reaction is likely to be mild. With open interventions, the administration states reasons, usually more than one; and even though the reasons given are not genuine, the media are not too probing, nor does the public object, at least if the operation is over soon.

The essential issue in both types of intervention is whether the public gets the truth, which it rarely does. The United States, of course, is hardly alone in inventing reasons to go to war. In September 1939, when Germany invaded Poland, Chancellor Adolf Hitler accused Poland of border violations. Hitler gave no details but said that the violations were serious enough to justify the German troop entry into Poland that started World War II.[1] No evidence of Polish border violations ever surfaced, however, and Hitler's story was generally disbelieved.[2]

In 1956, Egypt nationalized the Suez Canal, and a few months later Israel invaded Egypt. Britain and France, who had controlling interests in the canal, argued that the fighting between Israel and Egypt war might jeopardize free passage through it, so they sent troops into Egypt.[3] In fact, the invasion of Egypt had been planned jointly by Israel, Great Britain, and France, the three agreeing that Israel would attack first, with Britain and France joining in later, claiming they were trying to stop the fighting between Israel and Egypt.[4] This pretext was quickly laid bare, however; the Eisenhower administration, acting in cooperation with the United Nations, pressured Britain, France, and Israel to withdraw.[5]

Also in 1956, the Soviet Union sent troops into Hungary, after a reform-oriented administration assumed power there. The Soviet government claimed that it had been "invited" by the Hungarian administration, although it could show no evidence of such an invitation, and its intervention was widely condemned.[6]

In 1967, when Israel attacked Egypt, it falsely accused Egypt of having stormed three Israeli towns, which Israel named. In fact, Egypt had taken no military action against Israel; at the United Nations Israel's story was challenged by Arab and Soviet-bloc countries but accepted by most others. After a few weeks, Israel changed its story to say that Egypt had been about to launch an attack, and that it had to attack first to prevent it. That story, inconsistent with the first, also gained wide acceptance, but it, too, was false. Although belligerent rhetoric was exchanged between Egypt and Israel, Israel did not expect an armed attack when it invaded Egypt, as a number of Israeli officials later acknowledged.[7]

In 1968, the Soviet Union had less success with its explanation of why it sent troops into Czechoslovakia. Unnamed "party and Government leaders of the Czechoslovak Socialist Republic" had, like the Hungarians, invited it, the story went.[8] The Soviet Communist party newspaper *Pravda* published a letter explaining the reasons for the request, purportedly from a "group of members of the Central Committee of the Communist Party of Czechoslovakia, of the government and National Assembly who asked for the assistance of the governments and Communist parties of the fraternal countries."[9] Immediately, the Czech Communist party issued a denial that the Czech government had asked for intervention.[10] Finding little acceptance of its request story, the Soviet government shifted to a different justification, namely, that socialism in Czechoslovakia was being undermined by outside forces, and that the Soviets must protect Czechoslovakia from a possible invasion by Western countries.[11] This rationale, which came to be called the Brezhnev doctrine, was apparently not based on any serious facts about actual or threatened external actions against Czechoslovakia, at least none that ever came to public attention.

We see, then, that the United States is by no means unique in disguising its reasons for interventions abroad. However, the U.S. has intervened more often than anyone else, and has been more successful in getting its pretexts for war believed. This being the case, the question of truth in packaging American interventionism is one that needs to be raised.

When a country deploys its troops abroad, a favorable version of events is necessary for three reasons. First, the country must convince its own troops of the need to fight. A cause perceived to be just is essential, because soldiers will not willingly go to their possible death unless they think they are fighting for a valid reason.

Second, the country must also gain the support of its public. Even for countries that are not particularly democratic, it is hard to maintain a war effort for long if popular opinion is against it. The public, too, must believe that the cause is just.

Third, the country must neutralize opposition from other countries and the world community. If it is a strong nation, that will be easier; it may ignore the opinion of other countries, but in any event an intervention is more easily carried to completion if outside states approve, or at least do not strenuously object.

Often governments feel they cannot state their true reasons publicly, particularly if those reasons have little to do with the interests of the country being invaded. A government may be in trouble with its own public because of high taxes, for example, and therefore desire a foreign enemy to divert the public's attention; but that is hardly a motive it can afford to see printed in newspaper headlines.

If governments send troops to overthrow a foreign government for ideological reasons, they usually avoid mentioning this, because countries are expected to act on the neutral principles stated in the United Nations Charter. If they give an ideological justification, as the Johnson administration did in the Dominican Republic, or the Soviet Union in Czechoslovakia, they may do so only as a last resort. Remember that Johnson had first tried a rescue rationale for the Dominican Republic, while the Soviet Union first elaborated an invitation scenario for Czechoslovakia. Ronald Reagan, on the other hand, was less chary about stating openly he was intervening for ideological purposes, arguing that it was permissible to offer military support to "freedom fighters" in Nicaragua opposing a Communist government. But even with Nicaragua, Reagan argued at the same time on the basis of the universally accepted neutral principles, claiming that he was opposing Nicaraguan aid to El Salvador insurgents.

With ideological motivations, a government may genuinely believe that what it is doing is for the best, and therefore that it is justified in inventing a cover story. With the Dominican Republic and Czechoslovakia, both Johnson and Brezhnev probably believed they were doing the right thing and, therefore, harbored no guilty conscience for what they said publicly.

For the United States, the cold war provided a powerful rationale for misrepresenting the facts. A report prepared in 1954 for President Eisenhower stated that "we are facing an implacable enemy whose avowed objective is world domination by whatever means and at whatever cost. There are no rules in such a game. Hitherto acceptable norms of human conduct do not apply. If the U.S. is to survive, long-standing American concepts of 'fair play' must be reconsidered."[12]

Some U.S. officials have even taken the philosophical position that prevarication in a good cause is ethically permissible, that the end justifies the means. In 1962, Assistant Secretary of Defense Arthur Sylvester said that lying is sometimes necessary to serve the national security.[13] In crisis situations, Sylvester believed in "the inherent right of the Government to lie." He spoke of lying euphemistically as "generation" of news, with "news management" being "part of the arsenal of weaponry" of government.[14] Sylvester may have been stating a widely accepted position, sometimes expressed in the classic definition of a diplomat as one who is paid to lie for his country. However, when it deceives its citizens about a military intervention, the American government regards the public as the enemy, to be managed, to be led to acquiesce.

If that means giving the public a false version of events, then a cover story is invented.

In 1986, as we saw, the Reagan administration planted false press releases about terrorist activity by Libya; when this disinformation campaign was revealed, National Security Advisor John Poindexter justified it in terms similar to Sylvester's, arguing that "deception" was a "tool that the government can use in combatting a very significant national security problem."[15] The public did not appreciate the deceptions over Libya, however. A *New York Times*/CBS poll found that 73 percent of those surveyed thought that the government has no right to lie, even on foreign policy matters. The poll also revealed that the prevarication by successive administrations had left the public skeptical. Only 34 percent of respondents said that they thought the government told the truth "most of the time."[16]

Thus, ethical considerations aside, lying may not always be as efficacious as it appears to an administration that practices it. Even if false stories suffice to keep the public at bay while a military action proceeds to its conclusion, the people may in the long run turn against the administration. Although President Johnson scored an initial success with his version of the Gulf of Tonkin incident, once the public perceived that he was not being forthright in explaining our actions in Vietnam, confidence in his leadership eroded, which led to Johnson's decision not to run for reelection in 1968.[17] In the 1968 presidential campaign, the "credibility gap" became a central issue.[18] In 1971, the publication of the Pentagon Papers gave further evidence of falsehoods about Vietnam, and public cynicism widened, even a sense of alienation from government.[19] This prevarication also undermined public confidence in the press, which was held responsible for passing along the administration's untruths.[20]

By 1990—if one poll can accurately reflect prevailing opinion—the public all but expected our government to lie in order to provide a pretext for war. Shortly after Iraq invaded Kuwait, interviewees were asked about U.S. intentions toward Iraq. Would we invade it, and if so, how? Half the respondents said that if we invaded Iraq, the government would make up a false story to the effect that Iraq had inaugurated the hostilities against us.[21]

Still, this lack of confidence has not led the American public to rise up, since government lying about military actions overseas does not seem to be a priority issue to most people. The public has often been willing to overlook the lying, perhaps because it has perceived the prevarication being employed to fight what is perceived as a threat, namely, communism or terrorism. We accept "white lies" that people tell for social reasons, and perhaps the public put this kind of lying in that category.

Our prevarication regarding military actions has, as we have seen, typically drawn a harsher reaction abroad. Many of our interventions have been condemned by lopsided votes in the United Nations or the Organization of American States, while our reputation as a nation is of one that typically throws its weight around to serve its own interests. The low credibility we enjoy abroad, however, may impede our ability to act on a range of international issues, particularly on hostile actions by other countries. When we charged Iraq with aggression against Kuwait, a common reaction in the Arab world was that we were selective in our outrage over aggression. Not only had we ourselves committed this same offense on various occasions, but we had raised no international cry when Israel invaded Lebanon in 1982, or when Turkey invaded Cyprus in 1974.

One other downside of administration lying is that it feeds on itself. The false stories become part of a whole body of spurious information to be drawn upon in future intervention situations. When Adlai Stevenson addressed the United Nations during the Cuban missile crisis, he drew an analogy to the Korean war. Stevenson referred to "1950, when the Communists decided to test how far they could go by direct military action and unleashed the invasion of South Korea."[22] Stevenson used this statement to demonstrate an offensive Soviet intent in the installation of missiles in Cuba, even though what he said about Korea was inaccurate. He used one piece of false information to bolster a new false story.

When war broke out in Korea, President Truman stepped up our support for the French in Indochina, arguing that the Soviet Union was taking action to conquer the world. Truman's misinformed position that the Soviet Union was on a global quest in Korea drew us into Vietnam, leading to a military involvement there. One can only wonder how post-war history might have been different if the public had been aware in each instance of what the true facts were, and why the current president was committing troops to a foreign soil.

The problem of prevarication feeding still more prevarication re-surfaced when President Reagan, early in his first term in office, asked the CIA for an analysis of the dynamics of terrorist acts against U.S. citizens abroad. The CIA reported back that such acts were on the decline. Reagan, however, was not pleased with this result, since he planned to use anti-terrorism as a rationale for military intervention. Therefore, he asked the CIA to repeat the study using a broader defini-tion of terrorism, suggesting that the agency consult a recent book by Claire Sterling, which showed a higher incidence of terrorism.[23]

That directive was problematic for the CIA, however, because when its analysts checked the incidents Sterling recounted, they found that many of them were false, having been planted in the media by the CIA itself.[24] Nonetheless, the CIA gave Reagan what he wanted, by writing a new draft of the report showing that terrorist acts against American citizens were rising.[25]

Notes

1. Otto D. Tolischus, "German Army Attacks Poland," *New York Times,* Sep-tember 1, 1939, p. A1, col. 8.

2. Martin Gilbert, *The Second World War: A Complete History* (1989), p. 1.

3. GAOR, Emergency Session I, Plenary, p. 7, UN Doc. A/PV.561 (1956) (Britain); GAOR, Emergency Session I, Plenary, p. 30, UN Doc. A/PV. 562 (1956) (France).

4. Donald Neff, *Warriors at Suez* (1981), pp. 309–10.

5. Res. 997, GAOR, ES–I, *Resolutions,* p. 2, UN Doc. A/3354 (1956); Res. 1002, GAOR, ES–I, *Resolutions,* p 3.

6. Report of Special Committee on the Problem of Hungary, June 7, 1957, GAOR, 11th yr., Supplement No. 18, p. 137, UN Doc. A/3592 (1957).

7. John Quigley, *Palestine and Israel: A Challenge to Justice* (1990), pp. 161–65.

8. "Statement by T.A.S.S.," *Pravda,* August 21, 1968, p. 1, col. 1; Raymond H. Anderson, "Soviet Explains: Says Its Troops Moved at the Request of Czechoslovaks," *New York Times,* August 21, 1968, p. A1, col. 5.

9. "Letter of the Group of Members of the Central Committee of the Communist Party of Czechoslovakia, of the Government and National Assembly of the C.S.S.R.," *Pravda,* August 22, 1968, p. 1, col. 6.

10. Declaration of the Presidium of the Central Committee of the Czechoslovakian Communist Party, August 21, 1968, in *International Legal Materials* 7 (1968): 1285.

11. S. Kovalev, "Sovereignty and the International Obligations of Socialist Coun-tries," *Pravda,* September 26, 1968, p. 4, col. 1, translated as "Text of Pravda Article Justifying Invasion of Czechoslovakia," *New York Times,* September 27, 1968, p. A3, col. 1. (The *Times* gave the date of the *Pravda* article incorrectly as September 25.)

12. *Final Report: Foreign and Military Intelligence,* U.S. Senate, Select Committee to Study Governmental Operations with Respect to Intelligence Activities, Book I, 94th Cong., 2d sess., April 26, 1976, p. 9.

13. James Deakin, *Lyndon Johnson's Credibility Gap* (1968), p. 54.

14. "U.S.-'Generated' News Defended by Sylvester," *Washington Post,* December 7, 1962, p. A2, col. 8.

15. Norman Kempster, "Poindexter Defends Deception on Security Issues," *Los Angeles Times,* October 15, 1986, p. A16, col. 4.

16. "Poll Finds Anger on Official Lies," *New York Times,* October 31, 1986, p. A3, col. 2.

17. David Wise, *The Politics of Lying: Government Deception, Secrecy, and Power* (1973), p. 26.

18. John Mueller, *War, Presidents and Public Opinion* (1973), pp. 112–13.

19. Wise, *The Politics of Lying,* pp. 14–15; Deakin, *Lyndon Johnson's Credibility Gap,* p. 52.

20. Haynes Johnson, "The Irreconcilable Conflict between Press and Government: 'Whose Side Are You On?' " in Thomas M. Franck and Edward Weisband, eds., *Secrecy and Foreign Policy* (1974), pp. 165, 173–74.

21. Alexander Cockburn, "Beat the Devil," *Nation,* October 22, 1990, p. 442.

22. "U.N. Security Council Hears U.S. Charges of Soviet Military Buildup in Cuba," statement of Adlai E. Stevenson, DSB, vol. 47, p. 729 (1962).

23. Claire Sterling, *The Terror Network: The Secret War of International Terrorism* (1981).

24. Gregory F. Treverton, *Covert Action: The Limits of Intervention in the Postwar World* (1987), p. 165.

25. Francis A. Boyle, "The Law Is An Ass," *African Events,* May–June 1986, p. 53.

32

Why Intervene at All?

Fighting communism became a rationale for the effort to gain economic control. When in 1949 the Communists won the Chinese civil war and the Soviet Union developed atomic weaponry, the White House found it that much easier to convince Congress and the public of the danger of communism, even though China was caught up in its own problems, and we had developed atomic weapons first. The Truman administration spelled out its new policy of permanent militarization in 1950, in the National Security Council (NSC) directive 68, which we discussed earlier in the chapters on the Korean war. Truman used the three years of war in Korea to implement NSC 68, moving the annual military budget from $13 billion to over $50 billion. Although Eisenhower cut the military budget somewhat in the years that followed, the course of high-level militarization had been set.

While the menace of China and the Soviet Union was the rationale for our military spending, we undertook actual military activity in Latin America, Africa, and Asia. Senator Frank Church in 1976 accused the CIA, in its efforts abroad, of always targeting "small, weak countries."[1] Two former CIA operatives called that agency's overall objective one of keeping us "the dominant arbiter of social, economic, and political change in the awakening regions of Asia, Africa, and Latin America."[2]

In our efforts to influence the political direction in Third World nations, we tried less to keep them from orienting themselves to the Soviet Union and China, than to orient them to ourselves. Nationalism and neutralism we found as serious a threat to our control as leftism, because what we sought was access to the local economy. That is why we overthrew President Arbenz in Guatemala in 1954, and tried to do the same to President Sukarno in Indonesia in 1958. Both men were nationalists and neutralists with only the most marginal of connections to the Soviet Union or China. That is why the Eisenhower Doctrine, promulgated in 1957 as a policy of opposing communism in the Middle East, was applied in 1958 in the Lebanon-Iraq-Jordan situation, in order to counter Arab nationalism. In Korea and Indochina, our efforts were aimed less at keeping the Russians and Chinese out, than at drawing those areas into the market-economy sphere that included Japan, which we were also trying to orient in our direction.[3]

One can speculate over whether administration officials actually believed what they were saying about a Communist threat. With Korea, for example, many of them may have believed, despite contrary evidence, that we were being challenged by the Soviet Union or China. Soon, in any event, the red menace became accepted administration doctrine, and fighting communism the accepted rationale for government policy. After a time, policy makers probably stopped thinking too deeply about the reasons behind their actions, so entrenched became the cold war mentality.

Combatting communism gave philosophical rectitude to a fight to maintain access to markets and foreign labor and resources, because we appeared to be fighting not for material gain but for freedom of conscience, representative democracy, and the rule of law. The fact that we supported authoritarian governments that let us at their economies was not noticed. In the Nicaragua of Anastasio Somoza, the Cuba of Fulgencio Batista, and the Dominican Republic of Rafael Trujillo, there was little democracy, yet we supported these men for many years. Ironically, our backing of such men led to more of the leftism we were supposedly fighting.

When the cold war ended with the Soviet Union's dissolution, the United States declared victory. The military buildup of the 1980s by the Reagan administration, it was said, had forced the Communists to their knees. The way was now open for a world committed to democracy, a "new world order" with the United States as the only major power.

Whether it actually was the Reagan build-up that led to the changes in the Soviet Union is something historians can ponder. But whether it was or not, the idea that the United States emerged from the cold war the winner was not obvious. Certainly the Soviet Union was no longer a competitor. But did that leave the United States the unchallenged victor?

Some have viewed the end of the cold war less as a victory by one competitor over the other than as self-destruction by them both. Just as the cold war was ending, the United States went into an economic recession like none it had experienced in years. It was losing jobs, its standard of living was falling, and economists could hold out little hope to the next generation that they would be able to live as well as their parents. Young couples could no longer expect to be able to own a home. For older people, the lowering of interest rates meant that they might not be able to live on the savings they kept in fixed-rate accounts.

If the United States and the Soviet Union were two knights jousting, the field of battle after the cold war was a graveyard of rusting steel. The two giants had grappled mightily, and both had been vanquished. They had done each other in. Weapons without a sound economy were worth little.

The victors were those who did not participate, at least directly, in the cold war fray. The World War II "losers," forbidden to militarize in order to keep them in check, had quietly built themselves up without the need to maintain a military establishment. Japan and Germany emerged as more serious contenders than either the United States or the Soviet Union (or its successors) for economic superiority. With Japan's economic base in Asia, and Germany's in western Europe, these two powers seemed to be the harbingers of the future, with their goods enjoying predominance in foreign markets. American manufacturers, meanwhile, were losing market share abroad, and even within the United States itself. American companies, as well as American agricultural land, began to be bought up by foreign interests.

The quandary in which the United States found itself after the cold war raised the question of how we got into this situation. Was the cold war something thrust upon us, something that we had to fight to maintain our way of life? Are we now, like the characters in a Greek tragedy, the victims of circumstances over which we have no control?

Or did we bring this upon ourselves for no good reason? Were we really under threat of takeover by the Soviet Union all those years? Or else was the cold war an unnecessary episode that our leaders concocted, and which did us in?

The answer to these questions will occupy historians for decades to come. This book addresses only part of the puzzle, namely, military actions by the United States in the Third World during the period after World War II. With few exceptions, these military actions, which were numerous, had cold war trappings: we were either stopping Communists from taking over, or else booting them out. Even though the Soviet Union was rarely involved directly, it was still portrayed as the behind-the-scenes adversary. Had we not fought, our leaders said, we would have risked encroachment by the dark forces that wanted to eradicate our freedoms.

If this was the case, if we were under serious threat all those years, then the cold war was unavoidable. The unfortunate situation in which we now find ourselves was, therefore, thrust upon us by circumstance, and we are the unfortunate victims of a tragedy not of our own making.

The other possibility, of course, is that the threat was not real, and that our leaders, for whatever reason, told us there was a threat when there was none. The facts of the situations leading to the various military conflicts were typically not presented in detail to the public. The cold war, in a way, provided the facts. The president insisted that the Communists were at work, and that we needed to stop them. We knew what Karl Marx had said about the proletariat taking over the world, that capitalism must inevitably fall, and that communism must replace it. The leaders of the Soviet Union were committed to this way of thinking.

But did this mean that the inevitable dictatorship of the proletariat was happening in a particular conflict situation? If our military conflicts were not thrust upon us to protect the Third World from communism, we were entering wars that did not need to be fought; at least they did not need to be fought for the reasons the presidents gave.

From a financial standpoint the policy of exerting control abroad worked, because we prospered during the 1950s and 1960s as we expanded our control. Politically, however, the policy had serious costs. It is doubtful that even the interventions considered successful at the time were in our best interest in the long term. The Guatemala coup of 1954 left that impoverished country with seemingly endless violence and civil war. Its governments were so repressive that in the 1970s the

Carter administration virtually disowned Guatemala. In Grenada and Panama, the populations eventually turned against us when we did not come through with the financial aid they thought would flow in the wake of our military intervention.

The legacy we left in the Third World was not one calculated to make friends. The Soviet Union, with a message of anti-neocolonialism, was viewed with suspicion but generally got a better reception than we did. Asia came out of World War II anxious to be rid not only of the Japanese, but also of the former European rulers. Asians did not want us or anyone else to take the role of power broker. In the Middle East, the Arabs and Persians were not happy about our efforts to take over from France and Britain. Senator Frank Church said, regarding our secret interventions, that "we have lost, or grievously impaired, the good name and reputation of the United States." We are "regarded with distrust."[4]

Notes

1. Frank Church, "Covert Action: Swampland of American Foreign Policy," *Bulletin of the Atomic Scientists,* February 1976, p. 9.
2. Victor Marchetti and John Marks, *The CIA and the Cult of Intelligence* (1974), p. 4.
3. Thomas J. McCormick, *America's Half-Century: United States Foreign Policy in the Cold War* (1989), pp. 100, 111.
4. Church, "Covert Action," p. 11.

33

Won't the Media Protect Us?

This book began with Hugo Black's exhortation to the press to protect our youth from dying in foreign wars for reasons that were hidden from them. Our media have remarkable technical capability, bringing instantaneous reports from any point on the globe. Yet many reporters and editors have not been inclined to inquire behind official stories. In the Dominican Republic, the American press was split. Some believed, and reported as fact, what was said by U.S. Embassy officials, while others wrote skeptically.[1]

With Grenada, a few media outlets challenged official stories, but most reported the government versions as fact, which meant they gave a false picture. What came across in most media coverage about Grenada was that it was a rescue mission, that the Cubans there were "troops" that attacked us, that the airport under construction was a military airport (the press did not bother to interview the British general contractor), that Grenada threatened other Caribbean countries, and that the operation was carried on by us jointly with the Caribbean countries, at the request of the Grenadian head of state.[2]

In an intervention situation, of course, the administration is aware that accurate media reporting will jeopardize its ability to convince the public of the truth of its version of the facts, so typically presidents try to keep the media from broadcasting any contrary information.[3] On occasion, journalists have voluntarily kept quiet about such information out of considerations of patriotism. In 1954, just before the CIA overthrew the Guatemalan government, a *New York Times* reporter was writing about Guatemala in a way that CIA Director Allen Dulles found too sympathetic to President Arbenz. After Dulles complained, the *Times* editors decided to keep the reporter out of Guatemala during the overthrow. When the Bay of Pigs was in the planning stage, a *Miami Herald* reporter discovered that the CIA was training Cuban exiles at secret locations in Florida and wrote an article divulging this fact. The paper's editor made the reporter show his draft to CIA Director Dulles, who subsequently asked the *Herald* not to publish the story, and the story was duly killed.[4] A few days before the landing at the Bay of Pigs, a *New York Times* reporter found out and wrote a story to the effect that the invasion was about to jump off; however, a *Times* editor, after consulting with President Kennedy, altered the story to obscure the fact that such an invasion was imminent.[5]

The CIA, of course, has taken direct action to influence the news. As we saw in the Angola operation, it has its own agents functioning as journalists abroad, who can get a false story placed in a local newspaper; from there it may be picked up by an international wire service.[6] Beginning in the 1950s, the CIA established a worldwide media and publishing empire, owning wire services, newspapers, and magazines. It recruited American journalists abroad to provide information and convinced news organizations to hire its own agents to provide them "cover."[7] According to CIA insiders, the aim was to deceive the public both abroad and in the United States, to shape opinion in favor of CIA objectives. Agents declared that a major aim of the false information the CIA had planted on the Vietnam war was to influence public opinion in the United States, thus thwarting the public campaign against our involvement. These planted CIA stories were run by major newspapers.[8] The Senate committee on intelligence charged that such CIA efforts to abuse the media "for clandestine operations [are] a threat to the integrity of the press."[9]

In a more subtle vein, administration officials put a "spin" on events in order to influence public opinion. They may feed trusted reporters with background information that puts events in a particular light, and the reporter, considering the "inside" information a scoop, prints it, with attribution to a "senior official" or to "U.S. intelligence."[10] If the information is later demonstrated to be untrue, the officials may acknowledge it was erroneous, but that rarely detracts from the impact of the initial publication. During the 1965 conflict in the Dominican Republic, the U.S. embassy, seeking to discredit the pro-Bosch forces, told reporters in a not-for-attribution briefing that the main pro-Bosch military officer had met with Communists the previous day. After the officer denied the meeting, Ambassador Tapley Bennett acknowledged that the information was untrue.[11]

That the media generally follow a State or Defense Department lead is not surprising. For one thing, what these agencies say is considered news, simply because of what they are. For another, these agencies flood the media with reports and press statements through their public information services, which employ thousands and spend millions to get their messages across.[12] With secret operations, the media have no ready access to information and are largely dependent on tips from inside sources; but even an insider who talks may have a motive to distort reality.[13]

When reporters insist on writing objectionable material, administration officials may try to discredit them. President Nixon included journalists on an "enemies list" he had prepared. Reporters may shy away from questioning government-generated facts, once they learn that repeating the government's version is safer.[14] A reporter who relies on sources or information that contradicts the administration line may jeopardize government sources. From El Salvador, *New York Times* reporter Raymond Bonner wrote graphic accounts of the bombing of rural villages by the U.S.-backed Salvadoran government. His accounts were accurate, from what can be determined, but they threatened the Reagan administration's efforts to convince Congress that El Salvador was improving its human rights record. In reprisal, the U.S. embassy in San Salvador refused to let Bonner attend press briefings or interview embassy personnel. Once the *Times* saw that Bonner no longer had access to these sources, it pulled him from El Salvador.[15]

Even when reporters are skeptical, it may take them time to figure out that government spokespersons lied. For the government, what is important is that the public should back an intervention while it is in progress. If an intervention is of short duration, the government may not be concerned if reporters write after the fact that the operation was built on a house of cards. Typically, once a short-term operation is over, the media lose interest. So if, as with Panama, it later turns out that we killed many more people than originally reported, the media will not give that fact great prominence.

Increasingly as well, the television networks, news magazines, and leading newspapers are owned by large business corporations and financial institutions with far-flung financial interests.[16] These organizations have holdings abroad and thus are the very entities that may benefit from our military interventions. Although the media are not impartial bystanders on these issues, they may, nonetheless, criticize administration information about a particular intervention. But when they do so, they are working against their own interests.

The executive branch, of course, is funded by the very people the administration is trying to influence, the taxpayers.[17] And the taxpayers are supposed to control the executive branch, principally through the intermediary of Congress, which is the watchdog over the executive. So it falls to Congress to protect the public from administration deception.

Notes

1. Tad Szulc, *Dominican Diary* (1965), p. 202.
2. Michael Parenti, *Inventing Reality: The Politics of the Mass Media* (1986), pp. 182–83.
3. David Wise, *The Politics of Lying: Government Deception, Secrecy, and Power* (1973), p. 27.
4. John M. Crewdson, "The C.I.A.'s 3-Decade Effort to Mold the World's Views," *New York Times,* December 25, 1977, p. A1, col. 1.
5. Peter Wyden, *Bay of Pigs: The Untold Story* (1979), pp. 153–55; Arthur M. Schlesinger, Jr., *A Thousand Days* (1965), p. 261; William Colby, *Honorable Men: My Life in the CIA* (1978), pp. 181–82.
6. *Final Report: Foreign and Military Intelligence,* U.S. Senate, Select Committee to Study Governmental Operations with Respect to Intelligence Activities, Book I, 94th Cong., 2d sess., April 26, 1976, pp. 198–200, 454; Stuart H. Loory, "The CIA's Use of the Press: A 'Mighty Wurlitzer,' " *Columbia Journalism Review* (September–October 1974): 9.
7. Colby, *Honorable Men,* p. 182.
8. Parenti, *Inventing Reality,* p. 233; Crewdson, "The C.I.A.'s 3-Decade Effort to Mold the World's Views"; John M. Crewdson, "Worldwide Propaganda Network Built by the C.I.A.," *New York Times,* December 26, 1977, p. A1, col. 1; John M. Crewdson, "C.I.A. Established Many Links to Journalists in U.S. and Abroad," *New York Times,* December 27, 1977, p. A1, col. 5.
9. *Final Report: Foreign and Military Intelligence,* p. 455.
10. Theodore Draper, *The Dominican Revolt: A Case Study in American Policy* (1968), p. 89.

11. Ibid., pp. 89–90.

12. Edward S. Herman and Noam Chomsky, *Manufacturing Consent: The Political Economy of the Mass Media* (1988), pp. 19, 23.

13. Loch K. Johnson, *America's Secret Power: The CIA in a Democratic Society* (1989), p. 246.

14. Haynes Johnson, "The Irreconcilable Conflict between Press and Government: 'Whose Side Are You On?' " in Thomas M. Franck and Edward Weisband, eds., *Secrecy and Foreign Policy* (1974), pp. 165, 176–77.

15. Parenti, *Inventing Reality*, p. 57.

16. Benjamin Compaine, "Who Owns the Media Companies?" in Benjamin Compaine, ed., *Who Owns the Media? Concentration of Ownership in the Mass Communication Industry* (1982), pp. 451–65.

17. Herman and Chomsky, *Manufacturing Consent*, p. 22.

34

Won't Congress Protect Us?

The Constitution gives Congress vast authority over foreign affairs, most significantly the power of the purse. The president gets not a farthing unless Congress allocates it. So an administration cannot wage a war of any duration unless it gets funding from Congress. Besides, the Constitution states that it is the role of Congress to make the important decisions when it comes to war and peace. The framers of the Constitution did not envisage an imperial president who could commit the country to war under his own authority, so they gave Congress the all-important right to declare war as an exclusive power of Congress, meaning that the president may not make war without a congressional declaration.

The framers were also concerned about military actions short of full-scale war, like many of those recounted in this book. Although a military action may be minor in scope, or of short duration, it has the potential for getting us into a larger conflict. Since the framers were also concerned that a president might evade Congress's prerogatives by starting a minor military action that would lead to war, they wrote into the Constitution a clause giving Congress the power to issue so-called letters of marque and reprisal.[1] These were documents issued by eighteenth-century sovereigns to their military officers or to private persons, to authorize them to carry out a military attack on the sovereign's behalf. They were typically issued when the monarch had been affronted and wanted to take reprisal. Thomas Jefferson said that the Constitution gave this power to Congress, because minor attacks could lead to war. President John Adams approached Congress more than once to ask it to issue letters of marque and reprisal.

While in the eighteenth century, Congress was thinking of open interventions when it adopted the clause on letters of marque and reprisal, the concept probably covers covert military operations as well, because any military action abroad, open or secret, has the potential to entangle the country in war. Congress, however, has not invoked this power to object either to open or to covert operations. One constitutional scholar has argued that by failing to insist on this power, and by letting presidents carry out military operations on their own authority, Congress "has abdicated its constitutional responsibilities."[2]

Although the Constitution seems to give Congress the upper hand when it comes to military action abroad, the president has practical advantages that undermine Congress's power. In the matter of covert operations, Congress cannot exercise its power of the purse if it does not learn of the action. Moreover, the CIA may camouflage funding for an action behind general budget categories, so that Congress, having failed to insist on budget accountability, does not know what it is funding.[3]

Also, the president controls access to information, because he commands our intelligence-gathering agencies and obtains reports from embassies around the world. If Congress and the administration argue over agricultural subsidies, a member of Congress can get information from the folks back home; but if the issue is whether to invade Ruritania, he or she may be totally dependent on the administration for information. The president, using this knowledge, can present foreign policy options to Congress in a light favorable to his own plans. The Senate committee on intelligence has admitted Congress is "almost totally dependent on the executive branch for information on covert operations."[4]

One other advantage for the president is Congress's size. With one hundred senators and 535 members in the House of Representatives, and with half of Congress, more or less, being of the president's party, it is difficult to muster a majority to stop a president. With most interventions, as we have seen, Congress has "rallied around the flag." Many of its members are afraid to criticize a president who commits troops into combat, for fear of sounding unpatriotic or unsupportive of our soldiers.

In the matter of covert operations, Congress's abdication of authority means that important policy decisions are made secretly. One congressional member complained that paramilitary operations ordered by a president "commit us to a specific foreign policy that has never been openly defended and supported, and whose outcome cannot be guided by our own democratic institutions."[5] After the secret bombing of Cambodia in 1969–70, Senator Harold Hughes said that if the Defense Department were to continue withholding information about military operations, "there will never be a moment in the history of this country in the future when the people will have a hand in the declaration of war or the conduct of war over international borders."[6]

The Senate committee on intelligence expressed the same concern: "The secrecy covert actions require means that the public cannot determine whether such actions are consistent with established foreign policy goals. This secrecy also has allowed covert actions to take place which are inconsistent with our basic traditions and values."[7] The committee might have made the same comment about overt military operations that the government justifies with false reasons, because there, too, the public and Congress are deprived of a say.

Congress, on the whole, has been half-hearted in extracting information from the executive branch on military operations. The CIA, when it began covert operations in the late 1940s, did not volunteer information on them to Congress, which in turn has not put demands for disclosure on the CIA.[8] CIA Director William Colby, during his time in office, found that Congress was "in the thrall of the Agency's mystique," and thus prepared to let it act on the quiet.[9]

In the 1970s, after a number of covert operations were publicly revealed to Congress's embarrassment, it passed the Hughes-Ryan Amendment, which required the administration to report to it on covert operations.[10] The amendment did not, however, require prior notification of covert operations, so Congress was making no effort to exert a veto power over them. Two years after the amendment went into effect, the Senate committee on intelligence admitted that the amendment was only marginally effective.[11]

Since the mid-1970s, however, each house of Congress has had a permanent committee to oversee covert operations. The Hughes-Ryan language was tightened in 1980, to require prior notification of these committees of a covert operation; however, it leaves a loophole allowing the president to limit notification to Senate and House leaders rather than to the committees.[12] Congress tried to close that loophole in 1990, but President Bush vetoed the bill.[13]

At times, the Senate and House committees have pursued information diligently, but they have rarely been a match for the more experienced State Department and CIA personnel. Officials have tried to avoid appearing when called by congressional committees.[14] One CIA official even claimed that the agency doctored its files to keep sensitive material from Congress,[15] and that CIA Director William Colby routinely lied to Congress during briefings.[16]

In one congressional debate over our involvement in Vietnam, members of both the House and Senate quoted from a Vietnamese periodical, citing passages that made our involvement seem appropriate. What they did not know was that the periodical was not authentic at all but produced by the CIA.[17] Whether the blame should rest more on Congress, or more on the administration, oversight by Congress has hardly been effective.[18]

In giving the executive money for military operations, Congress, to be sure, has shared the administration's cold war assumptions. During the Korean war, convinced by the president that we were being threatened by world communism, Congress let military spending skyrocket. Korea cost so much that Congress stopped funding the Marshall Plan for Europe. With the beginning of our involvement in Indochina under John Kennedy, military spending shot up higher still. In the 1980s, at the urging of Ronald Reagan, Congress increased the military's budget still more.

The monetary aspect of the interventions raises a serious question of public policy. Taxpayers give Congress the money to run the country, and Congress in turn gives it to the president. With military interventions undertaken secretly or for reasons other than those stated, the administration spends the public's money fraudulently. It tells them that it is spending the money in a certain way and for certain reasons, when in reality it is doing something else entirely.

Administration prevarication about military intervention incurs a major breakdown in the democratic process. The public elects the representatives, deciding whom to elect, in part, on how they vote on budget matters. When the president conceals from Congress what he is spending money on and why, the public is thereby deprived of its role in the budget process.

In some instances the public might, if it knew the true facts, agree with what is being done, but in others it might not. In either case, it is being forced to pay for something it does not know about. While the blame does not rest entirely on Congress or the administration, Congress has not protected the public from presidents who commit us to combat under false pretenses.

Notes

1. Constitution of the United States, art. 1, sec. 8, para. 11.

2. Jules Lobel, "Covert War and Congressional Authority: Hidden War and Forgotten Power," *University of Pennsylvania Law Review* 134 (1986): 1041.

3. *Final Report: Foreign and Military Intelligence,* U.S. Senate, Select Committee to Study Governmental Operations with Respect to Intelligence Activities, Book I, 94th Cong., 2d sess., April 26, 1976, p. 384.

4. *Final Report: Foreign and Military Intelligence,* p. 447.

5. *Congressional Record,* vol. 128, p. H9158, December 8, 1982 (statement of Rep. David Bonior).

6. *Bombing in Cambodia,* Hearings before the Committee on Armed Services, U.S. Senate, 93rd Cong., 1st sess. (1973), p. 157.

7. *Final Report: Foreign and Military Intelligence,* p. 445.

8. Ibid., p. 150; Victor Marchetti and John Marks, *The CIA and the Cult of Intelligence* (1974), pp. 345–47.

9. William Colby, *Honorable Men: My Life in the CIA* (1978), p. 182.

10. U.S. Congress, *Statutes at Large,* vol. 88, p. 1804 (1974); U.S. Code, Title 22, §2422.

11. *Final Report: Foreign and Military Intelligence,* p. 151.

12. U.S. Congress, *Statutes at Large,* vol. 94, p. 1981 (1980); U.S. Code, Title 50, §413.

13. Michael Wines, "Bush, to Guard Secrecy, Kills Espionage Agencies' Budget," *New York Times,* December 1, 1990, p. A10, col. 5.

14. Aaron Latham, "Introduction to the Pike Papers," *Village Voice,* February 16, 1976, p. 70.

15. John Stockwell, *In Search of Enemies: A CIA Story* (1978), p. 273.

16. "Should the U.S. Fight Secret Wars?" *Harper's* magazine, September 1984, p. 43.

17. *Final Report: Foreign and Military Intelligence,* p. 454.

18. Loch K. Johnson, *America's Secret Power: The CIA in a Democratic Society* (1989), pp. 108, 247.

35

Will It Stop?

A recurring theme of the interventions we have reviewed is the suppression of communism. But the political reform that swept eastern Europe in 1989–90 left the cold war on the ash heap of history. Even so, our military interventions did not end. In 1989, we intervened to support a government in the Philippines and to overthrow one in Panama. In 1990, we sent a massive force to the Persian Gulf.

The continuation of military interventions is not, however, surprising, because the aim all along, as we have seen, has been less to fight communism than to maintain our own control. The end of the cold war did, however, require a new rationalization for intervention, and Washington set about the task. The Reagan administration appointed what it called the Commission on Integrated Long-Term Strategy, which in 1988 issued a report. The gist of it was a call to devote more attention and resources to minor wars in Asia, Africa, and Latin America. "Nearly all the armed conflicts of the past forty years," the report said, "have occurred in what is vaguely referred to as the Third World: the diverse countries of Asia, the Middle East, Africa, Latin America, and the Eastern Caribbean." Third World conflicts "have had and will have an adverse cumulative effect on U.S. access to critical regions, on American credibility among allies and friends, and on American self-confidence." The report warned that, "if this cumulative effect cannot be checked or reversed in the future, it will gradually undermine America's ability to defend its interests in the most vital regions, such as the Persian Gulf, the Mediterranean and the Western Pacific. In the coming decades the United States will need to be better prepared to deal with conflicts in the Third World."

The wars the report envisioned represented what it called "low-intensity conflict," insurgencies that operated at a modest level over an extended period. In most instances, we would not be involved with our troops but would provide "security assistance" to a government. But we also might support an insurgency, the report said, if it is anti-Communist. This kind of support, however, may embarrass neighboring countries that provide base areas for "freedom fighters," so our support should be done as "covert action." In that way, "the U.S. Government can maintain official silence." This can be done either by the military or by the CIA. In any event, the report concluded, security assistance should be increased substantially.[1] Despite the reference to "freedom fighters," the report implicitly acknowledged that U.S. control, rather than fighting communism, was our real objective.

Senator John McCain of Arizona, arguing for the need for more frequent intervention, was talking about those in Korea, Vietnam, and Grenada when he said, "If anything, the global conditions that led us to make these uses of force are likely to be even more important in the future." " 'Glasnost,' " McCain argued, referring to the Soviet political reforms, "does not change the fact that there has been an average of more than 25 civil and international conflicts in the developing world every year since the end of World War II." We are "critically dependent," he said, "on imports of virtually all our critical minerals and most of our other raw materials. . . . The U.S. may not be the 'world's policeman,' but its power projection forces will remain the free world's insurance policy."[2]

President Bush sounded a similar theme: "Notwithstanding the alteration in the Soviet threat, the world remains a dangerous place with serious threats to important U.S. interests wholly unrelated to the earlier patterns of the U.S.-Soviet relationship."[3] General A. M. Gray, commandant of the Marine Corps, wrote: "If we are to have stability in these regions, maintain access to their resources, protect our citizens abroad, defend our vital installations, and deter conflict, we must maintain within our active force structure a credible military power projection capability with the flexibility to respond to conflict across the spectrum of violence throughout the globe."[4] General Carl Vuono, army chief of staff, argued that "because the United States is a global power with vital interests that must be protected throughout an increasingly turbulent world, we must look beyond the European continent and consider other threats to our national security."[5]

These officials were not suggesting anything new in terms of our practice, since, as they acknowledged, our military interventions have been in the Third World, not in Europe. But with the cold war over, the president was hard pressed to convince Congress of the need to keep military spending at the high levels it reached in the 1980s, so he acknowledged what had been true all along, namely, that since the end of the Second World War, our military has taken the Third World as a main focus.[6]

Top military brass explained what kinds of conflicts might break out. According to General Vuono,

> Regional rivalries supported by powerful armies have resulted in brutal and devastating conflicts in the Third World. . . . The proliferation of advanced military capabilities has given an increasing number of countries in the developing world the ability to wage sustained, mechanized land warfare. The United States cannot ignore the expanding military power of these countries, and the Army must retain the capability to defeat potential threats wherever they occur. This could mean confronting a well-equipped army in the Third World.[7]

Iraq's invasion of Kuwait in 1990 presented an opportunity to put this new theory into practice. Vital resources, the administration said, were threatened by a Third World war. "What is at stake economically," explained Secretary of State James Baker, "is the dependence of the world on access to the energy resources of the Persian Gulf."[8]

President Bush presented the issue in apocalyptic terms, declaring that our goal in the Persian Gulf had to be "maintaining access to energy resources that are key—not just to the functioning of this country but to the entire world. Our jobs, our way of life, our own freedom, and the freedom of friendly countries around the world would all suffer if control of the world's great oil reserves fell into the hands of Saddam Hussein."[9]

Baker, too, painted the stakes as high: "It is not just a narrow question of the flow of oil from Kuwait and Iraq. It is about a dictator who, acting alone and unchallenged, could strangle the global economic order, determining by fiat whether we all enter a recession or even the darkness of a depression."[10] The public had doubts, however. Were our forces in Saudi Arabia because we had foolishly made ourselves dependent on Middle East oil? Or were they there so that gasoline at the pump would cost $1.05 instead of $1.50?

Bush argued that if Iraq were to control Saudi Arabia's oil, and perhaps that of the Gulf emirates, it would have 60 percent of the world's oil reserves. That argument was unrelated to the cold war and rested on protecting our financial and commercial situation. So the end of the cold war is unlikely to bring an end to interventionism, as there is no prospect that we will lose our interest in these factors. Indeed, with Germany and Japan rising as economic powers, we may have greater reason to intervene militarily to keep Third World countries in our orbit.

Even with the Russian bear in apparently long-term hibernation, our policy makers have continued to make the mistake that kept the cold war alive, construing events abroad in light of our own strategic interests. During the cold war the mistake was that they saw communism as the key factor when it was not. The post-cold war warriors have seen access to resources and free flow of commerce as overriding issues, ignoring the local consequences of military intervention.

In the Middle East, particularly, our policy makers ignored the possible impact of Western military action, and ignored what should have been an object lesson. In Iran in 1953, the CIA engineered the overthrow of an elected leader and put in his place a man who became unpopular for aligning Iran with the West, and who ultimately was overthrown. This man was replaced, however, by elements intensely hostile to the West; an immediate result of this was the taking of hostages at the U.S. embassy in Iran. The moral we should have drawn, but didn't, is that meddling is hazardous.

The troop deployment in the Persian Gulf in 1990, however, held the prospect of inspiring just such a reaction. Middle East analysts warned that "anti-American Islamic extremism in the region was likely to be fueled by the crisis."[11] Islamic fundamentalism had grown in the Arab world, taking Iran as the model, and largely for the same reason— as a reaction to Western penetration. Our support for Israel and our opposition to Palestinian nationalism discredited the Arab nationalist politicians whom we called "moderate," which created the political space for Islamic fundamentalism.

President Saddam Hussein, when he invaded Kuwait, capitalized on this sense of grievance against Israel and the United States by saying that negotiations over Iraq's withdrawal from Kuwait could be held only in the context of negotiations that would include the question of Israel's withdrawal from the occupied Arab territories. Hussein's position was approved by many Arabs, who viewed him as the first Arab leader in a generation to stand up to the humiliation represented by the continuing U.S. support for Israel. Thus, although cold war considerations were absent, the United States still failed to consider local issues. From the beginning of the twentieth century, we have set our military sights on weaker countries for their markets, cheap labor, and minerals. There was no reason to believe that the end of the cold war would end that orientation.

Far from eliminating interventions, the post-cold war period removed one factor that stood in their way. Formerly, the Soviet Union called us to account whenever we gave a false reason for an intervention. It denounced nearly all our interventions and typically disputed our portrayal of the facts. Sometimes, as in Guatemala, it did not have the evidence to back up its charges, but it would, either in press statements or at the United Nations, challenge what the president said. Even though our own press generally dismissed what it called Soviet propaganda, at least this denunciation was part of the public record. The collapse of the Soviet Union, however, removed this nearly constant voice of opposition to U.S. intervention.

The end of the cold war brought change at the United Nations that seemed to portend a new climate that might affect U.S. intervention. The United States' increasing control of the United Nations led it to work through that body more frequently, in lieu of acting unilaterally. The Bush administration threatened military intervention against Libya in 1992, demanding that Libya turn over two Libyan officials on suspicion of blowing up a Pan American plane over Scotland.

Whereas before it might, in a comparable situation, have bombed Libya (as happened in 1986), this time the United States got the Security Council to pass a resolution demanding the extradition of the officials within two weeks, and threatening to impose economic sanctions if Libya refused. The administration's victory was not complete, however, because five Third World governments voted against the resolution in the Security Council.

Those five governments thought that a government in Libya's position must either try the officers itself or turn them over to a government that would. In the Pan American case, Libyan authorities investigated the two officials but did not prosecute; U.S. officials, on the other hand, claimed they had evidence implicating the pair, although they refused to give it to Libya.

In any event, the situation, which might have given rise to still more American intervention, was handled through the United Nations. The new and broadened UN role, with the United States in a position to get its way in the Security Council, may give the United States new alternatives. It may, in some situations, be able to gain by UN action what it had previously obtained by military intervention.

Notes

1. *Discriminate Deterrence: Report of the Commission on Integrated Long-Term Strategy* (Fred C. Iklé and Albert Wohlstetter, co-chairmen) (prepared for Secretary of Defense and Assistant to the President for National Security Affairs), January 1988, pp. 13–17; "More Vietnams; The Federal Commission on Integrated Long-Term Strategy's Report Is Likely to Cause an Increase in U.S. Conventional Forces," *Nation,* January 23, 1988, p. 75.

2. John McCain, "The Need for Strategy in the New Postwar Era," *Armed Forces Journal,* January 1990, p. 46.

3. Maureen Dowd, "Backing Pentagon, Bush Says Military Can Be Cut 25% in 5 Years," *New York Times,* August 3, 1990, p. A13, col. 3.

4. Gen. A. M. Gray, "Defense Policy for the 1990s," *Marine Corps Gazette,* May 1990, p. 18.

5. Michael Klare, "Policing the Gulf—and the World," *Nation,* October 15, 1990, p. 418.

6. Michael Klare, "The U.S. Military Faces South," *Nation,* June 18, 1990, p. 841.

7. Klare, "Policing the Gulf," p. 418.

8. James A. Baker, "America's Stake in the Persian Gulf Crisis," Statement to House Foreign Affairs Committee, September 4, 1990, U.S. Dept. of State, Current Policy No. 1297 (1990).

9. George Bush, "Against Aggression in the Persian Gulf," August 15, 1990, U.S. Dept. of State, *Current Policy,* No. 1293 (1990).

10. Baker, "America's Stake in the Persian Gulf Crisis."

11. Judith Miller, "Gulf Impact: Experts See U.S. Gain, but a Long-Range Threat to Interests," *New York Times,* October 11, 1990, p. A8, col. 1.

36

How about Swearing Off?

Beyond violating the rights of Congress and the people, many of our military interventions have abused the rights of the people against whom we fought. Governments are not free to roam the planet with tanks, using them wherever their interests are threatened. Each nation has a right to determine for itself what kind of government it will have, and who should rule it. When a civil war rages in a country, others are supposed to keep hands off. When a government is ruling peacefully, outsiders are not permitted to come in and stir up an insurgency or to invade in order to remove a leader they don't like.

All this has been decided by the countries of the world, working through the United Nations, which was set up after World War II to make sure that one government doesn't use force against another. The world body's founding treaty, the Charter, stipulates that each member nation agree not to commit aggression. A country may use force only if it is attacked by another and has to defend itself, or if another country is attacked and asks for help in its defense.

Along with its World War II allies, the United States put forward the idea for a United Nations; the Charter was negotiated and signed at a meeting we hosted in San Francisco in 1945. The Charter binds all the countries that have joined the United Nations, including the United

States. Under our own Constitution, when we conclude a treaty, it becomes part of the law of the United States. The Constitution says that a treaty, like a bill enacted by Congress, is the "law of the land." So it must be followed by our own government, by Congress, and by the president.

So what of our various military interventions in other countries? If we were to review them all in light of the UN Charter, we would find little room for arguments in their support. That is why, in this study of American interventionism, we often saw the UN objecting. Since the United States has not been invaded since World War II, we can't say we have had to use force to defend ourselves.

Although on occasion, when we used military force, we argued that we were helping another country to defend itself, generally that was not the case. We claimed South Vietnam had asked us to defend it against North Vietnam; however, as we have seen, that was a civil war, not a war between two countries. El Salvador had supposedly asked us to defend it against Nicaragua, but Nicaragua had not attacked El Salvador; therefore, we were not entitled to defend El Salvador. In both cases, we had our own reasons for attacking.

Our covert paramilitary operations were typically aimed at getting rid of a government we didn't like or keeping in power a government we did. The UN Charter, however, prohibits this kind of operation, because each country is sovereign in its own territory and has the right to determine its own form of government.

Much of the activity recounted in this book was unlawful under the United Nations Charter, and therefore unlawful under the United States Constitution. That means, among other things, that these operations were illegal for the presidents who ran them. The Constitution requires that a president who violates the law be impeached. The founding fathers thought it was only natural that a president who violated the Constitution should be thrown out of office. Congress, however, has rarely had the political stomach to begin impeachment proceedings.

Although there is little one can do after the fact to reverse the effects of a military intervention, we would do well not to let our past interventions languish in a kind of perpetual purgatory. It might serve a salutary purpose, in terms of our relations with the rest of the world, if we would state on the record that we won't commit this kind of action again. We did it to fight communism, we could say, and now there is no threat from communism. So no more interventions, no more cover stories.

Instead of formulating new reasons to intervene, as the Reagan and Bush administrations quickly began to do, we should take the end of the cold war as a time for a change in policy. We might even approach the countries we wronged and tell them we're sorry. An apology isn't much, but it is something. In the spirit of the post-cold war era, other governments have apologized for their misdeeds. Japan apologized to both North Korea and South Korea for its occupation of those countries from 1910 to 1945, which involved considerable repression of the Koreans, and which left a deep wound even after Japan's withdrawal.[1]

The Soviet Union apologized for the forced resettlement of ethnic groups for collaborating with Germany during World War II.[2] The Soviet government also admitted that the secret protocols to the Soviet-German nonaggression pact of 1939, which set up spheres of Soviet and German influence in eastern Europe, "were from a legal viewpoint in contradiction to the sovereignty and independence of a number of third countries."[3] Also, "the decision to introduce Soviet troops into Afghanistan" in 1979 "deserves both moral and political condemnation."[4] The Soviets even condemned their 1968 military intervention in Czechoslovakia. "The bringing of armies of five socialist countries into Czechoslovak territory in 1968" was called "unfounded" and "erroneous."[5]

These were unusual admissions, because while governments are quick to act, they are not so quick to acknowledge their mistakes. Such self-criticism would cost us little, although it would be of considerable importance to the countries affected. A confession by the United States might engender good will in countries like Guatemala, Laos, or Grenada. A public apology would be a recognition of the right of those peoples to order their own affairs.

An apology would also be important domestically. The mothers and fathers whose sons died for reasons that the government never divulged might appreciate hearing the truth from the government, as might the children who grew up without fathers and the taxpayers who financed it all.

Perhaps for the Soviet government, which was making changes across the board, it was easier to admit past errors. The government of Mikhail Gorbachev was distancing itself politically from those regimes whose errors it criticized. For us, public confessions would be more difficult, because we have not repudiated the policies that led to the interventions. That fact, of course, would make apologies all the more significant.

Without a blanket repudiation of its predecessors, the current administration could single out improper actions and set the historical record straight. And our government is capable of doing so when the right pressures are put on it. In 1990, the Bush administration apologized to the Japanese-Americans whom Roosevelt had incarcerated during World War II, and even paid token monetary compensation.

Since administrations come and go, perhaps the proper body to take such measures on behalf of the United States is Congress. Indeed, in the Soviet Union it was the parliament that issued most of the confessions. Perhaps both the president and Congress should take a hand in the matter. Or the House and Senate could adopt a joint resolution that the policy of the United States is not to interfere militarily in the affairs of other states, and that the executive branch is always to explain the truth to the public when it sends troops into combat.

Congress, however, like the executive branch, has undergone no basic change of heart about our role in the world and the use of our military forces overseas. That means that if a change is to occur, it will probably have to start with the rest of us.

Notes

1. "South Korean Leader Accepts Japanese Emperor's Apology," *New York Times,* May 27, 1990, p. A17, col. 6; Steven R. Weisman, "Japan and North Korea Set Talks on Ties," *New York Times,* September 29, 1990, p. A3, col. 4.

2. Declaration of the Supreme Soviet of the U.S.S.R. On Recognizing as Illegal and Criminal the Repressive Acts against Peoples Subjected to Forced Resettlement and on Ensuring Their Rights, *Vedomosti s'ezda narodnykh deputatov SSSR i verkhovnogo soveta SSSR* [*Gazette of the Congress of People's Deputies of the U.S.S.R. and the Supreme Soviet of the U.S.S.R.*], No. 23, item 449 (1989).

3. Decree of the Congress of People's Deputies of the U.S.S.R. Regarding a Political and Legal Evaluation of the Soviet-German Nonaggression Treaty of 1939, *Vedomosti s'ezda narodnykh deputatov SSSR i verkhovnogo soveta SSSR* [*Gazette of the Congress of People's Deputies of the U.S.S.R. and the Supreme Soviet of the U.S.S.R.*], No. 29, item 579 (1989).

4. Decree of the Congress of People's Deputies of the U.S.S.R. On a Political Evaluation of the Decision to Introduce Soviet Troops into Afghanistan in December 1979, *Vedomosti s'ezda narodnykh deputatov SSSR i verkhovnogo soveta SSSR* [*Gazette of the Congress of People's Deputies of the U.S.S.R. and the Supreme Soviet of the U.S.S.R.*], No. 29, item 582 (1989).

5. "Prague 1968: Views Now in East Bloc," *New York Times,* December 5, 1989, p. A15, col. 1.

37

What Can We Do about It?

In 1950, President Truman asked the secretaries of state and defense to write an analysis of "our objectives in peace and war." Their report, which became the famous National Security Council directive 68, stated that "it is important that the United States employ military force only if the necessity for its use is clear and compelling and commends itself to the overwhelming majority of our people."[1]

Governments know that they must have public support to fight a war, which gives them an incentive to deceive the public if they think that is the only way of convincing them. So long as the American people feared an attack from Moscow, the administration had a ready justification for intervention, because confronting communism was necessary to keep it from confronting us. Now that that justification no longer applies, the public must be demanding of an administration that gives a rationalization for an intervention.

As consumers of food products, the American people have successfuly demanded that manufacturers give an accurate list of ingredients on package labels. But as consumers of foreign policy decisions, we have yet to demand the same truth-in-labeling. If the public feels the American government should end its interventionism, or that intervention should be done only if the people are given the real reasons, there are directions in which we can urge Congress and the administration. The public has the power to stop a president from committing us to war.

One important avenue for limiting our government's ability to prevaricate is to multilateralize the use of force. This brings other governments into the decision-making process and keeps one government from going to war for reasons that it conceals.

At first blush, the multilateralization of force may seem remote from the citizenry. But it is treaties that require that force be used only on a multilateral basis, principally the charters of the United Nations and the Organization of American States. Under the Constitution, a treaty is part of our law. Therefore, just as the public can demand that the administration adhere to civil rights laws or tax laws, so can it demand that it adhere to our treaties.

In 1945, when we signed the UN Charter, we made a commitment to limit ourselves to multilateral use of force, on the theory that the peace can best be kept by nations working together. The Security Council would organize military action to stop aggression. So long as the cold war continued, however, the Security Council was hamstrung by its veto rule. If the major powers didn't agree, no action could be taken.

Since the end of the cold war, however, the Security Council, for the first time, has been in a position to function as planned in the UN Charter. When it is the Security Council, rather than the Central Intelligence Agency or Joint Chiefs of Staff, that makes a decision, the chances are less that a false story will be invented, because the decision is taken in the light of day, with various governments remaining free to object.

In Korea, military action was taken under UN auspices on questionable factual premises, because the council let the Truman administration be, in effect, the multilateral force. In the Persian Gulf in 1990, the Security Council again was willing to delegate its powers in a way that gave considerable rein to the United States. Still, when a country has to give an accounting before other countries, its latitude is restricted.

In addition to the United Nations, an international organization that has figured in many of the U.S. military interventions is the Organization of American States (OAS). If a pollster were to pick people at random in the United States and ask them to describe the OAS, probably most would draw a blank. Yet the OAS, like the United Nations, has the potential of protecting us from our own government. As an association of the countries of the Western hemisphere, the OAS took action on Guatemala in 1954, Cuba in 1961 and 1962, the Dominican Republic in 1965, Grenada in 1983, and Panama in 1989.

The OAS, unfortunately, has always labored under the strong influence of what the Latins call the "colossus of the North." Because it gives economic aid to Latin America, and because its economy predominates in the hemisphere, the United States has often been able to get its way in the OAS. In 1954, when the Arbenz government of Guatemala wanted the United Nations to do something about the efforts to overthrow it, the United States wanted the OAS to deal with it instead, because in the 1950s and 1960s the OAS countries were strongly on our side in the cold war.

More recently, however, the OAS has been less willing to bend to Washington's will. Despite their dependence on the United States, the Latin countries have a knee-jerk reaction against U.S. military intervention. One of the reasons they were anxious to form the OAS in 1948, in fact, was to stop our interference. They wrote into the OAS Charter a provision outlawing intervention in stronger terms than the UN Charter. When we invaded Grenada in 1983 and Panama in 1989, the OAS condemned us.

When, however, the United Nations or OAS has condemned a U.S. military intervention, the administration has been able to shrug off the condemnation. The press has not given it much play, and the public has remained largely unaware of it. That is where the citizenry comes in. Since the treaties establishing the United Nations and the OAS are the law of the land, the American people should demand that the administration comply with the will of these organizations. That requires, first, a public awareness of the existence and role of these organizations, and then a willingness to take action when the time comes.

Another avenue of redress for the citizenry is to pressure Congress. If Congress does not assert its powers—and we have seen that it often does not—the public must make Congress do so. This is not an easy task, however. If it is difficult for a member of Congress to get adequate information in a crisis situation, it will be more difficult still for the average citizen.

Moreover, when citizens try to figure out what is going on, they may ruffle feathers in high places. In the early 1980s, a citizen group was formed to keep tabs on our activities in El Salvador. The Committee in Solidarity with the People of El Salvador thought that our intervention was wrong, and it didn't believe the government's white paper. The FBI received information that the group was supporting terrorist activity, and it began an investigation. FBI headquarters sent a directive to its Chicago office to infiltrate the group, and agents joined and used informers. Agents attended meetings of the group and got their telephone and bank records in an effort to identify individual members. The FBI soon discovered out that its original information about supporting terrorism was false, yet it kept up the investigation. The group sued, and while the case was before a federal court in 1981, the FBI agreed to end its campaign, although it did not do so until 1985. Finally, in 1991, a federal judge, still unsure that the FBI would not resume its investigation, ordered a stop.[2]

Despite such difficulties, the citizen is the last defense for calling authorities to account for what they do. At the end of World War II, the international community first said that each individual has a responsibility for war and peace. In war crimes tribunals in Germany and Japan, German and Japanese officials were charged with planning and waging a war of aggression. The idea was that war is not something done by a faceless bureaucracy, but by individuals who make the decision to commit troops to combat. Just as government leaders are responsible as individuals for sending troops, so do the citizens bear a responsibility because, at least in a democratic system, they are ultimately responsible for tolerating action taken by the leaders.

Whatever system of governance prevails in a country, it can function only so long as it is tolerated by the public. The Vietnam war made it clear that a war cannot continue if the people do not acquiesce. Broad segments of the public took action to oppose that war, overcoming the difficulties of collecting the necessary factual information. The Vietnam experience showed that it rests ultimately with the citizenry to play the role of backstop when Congress does not act on its own to restrain an administration.

If past practice is any guide, our administrations will continue to commit our troops to combat and will not be forthright about the reasons. It will send more young men, and, increasingly, young women, to their deaths for reasons that have not been explained to them. It is, finally, up to the American people to put on the brakes.

Notes

1. "A Report to the President Pursuant to the President's Directive of January 31, 1950," April 7, 1950, FRUS 1950, vol. 1, p. 267.
2. *Alliance to End Repression* v. *City of Chicago,* Nos. 74-C-3268 & 75-C-3295 (slip opinion, U.S. District Court, Northern District of Illinois), October 2, 1991.

Bibliography

Acheson, Dean. *Present at the Creation*. New York: Norton, 1969.

Allison, John M. *Ambassador from the Prairie: Or Allison Wonderland*. Boston: Houghton Mifflin, 1973.

Appleman, Roy E. *United States Army in the Korean War: South to the Naktong, North to the Yalu (June–November 1950)*. Washington, D.C.: Office of the Chief of Military History, Department of the Army, 1961.

Barnet, Richard. *Intervention and Revolution: The United States in the Third World*. New York: World Pub. Co., 1968.

Berry, William. "Ten Days of Urgent Fury." *All Hands*, May 1984, pp. 18–29.

Bennett, Ralph Kinney. "Grenada: Anatomy of a 'Go' Decision." *Reader's Digest*, February 1984, pp. 72–77.

Bennouna, Mohammed. *Le consentement à l'ingérence militaire dans les conflits internes*. Paris: Librarie générale de droit et de jurisprudence, 1974.

Bill, Alfred Hoyt. *Rehearsal for Conflict: The War with Mexico 1846–1848*. New York: Knopf, 1947.

Bonner, Raymond. *Weakness and Deceit: U.S. Policy and El Salvador*. New York: Times Books, 1984.

Branfman, Fred. *Voices from the Plain of Jars: Life under an Air War*. New York: Harper and Row, 1972.

Burns, Richard Dean, and Milton Leitenberg. *The Wars in Vietnam, Cambodia, and Laos, 1945–1982: A Bibliographic Guide*. Santa Barbara, Calif.: ABC-Clio Information Services, 1984.

Cabot, John Moors. *First Line of Defense.* Washington, D.C.: Georgetown School of Foreign Service, 1979.

Caro, Robert A. *The Years of Lyndon Johnson: Means of Ascent.* New York: Knopf, 1990.

Cavelier, German. *La política internacional de Colombia.* Bogota: Editorial Iqueima, 1960.

Church, Frank. "Covert Action: Swampland of American Foreign Policy." *Bulletin of the Atomic Scientists,* February 1975, pp. 7–11.

Cobban, Helena. *The Making of Modern Lebanon.* London: Hutchinson, 1985.

Cockburn, Leslie. *Out of Control: The Story of the Reagan Administration's Secret War in Nicaragua, the Illegal Arms Pipeline, and the Contra Drug Connection.* New York: Atlantic Monthly Press, 1987.

Colby, William. *Honorable Men: My Life in the CIA.* New York: Simon and Schuster, 1978.

Commander in Chief, U.S. Atlantic Command. *Operation Urgent Fury Report.* Norfolk, Va.: U.S. Department of Defense, 1984.

Compaine, Benjamin, ed. *Who Owns the Media? Concentration of Ownership in the Mass Communcation Industry.* White Plains, N.Y.: Knowledge Industry Pubs., 1982.

Conference for a New Direction in U.S. Korea Policy. New York: Committee for a New Direction for U.S. Korea Policy, 1977.

Cormier, Frank. *LBJ: The Way He Was.* Garden City, N.Y.: Doubleday, 1977.

Cumings, Bruce. *Liberation and the Emergence of Separate Regimes, 1945–1947.* Vol. 1, *The Origins of the Korean War.* Princeton, N.J.: Princeton University Press, 1981.

———. *The Roaring of the Cataract, 1945–1950.* Vol. 2, *The Origins of the Korean War.* Princeton, N.J.: Princeton University Press, 1990.

Davis, Nathaniel. "The Angola Decision of 1975: A Personal Memoir." *Foreign Affairs* (Fall 1978): 109–24.

Deakin, James. *Lyndon Johnson's Credibility Gap.* Washington, D.C.: Public Affairs Press, 1968.

Discriminate Deterrence: Report of the Commission on Integrated Long-Term Strategy. Fred C. Ilké and Albert Wohlstetter, co-chairmen. Prepared for Secretary of Defense and Assistant to the President for National Security Affairs. Washington, D.C., January 1988.

Donovan, Robert J. *Tumultuous Years: The Presidency of Harry S. Truman 1949–1953.* New York: Norton, 1982.

Draper, Theodore. *The Dominican Revolt: A Case Study in American Policy.* New York: Commentary, 1968.

Dupuy, René-Jean. "Agression indirecte et intervention sollicitée à propos de l'affaire libanaise." *Annuaire Français de Droit International* (1959): 431–67.

Edwards, Albert. *Panama: The Canal, the Country, and the People.* New York: Macmillan, 1912.

Eisenhower, Dwight D. *Mandate for Change 1953-1956.* Garden City, N.Y.: Doubleday, 1963.

Eveland, Wilbur Crane. *Ropes of Sand: America's Failure in the Middle East.* New York: Norton, 1980.

Fall, Bernard B. *Vietnam Witness 1953-66.* New York: Praeger, 1966.

Foot, Rosemary. *The Wrong War: American Policy and the Dimensions of the Korean Conflict, 1950-1953.* Ithaca, N.Y.: Cornell University Press, 1985.

Franck, Thomas M. "Who Killed Article 2(4)? or: Changing Norms Governing the Use of Force by States." *American Journal of International Law* 64 (1970): 809-37.

Franck, Thomas M., and Edward Weisband, eds. *Secrecy and Foreign Policy.* New York: Oxford University Press, 1974.

Gettelman, Marvin E. *Vietnam: History, Documents, and Opinions on a Major World Crisis.* Greenwich, Conn.: Fawcett Pubs., 1965.

Gettelman, Marvin, E., et al., eds. *El Salvador: Central America in the New Cold War.* New York: Grove Press, 1986.

Geyelin, Philip. *Lyndon B. Johnson and the World.* New York: Praeger, 1966.

Gibson, James William. *The Perfect War: Technowar in Vietnam.* Boston: Atlantic Monthly Press, 1986.

Gilbert, Martin. *The Second World War: A Complete History.* New York: Henry Holt, 1989.

Gleijeses, Piero. *The Dominican Crisis: The 1965 Constitutionalist Revolt and American Intervention.* Baltimore, Md.: Johns Hopkins University Press, 1978.

Gott, Richard. *Rural Guerrillas in Latin America.* Harmondsworth, England: Penguin, 1973.

Goulden, Joseph C. *Truth Is the First Casualty: The Gulf of Tonkin Affair—Illusion and Reality.* Chicago: Rand McNally, 1969.

Grenada: Whose Freedom? London: Latin America Bureau, 1984.

Grenada: The World against the Crime. Havana: Editorial de Ciencias Sociales, 1983.

Gunther, John. *The Riddle of MacArthur.* New York: Harper, 1950.

Handy, Jim. *Gift of the Devil: A History of Guatemala.* Boston: South End Press, 1984.

Hastings, Max. *The Korean War.* New York: Simon and Schuster, 1987.

Herman, Edward S., and Noam Chomsky. *Manufacturing Consent: The Political Economy of the Mass Media.* New York: Pantheon, 1988.

Hersh, Seymour. "Target Qaddafi," *New York Times,* February 22, 1987, p. F17, col. 1.

Hernandez, Manuel Arteaga, and Jaime Arteaga Carvajal. *Historia política de Colombia.* Bogota: Intermedio Editores, 1986.

Hitchcock, Wilbur. "North Korea Jumps the Gun." *Current History* 20 (March 1951): 136-44.

Howarth, David. *Panama.* New York: McGraw Hill, 1966.

Hoyt, Edwin C. *Law and Force in American Foreign Policy.* Lanham, Md.: University Press of America, 1985.

Hughes, Emmet John. *The Ordeal of Power: A Political Memoir of the Eisenhower Years.* New York: Atheneum, 1963.

Immerman, Richard H. *The CIA in Guatemala: The Foreign Policy of Intervention.* Austin: University of Texas Press, 1982.

Johnson, Loch K. *America's Secret Power: The CIA in a Democratic Society.* New York: Oxford University Press, 1989.

Johnson, Lyndon B. "An Assessment of the Situation in the Dominican Republic." *Department of State Bulletin* (1965): 19–21.

Kadane, Kathy. "U.S. Officials' Lists Aided Indonesian Bloodbath in '60s." *Washington Post,* May 21, 1990, p. A5, col. 1.

Kaiser, Robert G. "White Paper on El Salvador Is Faulty." *Washington Post,* June 9, 1981, p. A1, col. 2.

Kalb, Madeleine. *The Congo Cables: The Cold War in Africa from Eisenhower to Kennedy.* New York: Macmillan, 1982.

Knightley, Phillip. *The First Casualty: From the Crimea to Vietnam: The War Correspondent as Hero, Propagandist, and Myth Maker.* New York: Harcourt Brace Jovanovich, 1975.

Kirkpatrick, Lyman B., Jr. *The Real CIA.* New York: Macmillan, 1968.

Kolko, Joyce, and Gabriel. *The Limits of Power: The World and United States Foreign Policy, 1945–1954.* New York: Harper and Row, 1972.

Kwitny, Jonathan. "Apparent Errors Cloud U.S. 'White Paper' on Reds in El Salvador." *Wall Street Journal,* June 8, 1981, p. A1, col. 6.

———. *Endless Enemies: The Making of an Unfriendly World.* New York: St. Martin's Press, 1984.

Lacouture, Jean. "Viet Cong. Who Are They, What Do They Want?" *New Republic,* March 6, 1965, pp. 21–24.

Laffin, John. *The War of Desperation: Lebanon 1982–85.* London: Osprey, 1985.

Liebenow, J. Gus. *Liberia: The Quest for Democracy.* Bloomington: Indiana University Press, 1987.

Lowenthal, Abraham F. *The Dominican Intervention.* Cambridge, Mass.: Harvard University Press, 1972.

McClintock, Michael. *The American Connection.* Totowa, N.J.: Zed, 1985.

McCormack, Gavan. *Cold War Hot War: An Australian Perspective on the Korean War.* Sydney Hale and Iremonger, 1983.

McCormick, Thomas J. *America's Half-Century: United States Foreign Policy in the Cold War.* Baltimore, Md.: Johns Hopkins University Press, 1989.

McCoy, Alfred W. *The Politics of Heroin in Southeast Asia.* New York: Harper and Row, 1972.

McGehee, Ralph. *Deadly Deceits: My 25 Years in the CIA.* New York: Sheridan Square Pubs., 1983.

Malone, Linda A. "The Kahan Report, Ariel Sharon and the Sabra-Shatilla Massacres in Lebanon: Responsibility Under International Law for Massacres of Civilian Populations." *Utah Law Review* (1985): 373–433.

Marchetti, Victor, and John Marks. *The CIA and the Cult of Intelligence*. New York: Knopf, 1974.

Marcum, John. "Lessons of Angola." *Foreign Affairs* (April 1976): 407–25.

Martin, David, and John Walcott. *Best Laid Plans: The Inside Story of America's War against Terrorism*. New York: Harper and Row, 1988.

Martin, John Bartlow. *Overtaken by Events: The Dominican Crisis from the Fall of Trujillo to the Civil War*. New York: Doubleday, 1966.

Martinez, Milton. *Panama 1978-1990: Una Crisis sin Fin*. Panama: Centro de Estudios y Acción Social Panameño, 1990.

May, Brian. *The Indonesian Tragedy*. London: Routledge and Kegan Paul, 1978.

Miller, Merle. *Lyndon: An Oral Biography*. New York: Putnam, 1980.

Mosley, Leonard. *Dulles: A Biography of Eleanor, Allen, and John Foster Dulles and Their Family Network*. New York: Dial Press, 1978.

Mossman, James. *Rebels in Paradise: Indonesia's Civil War*. London: Cape, 1961.

Mueller, John E. *War, Presidents and Public Opinion*. New York: Wiley, 1973.

Neff, Donald. *Warriors at Suez: Eisenhower Takes America into the Middle East*. New York: Simon and Schuster, 1981.

O'Ballance, Edgar. *The Wars in Vietnam, 1954-1980*. New York: Hippocrene Books, 1981.

O'Shaughnessy, Hugh. *Grenada: Revolution, Invasion and Aftermath*. London: Observer, 1984.

O'Toole, G. J. A. *The Spanish War: An American Epic-1898*. New York: Norton, 1984.

Paige, Glenn D. *The Korean Decision June 24-30, 1950*. New York: Free Press, 1968.

Panikkar, K. M. *In Two Chinas: Memoirs of a Diplomat*. London: George Allen and Unwin, 1955.

Parenti, Michael. *Inventing Reality: The Politics of the Mass Media*. New York: St. Martin's Press, 1986.

The Pentagon Papers As Published by the New York Times. New York, Toronto: Bantam Books, 1971.

The Pentagon Papers: The Defense Department History of United States Decisionmaking on Vietnam (Senator Gravel ed.). Boston: Beacon Press, 1971.

Phillips, David Atlee. *The Night Watch*. New York: Atheneum, 1977.

Piller, Charles, and Keith R. Yamamoto. *Gene Wars: Military Control over the New Genetic Technologies*. New York: Beech Tree Books, 1988.

Potter, Pitman B. "Legal Aspects of the Beirut Landing." *American Journal of International Law* 52 (1958): 727–30.

Powers, Thomas. *The Man Who Kept Secrets: Richard Helms & the CIA*. New York: Knopf, 1979.

Prados, John. *Presidents' Secret Wars: CIA and Pentagon Covert Operations since World War II*. New York: Quill, 1986.

President's Special Review Board. *Report of the Special Review Board* (Tower Commission Report). New York: Bantam Times Books, 1987.

Prouty, Col. L. Fletcher, U.S. Air Force, Ret. *The Secret Team: The CIA and Its Allies in Control of the United States and the World.* Englewood Cliffs, N.J.: Prentice-Hall, 1973.

Public Papers of the Presidents of the United States: Harry S. Truman, 1950. Washington, D.C.: U.S. Government Printing Office, 1965.

Quigley, John. "The Legality of the United States Invasion of Panama." *Yale Journal of International Law* 15 (1990): 276–315.

———. *Palestine and Israel: A Challenge to Justice.* Durham, N.C., and London: Duke University Press, 1990.

———. "Parachutes at Dawn: Issues of Use of Force and Status of Internees in the United States-Cuban Hostilities on Grenada, 1983." *University of Miami Inter-American Law Review* 17 (1986): 199–248.

———. "The United States Invasion of Grenada: Stranger than Fiction." *University of Miami Inter-American Law Review* 18 (1986–87): 271–352.

Randal, Jonathan. *The Tragedy of Lebanon: Christian Warlords, Israeli Adventurers and American Bunglers.* London: Chatto & Windus, 1983.

Rickover, H. G. *How the Battleship Maine Was Destroyed.* Washington, D.C.: U.S. Department of the Navy, 1976.

Ridgway, Matthew. *The Korean War and How We Met the Challenge, How All-Out Asian War Was Averted, Why MacArthur Was Dismissed, Why Today's War Objectives Must Be Limited.* Garden City, N.Y.: Doubleday, 1967.

Roosevelt, Kermit. *Countercoup: The Struggle for the Control of Iran.* New York: McGraw-Hill, 1979.

Schapp, Bill. "Disinforming the World on Libya." *Covert Action Information Bulletin,* No. 30 (Summer 1988): 71–76.

Schlesinger, Arthur B., Jr. *A Thousand Days.* Boston: Houghton Mifflin, 1965.

Schroeder, John H. *Mr. Polk's War: American Opposition and Dissent, 1846–1848.* Madison: University of Wisconsin Press, 1973.

Searle, Christopher. *Grenada: The Struggle against Destabilization.* London: Writers and Readers Pub. Cooperative Society, 1983.

Shawcross, William. *Sideshow: Kissinger, Nixon and the Destruction of Cambodia.* New York: Simon and Schuster, 1979.

"Should the U.S. Fight Secret Wars?" *Harper's* magazine, September 1984, pp. 33–47.

Smith, Joseph Burkholder. *Portrait of a Cold Warrior.* New York: Putnam, 1976.

Sorensen, Theodore C. *Kennedy.* New York: Harper and Row, 1965.

Sterling, Claire. *The Terror Network: The Secret War of International Terrorism.* New York: Holt, Rinehart and Winston, 1981.

Stevenson, Charles A. *The End of Nowhere: American Policy toward Laos since 1954.* Boston: Beacon Press, 1972.

Stockwell, John. *In Search of Enemies: A CIA Story.* New York: Norton, 1978.

Stone, I. F. *The Hidden History of the Korean War.* New York: Monthly Review Press, 1952.

Szulc, Tad. *Dominican Diary.* New York: Delacorte Press, 1965.

Talbott, Strobe, ed. *Khrushchev Remembers.* Boston: Little, Brown, 1970.

Thomasson, Gordon C. "Liberian Disaster: Made in the U.S.A." *New York Times,* July 14, 1990, p. A21.

"Tonkin—Dubious Premise for War." *Los Angeles Times,* April 29, 1985, p. A1, col. 1.

Treverton, Gregory F. *Covert Action: The Limits of Intervention in the Postwar World.* New York: Basic Books, 1987.

Tully, Andrew. *CIA: The Inside Story.* New York: Morrow, 1962.

Turley, William S. *The Second Indochina War: A Short Political and Military History, 1954–1975.* Boulder, Colo.: Westview Press, 1986.

United States-Vietnam Relations 1945–1967: Study Prepared by the Department of Defense. Washington, D.C.: U.S. Government Printing Office, 1971.

Uribe, Antonio Jose. *Colombia, Estados Unidos y Panamá.* Libreria colombiana, 1976.

U.S. Congress. House. *Mutual Security Appropriations for 1959.* Hearings before the Subcommittee of the Committee on Appropriations. 85th Cong., 2d sess., 1958.

————. *Situation in Lebanon and Grenada.* Hearing before a Subcommittee of the House Committee on Appropriations. 98th Cong., 1st sess., 1983.

————. *United States Policy on Angola.* Hearing before the Committee on International Relations. 94th Cong., 2d sess., 1976.

————. *U.S. Aid Operations in Laos.* Seventh Report by the Committee on Government Operations. House Report 546, 86th Cong., 1st sess., 1959.

————. *U.S. Military Actions in Grenada: Implications for U.S. Policy in the Eastern Caribbean.* Hearing before the Subcommittees on International Security and Scientific Affairs and on Western Hemisphere Affairs of the House Committee on Foreign Affairs. 98th Cong., 1st sess., 1983.

U.S. Congress. Senate. *Alleged Assassination Plots Involving Foreign Leaders: An Interim Report of the Select Committee to Study Governmental Operations with Respect to Intelligence Activities.* 94th Cong., 1st sess., 1975. Report no. 94-465.

————. *Angola.* Hearings before the Subcommittee on African Affairs of the Committee on Foreign Relations. 94th Cong., 2d sess., 1976.

————. *Bombing in Cambodia.* Hearings before the Committee on Armed Services. 93rd Cong., 1st sess., 1973.

————. *Final Report: Foreign and Military Intelligence.* Select Committee to Study Governmental Operations with Respect to Intelligence Activities, Book I. 94th Cong., 2d sess., 1976.

————. *Military Situation in the Far East.* Hearings before the Armed Services and the Committee on Foreign Relations. 82d Cong., 1st sess., 1951.

————. *Mutual Security Appropriations for 1955.* Hearings on H.R. 10051, an Act Making Appropriations for Mutual Security for the Fiscal Year Ending June 30, 1955, and For Other Purposes. Committee on Appropriations. 83rd Cong., 2d sess., 1954.

U.S. Congress. Senate. *Refugee and Civilian War Casualty Problems in Indochina.* A Staff Report Prepared for the Use of the Subcommittee to Investigate Problems Connected with Refugees and Escapees of the Committee on the Judiciary. 91st Cong., 2d sess., 1970.

————. *Situation in Grenada.* Hearings Before the Senate Committee on Foreign Relations. 98th Cong., 1st sess., 1983.

————. *United States Security Agreements and Commitments Abroad: Kingdom of Laos.* Hearings before the Subcommittee on United States Security Agreements and Commitments Abroad. Comm. on Foreign Relations. 91st Cong., 1st sess., 1969.

————. *War-Related Civilian Problems in Indochina. Part II: Laos and Cambodia.* Hearings before the Subcommittee to Investigate Problems Connected with Refugees and Escapees of the Committee on the Judiciary. 91st Cong., 1st sess., 1971.

U.S. Department of State. "Communist Interference in El Salvador." Special Report, no. 80, February 23, 1981. Washington, D.C.: U.S. Government Printing Office, 1981.

The U.S. Invasion of Panama: The Truth Behind Operation 'Just Cause.' New York: Independent Commission of Inquiry on the U.S. Invasion of Panama, 1990.

Walker, Thomas, ed. *Reagan versus the Sandinistas: The Undeclared War on Nicaragua.* Boulder, Colo., and London: Westview Press, 1987.

Weems, John Edward. *The Fate of the Maine.* New York: Holt, 1958.

Weissman, Stephen R. *American Foreign Policy in the Congo 1960–1964.* Ithaca, N.Y.: Cornell University Press, 1974.

————. "CIA Covert Action in Zaire and Angola: Patterns and Consequences." *Political Science Quarterly* 94 (Summer 1979): 263–86.

Wise, David. *The Politics of Lying: Government Deception, Secrecy, and Power.* New York: Random House, 1973.

Wise, David, and Thomas B. Ross. *The Invisible Government.* New York: Random House, 1964.

Woodward, Bob. *The Commanders.* New York: Simon and Schuster, 1991.

————. *Veil: The Secret Wars of the CIA 1981–1987.* New York: Simon and Schuster, 1987.

Wright, Quincy. "United States Intervention in Lebanon." *American Journal of International Law* 53 (1959): 112–25.

Wyden, Peter. *Bay of Pigs: The Untold Story.* New York: Simon and Schuster, 1979.

Yant, Martin. *Desert Mirage: The True Story of the Gulf War.* Buffalo, N.Y.: Prometheus Books, 1991.

Name Index